Our Cuba

Our Cuba
Contextualizing a Vibrant History

Edited by
Nancy Wright, John Winterdyk,
and Vilma Páez Pérez

Rock's Mills Press
Rock's Mills, Ontario • Oakville, Ontario
2025

Published by
Rock's Mills Press
www.rocksmillspress.com

Copyright © 2025 by Nancy Wright, John Winterdyk, and Vilma Páez Pérez.

All rights reserved. No part of this publication may be reproduced, distributed, or transmitted in any form or by any means, including photocopying, recording, or other electronic or mechanical methods, without the prior written permission of the publisher, except in the case of brief quotations embodied in critical reviews and certain other noncommercial uses permitted by copyright law. For permission requests, contact the publisher at:
customer.service@rocksmillspress.com

The trademark Rock's Mills Press® (the name itself and its styling in the font Rockwell Bold) is used under licence.

We dedicate this book to everyone who is interested in social justice, and particularly to the people of Cuba, who continue to endure the social and economic injustice of the legacy of the embargo! Your spirit and resistance are a testament to the strength of the nation.

Special Note

Whatever I read or hear in English about Fidel, he is called Castro, and most of the time it is pejorative. Those who despise Cuba give the Castro dictatorship or Castroism a negative connotation. The use of his first name, Fidel, as we normally called him, implies familiarity, friendship … someone close. So, we are using Fidel here … the way Cubans, and friends all over the world, refer to him … even today.

—*Vilma Páez Pérez*

Contents

Preface by José Vega Suñol / ix
Acknowledgements / xv

CHAPTER ONE
A Brief Historical Overview of Cuba: 1492–2020
Carlos Córdova Martínez and José Novoa Betancourt
1

CHAPTER TWO
Cuba and Its Transformations in the New Millennium
Luis Orlando Aguilera García
26

CHAPTER THREE
Some Considerations on the Updating of the Cuban Economic Model: Evolution of the Cuban Economy, 1989–2016
Miguel Ramón Torres Pérez
42
Afterword: A Brief Update on the Cuban Economic Model from 2016 to 2023 / 60

CHAPTER FOUR
Blockade? Embargo? It's More Than Just Semantics…
Salvador Escalante Batista and Paul Sarmiento Blanco
68

CHAPTER FIVE
Guantanamo: A U.S. Thorn in Cuba's Side
Vilma Páez Pérez and Salvador Escalante Batista
96

CHAPTER SIX
Social Justice and Democracy in the Cuban Revolution
Vladimir Pita Simón, Julio Eduardo Ávila Pérez,
and Violeta Rosa Mejías Rojas
116

Contents

CHAPTER SEVEN
The Cuban Socialist Constitution and Legal System
José Augusto Ochoa del Río
151

CHAPTER EIGHT
The Cuban Criminal Justice System: A Social Reintegration Model
Manuel Alberto Leyva Estupiñán, Larisbel Lugo Arteaga,
and Luis Manuel Probance Labrada
182

CHAPTER NINE
Sociocultural Anthropology in Cuba: Historical Overview
José Vega Suñol
216

CHAPTER TEN
Education in Cuba: A Model of Justice and Social Equity
Yohannia Ochoa Ardite and Vilma Páez Pérez
234

CHAPTER ELEVEN
**The Cultural Policy of the Cuban Revolution:
Roots, Utopia, and Reality**
Rolando Bellido Aguilera
270

EPILOGUE
An "Outsiders'" Perspective
Nancy Wright and John Winterdyk
287

Preface

José Vega Suñol

Cuban universities have, among their multiple tasks, promoting scientific exchange both nationally and internationally, by sharing and circulating achievements in their respective areas of expertise. This is a practice comparable, in general, to that of higher education institutions worldwide. The University of Holguín (UHo), located in northeastern Cuba in the capital city of Holguín province, organizes a unique scientific event related to such exchange: the International Seminar on Canadian Studies (SECAN), which is celebrated in conjunction with the annual International Conference on Foreign Languages, Communication, and Culture (WEFLA). The seminar has contributed to consolidating knowledge over time through necessary exchanges in Cuba among academics, faculty, and students from several Canadian universities, as well as a few independent researchers, and other educational and social institutions in Cuba, Latin America, and Europe. Participants in both congresses are inspired by bilateral respect, professional responsibility, and mutual benefit in dealing with issues related to the common good of the peoples and cultures involved.

It is worth recognizing the active role played by the Canadian Studies Centre of the University of Holguín, which since its inception in 2006 has been successful in working to strengthen the ties between Cuban and Canadian scholars. The links between the University of Holguín and Canadian universities have strengthened our university's ability to attract more professors and students, not only from the University of Holguín itself and other Cuban universities, but also from Canadian universities and other institutions. In 2017, because of the climate of cooperation between the two countries, the UHo welcomed Canadian editor and translator Nancy Wright, from the province of Quebec, to take a doctoral-level course on Cuban transculturation. The course involved several professors and included workshops and lectures on Cuban topics. The subject matter so enthused our colleague that she proposed the publication of a book conceived and written by Cuban authors but edited contextually for foreign readers by two Canadians (Nancy Wright and John Winterdyk) and one Cuban (Vilma Páez Pérez). *Our Cuba: Contextualizing a Vibrant History* illustrates various areas of the Cuban reality that are currently being debated in our academic fields.

This task required the collaboration of a multidisciplinary group composed of Cuban academics and active participants in the social project that the Cuban nation has been carrying out for more than six decades. Following an organizational meeting at UNEAC* with the editors, an interesting debate about the book's contents was held at the Research Centre on Culture and Identity (CECI) of UHo's Faculty of Social Science. Considering the socio-humanist profile of the professors and the aspects to be included, a consensus for a broad and diverse assumptive theme straddling three epistemic blocks was reached. The chosen topics were distributed amongst those professors and others willing to undertake the project.

Given the extended duration of this project—lengthened by language, geographic distance aggravated by the pandemic, standard publication delays, and a host of other factors beyond anyone's control—many chapters required some updating to reflect the significant changes introduced in Cuba, starting with the new constitution in 2019. The authors and editors made efforts to include such things or offer brief updates in footnotes. However, as this book finally reaches publication in 2025, new geopolitical shifts have emerged, including the resurgence of Trump-era policies, a renewed push for U.S. protectionism, and continued expansionist ambitions, along with revived debates around Guantanamo. While these developments could not be incorporated into the chapters, we acknowledge them here as part of the evolving context in which Cuba continues to navigate its future.

Block 1. Historical Description (5 chapters):

Chapter 1: Brief Historical Overview of Cuba: 1492–2020. By **Carlos Córdova Martínez**, Ph.D. Philosopher and historian. Professor Emeritus and leading principal researcher at the Research Centre on Cultural and Identity Issues. University of Holguín; and by **José Novoa Betancourt**, Ph.D. Director of the Research Centre on Cultural and Identity Issues. University of Holguín.

Chapter 2. Cuba and Its Transformations in the New Millennium. By **Luis Orlando Aguilera García**, Ph.D. Philosopher. Director of the Re-

---

* Established in Havana, Cuba in 1961, the UNEAC (*Unión de Escritores y Artistas de Cuba* [writer and artist union]) is a social, cultural and professional non-governmental organization in Cuba, a member of the Economic and Social Council of the United Nations (ECOSOC) from 1988 to 2014, except 1991, elected to subsidiary bodies of the UN: Social Development Commission (2025–2029) and Crime Prevention and Criminal Justice Commission (2025–2027) in 2024, after the writing of this book.

search Centre for the Management of Local Development. University of Holguín.

Chapter 3. **Some Considerations on the Updating of the Cuban Economic Model.** By **Miguel Ramón Torres Pérez**, Ph.D. in Economic Sciences. The author is currently working in Equatorial Guinea.

Chapter 4. **Blockade? Embargo? It's More Than Just Semantics...** By **Salvador Escalante Batista**, Associate Professor, University of Medical Sciences, Holguín; and by **Paul Sarmiento Blanco**, Ph.D. in Historical Sciences. Researcher at the Research Centre on Cultural and Identity Issues. University of Holguín.

Chapter 5. **Guantanamo: A U.S. Thorn in Cuba's Side.** By **Vilma Páez Pérez**, Ph.D. in Education. Researcher at the Research Centre on Cultural and Identity Issues. President of the Canadian Studies Centre. University of Holguín; and by **Salvador Escalante Batista**, Associate Professor, University of Medical Sciences, Holguín.

Block 2. Constitutional Framework and Legal System (3 Chapters):

Chapter 6. **Social Justice and Democracy in the Cuban Revolution.** By **Vladimir Pita Simón**, Ph.D. in Legal Sciences. Researcher at the Research Centre on Cultural and Identity Issues; by **Julio Eduardo Ávila Pérez**, Master's Degree in Constitutional and Administrative Law; and by **Violeta Rosa Mejías Rojas**, Master's Degree in Social Sciences and Axiology. University of Holguín.

Chapter 7. **The Cuban Socialist Constitution and Legal System.** By **José Augusto Ochoa del Río**, Bachelor of Laws and Ph.D. in Education. Researcher at the Research Centre for Culture and Identity Issues. University of Holguín.

Chapter 8. **The Cuban Criminal Justice System: A Social Reintegration Model.** By **Manuel Alberto Leyva Estupiñán**, Ph.D. in Legal Sciences. Non-Permanent Alternate Professional Judge of the People's Provincial Court of Holguín in the Criminal Division. President of the Union of Jurists of Cuba in Holguín province; by **Larisbel Lugo Arteaga**, Associate Professor of Criminal Law; and by **Luis Manuel Probance**, Associate Professor of Criminal Procedure Law. University of Holguín.

Block 3. Special Topics: Society and Culture (3 Chapters):

Chapter 9. **Sociocultural Anthropology in Cuba: Historical Overview.** By **José Vega Suñol**, Ph.D. in Historical Sciences. Corresponding Member of the Academy of History of Cuba. Researcher at the Research Centre on Cultural and Identity Issues. University of Holguín.

Chapter 10. Education in Cuba, a Model of Justice and Social Equity. By **Yohannia Ochoa Ardite**, Ph.D. in Education. Associate Professor. Dean of the Faculty of Arts and Communication; and by **Vilma Páez Pérez**, Ph.D. in Education. Researcher at the Research Centre on Cultural and Identity Issues. President of the Canadian Studies Centre. University of Holguín.

Chapter 11. The Cultural Policy of the Cuban Revolution: Roots, Utopia, and Reality. By **Rolando Bellido Aguilera**, Ph.D. in Philosophy. Member of Honour of the Hermanos Saíz Association of Young Creators and member of the Union of Writers and Artists of Cuba (UNEAC).

Epilogue. By **Nancy Wright**, P.W., M.A. (Comparative Literature). Professional editor and translator in Quebec; long-time Editor-in-Chief of a Canadian criminal justice publication for one of Canada's longest-standing criminal justice associations; and by **John Winterdyk**, Ph.D. Canadian criminologist and professor (now retired) at Mount Royal University, Calgary, Alberta.

The first of these blocks, Historical Description, reviews the main periods comprising the island's historical base. Cuba has a unique history in this hemisphere. The Cuban apostle of independence and national hero José Martí (1853–1895) symbolically situates the island as the *balance of the world*. Cuba, geopolitically, is located at the crossroads of the two Americas. Its geographic and cultural scope is the Caribbean, the fundamental historical space of the encounter of races and cultures in this part of the world, which gave origin to the *Homo Americano*. The Caribbean was the first take-off point from which the European metropolis set out to conquer the mainland in the *Novo Orbis* (New World). Modern history in this hemisphere begins in the Caribbean, a space in which Cuba occupies a visible place from whence the conquering armies of Mexico and Florida were organized and departed during the 16th century; this represents a vital scenario for the study of transculturation resulting from the mixing of Indigenous, European, and African populations.

Some of the peculiarities of the island are shown through longitudinal-historical cuts in time. Also, studies of our nation's history are usually divided into three periods (i.e., Colony-Republic-Revolution), and defined more by ruptures rather than continuities; our national discourse has been dotted with events, sometimes unexpected and sometimes violent, that have driven long-term gradual and radical changes. For instance, Spanish colonialism lasted longer in Cuba than in the rest of Hispanic America, as the domination of our island lasted almost four centuries (1510–1898). In addition, Spanish anti-colonial emancipation wars here were not only the longest (1868–1898) but among the bloodiest of any on American soil, due to the high number of casualties relative to the total population.

Historically and geographically, Cuba is also a bastion of resistance to U.S. imperialism. The island's prominent location alone has made it a central focus of the U.S. territorial expansionism deployed since the Jefferson administration and subsequent sequels of U.S. interventionism and military occupation (1898–1902 and 1906–1909). This epistemic block also incorporates an updated analysis on the Cuban socialist project in terms of the economy and society (see Chapters 2 and 3) along with other specific issues that have played an essential role in recent history, such as six decades of U.S.-driven blockade (Chapters 3 and 4) or more than a century of illegal occupation through the U.S. government's installation of a military base on a portion of Cuban soil, at Guantanamo Bay (Chapter 5).

This book's second block is entirely devoted to the sphere of legal sciences in Cuba, locating the Hispanic-Roman and French heritage in different areas of constitutional and civil law, along with matters of vital importance today, such as explaining the legality of the Cuban political system, its characteristics, and the way socialist democracy is exercised in Cuba (Chapters 6 and 7). Penal law and critical legal issues, probed by a competent body of dedicated jurists, including rehabilitation and social reinsertion of prisoners (referred to as inmates in Cuba) and youth justice, are also included in this block. These susceptible issues have been the focus of controversy and manipulation by enemies of the Cuban revolution. The fact remains, however, that Cuba has one of the lowest crime rates in the hemisphere, something to which most of the many tourists from Canada who visit the island every year will attest. As a preview, it is thought-provoking to read that "Through social justice promotion, public safety is among the highest in Latin America and the Caribbean. This is considered one of the most significant achievements since the Cuban political project was consolidated by the Cuban Revolution in 1959" (Chapter 8).

Next, we could not miss examining the sphere of Cuban culture and cultural thought, taking an anthropological, sociocultural, and educational approach to development that emphasizes prevention and aims for integral human development. These matters are grouped in the last block of this anthology (Chapters 9, 10, and 11). Although the proposed selection of topics does not cover the entire spectrum of interests that we would have wanted to include, it allows a comprehensive and concise overview of Cuban reality from the perspective of some leading academic practitioners.

The book presents and contextualizes a vibrant history, allowing readers to see inside present-day Cuba through the prism of Cuban social sciences, with no propagandistic information or artificial sweeteners. How transculturation performs through economic and legal-political systems and institutions is briefly visualized in some chapters to help readers better understand the Cuban reality. What appears on these pages is the result of rigorous research by a group of Cuban authors whose arguments are supported with scientific rigour and bolstered by the critical eye of their expertise and experience as involved members of a reality in permanent flux and transformation, exposed to immeasurable and costly foreign pressures, and willing to improve itself without abandoning its principles and sovereignty.

May this collaboration between Cuban and Canadian academics and professionals bridge dialogue and understanding between the peoples of Cuba and those of Canada and other nations. It is a way to ratify the friendship and collaboration sustained throughout more than a century of relations and proof of the power of cultural ties in promoting understanding between equals and respecting differences.

José Vega Suñol
2022

Acknowledgements

I, Nancy Wright, extend heartfelt gratitude to Dr. Vilma Páez Pérez, not only for being an exceptional co-editor but also for thinking outside of the box and initiating my three-month independent doctoral course in transculturation at Universidad de Holguín (UHo) in 2017. Unbeknownst to us then, that course spanned multiple departments (UHo professors J. Ochoa, J. Vega, V. Pita, J. Novoa, and M. Leyva) and ultimately sparked the idea for this book. I am also grateful to our co-editor, Dr. John Winterdyk, for joining this project and generously contributing his expertise as a Canadian criminologist and prolific author/editor. I deeply appreciate all the Cuban authors for their dedication to crafting this nuanced and contextualized history of Cuba, and special acknowledgement goes to Salvador Escalante for also making rich contributions to the editing. I am also grateful to our Canadian publisher, David Stover, for bringing this book to fruition. Vilma and Salvador, this journey has been an eye-opening experience, and I am eternally grateful to you and your niece, Elianis, for sharing Cuban wisdom by being my "Cuban family." I also extend my appreciation to retired professor Roxanne Rimstead. The Canada-Cuba mini-conference you organized at Université de Sherbrooke in 2016 became my gateway to Cuban academia. Credit also goes to Anabel Gonzalez (UHo, Cuba) for making excellent contributions to the English translation of the initial working versions of Chapters 6, 7, and 8. Finally, to the late Waldemar, a remarkable Cuban tourism expert and dear friend, thank you for sharing your wisdom and for making José Martí's words resonate with such meaning and life.

I, John Winterdyk, would like to express a special thanks to my co-editors, Nancy Wright and Vilma Paez-Perez, for beckoning me into this project. I particularly appreciate Nancy's dedication and tireless efforts; she deserves to be acknowledged as the lead editor of this anthology. I also extend my heartfelt gratitude to the diverse and rich collection of Cuban scholars who contributed to this volume. Most wrote in Spanish, the first language of all the authors, which posed its share of challenges, but brought a unique perspective to this anthology that would otherwise not likely have been captured. To David Stover, the publisher of Rock's Mills Press, your patience and professionalism in helping guide this anthology to fruition is deeply appreciated.

I, Vilma Páez Pérez, would like to express what a privilege it has been for me to be part of this project. It was my first experience as a book co-editor, and I had some self-doubt. It was a journey into the unknown, and I was also very afraid we would not be able to meet the expectations of a book. That we—as Cuban academics working, dreaming, and living in Cuba—would be writing and contextualizing our history for publication in Canada only increased my qualms.

The whole project was Nancy Wright's idea. She put great enthusiasm and effort into it, never questioning for a minute that such a book was possible. To her goes the credit; she became the heart and soul of a project that took a lot of work; however, listening to her talk about the book with conviction and passion made us—all Cuban authors—contribute no matter the difficulties or hardship. It was her dream, and when she asked Dr. Winterdyk, a well-known Canadian academic and editor, to get involved, he accepted the challenge. It has been a long and eventful journey. Each Cuban author strove to write their chapters first and then respond to the questions and demanding comments by Nancy, John and, later, by David Stover of Rock's Mills Press.

I join my fellow authors in expressing our gratitude to you, Nancy, John, and David. Thank you for the support and for making this book come to life. Thanks to you, we are making a little piece of our beloved Cuba available to American readers. Our Cuba, despised by some but loved by so many, inside and outside the island, is worth trying to defend, whatever the cost. We, Cubans, may be sailing in turbulent waters, but our journey is safe and forever driven by our determination that being independent is the only way to create our own future.

Our Cuba

CHAPTER ONE

A Brief Historical Overview of Cuba: 1492–2020

Carlos Córdova Martínez and José Novoa Betancourt

Abstract

Contextualizing the history of Cuba briefly is challenging. Cuba has a rich history marked by heroic events in the constant pursuit of national independence. Offering a general panorama from the moment Cristóbal Colón set foot on Cuban shores in 1492 until now is not easy either, since we are still engaged in a struggle to remain free from our neighbors to the north, who for more than a century have treasured the idea of holding the island. The U.S. has spared no effort, starting with a military intervention near the end of the Cuban War of Independence against Spain in the late 19th century when Cuba was already confident of winning on its own. U.S. military intrusions in Cuba were followed by pressure on the bootlicker governments that succeeded each other on the island from 1902 until 1959. The Revolutionary Government put an end to these forms of domination and set our country free. The path has been strewn with difficulties every step of the way, but Cubans' will to be independent and live according to the ideal of freedom and self-determination has proven that even the most ironclad blockade has not been able to defeat us.

Keywords: history, intervention, independence, self-determination

Carlos Córdova Martínez, Ph.D. Professor Emeritus. Full professor and researcher at the Research Center for Identity and Culture, University of Holguín. Coordinator of the Ph.D. Program in Historical, Philosophical and Legal Studies on National Identity. Recipient of the Hacha de Holguín, the highest award granted by the Government of the Province of Holguín, his area of expertise is in regional history and identity with a social history approach. Córdova Martínez's investigations into the genesis and formation of the Cuban nationality are expressed in studies on the formation of the Creole in the Eastern Central Region, the evolution of land ownership from the 17th century to the end of the colonial period and its impact on the economy and settlement, as well as on the origins of Holguín and evolution of its jurisdiction. Main publications: "El criollo una nueva hispanidad." *Héroes volcánicos del sur.* Editorial La Mezquita. Holguín, 2014. *De las Alturas de Maniabón a Ciudad.* Editorial Holguín, Holguín, 2017. *Terapia y Religión: ensayos antropológicos.* Ediciones Holguín. Holguín, 2017. *Pueblo San Isidoro de Holguín: 300 años de historia* (main author). Editora ConCiencia. Universidad de Holguín (university). Holguín, 2020.

José Novoa Betancourt, Ph.D. Assistant professor and researcher. Director of the Research Center for Identity and Culture, University of Holguín. He was awarded the José Vasconcelos Prize in 2018 by the Frente de Afirmación Hispanista A. C., México. Novoa Betancourt specializes in Contemporary European History, Regional History, History of Philosophy and Contemporary Philosophical and Social Thought. Corresponding member of the Academy of Cuban History, the Union of Writers and Artists of Cuba (UNEAC), the José Martí Cultural Society, and the National Union of Historians of Cuba (UNHIC), his research area covers the historical evolution of the Cuban nationality.

Introduction

This chapter aims to contextualize the complex process that would lead, starting in January 1959, to the construction of a national model unprecedented in the western hemisphere. Cuba simultaneously became a stronghold for the banners of anti-imperialism, social justice, popular democracy, and solidarity, despite interference and aggression by successive governments of the United States of America. Profound reasons explain not only the survival of an autochthonous project built in this underdeveloped country with few natural resources and located a scant 90 miles from U.S. territory—but also the seemingly unusual act of surviving the disappearance of the so-called "real socialism" of the Eastern bloc in the early 1990s. The former Soviet Union had been Cuba's main ally and trade partner since the U.S. imposed its embargo against our country almost 60 years ago. To offer a better general understanding of the history of Cuba, this chapter is divided into three sections:

- Colonial (1492–1898)—covering the Spaniards' arrival on the island in 1492 up to the United States' unbidden intervention in the Cuban War of Independence against Spain through the wrongly named Spanish-American War in 1898.
- Bourgeois Republic (1902–1958)—starting with the successive U.S. oc-

cupations of Cuba between 1899 and 1902 up to the establishment of the Republic of Cuba on May 20, 1902 under U.S. interference. This section also includes an analysis of how successive Cuban governments sold out to the United States, before the start of the Cuban Revolution on July 26, 1953.
- Popular-Democratic Socialist Republic (1959 onward)—explaining, in broad terms, the critical events of the Cuban Revolution, from January 1, 1959 to the present day.

> **Box 1.1**
>
> *It is not enough, Ortiz insisted, to have in Cuba a birthplace, nation, life, and behaviour. Something more is needed: "the consciousness of being Cuban and the will to be so are necessary." Fernando Ortiz invited us to embrace our condition as Cubans with an ethical commitment to the collective efforts of this people, to work on a common project to develop "a full, heartfelt, conscious, and desired Cuban identity." Let us listen to him and continue to nurture his work. (Prieto/Granma, 16 August 2019)*

Development
Colonial Period (1492–1898)

Unlike many states, in Europe as elsewhere, Cuba's national formation cannot be said to have resulted from the fusion of social components over the millennia. The arrival of Grand Admiral Christopher Columbus in what Europeans later named the New World, on October 28, 1492 in the case of Cuba, is a memorable event for the history of humankind because it initiated a fusion of the world's hitherto separate continental histories. It also marks the definitive advent of capitalist society, a hegemonic power that would rise to shape economic-social processes at a global scale.

For the Cuban archipelago, the brutal Spanish conquest nipped the evolution of the native cultures in the bud and brought about the integration of a new people emerging from descendants of the Spanish settlers and the African slaves they imported, along with the remnants of the Indigenous people, under the aegis of the dominant Spanish culture.

This represents a transculturation process that took place relatively quickly—over roughly 400 years—and through which the Cuban people emerged. First theorized and the term coined by the Cuban Don Fernando

Ortiz (1940),* the concept of "transculturation" marked the birth of definitively Cuban anthropology. Transculturation expresses the complex social phenomenon characterizing the formation of the Spanish Criollo† through the early colonial centuries. Later, towards the start of the 19th century, the first traces of Cuban national feeling emerged under the influence of the Enlightenment. This process culminated on October 10, 1868 with the beginning of Cuba's fight for national liberation. Through this and the subsequent fights for independence until 1959, the different classes and social strata would become definitively merged in Cuba.

Although formally added to the Spanish Empire in 1492, the actual conquest of Cuba did not begin until mid-1510. Spain prioritized its settlement of the island of Hispaniola (now Haiti and the Dominican Republic), which possessed untold wealth in precious metals and could serve as a strategic base for further conquests. Diego Velázquez de Cuellar (1465–1524), a conquistador who would become the first governor of Cuba (1511–1524), led the Spanish conquest. The Indigenous people resisted tenaciously between 1510 and 1512 under the guidance of the Arawak Cacique Hatuey, who had fled Hispaniola to help stop the Spanish advances in Cuba. Captured and burned alive by the conquerors, Hatuey became a Cuban symbol of Indigenous resistance and, with the subsequent development of anti-colonialist sentiment, the first martyr to the Cuban struggle for national freedom.

Hispanic colonization got underway by constructing a system of villas (i.e., towns), each endowed with a local government (town council) having its own jurisdiction. The colonial territory was divided into villas and their outlying areas. The first seven villas were founded between 1511 and 1516 along the coast: La Asunción de Baracoa; San Salvador (later Bayamo); Santa María del Puerto del Príncipe, first located at Nuevitas Bay but transferred to the interior, now Camaguey); Santísima Trinidad; Sancti Spíritus; San Cristóbal (moved from the south coast to Havana Bay; now Havana);

---

* Fernando Ortiz (trans. Harriet de Onís), *Cuban Counterpoint: Tobacco and Sugar* (Durham, 1947; orig. pub. in Spanish, 1940). See also Ortiz' 1949 essay, "Los factores humanos de la cubanidad" [The human factors of Cubanness].

† The term criollo comes from the Portuguese *crioulo*, meaning "raised locally," and originally distinguished people born in the Americas from those born in Spain or Portugal. Over time, it expanded to include American-born Spaniards, Africans, Indigenous, and some mixed-race groups. Fernando Ortiz redefined the term within Cuban identity, emphasizing that Cuba's criollo population was a fusion of Spanish, African, and Indigenous influences. In *Cuban Counterpoint: Tobacco and Sugar* and his lecture, "The Human Factors of Cubanidad," Ortiz (1940; 1939) explored how transculturation shaped Cuba's unique identity. Criollos born in Cuba identified as Cuban but were considered Spanish-American until the independence war began on October 10, 1868.

and Santiago. More villas were established to meet the political interests of the metropolis as economic activity and population growth reached a certain level in other areas, such as San Juan de los Remedios, Matanzas and Santa Clara. From Baracoa, the capital quickly migrated to Santiago de Cuba in 1515 and finally to Havana in 1563.

The construction of colonial rule required various political adjustments, but first the Crown rebuilt its relations with Columbus. Prior to his voyage, the Crown signed the Capitulations of Santa Fe (April 1492) giving Columbus the right to 10 percent of the profits from the gold, silver and merchandise obtained, with the remaining 90 percent reserved for the Crown. Once the news that Columbus had not reached East Asia but instead found a new, enormous and rich continent was out, Columbus and his family were humiliated, and their enormous privileges withdrawn after receiving just a bit of their due.

For the Spanish Empire, the principles of commercial monopoly were master keys to the system. Regulations evolved through the turbulent struggle between conceptions of the medieval spirit, absolutism, Christian humanism, mercantilism, and the ambition of men. This was the historical background behind the rise of many significant conflicts and rebellions and the birth of Criollo political aspirations against the Spanish metropolis, the so-called Motherland. At a political level, Cuba was subordinated to the monarchy's will by the legal and economic power delegated to the Governors, the *Audiencia* (Royal Courts) of Santo Domingo, and the House of Trade in Seville (Spain), which held exclusive trade rights for the new world.

The Spanish colonial model ushered the slave system and social stratification into Cuba. Following a bloody doctrinal struggle in which the Dominican Friar Bartolomé de Las Casas was the leading defender of the Indigenous People, Spain declared them vassals of the Crown under the Encomienda (labour-holding) system. This system constituted a genocidal form of slavery disguised as serfdom by which Spanish conquistadors received land in the colony and were assigned several natives to work in exchange for their own protection. Starting in 1513, these workers were ensnared in the conquistadores' frantic search for gold.

The Cuban educator and historian Ramiro Guerra suggests that the Indian was even worse off than the African slave in some ways. Legally embraced as vassals of the Crown, the Native people realized too late they were caught up in a genocide exterminating them through brutal forced labour while denying promised rights (Ramiro Guerra, 1922, p. 242). Their numbers were also rapidly reduced during new anti-colonial insurrections from 1520 to 1540, all of which produced outcomes putting the Indigenous Cubans at risk of the scourge of diseases such as smallpox. The brilliant ideas of Ramiro Guerra, a positivist, were later recalled in the Cuban ideological resistance against the negative impacts of social stratification related to systems of land tenure, caste and slavery designed to extract untold wealth from colonial sugar in the Caribbean by any means.

The migration of Europeans between the 15th and 19th centuries involved dramatic mass displacements of a large number of Africans from sub-Saharan Africa and the Taino Aborigines inhabiting the island. According to calculations by Cuban demographer Juan Pérez de la Riva, of the original 112,000 Indigenous population on the island before the conquest, fewer than 1,800 survived to be freed through the abolition of slavery in 1542. In addition to these were some 200 Indigenous slaves, brought in from the continent, and a few thousand runaway slaves (*cimarrónnes* / maroons) inhabiting the mountains (Pérez de la Riva, 2004, pp. 32 and 54).

As the Indigenous culture was being extinguished, the African slaves gradually assumed their place in society. Through this process, they absorbed components of the Indigenous culture and aspects of both were injected into the dominant local Hispanic matrix. The groups shared traditions of resistance, such as their collusion during the rebellions at the gold mines of Jobabo in 1533. At the turn of the 19th century, in a study of the various influences of European colonization, José Martí Pérez succinctly observed that "North America was born from the plough but the Caribbean (i.e., Hispaniola) was born of the prey dog" (Martí, 1963 [1853-1895]).

With the gradual depletion of gold and near extinction of the Indigenous population, depopulation of the colony was furthered by the departure of many conquerors to other promising centres of wealth such as Mexico and Peru. The Cuban economy was reoriented around 1520 to the exploitation of livestock—particularly bovine, porcine and equine—animals introduced by the colonizers and rapidly multiplying. A wealthy landowner social class/caste emerged from the cattle ranches, which complemented the sugar industry with leather, salted meats and animal fat. Tobacco was included in the mix by the mid-17th century. Peasant farmers were mixed with the surviving Indigenous people, blacks, free mulattos, and members of the Canarian diaspora through these agricultural practices.

The fleet supported the Spanish commercial monopoly over its colonies, moving back and forth from Spain to Cartagena de Indias (i.e., now Cartagena, Colombia). The fleet carried wealth taken from northern South

America and goods from Peru. The goods were transported by mule across the isthmus to Panama and shipped again, from Portobello to Cartagena and then to Havana. Treasures from Mexico were shipped from the port of Veracruz to Havana, the fleet's meeting point before the dangerous crossing of the Atlantic. Galleons of war protected the fleet's departure for Seville.

Havana was chosen for its strategic location in the western Caribbean. It had easy access to the Gulf Stream, favouring navigation to the European coasts and making Havana the strategic center of Spanish colonial trade. The fleet was located next to the sheltered bay housing the Havana exchange, among the largest Latin American stock exchanges. The stay of the fleet and the numerous garrisons protecting the city provided the economic impetus to make Havana the colony's capital city. By the middle of the 16th century, commerce proliferated, money circulated, and populations soared in Havana.

From that moment on, however, regional development in Cuba was no longer balanced, making the western part of the Cuban archipelago the center of economic growth. The commercial monopoly ensured extraordinarily high profits for the Spanish Crown and induced a thriving black-market smuggling trade—especially in the eastern town of Bayamo.

The Rise of Criollo and a Popular Piety

The first manifestations of Criollo culture are reflected in the epic poem "Espejo de Paciencia" ("Mirror of Patience"), written in Cuba in 1608 by the Canarian Silvestre de Balboa Troya Quesada (1563-1644). It fables an incident between Criollos and pirate smugglers near Manzanillo, Cuba. It casts a black Criollo slave as the hero—something that would have been almost unthinkable in the later plantation days—together with descendants of Indigenous people and Spaniards. Balboa Troya Quesada would later elaborate, in 1612, the legend of the Virgen de la Caridad del Cobre. It was based on a small sculpture found in Nipe Bay at Holguín by two native Indigenous descendants and a black child slave rowing through lurching seas. The miniature effigy was taken to the *minas de cobre* (the copper mines near Santiago de Cuba), where it became the subject of popular piety known in Spanish as the Virgin of Charity. Devotion to the Virgin of Charity was one of the expressions of Cubanness during the Cuban wars for independence. In 1915, a group of war veterans asked the Vatican to name her the Patron Saint of Cuba, which it did in 1936.

Spain's socio-economic backwardness compared to other European powers was reflected in the plundering of its colonies (not only in Cuba but throughout the Latin American territories). The situation intensified under the Bourbon Dynasty of the 18th century and peaked under the Spanish liberal governments of the 1840s with the development of sugar-plantation slavery. Sugar plantations predominated in the western part of the island—the Havana-Matanzas plain, extending into Trinidad and Cienfuegos—and coffee plantations in the east, in particular at Santiago de Cuba-Guantánamo. This saw the forced introduction of no less than 1,110,000 Africans (Betancourt and Obregón, 2013: 119). The old cattle-ranching structure was essentially maintained in the rest of the country.

As the demographics show, there were 272,300 inhabitants in the slave colony in Cuba in 1792, a number that jumped to 1,007,624 in 1841 and to 1,396,530 in 1861. The registers show that slaves represented 23.72 percent, 43.32 percent and 26.53 percent of the population, respectively. However, the breakdown did not include people classified as mulatto (i.e., Afro-European) and Black freedmen; with them, the population sector of African origin would have risen to 43.61 percent, 58.49 percent and 43.14 percent (Abreu 2013: 116), respectively.

Underlying this significant demographic and economic transformation was Spain's desire to make Cuba the new Haiti, which was the main sugar and coffee producer both before and after the slave-driven, anti-colonial Haitian Independence revolution at the dawn of the 19th century. The institution of slavery and the class/caste system imported from Europe were—along with terror—the mainstays of colonial socio-economic and political domination. Afraid that news of the bloody insurrection in Haiti might trigger similar revolts in other colonies, the colonizers projected anti-Black fear into the social imagination of Cubans while Spain set about whitening the population through greatly increased immigration from the Motherland. This stalled any progress in race relations in Cuba until 1868.

The process of Christian Catholic evangelization was less intense in Cuba than in other areas of the continent. This period of transculturation transformed the ethos around cultural life, especially involving the animistic cults of African derivation that had co-existed in the same period. In the 19th century, the liberal governments of the metropolis Hispanicised by giving privileges to the priests coming from the peninsula and also by, gradually, closing the convents. As a result, the local population diverged even more from the spiritual command of the church and from the church itself (Segreo Ricardo, 2000, pp. 6, 159,160).

As the 19th century progressed, various schools of thought or ideological currents emerged, offering visions for the country's destiny. Some aspired to reforms from Spain to remain integrated with the Motherland, others sought annexation to the United States as a way to ensure the continuation of slavery in the country, and yet others were fighting for the complete independence of Cuba and the simultaneous abolition of slavery.

This phase of Cuban history is also distinguished by a high-flying Cuban intelligentsia. The eminent Criollo priest and law professor Felix Varela y Morales (1788-1853) stands out for pioneering a new methodology that would eventually outmode the rote-memory learning entrenched by Scholasticism. The independence ideology also changed amid reformist and annexationist attempts spanning over half a century. Varela y Morales is celebrated as the first to actively theorize Cuban independence. He defined Cuba as having a national identity apart from Spain's and was the first intellectual to support independence wrought through revolution rather than evolution.

Varela y Morales insisted that Spain's colonial oppression and rejection of reforms would likely mean a non-peaceful revolution, but that the independence of the Island of Cuba was a matter of necessity not choice (Varela y Morales, 2001). He defended the principle of Cubans carrying out the revolution themselves rather than through a foreign invasion of troops from Mexico or Colombia, for example.

The movement gained strength until, under Carlos Manuel de Céspedes López del Castillo (1819-1874), the Cuban War of Independence commenced on October 10, 1868. This phase is known as the Ten Years' War (1868-78), and was followed by two more phases (1879-80; 1895-98) extending over 30 years, interspersed with several stormy intervals of peace. Céspedes, a lawyer by profession, was the leader of the Manzanillo revolutionary group and owner of a small sugar mill operating with about 50 slaves. He ended delays in the uprising that had divided the insurgents. Céspedes began the insurgency by declaring his slaves free and inviting them to join in the fight for a free Cuba. A competent *Mambi* (Cuban Liberation Army) officialdom was formed by men from the emerging middle classes and popular (i.e., blue-collar) sectors such as Máximo Gómez Báez (1836-1905), Antonio Maceo Grajales (1845-1896), and Calixto García Iñiguez (1839-1898).

Cubanness, the Quality of Being Cuban

From that first flash in 1868 under Céspedes, the independence movement pervaded the Cuban people, binding social classes/strata together in the Cuban fight for freedom. This process was strengthened by the wellspring of ideas emanating from the French Revolution, which had provided the ideological rationale of the insurrection by Haiti's black francophone slave population at the turn of the 18th century. Following the Haitian Revolution (1804), however, the social and economic structures, colonial ideology and resulting hierarchical value system fostered the rise of a neocolonial socio-economic reality.

As noted in Insert 1.1, the eminent Cuban author Alejo Carpentier (1957) depicted the colonial development of the Americas within a framework of slavery and anti-Black racism in his celebrated novel, *The Kingdom of This World*. Written just a few years before the successful conclusion of the Cuban Revolution, Carpentier's novel also illustrates how vestiges of colonialism/imperialism can thwart successful independence movements over the long term. Warnings about colonial legacies affecting the post-colonial period were at the forefront of the black African and Caribbean literary traditions and critical thought of the 20th century. A sociological study by the Tunisian sociologist and author Albert Memmi (1957), *Portrait of the Colonized*, explains the rise of an oppressive bourgeoisie from among the once-colonized (Wright, 2007, p. 42). The impacts or legacies of the colonial system continue to plague the African people and their descendants in ways that no Western nation, including Cuba, has yet to completely understand.

José Martí (1853–1895): The Final Phase of the Cuban War of Independence

In Cuba, the final stage of the national struggle for total independence resumed in 1895 when José Julián Martí Pérez (1853–1895) emerged as a main leader, overcoming regional, classist and racist disagreements in favour of uniting all Cubans. Martí created a political party to organize the final stage of the war initiated in 1868 for national independence.

Known as the apostle of Cuban independence, José Martí forged the necessary unity among the revolutionaries. He made it clear that his ideas for the future of the Republic meant acting together for the just cause of all Cubans by moving beyond racism and embracing the exercise of human dignity and honest work, along with the broader struggle for world peace and equity.

With considerable diplomacy, Martí expressed his growing concerns about the expansionist goals of U.S. policy and politicians. Martí's final letter, which he started writing to his Mexican friend Manuel Mercado on May 18, 1895 before heading into his last battle, would remain unfinished but contained a warning that prophesied not only his own imminent death but the U.S. intervention in the Cuban War of Independence:

> *I can write: I can tell you how tenderly and gratefully and respectfully I love you, as I love that house that is mine, and my pride and obligation; I am already in danger every day now of giving my life for my country, and because of my duty—since I understand it and I have*

Insert 1.1
The Kingdom of This World (1957)

The Haitian Revolution (1791–1804) marked the first successful anticolonial fight in the New World. The Haitian people emerged celebrating freedom, yet failing to see how the structures of the New World would thwart the new nation's success. In effect, the successful culmination of the Haitian Revolution faced three hurdles that would prove impossible to overcome.

First, it made Haiti the only nation in the "free" world competing without slave labour. Secondly, France refused to recognize Haitian sovereignty until 1925, the time it took for the new nation to pay France "more than £17bn, in gold from Haiti—under the threat of a blockade." This was how "Haiti gained immunity from French military invasion, relief from political and economic isolation—and a crippling debt that took 122 years to pay off" (Sperling, December 6, 2016). "In 2003, when the Haitian government demanded repayment, the French government responded by helping to overthrow that government" (*The Guardian*, 2010).

By the end of the 19th century, José Martí had identified "the non-realization of revolutionary change and the content of such change" as a post-revolutionary problem for the United States of America. He advocated "making the cultural revolution, to break away from the colonial mechanisms and mentalities, for which the participation of the oppressed [the peasant, the black, the Indian] was fundamental" (López-Civeira, 2019).

Just a few years before the successful conclusion of the Cuban Revolution, Cuban author Alejo Carpentier (1957) explored the colonial development of the Americas within a framework of the Haitian Revolution in his celebrated novel, *The Kingdom of This World*. In Carpentier, we see Fernando Ortiz's concept of transculturation in negative social transformation brought about by the pull of the colonial and imperialist paradigm which the world trade system (i.e., the economics of slavery, sugar, and tobacco) had come to embrace.

This pull compelled Haiti's despotic rulers following the Haitian Revolution to replicate a serfdom. The popular ideology of humanism underlying the Cuban socialist democracy's focus on cultural development has prevented this failure in Cuba. However, the colonial legacy of anti-Black social mindedness has not been wholly eliminated even here where almost every Cuban has some African heritage.

This situation is being reported in Cuba's *Granma* newspaper, the official voice of the Cuban Communist Party—an entity which has no political power but serves as a guide for the Cuban people and the ongoing development of Cuban socialism: "Racism, with its historical roots in the pursuit of the most brutal exploitation as a means of enrichment, is also necessarily a cultural phenomenon. That is why it does not end with the elimination of the economic bases sustaining it. It endures over time beyond the elimination of explicit or implicit laws codifying it, beyond the economic relations that need racism. A relentless struggle must be waged, on the economic, social and cultural planes, against racism, which not only persists but threatens to expand" (*Granma*, 2021).

> the courage to realize it—to prevent in good time that, with the independence of Cuba, the United States should extend its power over the Antilles and fall with that much more weight on our lands of America. All I have done so far and will do is for this.

With the death of Martí in 1895 and Maceo, the second-in-command military leader and eminent political personality in 1896, the leadership was left mainly in the hands of Salvador Cisneros Betancourt, Máximo Gómez, Calixto García and Bartolomé Masó. Having meager resources, Spain relied on terror alone to sustain its colonies from 1896 to 1897, so the Cuban victory was only a matter of time.

An intervention by the U.S. in July 1898 (the so-called Spanish–American War) prevented the inevitable defeat of Spain by the Cuban Liberation Army, and led Spain and the United States to refuse to allow the Cubans to participate in the post-war peace talks, resulting in the erasure from Western historical memory of the lengthy Cuban War of Independence. In one fell swoop, the U.S. occupied Cuba and seized two of the expiring Spanish Empire's other colonies, the Philippines and Puerto Rico, which is still in the hands of the United States.

Between 1899 and 1902 Cuba was occupied militarily by U.S. forces. Facing (Cuban) resistance not experienced with Puerto Rico, the U.S. opted for a more subtle solution, making Cuba an independent republic tied to the U.S. Empire by the Platt Amendment (1901). Imposed coercively as an appendix to the 1901 Constitution, the amendment allowed the U.S. to intervene in the island at will (Article III). The Platt Amendment also attempted to usurp Cuba's sovereignty over the Isle of Pines (Article VI) and ensured the use of Cuban land at Guantanamo for a naval base (Article VII), while facilitating the ongoing U.S. occupation of the island. This coincided with the signing of Order No. 62/1902 (Pérez, Louis A., Jr., 1985), allowing North American investors to take over Cuban lands and impose leonine treaties such as the Treaty of Commercial Reciprocity (1902) (Pichardo 1968, Volume II: 119–120, 180–198 and 212–217).

Even though the U.S. Congress had amended its War Measures Act with the Teller Amendment in 1898 to prevent a perceived risk of annexation attempts against Cuba during or following the impending war, Leonardo Wood, the post-war military governor of Cuba, suggested annexation to U.S. President McKinley (Cirules, 1976: 12). Cuba was again occupied militarily between 1906 and 1909, and U.S. troops also landed menacingly again in 1917 but did not occupy the country.

Bourgeois Republic (1902–1958)

On May 20, 1902, the Republic of Cuba emerged as a conservative political entity under a foreign protectorate. It seemed a disavowal of the inclusive Republic—with all and for the good of all—to which José Martí* had aspired. In all areas of the economy and society, U.S. economic penetration gave rise to a new economic and political model responsive to U.S. interests that has been described in Cuban historiography as neocolonial.

During the wars for independence, Blacks and mulattoes—a social mass that had grown with the introduction of thousands of Black West Indian seasonal farm labourers—had been integral to the Cuban Liberation Army. Still, they would find no solutions to their problems in the new Republic. The Black and mulatto (Afro-European) populations remained a vital labour force for the sugar industry. The response of the Independent Party of Color, which represented their interests, was an insurrection cruelly repressed by the army between May 20 and July 16, 1912, demanding recognition of their human rights. The plantation owners of the sugar republic joined with the U.S. interests in propagating a myth that this massacre of rebels would ensure everlasting internal peace for investors.

According to the U.S. census of Cuba, in 1899 the black population was 14.92 percent of the total. Together with mulattos (Afro-Europeans), this figure jumped to 25.4 percent in 1919. Between 1917 and 1930 Cuba imported 300,000 Antillean braceros to work in the sugar cane harvest (Pérez de la Riva, 1979, p.7). Around the same time, Fernando Ortiz,† a law professor at the University of Havana and an elected member of the House of Representatives (1917–1927), spoke out against anti-Black racism and called for Afrocuban studies in Cuba. It is noteworthy that the term Afro-Cuban was never popularized in Cuba because it is reductive to the goals of the Cuban Revolution. Here, everyone is an equal Cuban. The appropriate term is Afrodescendants or African descendants.

A complex ideological and political process fostered by growing criticism of this neocolonial reality awakened the national consciousness in Cuba between 1920 and 1933, against a backdrop of events such as Russia's Socialist Revolution of 1917, Argentina's University Reform in 1918, the world economic crises of 1921–1922 and the Great Depression (1929–

---

* "With all and for the good of all," a speech by José Martí delivered in the U.S. on November 26, 1891. Martí Pérez, J. *Obras Completas tomo 4*. Havana: Editorial de Ciencias Sociales, 1991.

† Fernando Ortiz (trans. Harriet de Onís), *Cuban Counterpoint: Tobacco and Sugar* (Durham, 1947; orig. pub. in Spanish, 1940). See also Ortiz' 1939 essay, "Los factores humanos de la cubanidad" [The human factors of Cubanidad].

1933). This process deconstructed colonial notions of progress, bringing Cuban intellectuals, students and workers together with various progressive political organizations, among them the communist party founded in 1925.

The growth of this popular anti-imperialist and anti-oligarchic movement led to the Revolution of August 1933, in which the main revolutionary political forces were not unified. On the contrary, there were differences between the nationalist bourgeoisie's interest in an anti-imperialist project, and the communists' promotion of an anti-capitalist revolution. Forging a united anti-imperialist or anti-capitalist movement proved undoable, yet the struggle between the two groups favoured the advance of the reactionary forces.

The impact of this unstable political situation smoothed the way for the rise to power of the U.S.-backed Cuban despot Fulgencio Batista Zaldívar (1901–1973), who had led a counterrevolutionary coup in January 1934 during which the outstanding leader of the left Antonio Guiteras Holmes (1906–1935) was assassinated. Between January 1934 and May 1940, Batista became the real power in the Republic. The six presidents* of that time were puppets kept in power by his grace. His ambition saw him become Constitutional President from 1940 until 1944, surprisingly gaining support from the communists. Such was the corruption and trickery that ruled Cuba at the time. Under popular pressure, the United States repealed the Platt Amendment in 1934 and established the Treaty of Commercial Reciprocity; however, by 1940, 78 percent of Cuban exports (mainly sugar) were destined for the United States (Hernández Castellón 1988: 63).

With the anti-fascist democratic activity of the day came a bit less repression and the approval of a new Constitution in 1940, which outlawed latifundia (private ownership of large land extensions) and incorporated broad democratic rights and responsibilities. This Magna Carta was not applied in its fundamental sections since the Cuban Parliament never approved the necessary complementary laws. For example, article 90 of the Constitution of 1940 prohibited latifundio, and to that end the Law would dictate the maximum size of property each person or entity could possess, but the regulatory laws were never put into practice.

Between 1944 and 1952 the Authentic Party governed under the presidencies of Ramón Grau San Martín (1881–1969) and Carlos Prío Socarrás (1903–1977). They presented themselves as bastions of the progressive

---

* Six presidents between 1934 and1940: Carlos Hevia y Reyes-Gavilán; Manuel Márquez Sterling y Loret de Mola (for 6 hours); Carlos Mendieta Montefur; José Agripino Barnet y Vinageras; Miguel Mariano Arias' Federico Laredo Bru.

conceptions of the Cuban people but were corrupt rulers bending to Washington's Cold War mandates (Vignier y Alonso, 1973). The obvious administrative and political corruption of the Authentic Party caused a split in their ranks in 1947, and the lawyer and radio announcer Eduardo Chibás y Ribas (1907–1951) founded the Party of the Cuban People (aka Orthodox Party). It embodied Chibás' well-known political slogan, "Shame on money." Its emblem was a broom, intended to sweep away the evils of the corrupt Republic. The Orthodox Party emerged as the indisputable winner of the 1952 elections, without Chibás. Accused of dishonesty in 1951 by President Prío (Chibás had written a public letter accusing him of sacrificing Cuban interests for personal gain) and then betrayed by others while trying to prove his innocence, Chibás committed suicide in resisting this injustice (Vignier, E. y G. Alonso, 1973).

Three months before the presidential elections and bolstered by Prío's inability to defend the republic, on March 10, 1952 General Fulgencio Batista led a coup d'état and seized power. Against this dramatic panorama, the young Cuban lawyer Fidel Castro Ruz (1926-2016) denounced the takeover and demanded action from constituted judicial authorities. He was not heard. On March 27, 1952, the United States officially recognized the Batista regime, ignoring widespread mass opposition. With the coup d'état, political ethics and justice became front and center of the political and popular struggle. Faced with the traditional parties' inability to confront the situation created by the Batista dictatorship, Fidel Castro (1953) sought new ways, such as the assault on the Moncada barracks of July 26, 1953.

In his defence plea known as "History will absolve me", Fidel declared José Martí the "intellectual author" of the July 26th (1953) revolutionary act and called the assault at the Moncada Garrison a tribute during what would have been Martí's centenary. Fidel also explained the revolution's program, pointing to the core problems besetting the republic, such as powerful foreign landowners with large companies amid a sea of landless, uneducated, illiterate peasants facing unemployment and increasing industrialization. The *Moncadistas* were liberated in 1955 with popular support, and Fidel founded the July 26 Movement as an instrument of unification for all forces fighting against the dictatorship.

Exiled to Mexico, Castro and a group of his followers organized an expedition on a small yacht to Cuba (the Granma Yacht) and landed on December 2, 1956 in the southwestern area of the then province of Oriente. From the Sierra Maestra, the first bastion of the Rebel Army, he led the struggle against the dictatorship. Faced with a potential military coup in Havana with U.S. collusion, Castro led the rebels to enter Santiago de Cuba and onward to Havana (Rioseco, P., 2020). This was in memory of Calixto García and the Mambisa insurgents who had been prevented from entering Santiago de Cuba when the Spanish troops surrendered to the U.S. Army in 1898).

The Popular-Democratic and Socialist Republic (1959–present)

The success of the revolution on January 1, 1959, cleared the way for attempts to solve the critical problems accumulated since the birth of the Republic of Cuba more than half a century before. The marvel of this opportunity lay in the fact that the Rebel Army and July 26 Movement was a leading force because it established a radical popular democracy with unlimited support of the vast majority of Cubans and increased the cohesion of the main revolutionary forces.

This integrative revolutionary leadership illustrates the unity of the revolutionary forces towards a common goal: to free Cuba from a bloody regime. The masses were demanding real solutions and change. The strategy of the three organizations fighting the tyranny—the vanguard of the July 26 Movement, the Student Revolutionary Directorate, and the Popular Socialist Party—was clear: to join forces for social justice through national independence. A verse in *Se acabó* (*It's Over*), a poem by the Cuban National Poet Nicolás Guillén (1960), a mulatto, illustrates the deep roots of Cuban national identity: *Martí promised it and Fidel fulfilled it*. The Constitution of 1940 was reinstated by the Revolution and soon began to be filled with new content.

The Law of Agrarian Reform issued on May 17, 1959, initiated a confrontation between the Revolution and U.S. imperialism that would escalate into the U.S. military attack at Playa Girón (Bay of Pigs) in April 1961. This was an attempt, with Cuban mercenaries, to conquer a portion of the Cuban coast and install a so-called Provisional Government manufactured by the CIA in Miami. The goal was to have this latter ask for U.S. military intervention "in the name of the Cuban people." This flimsy political maneuver was followed by the U.S. economic and financial blockade against Cuba and various assassination attempts against Fidel and other key leaders. Documents declassified over the years confirm the U.S. interest in Cuba as imperialist (Ramírez Cañedo and Morales Domínguez, 2015). The real goal behind the United States' intense public campaigning about an alleged lack of freedom in our nation was as imperialist as it could be: "Our [the U.S.] ultimate goal in Cuba is to replace the Castro regime with one that is fully compatible with the objectives of the United States" (Escalante 2016, p. 199).

The anti-Cuban aggression from Washington led to the nationalization of U.S. property and integration of an important quantity of Cuban land, mines, industries, trade, and other economic and social enterprises. The Soviet Union assumed responsibility for the Cuban sugar quota and provided petroleum, solving the demand for oil as well as other pressing economic problems. This forged a line of defence for the Cuban Revolution.

The consolidation of the new political path chosen by Cuba was evidenced by Fidel's declaration, on April 16, 1961, of the socialist character of the revolution. The day before, several attacks at small airports aimed to destroy the Revolutionary Government's small air force brought about several casualties. On April 16, 1961, at the funeral honouring those who had fallen in the bombings, Fidel confirmed the political unity of the revolutionary forces and laid the basis for the founding of the Communist Party of Cuba (PCC) in 1965. (Martí had renamed the original Communist Party [of 1925] as the Popular Socialist Party in 1944.)

The Cuban political structure is as much the result of integration as are many other aspects of Cuban development. The traditional historical parties, proven incompetent in the face of the U.S.-backed Batista dictatorship, fell apart as membership dropped away. The Cuban Revolutionary Party founded by José Martí was dissolved as early as 1898 and Ramón Grau's Authentic Party in 1959. The new PCC represented the political integration of the three primary forces that united in opposing the Fulgencio Batista dictatorship: the July 26 Movement, the Student Revolutionary Directorate, and the Popular Socialist Party. These three entities would unite into the Integrated Revolutionary Organization (ORI), which morphed into the United Party of the Cuban Socialist Revolution (UPURSC) in 1962 and the Communist Party of Cuba (PCC) in 1965.

It promoted a concept of social justice in which Martí's humanism and call for education for the masses would remain fundamental. Within the basic ideas of the Cuban Revolutionary Party (dissolved by the intervention government in 1898), the PCC's objective to organize the war was deemed necessary for the definitive liberation of our homeland, and to build "a nation capable of ensuring the lasting happiness of its children and assuming, in the historic life of the continent, the difficult duties that its geographical location dictates"; herein lies the embryonic components of the current political vanguard of our people, the Communist Party of Cuba (Castro, Raúl, 2021).

Therefore, as Fidel once stated, "there has only been one revolution in Cuba—the one which Carlos Manuel de Céspedes began on 10 October 1868!" (Castro, R. F., 1968). The Communist Party, an extension of that Revolutionary Cuban Party founded by Martí, a humanism-centred party, was the first to embrace all the revolutionaries who fought for independence. The PCC also assumed the task of organizing and directing the defence of national sovereignty against the hegemonic interests of U.S. imperialism. For these reasons, the PCC is considered to be the legitimate heir of the Cuban Revolutionary Party founded by José Martí in 1892. The Communist Party of Cuba (PCC) is in place to guide the Republic. It continues to support the genuine, popular interests of the people and their commitment to the Cuban Socialist Democracy.

The turbulence of the 1960s was manifested in acute class struggle, and counter-revolutionary destabilization attempts also characterized the period. All this happened amid the international siege of the Revolution, first under threat of direct military intervention by U.S. military forces and following their attack at the Bay of Pigs (*Playa Giron*, Cuba). In October 1962, Soviet medium-range nuclear missiles were moved by the USSR into Cuba, triggering the Cuban Missile Crisis. After a 13-day political and military standoff, the missiles were withdrawn by the Soviet government following secret conversations with the Kennedy administration that did not include Cuba. In exchange, the United States agreed not to invade Cuba. However, the economic blockade and subversive activities against Cuba continued.

At the same time, however, this drove Cuban revolutionary thought away from the dogmatism of Soviet socialism and, as discussed below, would prevent Cuban socialism from becoming a carbon copy. Remember that the colonial economic (trade) structures established in the 1500–1600 period favoured foreign natural-resource ownership, and this facilitated U.S. control of such resources in Cuba after the Spanish-American War. When control could no longer be maintained by the U.S. after 1959, the U.S. focussed its efforts on genocidal economic policies. The revolutionary project's attempts to use Cuban sugar production as a basis for national finances were doomed to fail within such a context; however, an ambitious plan of sowing 10 million tons of sugar was devised in 1970. The failure to harvest the sugar, after over-investing economic resources and human labour in the national project, forced Cuba to deepen its relations with the USSR and increased the Soviet influence on the Cuban economy.

The first Congress of the Communist Party of Cuba, in December 1975, gave shape to a socialist state imbued with Cuban features. Fidel warned against what we today would call "copying and pasting" models from other countries, especially as regards their economic mechanisms, that could undermine Cuba's revolutionary consciousness. The institutionalization of Cuban Socialism enjoyed overwhelming approval by the Cuban People.

Around the same time, the Cuban government recognized the growing economic potential of tourism, owing to the decreased airfares making travel to the Caribbean more feasible for the Western masses. Cuba's *Instituto Nacional de Turismo* (INTUR) has been operating in national and international tourism since 1976 and was joined by Cubanacan in 1987 and the Grupo de Turismo Gaviota S.A. in 1988. In certain respects, which are being monitored, the rollout of tourism has not been compatible with Cuban socialism.

Bartenders and wait staff can receive more in tips in one day than a university professor earns in a month, affording them a visibly higher lifestyle than the majority of Cubans (see Chapter 2). This has drawn human resources away from other sectors, especially education, and created pockets of relative wealth over time (see Chapters 3, 10). The relational social impact of the individual "fortunes" accruing from tourism to certain service-sector employees can be damaging for those who have less.

Social transformations naturally arise from economic processes, which will also be true of the 'free-market" activities newly introduced in Cuba, such as independent workers and small businesses. Since 2011, this has been the subject of intense scrutiny under two government initiatives: the Conceptualization of the Cuban Economic and Social Model of Socialist Development and the National Economic and Social Development Plan Through 2030: Vision of the Nation, Axes and Strategic Sectors.

Historically, foreign policy was the main battlefield of the revolution, and Cuba became synonymous throughout Latin America with the fight for non-alignment, anti-imperialism, and internationalism. Since 1959 Cuba has supported anti-colonial and anti-imperialist movements in Africa, in fulfillment of a perceived historical moral obligation to the African peoples. In 1975, Cuba gave military support to the legitimate government of Angola against the invasion of troops from the apartheid government of South Africa. The war in Angola culminated in 1991 with the defeat and disappearance of the racist regime, following the liberation of Namibia in 1990, and the consolidation of peace in Africa.

At this time, we were facing a complex internal environment still being manipulated to some extent by the United States. In the late 1970s and early 1980s a cultural movement, enveloping the visual arts in particular, brought to light social conflicts linked to ongoing destabilization attempts in Cuba by the U.S. A deeper appreciation of work, ethics, education and criticism was needed in order to safeguard the Cuban dream in accordance with the socialist will of the Cuban people.

Illegal immigration and acts of violence were stimulated through the

U.S. "dry foot/wet foot" policy, which encouraged illegal immigration from Cuba. Since 1966, under the Adjustment Act, Cubans who arrive illegally in the United States automatically receive aid programs and the right to citizenship. This does not happen with any other group of immigrants. It created a false impression, that people were being prevented from leaving Cuba. That was not the case, as evidenced by the revolutionary government's opening of the Mariel port, the closest port to the U.S. in 1980. This facilitated the exodus of more than 120,000 Cubans to the United States in what was dubbed the "Mariel boatlift." For many of them, the American Dream didn't become a reality. The United States defined a group it considered unacceptable, returning them to Cuba, and the rest were later able to return as visitors under Cuba's immigration laws (Satin, M.A., 1996).

In 1985, at the Third Congress of the Cuban Communist Party, Fidel Castro denounced the existence of enormous deficiencies in the management of the economic system and called for the rectification of errors and the negative tendencies damaging the country. It was an active political process that began with the strengthening of the Communist Party and reached all levels of the country's economic, social and intellectual life. This process preceded the famous Perestroika in the Soviet Union and underlined the authenticity of the Cuban process, making it possible to definitively remove Cuba from the bankruptcy of the political processes that led to the collapse of the Soviet Union and Eastern Europe socialist countries.

The disappearance of the Soviet Union and the European socialist community in the 1990s meant that Cuba had to contend with the demise of the trading partner that had served as its lifeline during the U.S. blockade. This development led to the so-called Special Period in Times of Peace, which caused euphoria in anti-Cuban circles. Cuba's link with Russia and the European socialist community dated back to the Cuban Missile Crisis in 1961. This was the original rationale for the U.S. embargo, which should have been ended by the U.S. Congress upon the fall of the USSR. Instead, Congress passed the Cuban Democracy Act (aka the Torricelli Law, 1992) and finally the Cuban Liberty and Democratic Solidarity (LIBERTAD) Act (aka the Helms-Burton Act, 1996), both of which are interventionist, antinational, genocidal, and extraterritorial, given their intended impact on the Cuban economy.

The Cuban Revolution remains strong and with the necessary vitality to withstand shortages and serious economic hardships, thanks, mostly to the unity of the people in their determination to maintain its achievements. The unity of the Cuban people around Fidel and the Party, active citizen participation in the decision-making of mass and social organizations, a nimble foreign policy that brought in new economic allies from different parts of the world, and reinforcement of the tourism industry, together with opening up to foreign capital and, more recently, to self-employment, have all proved important. These new sources of income arose due to the great destabilization of the Cuban sugar market in 1991.While these changes seem significant for the Cuban system, it is essential to remember that half the Cuban sugar industry between 1961 and 1991 had been sustained by the Russian market, which had vanished. Tourism and the export of services in public health as well as of some medicines, technicians from various specialties and other professionals such as teachers/professors, have been Cuba's principal sources of income since 1991. The Cuban development of COVID-19 vaccines to vaccinate Cuban citizens and for export is another testament to the Cuban government's unwavering fiscal and ideological commitment to education and healthcare since 1959. As José Martí put it, "There is no freedom without education."

Even before 1990, and especially after, the Cuban Government has found ways to move the Cuban economy forward while staying true to the social justice policies supported by the vast majority of Cubans and without causing shock to the economy, which would have a relational negative impact on society. Numerous assessments have illustrated the significance of the impacts on the Cuban economy and society of the longstanding economic stranglehold of the U.S. embargo.

President Obama called for an end to the embargo and re-established diplomatic relations between the U.S. and Cuba. As the Cuban Minister of Foreign Affairs, Bruno Rodríguez Parrilla (2020), has pointed out, however, President Trump introduced 243 new measures during the pandemic to reinforce the blockade in a way that opportunistically made deliveries of medical supplies that traditionally came to Cuba from Asia fall under the U.S. embargo, causing incalculable suffering for Cuban families. Rodríguez Parrilla's report also confirms that the Biden administration has maintained the same policy, adding more than $5.57 billion in damages when the pandemic was at its peak to an already astonishing total of losses related to the embargo:

> The accumulated damages caused by the blockade during almost six decades, at current prices, have reached the colossal figure of 144 billion 413 million dollars. For a small economy like the Cuban economy this is a truly overwhelming burden. However, if one takes into account the devaluation of the dollar against the price of gold, accumulated damages reach the extraordinary figure of 1 trillion 98 billion 8 million dollars. (Rodríguez Parrilla, B., 2020)

Not all of Cuba's present and past problems can be blamed on the embargo, but a simple analogy illustrates that most of Cuba's current problems are attributable to the blockade: If you own a store and a neighbour prevents the majority of shoppers from entering it, you won't survive. As noted at the outset of this chapter, Cuba continues to beat all the odds of this happening. This is partly because of Cuba's longstanding, ongoing, and costly commitment to the Cuban People in terms of education and healthcare. Cuba is the only country in Latin America that produced vaccines to fight COVID-19.

Despite all the economic difficulties, this downtrodden yet unwavering island has maintained the socialist principle of distribution, such as continuing to provide housing and ensuring at least a minimum of nutritional needs. Even though salaries have risen, they are still low considering the high prices. Efforts are being made to encourage domestic production of agricultural products and other products in high demand. Cuba is no threat to any person, group, or nation. Our history of humanitarian aid dates back to our early revolutionaries who fought for Cuban independence.

Following Fidel's illness and retirement from his positions and responsibilities, his brother Raúl was officially made acting President of the Council of State and the Council of Ministers from 2006 to 2008 by the National Assembly of People's Power. He served as defence minister from 1959 to 2006 and President-elect from 2008 to 2018, after which he did not seek re-election. Raúl Castro was chosen for proven political and personal merit. He was a key and respected figure in the Cuban Revolution and then as defence minister. The succession also demonstrated that the Cuban system was sustained by its popular bases and institutions and not by a single man, even one so symbolically suited to the purpose. The general elections of April 19, 2018 culminated with Miguel Antonio Díaz-Canel Bermúdez becoming President, confirming the historical continuity of the Cuban Revolution.

Public discussions around the 2019 Constitution included possible future changes to the presidential electoral process to include a selection of presidential candidates. Civil changes permitting same-sex couples to marry were implemented following approval by the Cuban people in a national referendum by secret ballot in 2022. Like China and Vietnam, Cuba has a unique model of socialism based on its evolving characteristics and needs. The current process of updating underway since 2011 is completely in step with the historical direction of the revolution as new generations of leaders emerge.

References

Abreu Cardet, J.M. (Ed.) (2013). *La historia de Cuba*. Archivo General de la Nación, Santo Domingo, R. D.

Betancourt, J.N., and Obregón, A.P. La colonia [the colony] (1492–167). In Abreu Cardet, J.M., *La historia de Cuba*.

Castro Ruz, F. (1953) (1968). *History will absolve me: The Moncada trial defence speech, Santiago de Cuba, October 16th, 1953*. London: Jonathan Cape.

Castro Ruz, F. (1968). Speech by Cuban Prime Minister Fidel Castro at the principal ceremony marking the centennial of Cuba's struggle for independence at La Demajagua National Park near Manzanillo, Cuba. Latin American Network Information Center (LANIC). Castro speech database. http://lanic.utexas.edu/project/castro/db/1968/19681011.html

Castro Ruz, R. (2021, April 22). Central Report to the Eighth Congress of the Communist Party of Cuba. *Granma International*. April 22, 2021. https://en.granma.cu/cuba/2022-01-07/central-report-to-the-eighth-congress-of-the-communist-party-of-cuba

Cirules, Enrique. (1976). *Conversación con el último norteamericano* [conversation with the last American]. Mexico: Siglo XXI editores.

Cuban Liberty and Democratic Solidarity (Libertad) Act of 1996. [Codified in Title 22, Sections 6021-6091 of the U.S. Code. P.L. 104-114]. Washington, DC: One Hundred Fourth Congress of the United States of America. https://home.treasury.gov/system/files/126/libertad.pdf

Escalante Font, Fabián. (2016). *Más allá de la duda razonable. El asesinato de Kennedy y la inculpación a Cuba* [Beyond reasonable doubt, the Kennedy assassination and indictment of Cuba]. Havana, Cuba: Editor Política.

Estévez Rams, Ernesto/*Granma*. (2021, July 17). In black and white: A relentless struggle must be waged, on the economic, social and cultural planes, against racism that persists, despite the immense efforts of the Revolution. *Granma*. Havana: Cuban Communist Party (CPP). Retrieved from https://en.granma.cu/cultura/2020-07-17/in-black-and-white

Gámez, T. N. (2018, February 11). U.S. promise to issue 20,000 visas to Cubans is jeopardized by cuts at Embassy in Havana. *Miami Herald*.

Guardian, The. (2010, August 15). France urged to repay Haiti billions paid for its independence [Leading activists write to Nicolas Sarkozy urging president to repay more than €17bn to help earthquake-hit country rebuild]. https://www.theguardian.com/world/2010/aug/15/france-haiti-independence-debt

Guerra, Ramiro. [1555–1607] (1922). *Historia de Cuba*. Vol. II. 2nd ed. [History of Cuba]. Havana, Cuba: Librería Cervantes.

Guillén, Nicolás. (1960). *Se acabó* [It's over]. Ministry of Foreign Affairs of Cuba (MINREX). December 31, 2018. https://misiones-minrex-gob-cu.translate.goog/es/articulo/te-lo-prometio-marti-y-fidel-te-lo-cumplio?_x_tr_sch=http&_x_tr_sl=es&_x_tr_tl=en&_x_tr_hl=en&_x_tr_pto=sc

Hernández Castellón, Raúl. (1988). *La revolución demográfica en Cuba* [Demographic revolution in Cuba]. Havana: Editorial Ciencias Sociales.

López-Civeira, F. (2019). The concept of nuestra américa [Our américa], in José Martí. Havana, Cuba: University of La Habana, Cuba. School of Philosophy and History. doi.org/10.15359/tdna.35-65.4. ISSN 0259-2339–EISSN 2215-5449. Retrieved from file: ///C:/Users/Client/Downloads/12800-Texto%20del%20art%C3%ADculo-48495-1-10-20191123.pdf

Martí, J. (1963) [1853-1895]. *Obras completas*. Volume 4 of 27. Havana: Editorial Nacional de Cuba, 1963–1973.

Martí, J. (1991). *Obras completas* [Martí's complete Works]. Tome IX. Havana: Editorial de Ciencias Sociales.

Martinez, Maria Elena. (2008). *Genealogical fictions: Limpieza de Sangre, religion, and gender in colonial Mexico*. Stanford, California: Stanford University Press.

Memmi, Albert. [1957] (1991). *The Colonized*. (Trans.) Boston: Beacon Press. [*Portrait du colonisé*. Paris: Éditions Corrêa. 1957].

Museum of Anthropology (MOA). (2013–2014). The marvellous real: Art from Mexico, 1926–2011. Vancouver, BC: Museum of Anthropology, University of British Columbia. https://moa.ubc.ca/exhibition/the-marvellous-real-art-from-mexico-1926-2011/

Ortiz, Fernando. (1940) [1947]. *Contrapunteo cubano del tabaco y el azúcar*. Havana: J. Montero. [*Cuban counterpoint: Tobacco and sugar*. (Trans. H. de Onis). New York: A. Knopf.]

Ortiz, Fernando. (1939; 1940). Los factores humanos de la cubanidad. [Lecture]. University of Havana, Cuba. Revista Bimestre Cubana. Havana, Cuba: Printed by Molina y Cía. 1940. [The human factors of cubanidad (Trans. H. N. Eissler). *HAU: Journal of Ethnographic Theory* 4(3): 407–434].

Pérez de la Riva, J. (1979). Cuba y la migración antillana 1900–1931. In *La República neocolonial*. [Cuba and Antillean migration 1900–1931. In *The Neocolonial Republic*.] Yearbook of Cuban Studies. Havana: Editorial de Ciencias Sociales.

Pérez de la Riva, Juan. (2004). *La conquista del espacio cubano*. Havana, Cuba: Fundación Fernando Ortiz.

Pérez, Louis A., Jr. (1985) Insurrection, intervention, and the transformation of land tenure systems in Cuba, 1895–1902. *The Hispanic American Historical Review*, 65(2): 229–254 (26).

Prieto Abel and *Granma*. (2019, August 16). Cubanness and Cuban identity: Fernando Ortiz invited us to work on a common project to develop "a full, heartfelt, conscious, and desired Cuban identity." Havana: *Granma*. http://en.granma.cu/cultura/2019-08-16/cubanness-and-cuban-identity

Ramírez Cañedo, E., and Morales Domínguez, E. (2015) J. F. Kennedy y la diplomacia secreta con Cuba. In *De la confrontación a los intentos de 'normalización'. La política de los Estados Unidos hacia Cuba*. Havana: Editorial Ciencias Sociales. http://www.cubadebate.cu/opinion/2015/01/19/j-f-kennedy-y-la-diplomacia-secreta-con-cuba/

Rioseco, Pedro. (2020). La Operación Santiago y preludios del triunfo de la Revolución Cubana. https://www.contraloria.gob.cu/en/node/13930

Rodríguez Parrilla, Bruno. (2017). Cuba vs blockade report. Report. Informe de Cuba. Sobre la resolución 71/5 de la Asamblea General de las Naciones Unidas, titulada "Necesidad deponer fin al bloqueo económico, comercial y financiero impuesto por los Estados Unidos de América contra Cuba." Digital. Havana: Cuban Minister of Foreign Affairs (MINREX). http://misiones.minrex.gob.cu/es/articulo/informe-de-cuba-sobre-la-resolucion-715-de-la-asamblea-general-de-las-naciones-unidas-5

Rodríguez Parrilla, Bruno. (2020, October 26). Cuba's Report under Agenda item 74/7 of the United Nations General Assembly entitled "Necessity of ending the economic, commercial and financial blockade imposed by the United States of America against Cuba." http://www.minrex.gob.cu/en/node/3608

Satin, M. A. (1996) Detention of Cuba excludable aliens in the United States. *New England Journal on Criminal and Civil Confinement*, 22(1): pp. 139–174.

Segreo Ricardo, Rigoberto. (2000). *De Compostela a Espada, Vicisitudes de la Iglesia Católica en Cuba*. Havana: Editorial de Ciencias Sociales.

Sperling, D. (2017, December 6). In 1825, Haiti paid France $21 billion to preserve its independence—time for France to pay it back. Guest Commentary. Forbes. https://www.forbes.com/sites/paulhsieh/2020/06/23/delayed-cancer-care-due-to-covid-19-could-cost-thousands-of-lives/?sh=1f2f7be35ba9

Varela y Morales, F. (2001). *Obras*. [works]. Vol. II. Editorial CP. Havana: Ediciones

Imagen contemporane/Cultura popular. University of Havana. Volume II, p. 225. http://ufdcimages.uflib.ufl.edu/AA/00/00/86/90/00002/FV2.pdf

Vignier, E. y G. Alonso. (1973). La corrupción política administrativa en Cuba 1944 – 1952. [political corruption in Cuba 1944-1952]. Havana, Cuba: Editorial de Ciencias Sociales.

Wright, Nancy. (2007). *Pre-sent realities: Counter-memory in Brand, Clarke, Dorsinville, and Laferrière*. Master's Thesis, 2006. Comparative Canadian Literature. Quebec (Canada): Université de Sherbrooke. Ottawa: Library and Archives Canada/Bibliotheque et Archives Canada, [2008].

CHAPTER TWO

Cuba and Its Transformations in the New Millennium

Luis Orlando Aguilera García

> ... his comprehension does not, as Hegel thinks, consist in everywhere recognising the determinations of the logical concept, but rather in grasping the proper logic of the proper object.
> —Marx, *Critique of Hegel's Philosophy of Right*

Abstract

This chapter analyzes the socio-cultural transformations unfolding in Cuba in the second decade of the 21st century through a process known as "Updating the economic and social model of socialist development." The Cuban Revolution is an unprecedented experience and not just for the island; its differences from similar processes in other latitudes give it entrenched historical-cultural singularities that find expression in all aspects of social life. This chapter draws on original approaches to illustrate the current trajectories of the Cuban Revolution and point out possible future directions. The author proposes a reflective dialogue with the reader to explain the updating process and its impact on all components of the Cuban social framework. Only by fathoming the interaction between the political, ideo-cultural, economic, social, technological, and scientific spheres can one gain a holistic view of a process designed to build a sovereign, independent, socialist, democratic, prosperous, and sustainable society in Cuba.

Keywords: democracy, socialism, socialist revolution, Cuban Revolution, political science

Luis Orlando Aguilera García, Ph.D. Email: loag56@gmail.com, loag@uho.edu.cu. Member of the Cuban Society of Philosophical Research; Professor of Political Science (South Approach); Professor of Science, Technology, and Society, University of Havana; Chair Member of the National Accreditation Board of the Republic of Cuba and of the Provincial Council of Social and Humanities Sciences in Holguín.

Introduction

The Cuban Revolution, which in 2019 celebrated its 60th anniversary of progress in the midst of economic zigzags and social consolidations, still bears scars from the 1990s, a difficult time known as the "Special Period in Times of Peace." Its consequences can still be clearly seen, etched into the facets of everyday life in Cuba, and there is a real need to improve the socio-economic system of the country to ensure sustainability. The process was initiated in 2011 and is known as "Updating the economic and social model of socialist development." A capricious interweaving melding the traces of the Special Period in the intricate social fabric with the goals and transformations of the new socio-economic model, is the background against which the processes we are about to present to the reader will be outlined.

The objectives of this chapter are to lay out the fundamentals of the socio-cultural processes developing in Cuba since 2000 and to identify the tensions and challenges that lie ahead for our country. The chapter consists of two sections and some brief conclusions. The first section sets out the conceptual and social bases of the updating process and its direct historical precedents. Within a framework of these elements, the second section analyzes the tensions and challenges generated by the multidimensional effects of the social transformations being brought about through the process of updating the economic and social model of socialist development currently being undertaken by Cuba.

I. Updating the Economic and Social Model of Socialist Development in Cuba: Transformational Concepts and Changes (2011–2017)

While the first expressions of the transformations being driven by Cuba's updating process only came into view around 2008, they are a continuation of changes initiated in the 1990s to reverse the deep crisis then facing the country and threatening the collapse of the entire social system. In 2008, situations in the international and national spheres converged to produce severe impacts on the island's economy. The countries that constitute the great world economic centre fell into a systemic crisis that shook international finance and the global economy. All nations felt the effects, and Cuba was no exception. Three tropical hurricanes also ripped through Cuba that year, having devastating effects on all spheres of the social network in a country not yet able to recover from the deep crisis of the 1990s. Signs in the economy indicated a need to rethink various components of the country's chosen path. These key factors would lead to the introduction of delicate and important changes to the national economy and open the door to a rethinking of the country's development strategy.

Such was the preamble to the VI Congress of the Communist Party of Cuba (hereinafter PCC, its Spanish acronym) in 2011, which pursued the approval of important concepts and various documents needed to give coherence to the necessary changes, some of which were already underway, including expansion of a small private-sector economy. It was within the framework of this Congress that the process of updating the social and economic model of socialist development (2011) was officially defined and launched. In the author's opinion, this updating process encompasses a complex process of multiple, successive, and simultaneous transformations that will impact the most dissimilar spheres of social life and has productive economic and financial relations as a core dimension, political relations as a guiding dimension, the ethics of Cuban revolutionary thought as a regulatory framework, and the construction of a sovereign, independent, socialist, democratic, prosperous, and sustainable society as a main objective (Aguilera, 2017, p. 55).

Among the changes being carried out through the process of updating the social and economic model, the following are key to the analysis in this chapter:

- The five forms of property ownership in Cuba:
  - socialist state property, which is the property of the Cuban people,
  - cooperative ownership,
  - mixed ownership,
  - private ownership, and
  - ownership of political, mass, social and other organizations;
- The relations between these forms of ownership and emerging forms of associated management, as well as the productive, service, and value chains opening up, and their consolidation within the primary framework of socialist ownership of the means of production, which hinges on the efficient performance of enterprises owned by the people and conjoined with the other forms of ownership;
- The socialist character of the fundamental relations of production;
- The socialist character of the state and its functions;
- The definition of the strategic axes of development, in which infrastructure consolidation *vis-à-vis* human capital, science, technology, and

innovation, cultural transmission and social expression, human development, and social justice are related to the need for international insertion, productive transformation, and a government that is socialist and practical;
- The ratification of the updating model's strategic objective, which is to promote and consolidate the construction of a socialist society that is prosperous and sustainable across the economic, social, and environmental spheres and committed to the ethical, cultural, and political values forged by the Revolution in an independent, sovereign, and solidary nation;
- The achievement of balanced rhythms of economic growth and structural change that will safeguard the society's twin goals: prosperity and social justice;
- The primary role of an efficient economy as the basis of material support for a socially just distribution of wealth;
- The new Constitution (2019) reaffirming the Communist Party of Cuba (PCC) as the superior guiding political force and the commitment to a **socialist political framework** (PCC, 2017a, p. 22; Aguilera, 2017, pp. 53–54).

These go hand in hand with important new government purposes related to decentralization and the subsequent need to consolidate leadership among local government bodies (PCC 2017(a), p.17, 32, 40; 2017(b), p.17, 39). The sweeping changes planned for the future and those already underway can, in the author's opinion, be classified according to the following logical groups:

1. Changes to the economic management model;
2. Changes to macroeconomic policy;
3. Changes to social policy; and
4. Changes to sectoral and other microeconomic development.

As explained above in relation to the updating process, the entire set of economic changes undertaken in Cuba will reverberate in all facets of Cuba's economic, political, and sociocultural spheres and the daily lives of individuals and groups across the island. For Cuba, this multiplicity of processes and effects can be seen in the latent relationships between economic change, political effects, and social ethics, which the author expresses as the "Economy–Ethics–Politics Complex." In general, any analysis of the ongoing development of the Cuban Revolution must recognize the pivotal

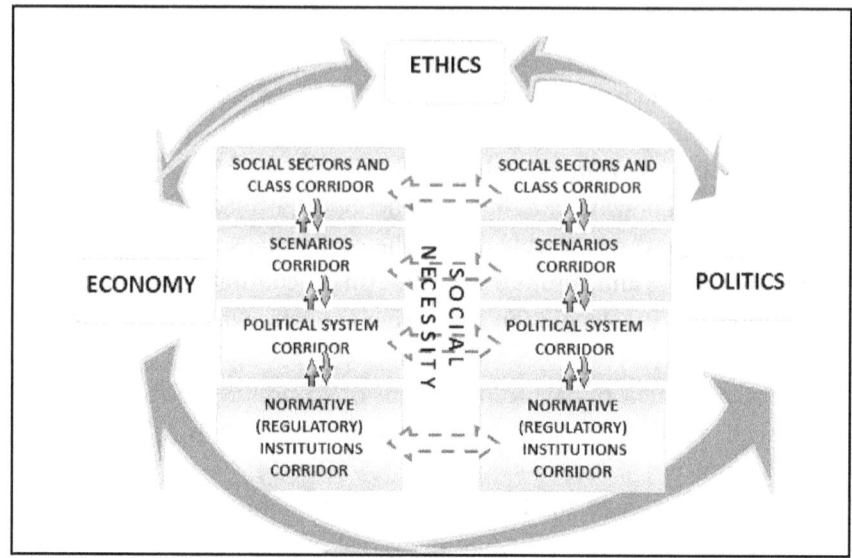

Figure 2.1. Economy–Ethics–Politics Complex (Aguilera, 2013, p.18).

importance of the interconnectivity of these three spheres. Some would say, with absolute reason, that this is true for the study of social processes in any nation; but for Cuba, these relationships are the crux of socio-classist confrontations against which the Revolution has had to advance since its inception, and the U.S. government stands as a representative par excellence of positions opposed to this process.

As shown in Figure 2.1,* the Complex's three spheres are connected through relational determination to the social system, where they intercondition, interact, and mutually determine each other in such a way that a change in one leads to changes in the others, directly or indirectly and sometimes in the most unusual and unpredictable ways. The character of the Economy–Ethics–Politics Complex is indivisible and its connections play out in the social fabric, affecting every sector, group, and class, in all the institutional structures, norms and in every person and their values—because any change in the economy reaches politics through the ethics of the social subjects who carry the Revolution, to become, also through ethics, a concerted political expression of economic change.

The notion of a complex (Economy–Ethics–Politics) is given by the interconnectivity of the spheres, which the author terms "Corridors" to reflect an inherently constant and permanent flow of dialectic relationships:

---

* The author elaborated on this figure, which appears in Aguilera, 2013, and has been updated and translated into English for the present book.

1. Social Sectors and Class Corridor: The socio-class structure in Cuba: working class, petty bourgeoisie,* intellectuals, and other social sectors.
2. Scenarios Corridor: Where and by which means people undertake and are influenced by their daily lives as a function of where they live and work: urban areas vs. rural areas and industry vs. academia.
3. Political System Corridor: The fundamental elements of political power, the role of the state, the characteristics of governance at both the national and regional (local) levels.
4. Regulatory (Normative) Institutions Corridor: Specifically, the body of law that defines the national characteristics, from the constitution to the accompanying legal institutions. The relationship between law and social values is very important to the present analysis.

As the Cuban philosopher R. Pupo (2011) observed in his brilliant work on ecosophy, culture, and transdisciplinarity, the very notion of "dialectical corridors"† imparts the idea of constant and permanent flows that produce a synergistic effect (i.e., the whole is greater than the sum of its parts) under which the combined actions (changes to economic policy) produce an effect (transformation) far greater than the sum of the individual effects (transformations). The "dialectic corridors" metaphor was coined by Dr. Thalía Fung Riverón (2011) as a process that reveals and reinforces the dynamics of social life, which makes it highly applicable within the unique framework of the present author's notion of an Economy–Ethics–Politics Complex involving the dialectics of change and the evolutive character of Cuban society.

In the author's Economics–Ethics–Politics Complex, social factors are affected by the dialectical relations of the spheres, and it is the determining link of the development context, which aims to bring about the desired social ends. In the author's opinion, these relationships act as a complex because of the apparent cohesion of the designated spheres of social life as otherwise explored by Nuñez Jover (2010). As a complex, the spheres interact to overcome dysfunctions and preserve the social balance; however, the same forces that can lead to improvements aimed at strengthening social justice can also be seen as the seeds of oligarchic interests, depending on the development context and the particular character of the

---

* See Marx and Engels (1848); Engels (1847); Marx (1871); Lenin (1917).

† In a private communication, the author discussed the notion of "dialectic corridors" with Dr. Thalía Fung Riverón, who coined the expression and used it in a variety of works. For the author, Riverón's term connotes an idea force that reveals the dynamics of social life with great accuracy, hence the decision to incorporate it into the notion of the Economy–Ethics–Politics complex.

social transformations being brought about by changes in each of the three spheres of the complex.

This signifies the ethical implications that the economic changes and ensuing social transformations may have on the political life of the nation and the demands this places on every component of the political system, the various social actors, etc. There is a real need to effectively identify the social impacts and ensuing transformations being brought about in the sphere of social relations by the changes to the economy. Thus, while the overwhelming majority of the measures adopted concern economic relations, the application of the updating process has inevitably led to deep constitutional reform (see Proyecto, 2018; Referendum, 2019). The Constitutional Referendum was held on February 24, 2019, when 7,848,343 Cubans exercised their right to vote. With 86.8 percent (6,816,169) voting in favour of the Constitution, 9 percent (706,400) voting "Nay," and 4.1 percent spoiling their ballots (Doimeadios, 2019), Cuba ratified its new Constitution.

Of course, for Cuba—located a scant 90 miles from what in all respects is the most powerful nation on the globe and one which has not "forgiven" Cuba for having advanced a socialist revolution in its backyard—everything that occurs within its watery limits provokes an immediate policy response by the U.S. government designed to limit, curb, and topple our system. This phenomenon reached an acute phase under President Trump's first administration (Mojena, 2019; Capote, 2019), including his full implementation of the Helms-Burton provision of the U.S. embargo against Cuba.

Cuba is among the countries most strongly affected by an endless cascade of U.S. policies. They aim to cripple our economic and social system within a framework of a confrontation that has already lasted more than 60 years. This economic blockade waged against the island by its closest neighbour constitutes one of the cruelest violations of human rights in the world. Any changes carried out by the Cuban Revolution have thus had to be designed with a built-in capacity for detecting signs that the process might be leaving itself open to the political intentions of the government of the United States.

This means that any processes of change carried out by the Cuban Revolution must be conducted under conditions of latent risk, and their conception, execution, and implementation also must be tempered to that reality. This approach will also qualify the rates of progress and allows for any adjustments or backtracking regarding the updating of the economic model. The multiple transformational social effects of each of the changes must be weighed and balanced against this perceived threat to ensure that the systemic set of those effects serves to advance the Revolution while minimizing political risks. The influence of relations with the United States is an element that always affects any changes under development in Cuba. That country's policy towards the island has steadied it on a course of permanent aggression. This is why any change must here be designed so that it is ready to prevent or offset the negative impact of external interests on the internal social processes supported by the Revolution and thus, the Cuban people.

Smart Revolution

The author, to coin a version of a term widely associated with the smartphone, associates this process with the metaphor of "smart revolution" (Aguilera, 2013), which is ideologically and politically contrary to the "smart power" orchestrated by the power circles of the government of the United States.

Some of the early tensions and challenges that emerged from Cuba's process of updating our economic and social model over the fourth and fifth years of this century are described in the following section.

II. The Updating of the Economic and Social Model in Cuba amid Challenges and Tensions

The far-reaching transformations that will result from the changes discussed in Section I illustrate the degree and scope of the changes that are underway, which encompass the economic, financial, political, administrative, legal, cultural, social, and, of course, ideological spheres. Their combined action produces effects on the everyday lives of everyone in the nation, both individually and within groups, families, institutions, and communities. These changes thus impact a wide range of social scenarios and processes.

The impacts are economic, financial, organizational, cultural, ethical, political, legal, and, of course, social and ideological. In this context, the word "impacts" is understood as changing or transforming what already exists into something superior to benefit the people, the economy, society, etc. The impacts must be long-lasting rather than transient and will be seen not only in the economic results but also in the transformational effects of change and repercussions on people, their values, and the environment (Quevedo and Chía, 2010). The impacts result from the tensions generated within and without each sphere of the dialectical triad given by Economy–Ethics–Politics. In turn, these tensions take various forms and degrees of radicalism (such as private ownership and free-market activity) and, in different ways, will affect the social stakeholders of the five political generations of Cubans living on this island. The Cuban researcher Luis Suárez, in an interview (Granovsky, 2014), characterizes these generations as: (1) the historical generation, (2) the Guevarian generation, (3) the institutionalized-revolution generation, (4) the special-period generation, and the (5) battle-of-ideas generation.

The design, implementation and effects of economic measures generate tensions of various magnitudes and degrees of radicalism, as explained by the following relations and reflections:

- **Economics–Politics:** What political implications can be generated by the deployment of economic changes such as the forms of property discussed above? Do all these implications contribute to strengthening the legitimacy of the Revolution, or can they hurt it? What actions will be necessary in the political sphere to counteract unwanted effects of drastic economic measures?
- **Market–Plan:** What are the necessary and possible measures of market relations in a society that has gone more than 50 years without any such relations and is therefore unprepared for the consequences, which find expression through the law of supply and demand? What economic actions should be incorporated to help protect those sectors of the population still working within the realm of the state economy, and what will the effects of these market relations be on such sensitive matters as, for example, wages and prices?
- **Equality–Equity–Social Justice:** To what extent is it possible and necessary to maintain a subsidized distribution of benefits to the entire population in the face of an economic scenario in which private ownership will ensure comparatively higher incomes to some of the recipients of these subsidies? Is it socially possible and morally correct to proceed instead with a subsidy program based on relative need?
- **Ethics–Economics:** How can the ethical positions of integrity and anti-corruption be defended in an economic environment in which the salaries of state workers fail to sustain the adequate quality of life enjoyed by the majority of Cuban families back in the 1980s when scarcities existed, but both salaries and the prices of available products were low? What actions on the political and education fronts can counteract the tendencies toward alienation and corruption that will arise?
- **Economy–Scientific Research–Academic Life:** Will it be possible to deploy a retention policy for professionals educated and trained under public policies implemented through the Revolution in a way that encourages people to continue to take up these fields, thus safeguarding

their contribution to national development, and that takes into account the benefits of such as opposed to the enormous economic cost incurred to the nation when such professionals emigrate for economic reasons?*

It is worth mentioning that a very positive approach to assessing the social impact of changes made to the economic system was introduced in the Province of Holguín in 2013. It promotes the broad participation of all citizens in solving the more pressing problems afflicting the social life of cities, municipalities, and families in the territory. It involved talking with the people to identify and better understand the transformations, and reporting back to them via television and radio (Diálogo Público, 2013).

Many other tensions are emerging through the arduous but necessary updating process. These tensions have generated a number of questions in the popular imagination:

- What increased level of productivity is needed to generate an equitable wage-price ratio for state workers?
- To what extent should and can the regulation of private initiatives impose restrictive price policies for their products and services without leading to their collapse?†
- Is wage reform possible and sustainable without triggering further increases in prices for basic products, or should wage reforms be designed with the principle of "to each according to their ability, to each according to their work" in mind? Will these be mutually exclusive or not?

These key questions, among others, give us an idea of the magnitude of the tensions faced by Cuban policy makers *vis-à-vis* the design and implementation of the ongoing changes.

---

* As Fung Riverón (2014, p 211) has emphasized, the "economics-ethics relationship is mediated by a politics all the more complex because it will incorporate masses that capitalism has not fashioned the increase of productivity." In the author's opinion, the intimate relation between the understanding of politics and the worldview with respect to society must be emphasized. For Marxism, the transformational activity of the framework of social life correlates with economics and politics through complex mediations decided by man and his conceptions, interests, values, etc. They are the concentrating filter, the mediation that transmits politics to the economic occurrence.

† Evidence of the complexity of the relations between socialist social economy and private economy, in relation to the decision-making exercise of territorial governments (Havana province in this case), has been provided by the diverse reactions to the regulations on private transportation in the capital. Since 2016, the implementation of these regulations has been conducted in various ways and by the end of 2018 was legally reinforced by the reform concerning self-employment.

Those Cubans who boast, not without some reason, that we are experts in a wide array of fields including baseball, medicine, economics, and politics, will undoubtedly be "scratching their heads" over these questions, which pose real intellectual challenges as regards the entire nation's declared objective to persist in advancing the construction of a sovereign, independent, socialist, democratic, prosperous, and sustainable society. The goal is to mediate progress in such a way as to prevent the changes and ensuing tensions from becoming radicalized seeds of social conflict that will not benefit national progress in any way. How, especially given the urgent need to deploy this comprehensive change process, can the revolutionary process's legitimacy be ensured?

By 2018, the need for an appropriate legal framework for the gamut of successive changes had become obvious. Given the scope of what is being undertaken and the fact that some of the elements have long been well underway, such as the operation of small businesses through self-employment, the construction of a legal framework would require major constitutional reform in line with the envisioned purpose of the future society. In August 2018 the text of the Constitutional Reform was made public by way of the broadest widespread consultation on constitutional issues in the history of the nation. The text of the constitution was prepared with the participation of the entire population. This means that the Cuban constitution was being modified by the people through popular debate in the popular assemblies designed for that very purpose. To ensure that no Cubans of legal age were deprived of their rights under the law, the text of the constitutional reform was made widely available via various modes of communication, including traditional newsprint, radio, and digital media. In November 2018, the Reform debate closed with more than 7 million Cubans participating. The passion with which the Cubans expressed their opinions and supported the proposals—in favour, against, or proposing additions or modifications—was evident across the nation.

Cuban society discussed such crucial issues as the forms of ownership, the structure of government, the characteristics of the electoral process (including the election of the president and the governors), the amending of marriage laws to eliminate gender restrictions, the role of the party and its relationship to the state and the government, the upholding of civil rights, municipal (local) autonomy, and the dissolution of provincial assemblies, which marks an important de-concentration and decentralization of power, elimination of any form of social exclusion or discrimination, and many other vital issues. Starting with the proclamation of the new Constitution of the Republic on April 10, 2019, the process begins to elaborate the new norms into laws that will legalize the new economy characteristics defined in the constitutional text. The scope, limits, actors, and competencies of the articulations approved by popular constitutional referendum on February 24 of the same year will be defined through this process.

At the time of preparing this chapter, the author was also playing a passionate role in the constitutional debate, aware that it would have a transcendental impact on the island's fate. It was clear that the inclusive character of the process would go down in history. The entire nation had its say in the constitutional amendments. A constituent assembly of the people has long existed in Cuba and, accordingly, the vast majority of Cubans were also directly involved in this process. Although children were not directly involved in the constitutional project, many made their opinions known through family discussions—for example, Article 68 (one of the most debated) of the constitutional project (Proyecto, 2018), which concerned marriage laws regarding gender. Children also played their role in the referendum since they are the custodians of the safety and transparency of the elections.

This author, with no pretense of being a fortune-teller, locates in this reform process the "magic' formula that continues to ensure the legitimacy of the Cuban Revolution: the involvement of the vast majority of the Cuban people. Everything possible has been done to conduct the reform process as an everyday issue involving everyone at a design and implementation level and in terms of the attention given to the transformational impacts that will arise from each of the changes. Here we see a convergence of the wisdom of a people that is arguably the most well-educated in Latin America thanks to the tenets of the educational revolution deployed by the Cuban nation since 1959, which mandates cost-free, universal education at all levels and for all citizens.

Some Preliminary Observations and Conclusions

The process of updating the economic and social model of the Cuban Revolution has only just begun. There is more to come, and the most important changes involve Cuban state-run enterprises and monetary unification and fiscal consolidation. These are accompanied by the presidential change that took place in April 2018 when Raúl Castro Ruz (a symbol of the continuity of the historic generation) stepped down as Minister of the General of the Army and ceased to hold office as president of the Councils of State and Ministers in favour of the current president, a talented younger Cuban named Miguel Díaz-Canel Bermúdez.

These steps must strengthen the socio-classist nature of the revolutionary process, which is now enriched by the inclusion of new social actors given by the private economy whose economic presence is influencing the nation's social, cultural, and political life. It is clear that the socialist enterprise must guide the national economy and support the effective realization of socialist property in relation to the fundamental means of production, which means that the real owner is the Cuban nation, whose melting pot of classes and social sectors consolidated through the work of the Revolution is the class bearer of the process and its vanguard party. As stated in the Constitution, the working class is the essential class of the political power (Cuban Constitution, Ch. II, Sec. II, Art 18., P. 3).

Although the process is well underway, there is still a lack of a theoretical body, such as that given by the basic precepts of Marxism enunciated in the well-known platforms of Cuban revolutionary thought elaborated through the contributions of Fidel Castro Ruz, on something new: the construction of a sovereign society that is independent, socialist, democratic, prosperous, and sustainable and will finally achieve the goals originating with the Cuban Revolution and the outcome foreseen by Fidel in 1953 when he uttered the words "History will absolve me" before the court judging him for the attack on the Moncada Army Garrison in Santiago de Cuba (Castro, F., 1968). Even though the Cuban Revolution has been in power for more than 60 years, it has faced changing world conditions and other difficulties. As such, the unique nature of the Cuban Revolution is still under construction, and the theoretical body is being written on a daily basis.

Creativity is key to the process of safeguarding the Cuban social practice, which includes all of our social programs (education, health care services including for mental health, sports), celebration of culture and the arts, subsidized housing and rations, recreational activities and venues, and the organizations supporting the decision-making praxis given by the constituent assembly of people and the mass organizations that support it. For a long time, this social practice has been accompanied by new economic processes, scenarios, and stakeholders that now, for the first time, are officially recognized as part of the Cuban Revolution and its social transformations. New "partners" are being added to the nation's economy and certain capitalist relations of production have been legalized, and with them come the risks of various forms of exploitation of man over man.

The new scenarios are carriers of these relationships, which include economic competition at the level of the individual, for which Cuban society is unprepared. But in the light of the mission to reveal the special logic of the special object (Gómez Velázquez, N., 2014), these relationships, scenarios and actors are framed by the socialist relations of production, distribution, change, and consumption, defined in the social nature of ownership over the fundamental means of production.

What new features are required to reconcile these capitalist relations of production, and the implicit relations of human exploitation that such competition might, will, have under Cuban socialism? It is not enough to point out the existence of these phenomena, scenarios, relationships, and stakeholders; for the committed social scientist, it is a question of unveiling, proposing, substantiating and predicting the social transformations resulting from a mixed economic system in Cuba. The way the capitalist relations of production are expressed in other latitudes and how they have been understood in theory can and must be altered in a nation like Cuba, which is irrevocably and constitutionally bound to build a sovereign, independent, socialist, democratic, prosperous, and sustainable society.

The progress of the Cuban Revolution in the 21st century, as characterized by its process of updating the economic and social model, will undoubtedly encounter major obstacles that will not be easy to circumvent; however, our experience, which has been wrought through more than 60 years of revolution, political will, and unity of the people around this project of nation, offers a solid foundation for the consolidation of the Cuban model of socialist development.

References

Aguilera García, L.O. (2004). Un enfoque marxista de la gobernabilidad. *Una ciencia política desde el Sur*. Havana, Cuba: Editorial Félix Varela.

-----. (2013). *Lo participativo popular en los procesos electorales en Cuba.. Las elecciones de 1993 y de 2013*. In Fung Riverón, T. and Bauta Soles, M. (2014). *Intromisión en la participación política*. Havana, Cuba: Editorial Félix Varela.

-----. (2017). *Cuba: dialéctica de la actualización de su modelo económico y social*. Holguín, Cuba: Conciencia Ediciones.

Referendum, Cuban Constitution. (2019). National Assembly of People's Power. www.parlamentocubano.cu.

Constitution of the Republic of Cuba. (April 10, 2019). *Gaceta Oficial de la República de Cuba (Cuba Gazette)*, 5. *Constitución de la República de Cuba*. http://www.cubahora.cu/uploads/documento/2019/04/11/goc-2019-ex5.pdf.

Capote, F. R. (2019, April 30). La Ley Helms-Burton es inaplicable y no tiene valor ni efecto jurídico alguno. *Granma* Tabloid: 5. Havana, Cuba.

Castro, Fidel. (1968) [1953]. *History will absolve me: The Moncada trial defence speech, Santiago de Cuba, October 16th, 1953*. London: Cape.

Diálogo Público. (2013). Al Corriente. Holguín, Cuba: Radio Angulo. A radio program featuring public debates in the presence of the President of the Provincial Goverment and other authorities. www.holguin.gob.cu.

Doimeadios, G. D. (2019, February 25). Cuba ratifica la nueva Constitución con el 86.85% de los votos emitidos, según datos preliminares. Havana, Cuba: Cubadebate. www.cubadebate.cu.

Engels, F. (1847) [1969]. Principles of Communism. In *Selected Works*, vol. 1, pp. 81–97.

Moscow: Progress Publisher.
Fung Riverón, T. (2011). La sociedad civil internacional y global: ¿unitarias o antinómicas? *El mundo contemporáneo en crisis.* Havana, Cuba: Editorial Félix Varela.
Fung Riverón, T. (2011). *El mundo contemporáneo en crisis.* Havana, Cuba: Editorial Félix Varela.
-----. (2011). Las metadialécticas: metabioética y metapolitología. In *El mundo contemporáneo en crisis.* Havana, Cuba: Editorial Félix Varela.
-----. (2014). *La ciencia política: Enfoque sur desde la Revolución Cubana.* Havana, Cuba: Editora Política.
Fung Riverón, T., and Bauta Solés, M. (2014). *Intromisión en la participación política.* Havana, Cuba: Editorial Félix Varela.
Gómez Velázquez, N. (2014, October–December). Definiendo el pensamiento crítico. *Revista Temas,* 80: 106–113.
Granovsky, M. (2014, June 1). *Cuba es una isla, no una ínsula.* Interview with Cuban researcher Luis Suárez Salazar. Havana, Cuba: Cubadebate. www.cubadebate.cu.
Keeran R., and T. Kenny (2013*). Socialismo traicionado. Tras el colapso de la Unión soviética 1917-1991.* Havana, Cuba: Editorial Ciencias Sociales.
Lenin, V. I. (1917) [1964]. The tasks of the proletariat in our revolution. In *Collected Works* (trans. Bernard Isaacs), 4th English ed., vol. 24, pp. 55–91. Moscow: Progress Publishers.
Martínez Hernández, L. (2013, May 21). *Despejando potencialidades. Granma* Tabloid. Havana, Cuba.
Martínez Hernández, L. (2015, February 28). Analiza Consejo de Ministros temas relacionados con la actualización del modelo económico y social cubano. *Granma* Tabloid. Havana, Cuba.
Marx, K. (1843–44) [1970]. *Critique of Hegel's philosophy of right.* Oxford University Press. http://www.marxists.org/archive/marx/works/1843/critique-hpr/index.htm.
-----. (1871) [1933]. *The Civil War in France.* London: Martin Lawrence Ltd.
Marx, K., and F. Engels. (1848) [1969]. Communist Manifesto. In *Selected Works,* vol. 1, pp. 98–137. Moscow: Progress Publishers.
Mojena Milian, B. (2019, May 2). Mienten para justificar agresiones contra Cuba. *Granma* Tabloid. Havana, Cuba.
Murillo Jorge, M. (2012, December 15). Notas sobre su intervención en la Sesión Plenaria de la Asamblea Nacional del Poder Popular. *Granma* Tabloid. Havana, Cuba.
Nuñez Jover, J. (2010). *Conocimiento y Sociedad.* Havana, Cuba: Editorial. [University of Havana].
PCC [Communist Party of Cuba]. (2017a). *Conceptualización del modelo económico y social de desarrollo socialista en Cuba.* Santa Clara, Cuba: Partido comunista de Cuba (PCC).
PCC [Communist Party of Cuba]. (2017b). *Actualización de los Lineamientos de la política económica y social del Partido y la Revolución para el periodo 2016-2021.* Santa Clara, Cuba: Partido comunista de Cuba-PCC.
PCC-Communist Party of Cuba. (2017c). *Bases para el plan nacional de desarrollo económico y social para el periodo 2016-2030.* Santa Clara, Cuba: Partido comunista de Cuba-PCC.
Proyecto de Constitución de la República de Cuba. (2018). Cuba National Assembly of People's Power. Tabloid. Available in pdf at: www.parlamentocubano.cu.
Puig Meneses, Y. and L. Martínez Hernández. (2012, December 12). Insiste Raúl en continuar perfeccionando la política de cuadros. *Granma* Tabloid. Havana, Cuba.
Puig Meneses, Y., and L. Martínez Hernández. (2014, June 23). Tomando el pulso de la economía cubana [Speech by Marino Murillo Jorge, Council of Ministers meeting.]. *Granma* Tabloid, Havana, Cuba.
Pupo, R. (2011). Ecosofía, cultura, transdisciplinariedad. In Fung Riverón, T. *El mundo con-

temporáneo en crisis, p. 197. Havana, Cuba: Editorial Félix Varela https://patrialibros.org/book/1168.

Quevedo, V., Chía, J. and A. Rodríguez. (2010). Midiendo el Impacto. *Boletín de Área de Cooperación Científica de la OEI*. Newsletter. Organization of Ibero-American States for Education, Science and Culture (OEI). www.oei.es/salactsi/Cuba.pdf.

Rodríguez Cruz, F. (2012, December 17). De lo más sencillo a lo muy complejo. *Trabajadores* Tabloid. Havana, Cuba.

CHAPTER THREE

Some Considerations on the Updating of the Cuban Economic Model: Evolution of the Cuban Economy, 1989–2016

Miguel Ramón Torres Pérez

Abstract

As suggested by the title of this chapter, the following pages offer some perspective on the updating as well as the peculiarities of the Cuban economic model. The reader will gain insight into the ups and downs of the Cuban economy from 1989 to 2016, including the causes of the Special Period in Times of Peace and the Cuban government's efforts to shift what might be termed the "inertia economy" into a dynamic-growth scenario, which requires procurement of finance capital (foreign exchange), control over markets, and dollarization of the economy. Finally, an assessment of Cuba's economic model and the growth prospects for the economy are given, starting with the approval of the following policy documents: *Economic and Social Policy Guidelines for the Party and the Revolution for the 2016-2021 Period*; *Conceptualization of the Cuban Economic and Social Model of Socialist Development*; and *National Economic and Social Development Plan Through 2030: Vision of the Nation, Axes and Strategic Sectors*. A recent update on the Cuba economy has been provided as an afterword following this chapter.

Keywords: Simple reproduction, Special Period, development, guidelines, economy, dollarization.

Miguel Ramón Torres Pérez. Email: mtorresperez7@gmail.com or tmiguel48@yahoo.com. Ph.D. in Economics. Member of the National Association of Economists of Cuba (ANEC), of the Economic Society Friends of the Country (SEAP), of the National Board of Examiners of Scientific Degrees in Economic Sciences for the provinces of Eastern Cuba. Provincial and National Prize of the Academy of Sciences of Cuba (IANAS) in 2014 and 2015, respectively.

Introduction

Cuba has received an undue share of media attention over the past 60 years relative to its size and population. The country has an area of about 110,000 square kilometres making it the 104th largest country in the world; a population in 2022 of about 11.2 million, ranking 85th in the world; and a population density of 102 persons per square kilometre, 80th in the global rankings.* In area, Cuba is about the size of the Canadian provinces of New Brunswick and Nova Scotia combined, while its population is roughly equal to those two provinces plus the province of Quebec.† The attention given Cuba can be narrowed down to a single cause: the Cuban social model deviates from the Western norm. The objective of this chapter is thus to elucidate the peculiarities of the Cuban economic model. This will facilitate understanding of the evolution of the Cuban economy and the factors that have impacted it positively and negatively. The first section analyzes the forces that gave rise to what we call the Special Period in Times of Peace and pushed the country's economy into a period marked by inertia; the second section explores what is required to revitalize our economy; and the third section presents an analysis of the conceptualization of the Cuban economic model and development perspective. A recent update on the Cuba economy appears as an afterword at the end of this chapter.

Section One:
What Factors Gave Rise to the Special Period in Times of Peace?

While it is true the social achievements of revolutionary Cuba—in health, education, culture, sports, social security and public safety—have been recognized at the global level (UNICEF Cuba, 2017), it is also true that Cuba's economic model has been the main object of criticism by those opposed to the Cuban Revolution.

Cuba is going through a period of transition to socialism at a time when structural problems, remnants of the previous system, are hampering development and the effects are multiplied by the ongoing economic, material, and financial blockade imposed in February 1962 by the U.S. government as one of multiple unsuccessful attempts to stop the revolutionary process in its tracks; from the author's point of view, this is the root cause of the serious problems currently plaguing the Cuban economy.

This is not to ignore other factors that have weighed heavily in the sit-

---

* Cuba is an archipelago consisting of 4,195 islands and cays surrounding the main island; the national territory covers an area of 114,525 km.

† Compared to U.S. states, Cuba's area is about the same as that of Virginia, and its population comparable to that of Georgia.

uation, including such internal errors as over-staffing in public venues and state enterprises, neglecting equity and mistaking egalitarianism for equality, remuneration that is unaffected by employee performance, free products and services, and product subsidies requiring no qualifications in particular. These have resulted in reduced productivity, as did the collapse of socialism in Eastern Europe, and all of this landed Cuba in the most profound crisis the country has experienced since before the triumph of the 1959 revolution. This crisis is directly related to a lack of the essential elements (e.g., supply) needed by the state to maintain the rates of economic growth achieved in previous years.

When the Cuban government declared the Special Period in Times of Peace in August 1990, it announced a series of contingency plans originally conceived for use during wartime. A new series of austerity measures and rationing schedules were put in place to counter the deepening economic crisis. Available supplies of gasoline and fuel oil were severely cut. Blackouts became more frequent than periods with electricity. Industrial plants and factories reduced weekly work hours; some closed altogether.

In the 1990s, revenue shares from Freely Convertible Currency (FCC) oscillated between U.S. $2.3 billion and $5 billion, of which $1 billion to $1.7 billion was made available to the state.* This was below the so-called *breakpoint*, which is the level of state spending required to achieve positive economic growth and has been estimated at approximately $2 billion. As a result, the country did not achieve growth levels needed to sustain an efficient economy. The country's economy is now characterized by *inertia*, which results from a loss of sources of finance capital, supply of material resources, markets, national production, sources of employment, energy, and food—all which depend on circumstances that are hard to foresee or control. Figure 3.1† shows the allocation of scarce financial resources to the state at the beginning of the Special Period: 75 percent was allocated to acquisitions on the world food and fuel markets, and the remaining 25 percent went to combatting the widespread shortages. Three decades later, these proportions have not changed much.

The asphyxiation of our country's economy led to an excess of money in circulation (more than 11 billion Cuban pesos in 1992), which affected labour stability and productivity in the sectors that remained active to the point where the needs of the population could no longer be met. There was more money in the hands of people than goods in the normal market,

---

* All figures given in dollars in this chapter represent U.S. currency.

† The author's research is based on official data from the *Cuban Statistical Yearbook* (ONEI) (Havana, 1994). At the time of preparing this chapter no other data was available.

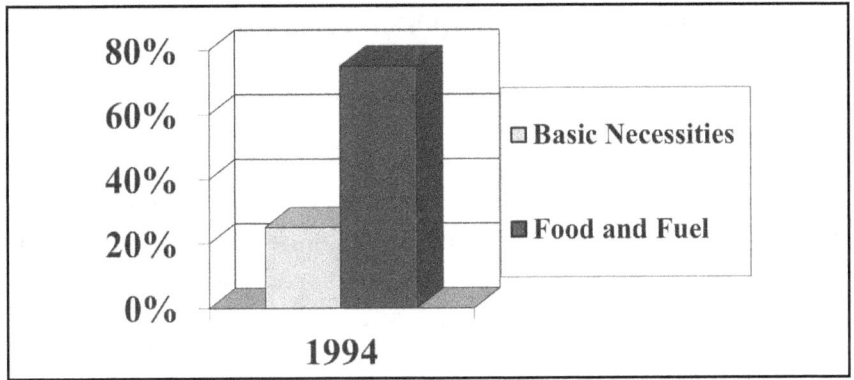

Figure 3.1. Allocation of Financial Resources, 1994.

which led to increased informal market activity. The Cuban peso became extremely devalued: 150 Cuban pesos for 1 U.S. dollar in 1993. Neither the state nor individual providers were able to satisfy the food needs of the population and the prices of such products skyrocketed as a result. Remedial measures were deployed in three fundamental directions:

1. **Create inflows of finance capital.**
   a) Development of tourism;
   b) Promotion of national products and industries that could compete in the world market (e.g., biotechnology, tourism, nickel, and sugar, among others);
   c) Openness to inflows of foreign capital (finance capital) through joint ventures or other forms of association;
   d) Increased donations from foreign governments, NGOs or individuals; and
   e) Decriminalization of foreign currency possession for Cuban citizens.

2. **Clean up/restructure the financial sector.**
   a) Increasing private initiative (self-employment activities);
   b) Development of an industrial market;
   c) Price increases for non-essential products such as alcoholic beverages and cigarettes; and
   d) Implementation of a taxation system, nonexistent in the country since before the triumph of the Revolution of 1959.

3. **Solve the food problem.**
   a) Creation of agricultural markets;

b) Implementation of territorial food programs;
c) Creation of agricultural quotas; and
d) Agricultural reform via the creation of Basic Units of Cooperative Production (UBPCs).

The social pyramid has clearly been inverted by the economic crisis, to the relative detriment of lower-income earners and those whose labour contributions should be better paid according to the socialist principle of distribution, "from each according to his ability; to each according to his needs…" (Lenin, 1917). Today, those who have more are not necessarily those who contribute the most, and this adversely affects work productivity. For example, the salary of a luggage porter, doorman, taxi driver, or other service-related position can be as high as $500 dollars per month, considerably more than the $30 per month they could earn practicing their professions. Many professionals prefer to let their jobs go and work in areas that generate higher incomes, even when this entails working outside their profession. This has an unfavourable impact on productivity in the key sectors of education, health, and among other state-owned enterprises in non-emergent sectors. The Cuban government applied a series of measures aiming to reverse the situation and move the economy from "inertia to growth." The question of what measures were taken is answered in the next section.

Section Two: How to Achieve Dynamic Economic Growth

To achieve the necessary dynamism of the Cuban economy since declaring the Special Period in Times of Peace, the government has foregrounded the use of internal capacities developed since 1959 and which put the following at its disposal:

1. A solid technical infrastructure.
2. Human capital able to embrace new technologies.
3. Indispensable natural resources.
4. Capacities for attracting the necessary finance capital.

For Cuba to act upon these factors, the following will be required:

1. Reduction of fuel imports.
2. Increased food production to meet food requirements using internal resources.
3. Increased production to enhance competitiveness and stimulate the inflow of Freely Convertible Currency (FCC).

The measures implemented by the Cuban state have had a significant impact on the majority of the population but did not constitute the shock therapy associated with International Monetary Fund (IMF) neoliberal recommendations, which have negative repercussions on society (CLACSO, Del Búfalo, 2008). The economic decisions taken by Cuba managed to stop the decline of the economy and turn the growth rate around. Figure 3.2 shows growth in gross domestic product (GDP) of 0.7 percent for 1994 compared to negative values in previous years of the Special Period.

Figure 3.2. Gross Domestic Product (GDP) 1989–2016 at 1981 CUC* Price (1 CUC = 1 USD)

Year	GDP per Capita	Growth Rate	Variance from 1989
1989	19585.8	-0.7	0
1990	19008.3	-2.9	-2.9
1991	16975.8	-10.7	-13.3
1992	15009.9	-11.6	-23.4
1993	12776.7	-14.9	-34.8
1994	12868.3	0.7	-34.3
1995	13184.5	2.5	-29.8
1996	14218.0	7.5	-22.3
1997	14572.4	2.5	-19.8
1998	14747.3	1.2	-18.6
1999	15661.6	6.2	-20
2000	16538.0	5.5	-15.6
2001	17530.9	6.0	-10.5
2002	17723.7	1.1	-9.5
2003	18166.8	2.5	-7.2
2004	19075.1	5.0	-2.6
2005	21077.9*	10.5	10.7
2006	23712.7*	12.5	12.4
2007	25443.763*	7.3	12.9
2008	26715.951*	5.0	13.6
2009	50200.675*	1.5	32.2
2010	56795.437*	2.4	33.3
2011	63258.768*	2.8	33.5
2012	65721.743*	3.0	33.9
2013	63031.243*	2.7	33.4
2014	61659.591*	1.0	32.6
2015	80457.361*	4.4	36.3
2016	80370.675*	2.0	35.2

* See Notes to Figure 3.2 on the next page.

Notes to Figure 3.2

Compilation by the author factoring sectors such as health and education into GDP data obtained from *the Statistical Yearbook of Cuba* (AEC 1989–2017), National Office of Statistics of Cuba (ONEI 1998–2017): Economic Report of Cuba's Central Bank (BNC 1990-2017); Cuban economy 1997–2017. Retrieved from https://www.datosmacro.com/pib/cuba, www.cubadebate.cu/etiqueta/pib.

*(2005–2016) Indicates a change in the base calculation to account for income aside from the productive sectors. Starting as early as 2003, Cuba for the first time factored social investment into its GDP, including the free social services, subsidized goods, housing, and exports of professional services to foreign countries in exchange for commodities such as oil. In 2008 (Reuters), the UN agreed with this methodology for calculating GDP.

· · · · ·

Informal market prices fell by 40 percent during the same period, which was reflected in the exchange rate on the informal currency market dropping from 120 Cuban pesos per U.S. dollar in May 1994 to 50 pesos per U.S. dollar in December 1994. The exchange rate is currently 25 Cuban pesos per U.S. dollar.

What Did Cuba Do to Achieve the Economic Growth Scenario of 1994?

1. Implemented measures to clean up and restructure the economy, such as eliminating subsidies on certain products, increasing prices for non-primary products such as alcohol and cigarettes, and increasing public funds by approving Cuba's first Tax Code (Decree Law 73, 1994), which imposed taxes only on those earning high incomes from non-state-owned activities, not on the general population.
2. Reduced excess money in circulation by 25 percent as of December 1994.
3. Controlled the money exchange markets; two each for national currency (CUP) and Freely Convertible Currency (FCC).
    a. National Currency (CUP):
        - Regulated (standardized).
        - Free (unregulated unofficial and official market exchanges).
    b. Freely Convertible Currency (FCC):
        - Foreign exchange bureaus belonging to state-owned entities.
        - Informal market.
4. Stimulated savings through increased interest rates.

5. Prioritized incentives to lower-income earners.
6. Imposed new personal income taxes.
7. Approved the Cuban Convertible Peso (CUC).
8. Made changes to Cuban business, including income taxes, staff/organizational restructuring, salary readjustments, and technological modernization.
9. Improved foreign policy to reduce constraints on foreign investment.
10. Managed the external debt—from creating a new image for the country to restoring the market confidence enjoyed before the Special Period.
11. Strengthened the inflow of foreign exchange from all possible sources.
12. Increased economic decentralization, enabling companies to execute their assigned tasks.
13. Utilized independent (intra) and competitive (extra) management.
14. Increased openness to self-employment.
15. Implemented flexible forms of ownership in various sectors.
16. Increased the country's geological prospecting initiatives.
17. Increased the national food production.
18. Aimed for a fair (equity) and uniform (equality) level of social compensation.
19. Developed export bases (e.g., biotechnology, medicines, human capital, etc.).
20. Decentralized foreign trade management.
21. Made foreign currency available for self-financing.
22. Introduced a managerial revolution emphasizing marketing and competition in the Cuban economy.
23. Introduced new roles or work cultures in Cuban companies.
24. Reformed wholesale prices.

As can be deduced from the above factors, the main focus is on procuring the finance capital upon which all the others rely; and this, for the good of the people and society and with respect to technological improvement.

Sources of Finance Capital (Foreign Currency)
1. Domestic savings;
2. Exports for foreign trade (external) and for foreign companies operating and selling products in Cuba (internal);
3. Inflow of money from outside Cuba (remittances, solidarity grants, loans and other); and
4. Foreign capital (private and mixed companies).

While joint ventures are viewed skeptically because some theorists have cast them as capitalist islands floating in a socialist ocean, the need for development capital under socialist formulas is obvious. Even though political and ideological factors hang heavily in the balance, opening Cuba up to foreign capital is a risk that must be run on pain of losing all that has been accomplished at a social level since 1959. There has been much discussion about the economic benefits of such ventures and whether they are worth the risk. This question and the impact of such ventures on the economy have been subject to much scrutiny over the years; and the benefits clearly outweigh the damages, because without such ventures Cuba could not have obtained the capital needed for its own development.

Foreign Investment

The inflow of foreign exchange into Cuba can be expressed as:
$$USD = g + y(1 + b) + t$$
g = proportional gain (rate of return to investors).
y = worker incomes, which Cuba receives from the foreign partner in convertible currency and pays out in FCC.
b = % (rate of return to social security).
t = tax on profit (+ 0 − 20%).

In order to stimulate investment, the Constitution of the Republic of Cuba was amended on July 26, 2002, through the inclusion of specific laws on foreign investment, property, share divisions, profit margins, mining and subsoil regulations, etc. A rise in the number of joint ventures increases incomes in hard currency, which grows domestic savings to be invested in the creation of new sources of employment, establishing cyclical growth. The international fairs of Havana and Santiago de Cuba contribute significantly to attracting foreign capital by annually bringing together a host of entrepreneurial representatives from various firms and countries.

Agricultural Capital

In agriculture, procurement of foreign capital has been slower, but the pace is picking up, especially from exportable items like sugar and its by-products as well as tobacco. While many companies from various countries were rushing to invest in Cuba, the United States persisted with its blockade and continues to enforce bans even on its own companies wishing to engage with a safe and nearby market to this day. A study carried out by the Association for the Study of the Cuban Economy recommended to the White House in September 1994 that the U.S. should maintain relations of the highest order with Cuba (ASCE, 1994). This same source indicates that the Cuban economy would need a capital inflow of $200 billion over the first five years after the end of the blockade just to recover from its effects.

Dollarization of the Economy

Dollarization is the subject that has elicited the most debate and opinions among the Cuban population, and abroad, in recent years. This is understandable, given that the decision to allow free movement of U.S. currency within the local Cuban economy was politically charged and very risky. The Cuban case is atypical, especially considering that the foreign currency in question is that of a self-declared political and economic enemy. But behold the wisdom that justified the means: to decriminalize U.S. currency was to expand the sources for its procurement.

It follows from international practice that a country may choose to safeguard its own currency by restricting the free movement of others; all operations must thus be carried out in national currency. Since the Cuban peso has no international convertibility and the country lacks the productive capabilities to secure its domestic market, Cuba depends on a large percentage of resources from abroad and must pay for them in FCC. Under the circumstances, it would make no sense to buy products in hard currency and sell them in national currency at subsidized prices because demand would quickly outweigh supply, causing a shortage of said products and thwarting the conditions of economic reproduction.

The Cuban government deemed it necessary to proceed with the decriminalization of the use of foreign currency in the following four stages:

- **Stage I.** Decriminalization of foreign currency holdings via Decree Law 140 (BNC—National Bank of Cuba, August 13, 1993). Free circulation in the domestic (internal) market of both FCC and the Cuban peso (CUP) and the creation of exchange houses (CADECA, 1994). This stage took place between 1994 and 2004.
- **Stage II.** Price tags (in stores) showing the price in both the Cuban Free Convertible Peso (CUC) and the non-convertible peso (CUP) as given by the official exchange rate. The country is currently in this stage, which began in November 2004.
- **Stage III.** Circulation in exchange bureaus of both currencies, CUP and CUC, with buy and sell prices established by the official exchange rate. This measure was first implemented in 2014.
- **Stage IV.** Projected exchange rate adjustments between FCC and the CUC and the Cuban Peso (CUP). This process took five years in China

and ten in Vietnam. Initial projections for Cuba pointed to fifteen to twenty years, but the forecasts were already surpassed by 2014. When this stage is complete, the CUP will have recovered its convertibility and the CUC will be put out of circulation.

Consider the exchange rate of money in relation to the work of the U.S.'s Max O. Lorenz, who developed a comparative model for measuring the relative wealth of different nations as a function of monetary parity with the U.S. dollar. As per Figure 3.3, the Lorenz curve illustrates that the wealth level of a country will be higher the closer its monetary exchange rate is to the U.S. dollar. Lorenz's model also assumes that the origin (e.g., where the x-axis and y-axis intercept) equals zero, because it considers nominal (money) wages as equal to real wages, which take the purchasing power of money into account. Consequently, when the currencies of poorly developed countries lose their value against the dollar, the real wealth reflected in their own currency will be resultingly lower.

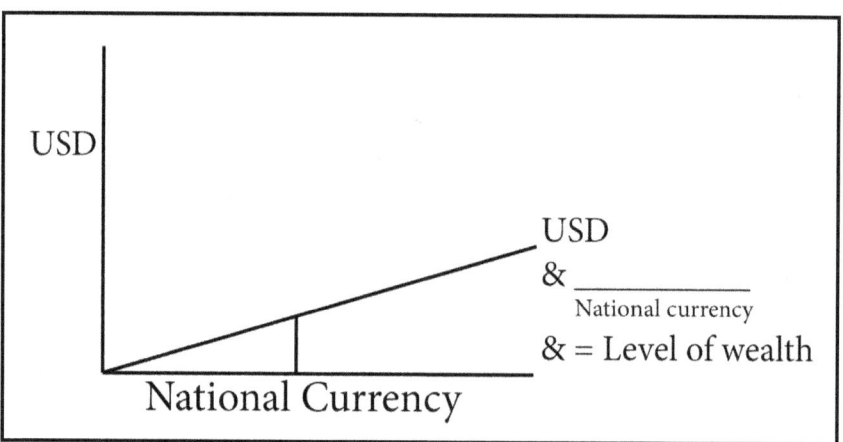

Figure 3.3. Calculating Cuba's Level of Wealth Based on the Lorenz Curve
Calculating Cuba's level of wealth based on the Lorenz Curve (Rosales, 2018) would illustrate that the level of Cubans' wealth was much higher than the sum of its revenues in 2018 as compared to 1993 in terms of buying power *vis-à-vis* the exchange rate:

$$1993: \quad \& = \frac{1 \text{ USD}}{150 \text{ CUP}} = 0.006$$

$$2018: \quad \& = \frac{1 \text{ USD}}{25 \text{ CUP}} = 0.040$$

& = Index of wealth of country

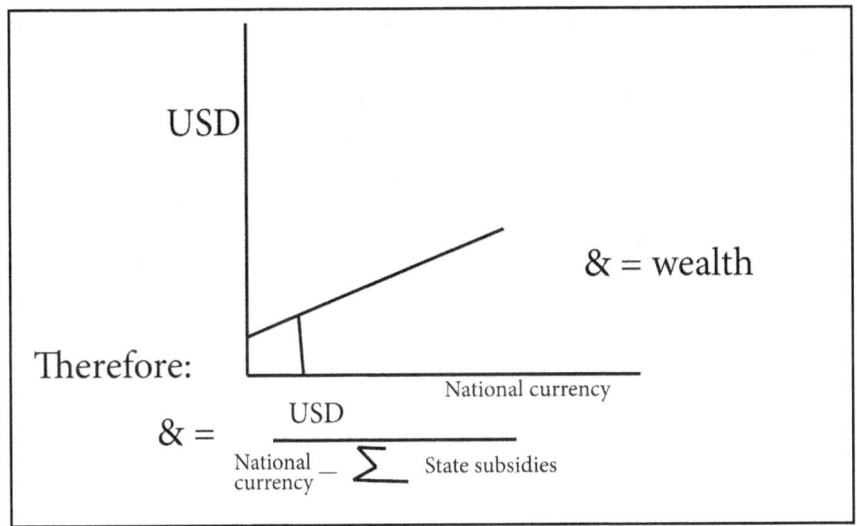

Figure 3.4. Author Elaboration of the Lorenz Curve for the Cuba Case (Torres Pérez, Miguel, 1999)

These results are unrealistic indicators of Cuba's wealth levels, however, because the Lorenz curve only considers total income. It is not enough to simply relate the purchasing power of hard currency with that of the national currency in Cuba, because the state uses national currency to obtain the foreign currency needed for the provision of products and services centrally guaranteed by the Cuban system, and this affects the value of the national currency (through internal demand for foreign currency and the principles of supply and demand), which means the curve's origin or starting point cannot be zero. As per Figure 3.4, the Lorenz curve can nonetheless be used to illustrate the Cuban case. That is to say, the calculation for Cuba must factor in the state subsidies of goods and services to all Cubans.

As shown in Figure 3.4, the level of a Cuban's wealth is higher than the sum of incomes. For example, in 2019, the average salary of 450 CUP was $18 (25:1), but we must factor in the value of state subsidies (food, medical and dental services, education, housing, communications, transportation, among others) received in kind by workers—which brings "real" wages up from $18 to $500 (USD) per month. In addition, Cuban studies have indicated that 49.5 percent of the population has access to foreign currency through personal remittances (in kind income) from different sources that must also be factored into total income (Rodríguez, J., 1998).* Many of the family remittances, such as from Cuban relatives living in the U.S., take the

---

* Estimaciones recientes indican que el 26% de los hogares cubanos reciben remesas desde el exterior (Orozco, M., 2022, https//www.wola.org).

form of (U.S.) dollars, since U.S. banks are restricted by the embargo from transferring money to Cuba. While it is impossible to accurately assess total foreign remittances in Cuba, they are significant.

In his address to the first session of the National Assembly of People's Power (1998), José Luis Rodríguez (then Minister of Economy and Planning) explained the increased supply of foreign currency available in Cuban exchange bureaus as the result of citizens working abroad or receiving funds from family members who live abroad, enhanced incentive programs for attracting freely convertible foreign currency, and growth in tourism (Rodríguez, J. Luis, 1998).

Cuba's 1994 decision to decriminalize possession and use of the U.S. dollar by Cuban citizens has led to deep social divides and ideological conflict. Today, most of those who receive funds do so through remittances from relatives residing abroad, who may or may not support the revolutionary process. The citizens most connected to the Revolution, the rank-and-file workers, are unlikely to have relatives sending funds from abroad and are thus unable to satisfy needs that can only be met with such extra funds. The solution to this problem lies in breaking the inertia and transitioning the economy through a dynamic growth scenario, where production supports the value of the national currency by virtue of an economic upswing that ensures salary increases and overall quality of life by virtue of increases in national productions, more efficient allocation of resources, improvements to the services regime, and overall well-being.

According to by Osvaldo Martínez in 2008, then Director of the Center for Research on the World Economy,* the future of Cuba lies in a strong state sector, greater market specialization, and better use of commercial relations. This is not synonymous with abandoning socialism; the Cuban economic model pursues a significant presence of foreign capital, a more robust tourism sector that will contribute more to the economy than the sugar harvest, solid biotechnological and pharmaceutical development, and greater integration with Latin America (Osvaldo, 2008).

Section Three: The Cuban Economic Model: Prospects for the Developing Cuban Economy

Various interpretations of the changes being undertaken by the Cuban government to resolve the problems associated with the Special Period

---

* Television appearance, as ex-director of University of Havana's Center for research on the world economy, within a framework of the *University for All* program. Multivision, October 2008.

have been advanced but all use qualifiers like "reform," thus locating a nexus between this and what happened with the former USSR and *perestroika*. This misconception is clearly contradicted by the recent re-affirmation of the socialist direction of the revolution, which lends a connotation of "improvement" rather than reform to the process of updating the Cuban economic model.

While the Cuban government has promoted fixes that will allow it to emerge from the current crisis situation, and slight improvements can indeed be discerned, there is no sign that a solution is at hand. The results thus far obtained owe their success to a great deal of effort and the procurement of loans whose high interest rates and short terms reflect the potential for penalties by the U.S. government (under its blockade against Cuba) on the foreign banks making the loans. Where some loans issued by foreign banks do offer reasonable interest rates and longer terms, these contain stipulations that earmark the funds exclusively for use in pre-existing markets. Trade links have also been maintained with countries whose political situations put their economies at risk and thus affect their ability to follow through on commitments. This all continues to undermine the outcome of the updating process conceived by the Cuban government.

It all comes down to efficient allocation of resources (e.g., allocating resources to their best uses), which has not always been achieved. After a long process of popular consultations, the *Guidelines of the Economic and Social Policy of the Party and the Revolution for the period 2016–2021* were submitted for approval at the Communist Party of Cuba's Seventh Congress. This core document, which laid out 274 recommendations including conceptualization of the direction of the Cuban economic model, was subsequently approved at the III Plenum of the Central Committee of the PCC on May 18, 2017, along with the other two main policy documents: *Conceptualization of the Cuban Social and Economic Development Model* and the *National Economic and Social Development Plan through 2030: Vision of the Nation, Axes and Strategic Sectors*. All three were subsequently approved by the National Assembly of People's Power on June 1, 2017 (PCC, 2017).

For Cuba to move in its chosen direction and implement the appropriate corrections, its economy must be dynamized from within (i.e., internal resources) and without (correct use of external factors). Predicting what will happen in the next few years in the Cuban economy may be a daunting task, but projections indicate that the *breakpoint* can be attained as follows:

- Stable annual sugar harvests of over 5 million tons and appropriate positioning in the international market.
- Redirection of GDP towards the productive (wealth-generating) sector (primary processing of raw materials and value-added secondary transformation). Higher production levels will stimulate and strengthen the economy, making possible a subsequent allocation of resources to the non-wealth-generating sectors such as health and education that stand as achievements of the Revolution.
- Increased domestic oil production representing 30 percent of the country's needs or 3 million tons; currently, only 1.3 million tons are being produced.
- Substantial increase in food production that surpasses current levels, given that the production of meat, foodstuffs, vegetables, and eggs has declined by 16 percent since December 1994.
- By the end of 2017, the Cuban economy had received an injection of more than $1.5 billion, the spending equivalent of 4.9 million tourists (Cubanet, July 13, 2017).
- Achieving a favourable trade balance. The solution here is to produce non-traditional commodities as permitted by the country's scientific and technological capacities as well as to increase exports.
- Reduce the money supply by cleaning up the national economy, which means keeping 3 billion pesos in stable circulation as opposed to the more than 9 thousand billion that had been circulating in the early 1990s.

As a policy document, *Conceptualization of the Cuban Social and Economic Development Model* presents the theoretical and conceptual bases of the socialist direction of the Cuban economy and is enriched by guidelines covering the gamut of the socio-economic aspects of our country's development priorities; the ultimate outcome is to safeguard past achievements while achieving economic stability by opening the economy up without resorting to neoliberal shock therapy. The *Conceptualization of the Cuban Social and Economic Development Model* policy document defines and sustains the essential guidelines underpinning the objectives of practical policy actions in both the social and economic spheres, in accordance with historical advancements and contemporary conditions that frame the construction of Cuban socialism and safeguard the strategic purposes being undertaken by our country (PCC, 2017).

The first of the policy document's four chapters is devoted to the principles underpinning the model and the principal changes, which lay the foundations for the strategic policy measures outlined in the *National Plan for Economic and Social Development up to 2030: Vision of the Nation, Axes, and Strategic Sectors*, which aims to "guarantee the irrevocability and continuity of our socialism by strengthening its sustaining principles, economic development and increase the standard and quality of life. All this will be carried out in conjunction with the necessary consolidation of ethical and political values that defeat selfish competitiveness and the individualism and alienation of predatory consumerism" (PCC, 2017).

Chapter 2 of the policy document deals with the structure of the forms of ownership in relation to the means of production, affirming the people's socialist ownership of the fundamental means of production as the guiding principle and recognizing different forms of ownership and management during specific stages of the country's development and the real need to mobilize human, material and financial resources, national or foreign, in order to sustain our nation through its construction of socialism. The existence of non-state forms of ownership and management serves the purpose of the state and the government in carrying out the complex tasks conferred upon them.

The following forms of property are included in the model (PCC, 2017):

1. People's socialist property ownership;
2. Cooperative property;
3. Mixed property;
4. Private property; and
5. Ownership of political, mass, social organizations and other entities of the Cuban civil society. This means that organizations like the Communist Party of Cuba, the Union of Young Communists, the Committees of Defence of the Revolution, the Federation of Cuban Women, the Association of Small Farmers, the National Union of Cuban Writers and Artists, religious organizations, etc., will have ownership over their premises, vehicles, and other assets.

Chapter 3 of the policy document clarifies that the steering system will be "the planned direction of economic and social development," which it defines as the instrument by which the state and government can organize, coordinate, execute, monitor and evaluate the actions taken by all stakeholders in the name of progress at the national and regional levels and the relations of these latter with the national and international economy" (PCC, 2017).

Finally, Chapter 4 presents the main characteristics of social policy and posits the fundamental object of said policy as the integral development of the human being. Constituting more than mere spending, the resources allocated for these purposes constitute an investment in both economic and social development (PCC, 2017).

For the majority of citizens, the accumulation of unmet needs requires flexible solutions that can be implemented and produce results quickly. While it is true that resolving unfavourable situations as quickly as possible is always in everyone's best interests, it is also true that internal and external obstacles to the Cuban economy make it very difficult to find solutions quickly enough.

Adherence to the strategies outlined and duly approved by the 7th Congress of the Communist Party of Cuba (PCC, 2017) is of utmost importance to the preservation of the strides made by the Cuban Revolution in the areas of health, medicine, education, sports, culture, social security and public safety, equal rights, and universal access to opportunity, etc. These remain the unwavering paradigms of the international left and embody the historical achievements of the Cuban Revolution now in the hands of a new generation. Even the slightest deviation from the plan could engender dire consequences for the future of the Revolution, which is why measures must be implemented "slowly but surely," as General Raúl Castro has recommended. It's about doing what needs to be done at the right time to avoid making mistakes that could lay to waste so many years of effort and sacrifice by the Cuban people.

Conclusions

Any global explanation of the Cuban economy must illustrate how internal and external situations have resulted in a non-linear and rocky path. To understand it, one must first come to terms with the peculiarities of the Cuban economic model. This present chapter has attempted to contextualize the underlying issues and challenges and the factors that have conditioned the model, from the start of the economic crisis of the 1990s (the Special Period in Times of Peace) to the present day. A country's economy generates social relations of production that form the basis of any society, constructing a superstructure that takes into account the degree of well-being enjoyed by its citizens; the conceptualization of the Cuban economic model aims to satisfy such a purpose by taking a realistic look at the current problems. The problems include the strict blockade measures imposed by the United States government, which together with internal errors are engendering lower productivity, a lack of the supply chains needed for development, financial insolvency, and energy insecurity. The recently approved updating model conceptually addresses these and other inadequacies with an objective and optimistic vision of the future; however, the rigour and vision with which it is applied and the global economic and geopolitical processes that may affect Cuba and its ability to control the necessary changes will have the last word on the stability of the Cuban economy.

References

AEC. (1989-2017). *Statistical yearbook of Cuba* (1994). Oficina nacional de estadística e información/national office of statistics (1998-2017). Havana, Cuba.

ASCE. (1991). Papers and Proceedings of the First Annual Meeting of the Association for the Study of the Cuban Economy (ASCE). *Cuba in transition 1*. Miami: Florida International University.

----- (1992). Papers and Proceedings of the Second Annual Meeting of the Association for the Study of the Cuban Economy (ASCE). *Cuba in transition 2*. Miami: Florida International University.

----- (1993). Papers and Proceedings of the Third Annual Meeting of the Association for the Study of the Cuban Economy (ASCE). *Cuba in transition 3*. Miami: Florida International University.

----- (1994). Papers and Proceedings of the Fourth Annual Meeting of the Association for the Study of the Cuban Economy (ASCE). *Cuba in transition 4*. Miami: Florida International University.

----- (1995). Papers and Proceedings of the Fifth Annual Meeting of the Association for the Study of the Cuban Economy (ASCE). *Cuba in transition 5*. Miami: Florida International University.

----- (1996). Papers and Proceedings of the Sixth Annual Meeting of the Association for the Study of the Cuban Economy (ASCE). *Cuba in transition 6*. Miami: Florida International University.

----- (1997). Papers and Proceedings of the Seventh Annual Meeting of the Association for the Study of the Cuban Economy (ASCE). *Cuba in transition 7*. Miami: Florida International University.

Cadena Vargas, Edel. (2018, April) *Una década de neoliberalismo en América Latina: el caso de México. Convergencia Revista de Ciencias Sociales*, [S.l.], 3. https://convergencia.uaemex.mx/article/view/10237

Castro Ruz, F. (1978). Informe Central. 1st CPC Congress. Havana, Cuba: Editorial Pueblo y Educación.

Castro Ruz, F. (1973). La historia me absolverá ("History will absolve me"). Havana, Cuba: Editorial Ciencias Sociales.

CLASCO. (2002). Del Búfalo. Enzo. Las reformas económicas en América Latina. Ed. Cristina Ruiz del Ferrier and Jorge Tirenni. *Venez de Economía y Ciencias Sociales*, 8(2): 129-182.

Comisión Económica para América Latina y el Caribe (CEPAL). http://www.biblawlioteca.clacso.edu.ar/ar/libros/venezuela/rvecs/bufalo.pdf.

CubaDebate. (2016, May 26). Descargue en Cubadebate documentos del VII Congreso del PCC que serán sometidos a consulta pública. http://www.cubadebate.cu/noticias/2016/05/26/descargue-en-cubadebate-documentos-del-vii-congreso-del-pcc-para-consulta-publica/.

Cubanet. (2017, July 13). Cuba estima en $1500 millones los ingresos por turismo en lo que va de año. https://www.cubanet.org/noticias/cuba-estima-en-1500-millones-los-

ingresos-por-turismo-en-lo-que-va-de-ano/.
Decree Law 73. (1994, August 4). Cuba tax code/Sistema Tributario. Havana: Cuba. www.parlamentocubano.cu/wp.../05/LEY-NO.-73-DEL-SISTEMA-TRIBUTARIO.pdf.
ONEI. (1998–2017). Anuario estadístico de Cuba [Statistical Yearbook of Cuba]. Havana, Cuba: Oficina nacional de estadística e información/national office of statistics (19982017). https://www.datosmacro.com/pib/cuba; www.cubadebate.cu/etiqueta/pib.
Informe presentado a la Asamblea Nacional del Poder Popular. (1998, January). Pamphlet. Havana: MEP.
Klein, Naomi. (2008, April). "La resistencia a la *'doctrina de shock'* en América Latina." Focus on the Global South. https://focusweb.org/la-resistencia-a-las-politicas-de-shock-en-america-latina/#
Lenin, V. I. (1917) [1963]. *El estado y la Revolución. August–September, 1917*. Havana, Cuba: Editorial Política.
Martínez, Osvaldo. (2008, October). Director of the centre for the world economy, University of Havana (Centro de Investigaciones de la Economía Mundial de la Universidad de La Habana). Television appearance. Cuba: Multivisión channel.
Marx, K. (1875) [1969]. "Critique of the Gotha programme." In *Selected Works 24*. Moscow: Progress Publishers.
PCC [Communist Party of Cuba]. (2011). *Lineamientos de la política económica y social del Partido y la Revolución para el periodo 2011–2016*. VI Congress of the Communist Party of Cuba. Havana, Cuba: Partido Comunista de Cuba (PCC) .
-----. *Lineamientos de la política económica y social del Partido y la Revolución para el periodo 2016–2021*. VII Congress of the Communist Party of Cuba. Havana, Cuba: Partido Comunista de Cuba (PCC).
----- (2017, June 1). Documentos del VII Congreso del Partido aprobados en el III Pleno del Comité Central del PCC [Documents approved at the 3rd Plenary Meeting of the Communist Party of Cuba on May 18 and by the National Assembly of People's Power on June 1, 2017]. *Partido Comunista de Cuba* (PCC). Tabloid. Havana, Cuba: Editora Política.
Reuters. (2008). Cuba says United Nations accepts GDP formula. https://www.reuters.com/article/cuba-statistics-un-idUKN1654470120081216.
Rodríguez, J. Luis. (1997, December 16). Economía cubana. Resultados económicos de 1997. *Granma* Tabloid. Havana, Cuba.
Rosales, José. (2018). Catedra de estadística social teóricos. UDELAR FCS. https://www.academia.edu/.../Curva_de_Lorenz_e_Indice_de_Gini.
Torres Pérez M. (1999). *La economía cubana actual: Realidad y perspectiva*. www.monografía.com.
UNICEF. (2017). UNICEF Annual Report. https://www.unicef.org/reports/2017-annual-results-reports.

Afterword: A Brief Update on the Cuban Economic Model from 2016 to 2023

Society constantly develops and changes under the influence of the economic system, which itself responds to events (including natural disasters, policy changes and currency devaluation) triggering chain reactions known as the domino effect. The world experience and the reality of the Cuban economy, in particular, make this obvious.

Correcting the distortions in Cuba's financial structure related to the dual currency system (CUC and CUP) implemented in 1994 by Cuba's

National Bank* is a necessary part of the nation's current socio-economic policy. In 1994, forecasts indicated that the CUP would regain its convertibility in 15 to 20 years, then be taken out of circulation. Its elimination was debated and articulated in the *Lineamientos*† at the 6th PCC Congress (2011) and consolidated in 2021. In fact, eliminating Cuba's dual currency through the withdrawal of the Convertible Peso (CUC) was the first order of business at the 8th Congress of the Communist Party of Cuba in 2021 as part of its approval of the *Updating of the Cuban Economic Model for the 2021–2026 period* (PCC, 2021).

Currency exchange unification will not, in itself, resolve all of the Cuban economy's current problems, but its implementation is crucial to re-establishing the value of the Cuban peso and its function as a unit of exchange. The dual currency had been introduced in 1994 as a means of offsetting the instability of the Special Period and keeping the new state-controlled capitalism separate from the state economy's CUP.

Over time, the problems inherent in running a dual currency led to a dual economy giving rise to inequities for most Cubans, as only those working in tourism or receiving personal remittances from family and friends, mainly in the US, could obtain the high-valued CUC needed to purchase certain goods. Among other impacts, such as a rise in informal markets, wage disparities related to the CUC's high value brought about a transfer of human resources from fields paid in CUP, such as education, medicine and engineering, into the lucrative tourist sector remunerated in CUC. In response to this, and as part of the reordering plan, state salaries were increased across the board in 2019—but no amount of planning could have saved the Cuban economy from the impact of the pandemic starting in 2020. With the CUC now out of circulation, the Cuban government is in the process of determining an ideal exchange rate and Cubans are able to formally exchange their pesos (CUP) for U.S. dollars at the fixed exchange rate.

Shifting the foundations of the national currency creates many follow-on effects in accounting platforms, in the cost calculations of state enterprises, in the productive layer, and in wage policy and incomes generally. When the state increased wage and pension scales in the state sector, the private sector began to justify its own, sometimes higher, increases; as one might logically expect, the higher wages increased demand, which trig-

---

* Cuba's National Bank (*Banco Nacional de Cuba*) was re-established as the Cuban Central Bank (*Banco Central de Cuba*) in 1997.

† *Guidelines of the economic and social policy of the party and the revolution for the period 2011–2016.*

gered higher prices. This inflationary result can only be curbed by ensuring that supply exceeds demand.

Neither did state price-cap regulations solve the problem. Given the insufficient level of government supply, which accounts for about 90 percent of the market, the growing demand for goods and services cannot be supported. Another process has also come into play. The private sector, seeing the supply constrictions, directs its products away from the formal market and into the informal market to get higher prices. The price increases in the informal market thus soar above state predictions for the regular market. If supply cannot be maintained, the delicate economic balance will repeatedly be thrown off.

Fear of Change

Calling for a paradigm shift is never easy. Humans tend to fear change, but it goes hand in hand with development. Cuba's monetary reordering process, necessary to correct the economic and financial distortions addressed in the 2021–2026 economic plan, has also had psychological and sociological impacts on the Cuban people. The measures taken by the Cuban government to implement the new monetary policy clearly represents a step towards a better society, but critics around the world have found fertile ground in exploiting the uncomfortable short-term effects.

Cuban citizens have displayed four main reactions to the reordering process, which has been extensively debated and discussed across the country including in forums such as televised roundtables.* Some Cubans, wrongly in the author's opinion, see the monetary policy as the definitive solution, while others feel the timing is wrong due to the embargo intensification and the pandemic's destabilization of the world economies. Others realize that monetary re-ordering is a necessary step but will not alone solve our country's economic problems. Still others come across as impatient cynics; disagreeing with everything or almost everything, losing hope and deciding to emigrate. The fourth group assumes that the reordering is necessary and will create some imbalances but is not the definitive solution to the problem. By now, most Cuban citizens realize that the solutions were not as simple as they had thought.

At a roundtable discussion on October 30, 2020, the President of the Commission for the Implementation of the Economic and Social Guidelines, Marino Murillo, made a few observations. He said that workers de-

---

* The Cuban TV network televises such roundtables to analyze and discuss important issues of concern to the general public. Renowned journalists and academics, politicians, ministers, and even the president participate when necessary.

pending on a salary will be better off than before once wages start growing faster than prices and supply can be increased to meet the new demand created by the higher wages. He also pointed out that excess money in circulation and the informal market both affect the state's ability to accurately forecast prices (Murillo, M., 2020). According to data provided to Cubadebate, on October 14, 2020, wage growth of 390 percent was projected, equivalent to an increase of the state wage fund by 4.9 times (Murillo, M., 2020). The Cuban pension fund has been increased, fivefold, and vulnerable groups are now uniquely prioritized to receive certain basic subsidies from the government that all citizens once received.

Establishing a New Official Devalued Exchange Rate for the Cuban Peso (CUP)

As part of the monetary reordering set in motion in 2019 and implemented in 2021 with the elimination of the CUC, the Cuban government is in the process of establishing a fixed foreign currency exchange rate for the national currency, the Cuban peso (CUP). In March 2022, a rate of 24 CUP to 1 USD was announced but over the summer reduced to 120 CUP to 1. Since this represents an overvaluation of the CUP relative to its real purchasing power and the demand for foreign exchange is so high, US dollars can be exchanged for 30 percent to 40 percent more by using informal currency exchangers (i.e., informal money market), which affects demand and pricing on the informal goods market and also puts excess money into circulation.* To counter the state's lack of hard currency needed to fulfill the demand for resources in various sectors of the economy, the U.S. dollar is being provisionally accepted in certain stores.

It was also announced that the price of the Cuban consumer price index basket of goods and services (CBBR), including pricing in the ration book, will be 1528 CUP as of "Day Zero"† (Yaffe, H., 2021), which represents enough "to cover the [monthly] needs of a worker and half a person more" (Anaya Cruz, 2020; Robreño, A., 2020; Pérez Villanueva, 2023). These calculations factored in the possibility of wages growing faster than prices;

---

* On February 25, 2024, the informal change rate was 310 CUP per USD.

† The first of January 2021 was known as "Day Zero" in Cuba, the day when President Díaz-Canel announced on Cuban National TV that Cuba's national peso (CUP) and its convertible peso (CUC) were unified. It was called "Day Zero" by the Cuban Government because it denotes the starting point of many changes for the Cuban economy: This monetary ordering also involves major price adjustments, the elimination of "excessive [state] subsidies and undue gratuities," and significant changes in salaries, pensions, and social assistance benefits (Yaffe, H. 2021).

however, the forecasted inflation levels have been greatly exceeded. According to Cuba's national statistics and information office (ONEI, 2024), Cuba closed 2023 with year-on-year inflation of 31.34 percent in its formal market, following 77.33 percent in 2021 and 39.07 percent in 2022 (OnCuba, January 19, 2023). Causes included excess money in circulation, global supply-deficit inflation brought about by the pandemic, the supply-smothering (and thus inflationary) impact of tightened embargo restrictions, and the persistence of the informal market. Retail inflation (i.e., change in the price-index) in Cuba as of November 2023 was 2.29 percent, lower than in the same period of 2022, when it reached 4.11 percent according to Cuba's deputy prime minister and head of economy and planning Alejandro Gil Fernandez.* According to the Cuban Office of Statistics and Information (ONEI), in 2023 the Consumer Price Index (CPI) rose to 41.77 from 33.32 in 2022 (de Barrio, October 4, 2023).

Our capacity to obtain the foreign currency needed to ensure supply suffered a double blow during the COVID-19 pandemic due to the 243 new measures added to the embargo by the U.S. government when presided over by Donald Trump in 2020 (MINREX, 2021). This new U.S. policy drove Cuba's economic, commercial, and financial difficulties to new limits. The policy reimposed a "measure preventing the importation [to Cuba] of products from any country containing more than 10 percent U.S. components. In a globalized economy, this constitutes a real obstacle to acquiring necessary inputs, regardless of the market of origin" (Tablada/MINREX in CubaNews, January 20, 2021). Combined with the economic effects of the COVID-19 pandemic, this U.S. interference ensured that the state could not fulfill its forecast of balancing the imbalances inherent to the low state salaries.

Comparing the increase in official prices with the increase in salaries in the state sector, we can see that wages have grown at a higher rate than prices in the state sector. Price ceilings in the private sector were also implemented to prevent this but have been gradually violated. The insufficient level of supply of goods and services in the state sector brought about by the lack of foreign currency, the diversion of resources from the state sector to the informal sector, the increase in wages in a general sense, and growing needs have caused prices to spiral beyond what is expected in the informal market. The government's efforts to enforce the established norms may slow these accelerated increases in prices but will not resolve the cause

---

* Facing a steep uphill battle, Alejandro Gil Fernandez, Cuba's deputy prime minister and head of economy and planning since 2018, was dismissed from his post on February 2, 2024.

of the problem, which originates in a manifest imbalance between supply and demand.

> **Insert 3.1**
> The Cuban government's most recent report, covering August 2021 to February 2022, indicates that the blockade cost the country US$3.807 billion during that six-month period, 49 percent more than estimated for the previous seven months and equivalent to 15 percent of GDP in 2022. Moreover, in early 2021, the United States government included Cuba on the list of state sponsors of terrorism, which imposes a further obstacle to participation in international trade and makes it more difficult to conduct financial operations or attract foreign direct investment (FDI). —*Economic Survey of Latin America and the Caribbean, 2023*.

A measure to increase supply is found in the approval to create private "Micro, Small, and Medium Enterprises" (MSMEs) (Martínez, J., and A. Pérez, 2021) that, with importing capacity, acquire products on the international market, avoiding the economic blockade since they do not operate state accounts; however, these prices obey the free play of supply and demand, and any setting of prices is carried out based on private interests and not in response to social needs. As well, where the Trump-era cap in 2019 limited family remittances to $1,000 every three months (Gámaz Torres, 2019) by putting in place sanctions that triggered a halt in Western Union money-transfer services (Reuters, March 2, 2023), then President Biden reversed this by "removing the current limit on family remittances [made by persons subject to U.S. jurisdiction] … and authorizing donative (non-family) remittances" (Wola, 2022).

However, since many of these remittances from the U.S. have historically been brought over in cash, via Western Union and by individuals, the actual total amount is unknown and makes imposing regulations, including any form of taxation next to impossible for Cuba. Such remittances from family and friends in the U.S., therefore, also contribute to the excess money in circulation in Cuba and, while benefitting the Cuban economy at the level of consumer expenditure, also arguably privilege those Cubans lucky enough to receive them, including when it comes to being able to establish an MSME.

Ultimately, even the most careful planning by the Cuban state is thrown off by the arbitrary, economy-smothering blocking measures of the U.S. blockade, making it impossible to ensure the stable links with the world market, such as for the sugar industry, needed to ensure the level of foreign exchange needed to fulfil the needed supply. In the meantime, price caps in the formal market will likely be rejected by those Cubans hoping to reap the unripe fruit from our new tree before it has time to grow. The economic imbalance itself will only be corrected with the joint productive effort of all the elements that intervene in the national economy, decreases in the effects of the pandemic, and the elimination of the arbitrary U.S. blocking measures via the embargo. Only through the restoration of stable links with the world market—which means an end to the U.S. embargo against Cuba—will Cuba be able to fully control our national economy.

At the Second Session of the National Assembly of the People's Power in December 2023, then deputy prime minister and head of economy and planning Gil Fernández said that Cuba is facing "a scenario of war economy, as it has been called, with the pressures of the intensified blockade, which hinders all the efforts we have to make for the economic performance of the country. … [W]e have to overcome; we have to find alternatives. It is about designing measures in accordance with our economic and social model, inclusive in our socialism, and that allow us, with objectivity, with realism, to move forward" (Trabajadores, December 28, 2023).

Correcting the distortions of the Cuban economy is a *must*. Measures that the Cuban government is about to take include price hikes in electricity, fuel, liquefied gas, and public transportation fares. According to President Diaz-Canel (2023), the measures are aimed at boosting the role of enterprises, increasing the production and export of goods and services, raising foreign exchange, and improving the money market to reinvigorate the economy, correct mistakes, and try to break the siege caused by the U.S. blockade. In his words: "No economy works in line with everybody's needs and wishes, but socialism aims at making it work for the majority."

References

Cruz Anaya, Betsy. (2020, July–December). Acceso a los alimentos en Cuba: prioridad, dificultades y reservas para mejorar." *Economía y Desarrollo*, 164(4). University of Havana. Cuba: Editorial UH.

de Barrio, Periodismo [Olivia Marin Álvarez]. (2023, October). Cuba. Creative Commons International License, 2015.

Diaz-Canel Bermúdez, M. (2023, December). Speech given at the Second Session of the National Assembly of the People's Power. https://cubaminrex.cu/es/discurso-pronunciado-por-el-presidente-miguel-mario-diaz-canel-bermudez-en-la-clausura-del-segundo

Gámaz Torres, Nora. (2019, September 6). Trump administration imposes new limits on remittances to Cuba. *Miami Herald*. https://www.miamiherald.com/news/nation-world/world/americas/cuba/article234796257.html

Martínez Molina, J., and A.F. Pérez Cabrera. (2021, October 25). Micro, small and medium-sized enterprises moving Cuba forward. *Granma* Newspaper, Havana, Cuba.

MINREX. (2021). Compendio de medidas del gobierno de D. Trump contra Cuba. Havana, Cuba: [Cuban ministry of foreign affaires (MINREX)]. https://cubaminrex.cu/es/node/4048

Morales, Emilio. (2024). Cuba: emigration grows, but remittances sink. Dossier Cuba 21. Cuba Siglo 21.

Murillo, J. M. (2020, October 30). *Información sobre el cercano proceso monetario y cambiario* [Information on the upcoming monetary and exchange process]. Round Table. Cuban Television Mesa Redonda. Cubavisión. Cuban televisión (Spanish). http://www.mesaredonda.cubadebate.cu/

Nova González, Armando. (2019). Unificación monetaria y cambiaria en Cuba: decisión impostergable. Cubadebate. http://www.cubadebate.cu/noticias/2019/03/28/unificacion-monetaria-y-cambiaria-en-cuba-decision-impostergable/comentarios/pagina-3/

OnCuba. (2024, January 19). Cuba cerró 2023 con una inflación interanual del 31,34% en su mercado formal [Cuba closed 2023 with year-on-year inflation of 31.34% in its formal market]. On-Cuba-News. https://oncubanews.com/cuba/cuba-cerro-2023-con-una-inflacion-interanual-del-3134-en-su-mercado-formal/#:~:text=Debido%20en%20lo%20fundamental%20a,Estad%C3%ADstica%20e%20Informaci%C3%B3n%20(ONEI).

ONEI. (2023, January). Consumer Price Index (base December 2010), Republic of Cuba. https://globaledge.msu.edu/global-resources/resource/5890

Partido Comunista de Cuba (PCC). (2021, April 16). Conceptualización del Modelo Económico y Social cubano de desarrollo Socialista. 8vo Congreso del PCC. 2021). https://www.mined.gob.cu/informe-central-al-8vo-congreso-del-partido-comunista-de-cuba-descargar/

Reuters. (2023, March 2). Western Union to open money transfers to Cuba from all 50 U.S. states. https://www.reuters.com/business/finance/western-union-open-money-transfers-cuba-all-50-us-states-2023-03-02/

Robreño, A. (2020, December 17). Ordenamiento monetario en Cuba, sin terapia de choque. Havana, Cuba: *Resumen Latinoamericano*. https://www.resumenlatinoamericano.org/2020/12/17/cuba-ordenamiento-monetario-sin-terapia-de-choque/

Trabajadores [via Cubadebate]. (2023, December 28*). Proyecciones del gobierno para corregir distorsiones y reimpulsar la economía* [Government's projections to correct distortions and boost the economy]. Trabajadores: Órgano de la central de trabajadores de Cuba. https://www.trabajadores.cu/20231228/proyecciones-del-gobierno-para-corregir-distorsiones-y-reimpulsar-la-economia/

Villanueva, Omar Everleny Pérez. (2023, April 17). Calculating the cost of living in Cuba. In *Cuba Capacity Building Project*. Columbia Law School. https://horizontecubano.law.columbia.edu/news/calculating-cost-living-cuba

WOLA [Mariakarla Nodarse Venancio]. (2022, May 19). The Biden administration takes constructive first steps on Cuba relations. Commentary. Washington, DC: WOLA [Human Rights in the Americas]. https://www.wola.org/analysis/biden-administration-takes-positive-steps-on-cuba/

Yaffe, Helen (2021, February 10). Day Zero: How and why Cuba unified its dual currency system. In *Cuba at a Crossroads*. London School of Economics and Political Science (LSE), 2024. https://blogs.lse.ac.uk/latamcaribbean/2021/02/10/day-zero-how-and-why-cuba-unified-its-dual-currency-system/

CHAPTER FOUR

Blockade? Embargo? It's More Than Just Semantics...

Salvador Escalante Batista and Paul Sarmiento Blanco

Abstract

The rationale and impact of the economic sanctions imposed on Cuba through the U.S. Embargo since 1962 do not fall within the category of an **embargo** but represent instead a **blockade** aimed at genocide, as evidenced by its destructive impact on the Cuban nation. By stifling the Cuban economy, the **blockade** risks destabilizing Cuban culture and society and, in so doing, limits Cubans' right to self-determination. While the fall of the USSR and the Eastern European communist bloc in the early 1990s should have put an end to this foreign policy and its Cold War agenda, the U.S. changed its rationale, from U.S. national security to Cuban democracy (i.e., "an Act to seek international sanctions against the Castro government ... to plan for support of a transition government leading to a democratically elected government in Cuba, and for other purposes"). This prevented U.S.-controlled companies in other countries from engaging in trade with Cuba while authorizing the U.S. president to use non-violent means to bring about democracy. In 1996, the U.S. strengthened its embargo under the auspices of the Cuban Liberty and Democratic Solidarity (Libertad) Act (aka the Helms-Burton Act). Cuba decries the benefits of traditional Western democracy for Cuba and maintains that the **blockade**, rejected by member-states of the United Nations, is designed to upend Cuban sovereignty as a means of gaining control over Cuba's markets, natural and human resources, and geostrategic positioning. The vast majority of Cuban citizens favour **Cuban socialism**, which enjoys a constitutional irrevocability upheld in the 2019 constitution approved by the national referendum on February 24, 2019. Despite the past, Cubans have faith that the American people will bring a timely conclusion to its embargo against Cuba.

Salvador Escalante Batista is a professor at Holguín University of Medical Sciences. **Paul Sarmiento Blanco** is a professor in the History Department of the University of Holguín.*

Introduction

From the end of the 18th century to the beginning of the 20th century, the United States of America constructed a discourse of domination based on the unfounded premise that the Cuban people were incapable of achieving independence on their own. As Cuba's first historian Emilio Roig de Leuchsenring (1889–1964) so eloquently pointed out, by 1791 U.S. president Thomas Jefferson had already euphemistically embraced an exclusionary political and cultural positioning of Cuba as one of "the stars of the northern patriotic pavilion." In the early 1800s, the independence-minded Cuban Catholic priest Father Félix Varela declared the U.S. power a threat to Cuban autonomy. He accurately predicted that the path to real Cuban sovereignty would only be found through our own efforts, without outside help (Varela, 1826, p. 77).

> **Box 4.1**
>
> *The persistent rejection by Cubans of annexation was a crucial component in the cultural construction of Cuban sovereignty over the first half of the 19th century.*

Near the end of the 1800s and not long before his untimely death, the influential and revered Cuban thinker and revolutionary José Martí—one of the foremost leaders of the Cuban War of Independence—warned Cuban patriots in Mexico of the latent threat to Cuban sovereignty posed by U.S. domination. A day before his death, Martí, who had "lived in the monster" [i.e., the U.S.], wrote a letter to alert his friend Manuel Mercado about the latent threat of U.S. domination "extending its hold across the Antilles and falling with all the greater force on the lands of our America" (Martí, 1895).

Martí's suspicions would be confirmed three years later when the U.S. appropriated the Cuban War of Independence as the only means of gaining control over the nation before it freed itself from the colonial grips of Spain. U.S. attempts to dominate and control the cultural-political-socio-economic reality of Cubans continued into the 1900s with the U.S.-backed Batista dictatorship, rejection of Cuban Socialism's democratic mechanisms, and the so-called embargo. The process of establishing Cuban sovereignty

---

* The authors would like to acknowledge Professor Vilma Páez Pérez of the University of Holguín, for her input on and support of this chapter.

was thus framed by an ideological-cultural confrontation with its closest northern neighbour for more than two centuries.

This chapter will provide a descriptive historical outline of Cuba-U.S. relations as characterized by successive U.S. attempts at domination. In the first section, we will explore some of the historical attempts by the U.S. to control and "conquer" Cuba. Part 2 will define the terms *embargo* and *blockade* and illustrate the genocidal implications for Cuba of this U.S. foreign policy. Part 3 will elaborate on the blockade against Cuba and how it threatens Cuban culture and society through the economy. The authors conclude the chapter by calling for an end to the embargo and summarizing the implications of then President Donald Trump's full implementation of the Helms-Burton Act in 2019.

A Necessary Preamble:
Background of the U.S. Embargo against Cuba

The Cuban right to self-determination is perhaps the value that the U.S. has tried hardest to undermine and delegitimize throughout our history. If one were to itemize every attempt by the U.S. to take possession of or otherwise control Cuba, the list would extend well beyond the length of this chapter. Even more than 60 years of actual Cuban independence has not convinced the U.S. that Cuba will never be a "ripe fruit" ready to fall into their hands (Fidel Castro, 2011; Franklin, 2016 [1997]). Yet today, almost two hundred years after U.S. Secretary of State Quincy Adams (1823) coined the "ripe fruit" metaphor concerning the annexation of Cuba, the Cuban fruit is none the riper for the proposed "picking"!

The U.S. Fixation on Cuba

At the dawn of the 1800s, President Thomas Jefferson confided in James Monroe that Cuba was "the most exciting addition which could ever be made to our system of States" (Jefferson, T., 1823. Considering Cuba "easy prey" (Roig, 1959), Jefferson did not look kindly on Cuban independence. He promoted his idea of annexation to Monroe, who would warn European countries away from interfering in the Americas once he took office in 1817 (Monroe Doctrine, 1823).

Throughout the 1840s and 1850s, the Cuban sociologist, journalist, historian, economist, leading anti-annexionist, and one of Varela's former students—José Antonio Saco—fueled a long, heartfelt, and heated controversy against annexation. For Saco, Cuba's induction as a U.S. state would mean the complete "absorption of Cuban nationality" (Saco, 1978). In 1854, the failed Ostend Manifesto—which was motivated by the desire to "expand U.S. slave territory" and to ward off any potential black uprising in Cuba motivated by the Haitian Revolution—laid out the U.S. self-imposed ultimatum to either buy Cuba for 130 million dollars or declare war on Spain (Ostend, 1854).

While the manifesto failed, the U.S. would gain economic domination over the island by 1877, controlling some 82 percent of Cuban exports – a clear sign the island's economic ties were already shifting from a weak Spain to the rising U.S. power. As the Cuban historian Ramiro Guerra (1927) pointed out, U.S. exports supplied the Cuban economy's strategic sectors, such as the sugar industry, through shrewdly invested American financial capital.

U.S. Appropriation of the Cuban War of Independence in 1898 and the Battleship Maine

In a message to the U.S. Congress, President William McKinley (1898) requested authorization for U.S. intervention to end the Cuban War of Independence against Spain by any means, in order to pacify Cuba and establish a stable government. Senator Henry Teller, a Democrat from Colorado, worried that the U.S. would use this to gain control over Cuba, called for a joint resolution including a provision that "disclaims any disposition or intention to exercise sovereignty over said island, except for the pacification thereof, and asserts its determination when that is accomplished to leave the government and control of the island to its people" (Randolph, 1901, p. 358; see also Rodríguez, 2006; Teller Amendment, 1898).

By authorizing the U.S. military to acquire Cuba by force if Spain would not sell its island territory or to intervene if any other nation tried to prevent the "self-determination of Cubans" through treaty or other means, however, the amendment nonetheless put the U.S. in a dominating position. It also resolved that Cuba would "sell land for coaling or naval stations" to be agreed upon by the U.S. government (see Chapter 5).

Leading up to this, in 1897 President McKinley had upped the ante on buying Cuba from Spain to 300 million dollars to no avail and used fearmongering to justify a war against Spain in Cuba (Guerra, R., 1934). McKinley employed "rumours of danger to U.S. citizens in Cuba to justify dispatching the USS *Maine* to Havana" (Franklin, 2016 [1997]). Newspaper baron William Randolph Hearst, whose use of "yellow journalism" (2019) concerning Cuba led somewhat directly to the coining of the term,* actively supported the war effort in Cuba by using those rumours to inflame public opinion (Castro, 2011; Franklin, 2016 [1997]).

With the stage so set, the U.S. used the explosion of the *Maine* as a (false) pretext to officially declare war on Spain (Cañedo, 2017) in a bald-faced attempt to gain control over the emergent Cuban sovereignty while there was still time (Castro, 2011; Xiqué Cutiño, 2018). "President McKinley declared a blockade of the northern coast of Cuba and its port at Santiago, an act of war [against Spain] according to international law" (Fidel Castro, 2011). The United States officially declared war on Spain the next day (April 1898), marking the start of the so-called Spanish-American War.

The pursuit of U.S. domination over Cuba thus moved from various pretexts of "helping" Cubans, by buying their island out from under them, to monopolizing Cuba's export market or appropriating a war that had already almost been won by the Cuban independence forces.

The Shaping of Cuban Resistance

Through these years, a Cuban culture of resistance was being shaped in the *Manigua*,† extending from the first cry for independence by Cuban landowner Carlos Manuel de Céspedes in 1868 to José Martí's role as leader of the Cuban War of Independence. The 19th century would culminate with a disintegrating Spain yielding Cuban sovereignty to the new world gendarme, the imperialist U.S., with President McKinley's signing of the Treaty of Paris and its ratification by the U.S. Senate with a 52-to-27 majority ("Chronology", 1898; CubaMilitar, [10 December 1898] 2019).

This did not end the exploitative presence of the U.S. in Cuba. It was consolidated by adding the Platt Amendment (1901) as a rider to the U.S. Army Appropriations Bill, legalizing U.S. military occupation of Cuba and mandating seven conditions for eventual withdrawal and an eighth condi-

---

* Cited in *Oxford English Dictionary* entry "Yellow," sense number 3.
† Manigua: A Cuban stronghold in the jungle during the battle against the Spanish Army.

tion for a treaty designed to uphold the first seven. These conditions were imposed as an appendix to the Cuban Constitution of 1901. Steeped in colonial fervour, the controls effectively ceded the Cuban people's right to self-determination by limiting their nation's ability to engage in treaties with other nations; by mandating the U.S. right to lease a 45-square-mile piece of land for a U.S. naval base at Guantanamo, Cuba (see Chapter 5); by giving the U.S. the right to take military action in the event of any attacks on itself or Cuba by other countries (such as Mexico or in Latin America); and by making it illegal for Cuba to transfer control or ownership of any part of the island to any nation other than the U.S.

This arrangement clearly aimed to ensure the continued U.S. domination of the Cuban share of the colonial sugar market (Zanetti and García, 2017).

1902–1958: Cuba Becomes a De Facto Neo-Colony of the U.S.

Thus, the Cuban Republic was born—as a de facto "neo-colony" of the United States of America. Between 1902 and 1958, the approval of the U.S. government was essential for any political action in Cuba. During this period, unceasing interventions and propagandistic rhetoric in the U.S. about Cuba shaped anew the image of this "independent nation" as a watched people and the U.S. as the "benevolent guardian."

In response to this oppression, resistance converged in the formation of "a Provisional Revolutionary Government" in September 1933 by a "loose coalition" of Cuban activists. The "Grau government"

The more things change, the more they stay the same…

(Whitney, 2000, 436), commonly known in Cuba as the "100-day government" (*Gobierno de los Cien Días*), was "directed by a popular university professor, Dr. Ramon Grau San Martin" and "promised 'a new Cuba' with social justice for all, agrarian reforms to give peasants 'legal title to their lands,' wage reforms, and 'arbitration'" (Whitney, 436).

The Cuban government under Grau was the first to be run "by people who did not negotiate the terms of political power with Spain (before 1898) or with the United States (after 1898), and its successes include the creation of a 'Ministry of Labour,' the 'universal abrogation of the Platt Amendment,' and 'woman suffrage'" (436). The Grau government "was overthrown by an equally loose anti-government coalition" headed by "a young sergeant, Fulgencio Batista" (437). Before this happened, however, "revolutionary struggle and mass mobilization had become part of the Cuban political landscape" through Grau's 100-day rule and "many of the demands of the failed revolution of 1933 became the constitutional edicts of 1940" (Whitney, 2000, 438).

U.S. Soft Power against Cuba

It is noteworthy that Prohibition (1920–1933) had made Havana an accessible hedonistic playground for U.S. citizens, replete with white-only beaches, where the U.S. rule of law and moral concerns around alcohol and prostitution could be thwarted a scant 90 miles off its shores. In March 1933, the Democratic administration of U.S. President Franklin Roosevelt (1932–1945) declared a new direction for U.S. foreign policy in Latin America. Cooperation became the call word in matters of trade and defence, officially ending the traditional interventionist (i.e., military) approach. This "Good Neighbor Policy" (Roosevelt, 1933), as it became popularly known, and the Cuban resistance to U.S. domination, would necessitate the abrogation of the Platt Amendment (1901–1934) with the notable exception of provisions regarding the U.S. naval base at Guantanamo.

Unfortunately, the soft power of the economic force wielded by the U.S. in Cuba was enough to continue to control its internal and external economic development and growth. Between 1934 and 1958, the U.S. monopolized a significant part of the island's sugar production, which remained the strategic core of the Cuban economy (Santos, 1960). Following the Second World War, the U.S. emerged as the global imperialist power, heightening its control over international relations. As a result of this process and within the scope of the General Agreement on Tariffs and Trade (GATT, 1947), which Cuba signed in good faith with permission to negotiate on (mainly) sugar. However, due to the neo-colonial positioning of U.S. interests in Cuba's domestic economy, the agreement had no reciprocity.

> **Box 4.2**
>
> *In his* New York Times *review of* Contesting Castro: The United States and the Triumph of the Cuban Revolution *by Thomas G. Paterson (1994), Thomas Carothers describes Fulgencio Batista as "the strongman who seized power in Cuba in 1952 and ran the country for seven tawdry years" and as "a corrupt, repressive leader backed by the United States for his anti-Communist and pro-business views." Batista faced "a rising but poorly understood nationalistic insurgency" while the U.S. pursued "a policy of strong support for the dictator until his imminent collapse prompted a vain, hurried search for some moderate alternative." Batista's fall was "coupled with the emergence of a revolutionary Government that viewed the United States with suspicion and hostility" (Carothers, 1994).*

The Personification of U.S. Soft Power in Cuba: Batista

Democracy was definitively expunged from Cuba when a petty-bourgeois political movement looking to increase its economic power on the island supported Fulgencio Batista's coup d'état of March 10, 1952. It soon became clear the U.S. had backed Batista because of his willingness to completely open the Cuban economy up to penetration by U.S. investors. An "urban planning" project in Havana, which had become a fiscal and tourist paradise, quickly converted the capital city into a profitable "playground" for the Mafia, thus opening it up to drug trafficking (Fernández Arias, October 2, 2018). Money laundering, gambling and prostitution became the norm. There were over 11,000 prostitutes in Havana alone at that time. "Beyond the outskirts of the capital, beyond the slot machines, was one of the poorest and most beautiful countries in the Western world" (Detzer, 1979, p. 17).

In the 1950s, with the process of socio-economic and cultural domination gaining ground, anti-U.S. resistance intensified among Cuban citizens. In short, the U.S.-backed Batista military dictatorship left Cubans with little choice but to revolt, driven by the need to end the horrendous conditions in which their country was mired. Rising crime rates and violations of fundamental human rights had become a way of life for Cuban citizens. Before the Cuban Revolution, journalists were prosecuted and several murdered, while hundreds of union and student leaders were forced into exile to avoid becoming victims of prosecution (López Civeira, 2009) through processes that today are considered aspects of human trafficking.

In a pact signed by the Batista government, the Mob engineered the construction of a chain of hotels and casinos, mainly in Havana and Varadero, so that the ports of the north coast of Cuba could be used as a transition point to guarantee the uninterrupted flow by air of drugs between Latin America and the U.S. (Fernández, 2018). However, the "Mob['s] dreams collided with those of Fidel Castro, who would lead an uprising of the country's socio-economically disenfranchised masses against Batista's hated government and its foreign partners" (English, 2009).

The increasing disenfranchisement of Cuban citizens fortified anti-U.S. sentiment and resistance in Cuba. In 1953, with the assault on the Moncada Army Garrison (named after General Guillermón Moncada, a hero of the Cuban War of Independence) in Santiago de Cuba, a group of young Cubans, commanded by Fidel Castro, showed the world a Cuba ready to face the beast, and the Revolution was on.

Why Didn't the U.S. Government Intervene Militarily This Time?
While one might think the U.S. would have reverted to its customary interventionist policy at this point, it is noteworthy that its non-military stance during this internal conflict in Cuba was the result of abject short-sightedness: Cuba's economic dependence on the U.S. economy, continually strengthened since formal independence from Spain, made the ruling circles in the U.S. confident that Cuba would remain controllable using soft power. The U.S. government failed to see that the new leadership in Cuba was emerging within a revolutionary context of resistance led by a man who could not be "bought." His name was Fidel Castro.

Naturally, support of Fidel and his rebels spread like wildfire among a Cuban population fed up with the Batista government's increasingly rampant corruption, brutality, and inefficiency. By the time the U.S. realized the new Cuban government was fulfilling its promises to the Cuban people, it would be too late to exert external pressure, and relations between the two countries rapidly deteriorated. "In January 1961, with mutual acrimony abounding, diplomatic relations were finally broken" (Klepak, 2000, p. 5).

Cuban Sovereignty Based on Socialist Development: 1959 to Present
Two essential issues have dominated U.S.-Cuba relations since 1959. First, Cuba has consolidated its sovereignty based on the Cuban socialist model, which first aligned with the values of communism—*from each according to his ability, to each according to his needs*—and later reverted to a principle of socialist distribution. The fervent post-WW II "better-dead-than-red" ideology had already tagged communism as a threat to global safety. During Fidel Castro's visit to the U.S. for a UN session in March 1959, Vice President Richard Nixon characterized Castro's support of communism as "incredibly naive" (Glass, 2013). The second issue is the U.S. embar-

go imposed against Cuba in 1962. As relations between the two countries continued to deteriorate, the United States conceived of this new vehicle to drive the continued staging of what, for all intent and purpose, was a complex political, economic and cultural encroachment on Cuba that had endured for more than 150 years.

A direct and aggressive hostility towards Cuba by the U.S. government dominated U.S.-Cuban relations through the attempts of 10 U.S. administrations to intervene in the Cuban sovereignty project. The Barack Obama administration (2008–2017) would become the exception, limiting the embargo slightly by easing travel restrictions, meeting with the Cuban President Raul Castro to re-establish diplomatic relations between the two countries, and removing Cuba from the United States State Sponsors of Terrorism list. Obama also announced the impending end of President Bill Clinton's dry foot/wet foot policy in the 1990s. However, this could all be seen as a yet another U.S. charade aimed at gaining the confidence of the Cuban people; for example, if Obama was intent on ending the embargo, why would he not have tried to lift it while the Democrats were in control of Congress during the early years of his administration?

Nonetheless, after two hundred years of disagreement between the two nations, Obama was the first U.S. president to deal with Cuba cordially and respectfully, to recognize the legitimacy of the Cuban government, and to voice disagreement with the embargo as a "policy of isolation designed for the Cold War [that] made little sense in the 21st century" and "was hurting the Cuban people instead of helping them" (Beckwith, March 22, 2016). Obama's policy towards Cuba thus seemed to signal a truce in a long and complicated period of dissent. But when Donald Trump came into power in 2017, the few steps Obama had taken to normalize relations were easily erased, practically overnight. Before looking at this, however, we will take a moment to define our terms.

Embargo? Blockade?

Since the best way to come to grips with conceptual terms is to look them up in the dictionary, the authors consulted the celebrated *Black's Laws Dictionary* for both *embargo* and *blockade* (Black, 1995): "EMBARGO— A proclamation or order of state, usually issued in time of war or threatened hostilities, prohibiting the departure of ships or goods from some or all the ports of such state until further order. The embargo is the hindering or detention by any government of ships of commerce in its ports." In the authors' opinion, therefore, the U.S. embargo on Cuba takes the form of a "CAPITAL BLOCKADE—A form of economic sanction in which a country or a group of countries attempt to limit or entirely stop the amount of investment capital going into another country that is seen to be performing questionable actions." Aside from prohibiting other countries from trade with Cuba and restricting almost all U.S. citizens from travel to Cuba, the so-called embargo (since 1962) is costing the Cuban nation a fortune in tourist dollars alone annually.

More U.S. Soft-Power Plays against Cuba

On March 14, 1958, during the armed conflict between the rebels led by Fidel Castro and Fulgencio Batista's soldiers, an embargo on the sale of arms was imposed (Wiskari, April 3, 1958). Ironically, the arms embargo had more of an impact on Batista's army than on the relatively ill-equipped rebels, who were seizing their arms. When the Revolutionary government came to power on January 1, 1959, Fidel Castro's overtures to the U.S. lasted until the failed U.S. invasion of Cuba at *Playa Girón* (Bay of Pigs), which was based on the false pretext of intervention for the good of the people. As early as "March [1960], [President Dwight Eisenhower] had begun making plans to help overthrow [Prime Minister Fidel Castro] and ordered the CIA to train Cuban exiles to invade their former country, [approving] $13 million for the project" (Smitha, 1998). Around the same time, Eisenhower also reduced Cuba's sugar quota after rejecting the "purchase of 700,000 tons already produced" (Rodríguez, 2010); Cuba was left with no market for its essential export product.

Nationalizations, as state acts, are based on a country's sovereignty. Therefore, every state is obliged to respect the independent right of all others to conduct such processes, which constitute acts of economic justice to benefit the entire people and, yes, do imply adequate compensation (Toledo, 2019). With its economic lifeline effectively severed, Cuba added several nationalization clauses in 1959, such as Law 851, to the Fundamental Law of 1959. Law 851 was a complement to the expropriation clause, Article 24, of the Fundamental Law of 1959. It "established the ways and means to award compensation for the nationalized property through government bonds issued for that purpose redeemable at maturity by the National Bank of Cuba" (Law 851, 1960; Capote, 2018). This compensation was accepted by the governments of claimants from several countries, all of whom received appropriate compensation, but the U.S. government refused any discussions on the matter (Cuba-MINREX, 2019).

The first nationalizations in Cuba took place with the birth of the Agrarian Reform laws (1959-1963) and established compensation with 20-year government-issued bonds, which accrued 4.5 percent annual interest. The

Revolutionary Government then proceeded to seize private land, nationalize hundreds of private companies—including several local subsidiaries of U.S. corporations—and impose taxes on American products; the substantial U.S. exports were halved in just two years. The U.S. sugar companies, having appropriated the country's best lands, began mounting a boycott of Cuba as early as March 1959, and the exorbitant prices charged by U.S. oil companies were otherwise draining the nation's economy (Miranda, 2000).

The Eisenhower administration responded on October 19, 1960, with the imposition of trade restrictions on everything but food and medical supplies (Fabry, 2015). At the apex of these transgressions and right after Cuba signed a trade agreement with the Soviet Union on February 13, 1960 (Walters, 1966 p. 74), the U.S. cut all diplomatic ties with the island.

Blockade

Operation Mongoose followed the CIA's failed attempt to overthrow Castro during the unsuccessful Bay of Pigs invasion (aka the "Cuban Project") (JFK, 2011; Cubadebate, 2013). It was a secret initiative by the Kennedy administration against Cuba aimed at removing Fidel Castro from power and dismantling the Cuban Revolution (Bohning, 2005). Such piratical attacks often turned deadly, such as in the fisherman's town of Boca de Samá, Cuba,* where a gang of mercenaries murdered two young men and seriously wounded many others, including children, in October 1971 ("Boca de Samá," 1971). On April 6, 1960, the tremendous support for the Cuban government and its movement toward communism made it clear to the U.S. that no future military occupation was possible and the best ploy would be "disenchantment and disaffection based on economic dissatisfaction and hardship" (Mallory, April 6, 1960).

Based on this assessment, U.S. Deputy Assistant Secretary of State of Inter-American Affairs Lester Mallory wrote a memorandum to the Assistant Secretary of State for Inter-American Affairs qualifying his earlier suggestion of an embargo aimed at interrupting the Cuban sugar industry as a possible means of ending the island's autonomy, using tactics "as adroit and inconspicuous as possible" to create "the greatest inroads in denying money and supplies to Cuba, to decrease monetary and real wages, to bring about hunger, desperation and overthrow of government" (Mallory, 1960, p. 886).

U.S. attempts to overthrow the Cuban government over the years have also included several plots to kill, maim or humiliate Cuban leaders (Maier,

---

* Boca de Samá is a humble fishermen's village in Cuba that was attacked by a gang of machine-gunning mercenaries in 1971, killing two and seriously wounding many others.

2018). For example, an assassination attempt on Fidel Castro, Raúl Castro, and Che Guevara was planned for July 26, 1961, by the CIA under the name "Operation Patty." The plot was uncovered by Cuban security forces and prevented. Proof of this was affirmed some "seventeen years later at an International Tribunal in Havana" by Humberto Rosales Torres, a Cuban who had been "arrested for his part in the plot and given a nine-year prison term." Torres also testified "that the plan also included an attack on the Guantánamo Naval Base that would have provided an excuse for sending in the U.S. Marines" (Franklin, 2016 [1997]).

After the U.S.-backed airstrike on Cuban airfields on April 15, 1961, just days before the Bay of Pigs invasion on April 17, Fidel delivered on April 16 a speech honouring the seven Cubans killed and emphasizing the socialist nature of the Revolution. At Havana's May 1, 1961, Workers' Day Parade, he declared Cuba socialist, and on December 2 he formally identified as Marxist–Leninist and affirmed Cuba's Soviet alignment. On September 4, 1961, attacks on Cuba were consolidated in the Foreign Assistance Act (1961), which authorized the U.S. president to establish a total embargo on trade with Cuba. This was followed in 1963 by the Cuban Assets Control Regulations (Rennack and Sullivan, 2018) of the U.S. Department of the Treasury, authorized under the Trading with the Enemy Act of 1917 (TWEA, section 5(b), 1958), regulating financial relations with Cuba.

Just after reportedly ordering 1200 Cuban cigars for himself (Salinger, 1992), President Kennedy declared the embargo, effective February 7, 1962. Within a few short years, at a time when Cuba's economy was dependent on U.S.-made factors of production, relations between the two countries devolved into a Cold War–type relationship such as that between the United States and the Soviet Union and their allies after World War II.

The darkest moment in U.S.-Cuba relations would be the morning of October 15, 1962, just over six months after the imposition of the embargo, when U.S. spy planes discovered the Soviet Union was building missile bases in Cuba. President Kennedy learned of the threat early the following morning, and for the next 12 days the U.S. and Russia were locked in a fierce nuclear stand-off known as the Cuban Missile Crisis that ended only when Russian President Nikita Khrushchev accepted Kennedy's secret proposal to remove U.S. missiles in Turkey in exchange for the de-arming of Cuba (Valido, 2012; Chomsky, May 1, 2012). Cuba dispensed with the Soviet missiles within six months (Díaz, 1999).

Central Intelligence Agency operatives reportedly employed several shameful tactics linked to anti-Castro terrorists, who introduced the African swine fever virus into Cuba in 1971. While the CIA denied the claim, both *Newsday* and the San Francisco *Chronicle* felt it worth printing on January 10, 1977, among numerous other newspapers. More importantly, mention appears in *Cuba and the United States*, a book compiled from such authentic sources as "once-secret documents now declassified" and written by the U.S. historian and scholar Jane Franklin (Franklin, 1997 [2006]). For example, within six weeks, the disease outbreak forced the slaughter of 500,000 pigs to prevent a nationwide animal epidemic. Early in the 1980s, a virulent strain of dengue fever was also introduced in Cuba. It was the first appearance of hemorrhagic dengue in the western hemisphere (Franklin, 1997 [2006]).

There is strong evidence that the virus was manipulated and introduced in Cuba (Escalante, 2006, p. 123). A study by María G. Guzmán, a distinguished researcher and full professor at the Pedro Kourí Tropical Medicine Institute, PAHO/WHO Collaborating Center for the Study and Control of Dengue, Havana, Cuba, has fathomed the extent of the situation:

> The epidemic was recognized as such in late May 1981. Retrospective epidemiologic studies found it had begun at the end of 1980 in three municipalities located in eastern, central, and western Cuba. Cases were reported during the same epidemiologic week in persons with no history of travel outside the country or their localities. A total of 344,203 cases were registered, including 10,312 severe and very severe cases, resulting in 158 deaths, 101 of them children (Guzmán, María G., 2012 s/p).

Eduardo Victor Arocena Pérez, a leader of the Omega 7 counter-revolutionary terrorist group based in Florida (Elfrink, 2008), has admitted that one of their groups had been mandated to "carry some germs to introduce them in Cuba to be used against the Soviets and the Cuban economy ... to begin what was called chemical war" (Franklin, 1997; Covert Action, 1984). Cuba subsequently suffered simultaneous outbreaks of hemorrhagic dengue fever, hemorrhagic conjunctivitis, tobacco mold, sugar cane fungus and a new outbreak of African swine fever (Blum, 1995).

The U.S. Embargo: Attempted Genocide during the Special Period in Times of Peace

Following the collapse of the Soviet bloc, the rationale for the embargo was updated, since Cuba could no longer in any way be considered a threat to

U.S. national security. In the new embargo sanctions, democracy (i.e., as opposed to U.S. security) became the word of the day. Virtually overnight, Cuba, a country whose economy had been flourishing through trade with the USSR and Eastern European bloc was turned into a nation almost entirely devoid of trade and commerce. This ushered in a period of famine and malnutrition known in Cuba as the Special Period in Times of Peace, which can easily be construed as the genocidal impact of the soft power wielded by the so-called embargo on Cuba.

The Cuba Democracy Act (CDA, 1992), signed by President George H.W. Bush, banned foreign subsidiaries of U.S. companies from trading with Cuba, and introduced the 180-day rule, barring ships that had docked in Cuba from entering U.S. ports for six months. As its title suggests, the law effectively reframed the embargo's justification—from U.S. national security concerns to a tool for pressuring sovereign Cuba into adopting U.S.-style democracy and advancing U.S. ideological and geopolitical interests. In a nutshell, the CDA was designed to prevent economic growth in the hope that the people would overthrow Fidel Castro, but that never happened because the Cuban Revolution was and remained a popular revolution. The new foreign policy also set coercive rules for other nations' policies by making U.S. aid contingent on their ceasing all trade with Cuba.

In 1996, the embargo against Cuba was again reinforced and codified into U.S. law through the Cuban Liberty and Democratic Solidarity (LIBERTAD) Act, along with amendments to the 1917 Trading with the Enemy Act (TWEA) that had enabled the embargo. Known as the Helms-Burton Act, LIBERTAD tied the embargo's termination to conditions such as a transitional government in Cuba and congressional approval. TWEA sanctions had previously been applied to China (1950 to 1975), Vietnam (1964 to 1994), and North Korea (1950 to 2008), but as of 2024, only Cuba remains sanctioned (federalregister.gov). TWEA "is part of the legal framework" that sustains the blockade, which includes several laws and administrative regulations, such as the Foreign Assistance Act (1961); Cuban Assets Control Regulations (1963); Export Administration Act (1979); Cuban Democracy Act (aka Torricelli Act) of 1992; and the Helms-Burton Law (1996); as well as Export Administration Regulations (1979) (Trading with the Enemy, *Granma*, 2019).

The U.S. Embargo on Cuba as an Act of Genocide

In 2019 and for "the 28th consecutive year, the UN General Assembly adopted the resolution calling for an end to the economic, commercial and financial embargo imposed by the United States against Cuba." Only the

U.S., Brazil and Israel voted against the resolution, while Colombia and Ukraine abstained (UN News, 2019; see Chart 4.1 below). In a pre-vote statement issued during the presentation of the resolution, the Minister of Foreign Affairs of Cuba, Bruno Rodríguez Parrilla, condemned the so-called embargo as "a flagrant, massive and systematic violation of human rights [that] qualifies as an act of genocide under Articles 2 (b) and (c) of the Convention on the Prevention and Punishment of the Crime of Genocide of 1948. There is no Cuban family that does not suffer the consequences" (Rodriguez Parrilla; UN News, November 7, 2019).

Rodríguez has also pointed out that the "blockade remains the fundamental obstacle to the economic development of the country" and "represents a hindrance for the updating of Cuba's Economic and Social Development Model, the implementation of its National Plan by the year 2030, the 2030 Agenda and its Sustainable Development Goals" (Rodríguez Parrilla, November 7, 2019). The U.S. Permanent Representative (Ambassador) to the United Nations Kelly Croft "defended the embargo" as an expression of the U.S. sovereign right to "choose which countries we trade with" but did not mention that the U.S. is also "forcing" other countries to comply. As shown in Chart 4.1, the U.S. is almost alone in its desire to perpetuate the blockade against Cuba.

Cuba has delivered a resolution on the so-called embargo to the United Nations every year for over two decades. In 2018, Rodríguez also qualified the blockade as "an act of genocide" that would constitute "a violation of the International Humanitarian Law, if it were a conflict" (Rodríguez Parrilla, November 1, 2018). Earlier that year, the UN said that this "blockade costs the Cuban people more than $130 billion at current prices and has left an indelible mark on its economic structure" (World News, May 8, 2018). The U.S. Permanent Representative to the United Nations, Nikki R. Haley, proclaimed that "the UN does not have the ability nor the authority to end the United States embargo on Cuba, and she had the added audacity to frame all this as a plea for "a better life for the Cuban people," saying that the resolution presented by Cuba "does not help a single Cuban family" (Nichols, November 1, 2018). This insinuates the Cuban people do not know what is right for them, recalling similar pretexts used in the past to "justify" U.S. intervention, such as during the Cuban War of Independence and subsequent foreign policy directed at Cuba. As usual, the overall vote against the embargo was almost unanimous in 2018 (Table 4.1, next page).

The U.S. government has voted against ending the embargo every year except 2016 when it abstained, following President Obama's policy of easing the relationship between the two countries.

Figure 4.1. United Nations Votes on Cuban Resolutions to End the Blockade

1991: Due to concerns that certain nations were powerless to vote freely due to their economic dependence on the U.S., Cuba withdrew its first resolution against the blockade.

Year	In Favour	Against	Abstention
1992	59	3	71
1993	88	4	57
1994	101	2	48
1995	117	3	38
1996	137	3	25
1997	143	3	17
1998	157	2	12
1999	155	2	8
2000	167	3	4
2001	167	3	3
2002	173	3	4
2003	179	3	2
2004	179	4	7
2005	182	4	1
2006	183	4	1
2007	184	4	1
2008	185	3	2
2009	187	3	2
2010	187	2	3
2011	186	2	3
2012	188	3	2
2013	188	2	3
2014	188	2	3
2015	191	2	0
2016	191	0	2
2017	191	2	0
2018	189	2	0
2019	187	3	2

Source: https://cubaminrex.cu/en/cubas-report-resolution-75289-united-nations-general-assembly-entitled-necessity-ending-economic (Cuba-MINREX, 2024). Editors' Note: This chapter was finalized in 2019. The afterword (an update) in Chapter 3 covers some of the early direct impacts of the U.S. embargo against Cuba through the COVID-19 pandemic. Most recently, in October 2024, 187 member-nations voted in favour of and two (U.S.; Israel) against the United Nations resolution put forward each year to end the economic, commercial, and financial embargo. Cuba's foreign minister again condemned the blockade as a crime of genocide: https://cubaminrex.cu/en/cubas-report-resolution-75289-united-nations-general-assembly-entitled-necessity-ending-economic.

Blockade as Genocide

As many readers will already know, the UN Convention on the Prevention and Punishment of the Crime of Genocide was adopted by the United Nations General Assembly in 1948. Genocide is defined in Article II as any of the following acts committed with intent to destroy, in whole or in part, a national, ethnical, racial, or religious group (UN, n.d.):

a. Killing members of the group;
b. Causing serious bodily or mental harm to members of the group;
c. Deliberately inflicting on the group conditions of life calculated to bring about its physical destruction in whole or in part;
d. Imposing measures intended to prevent births within the group; and
e. Forcibly transferring children of the group to another group.

Ralph Lemkin, who coined the term *genocide* and was instrumental in its codification as international law in 1948, identified two phases in genocide: "first, destruction of the national pattern of the oppressed group: secondly, the imposition of the national pattern of the oppressor" (Lemkin 1944, p. 79). Lemkin, "who was keenly interested in colonial genocides" (McDonnell and Moses), coined the term *cultural genocide* as well, as noted in his biography, but was unable to convince the UN committee to include it in the Convention on Genocide (Lemkin, 1958).

Cuba has consistently classified the blockade as having genocidal aims since 2018 (see Rodríguez Parrilla, 2018). Undersecretary of State L. D. Mallory clearly spelled out the genocidal tendencies of the so-called embargo for President Dwight D. Eisenhower in an official, since declassified, U.S. government document dated April 6, 1960:

> The majority of Cubans support Castro. There is no active opposition. The only foreseeable means of alienating internal support [from the government] is through disenchantment and disaffection based on economic dissatisfaction and hardship. (…) all possible means should be undertaken promptly to weaken the economic life of Cuba (…) denying money and supplies to Cuba, to decrease monetary and real wages, to bring about hunger, desperation and overthrow of the government. (Memorandum from the Deputy Assistant Secretary of State for Inter-American Affairs (Department of State [Mallory], 1960).)

2019: The U.S. Unleashes the Full Force of the Helms-Burton Act to Tighten Its Embargo (Blockade!) against Cuba

The death of Fidel Castro (November 25, 2016) and the election of Donald Trump in late 2016 created a propitious moment to rekindle debates over U.S.-Cuba policy. At a rally in Miami, President Trump announced the "cancellation" of some of the restrictions on travel and trade eased by the Obama administration. Instead, Trump tightened the "rules on Americans travelling there and restricting U S companies dealing with enterprises controlled by the island nation's military" but would not break the restored diplomatic relations ("Trump unveils new Cuba trade," June 17, 2017).

> Cuba had a 7 percent decline in overall tourism during the first three months of 2018, partly caused by a sharp drop in U.S. travel to the island. [It is] only 56 percent of what it was in 2017 due to various issues, such as the tightening of travel restrictions, mysterious health attacks, and the effects of Hurricane Irma. (Sesin, April 25, 2018)

Trump has repeatedly said U.S. sanctions will not be lifted until Cuba frees all political prisoners and holds free and fair elections, among other rights-related conditions that are exclusively Cuban matters. Such rhetoric has been used as a pretext for 10 U.S. administrations to intervene in Cuba. While holding political prisoners is a concern the world over, the U.S. and most other countries also hold a few prisoners of conscience (Amnesty International 2019), making it a weak rationale for the U.S. blockade on Cuba.

In September 2017, the Trump administration announced it was "pulling more than half of its diplomatic personnel" from Havana after twenty-one diplomatic staff suffered injuries, including hearing loss and cognitive impairment, believed to have been caused by sonic devices (Connor, September 29, 2017). The Cuban government had urged the United States not to cut diplomatic ties, denying any involvement and offering to provide any assistance to U.S. investigators. No evidence has yet been established, but the move suspended most of the embassy's functions, including visa processing. Initially, the U.S. directed Cubans seeking visas to the U.S. embassy in Bogota, Colombia, further complicating the process as Cubans require a visa to enter Colombia. Currently, Cubans who are trying to travel to the U.S. go to Georgetown in Guyana, which requires no visas for Cubans, to apply for a visa ("Cubans Seeking Immigrant Visas to USA," March 29, 2018; U.S. Embassy in Cuba, 2019).

Administration officials said the new restrictions would not disrupt existing U.S. business ventures; many U.S.-based companies, including Google and Starwood Hotels and Resorts, had signed deals and invested heavily in Cuba following the warming of relations (Smith, 2017). The U.S. embassy in Havana had only just opened two years earlier. "Senator Patrick Leahy, an advocate for closer relations between the U.S. and Cuba, said in a statement that the culprit 'obviously is trying to disrupt the normalization process'" (Connor, September 29, 2019).

Canada cut its embassy staff in Cuba after at least 14 citizens reported symptoms. The visa office in Havana, Cuba, was closed "starting May 8, 2018" and "[t]he visa office in Mexico now processes applications from Cuba" (Government of Canada, 2019). However, the findings of a Canadian government study run by Dr. Alon Friedman, who "headed up a multi-disciplinary team of experts at Dalhousie's Brain Repair Centre," to "find out why Canadian diplomats based in Cuba had become ill during 2016 and 2017" discount the idea of a "sonic attack" as the cause (Kimber, S., 2019).

2019: Application of Title III and Waiver Authority

Title III of the Helms-Burton Act (2019) states that any non- U.S. company that "knowingly traffics in property in Cuba confiscated without compensation from a US person" can be subjected to litigation. That company's leadership can be barred from entry into the United States. Furthermore, sanctions may also be applied to non-U.S. companies trading with Cuba. Title III includes a waiver authority, which was consistently used by U.S. Presidents every six months until January 16, 2019, when President Trump decided to suspend its application for only 45 days and pursue a review of the potential impact of full application—despite the extraterritorial, neo-colonial, and genocidal dimensions of the measure.

Most recently, the U.S. has bolstered its embargo arsenal by "dusting off" Title III to "tighten the blockade and dissuade foreign investors in Cuba" (Capote, 2019). "Its Titles I and II include a series of requirements

---

Box 4.3

Title III of the Helms-Burton Act is a central part of the U.S. embargo on Cuba: it officially writes the reactionary policy into law, prohibiting any president from unilaterally lifting it. Specifically, Title III allows U.S. nationals who owned property in Cuba that was seized by the Cuban government after the 1959 Revolution to sue U.S. and foreign companies for profiting from their former properties (Capote, 2019).

defining a transition government, and what constitutes a democratically elected government, according to the U.S," which some say "constitutes an intervention in the internal affairs of a sovereign country, in violation of international law" (Capote, 2019). Ironically, it recalls "the Monroe Document, proclaimed more than a century and a half ago" and "is an attack on the independence and dignity of Cuba, with openly annexationist, colonialist intentions" (Capote, 2019). In effect, "Title III creates a regime of extraterritoriality and permits U.S. nationals to file lawsuits against foreign companies despite no adverse action occurring within the jurisdiction of the United States" (O'Connor, 2019).

Several owners have already presented claims, likely anticipating juicy profits since Title III allows the "original owners of Cuban properties confiscated six decades ago to sue foreign companies 'trafficking' in them for three times their current value." One such lawsuit has been launched by the Múrias family, who "owned a sprawling beach neighborhood an hour from Havana" and several "apartment buildings in front of Havana's iconic sea wall," as well as "Cayo Ocampo," an island "off the province of Cienfuegos" (Sesin, NBC News, June 3, 2019). Although "experts now say the number [of properties involved] will more likely be in the dozens or hundreds at most" (Sesin, 2019), billions of dollars are at stake since many of the Cuban properties targetable under the Helms-Burton Act include such large multinational holding companies as the Grand Hotel Manzana Kempinski and Iberostar Grand Packard Hotel in Havana—large joint venture companies owned in part by major Canadian or European Union multinationals, Cuban ports (Havana and Santiago de Cuba), and even a pair of rum companies: Ron Caney and Ron Varadero (Sesin, 2019).

Much of the land in Cuba, its buildings, state institutions, private houses, sports fields, universities, schools, hospitals, playgrounds, much that the Cubans have held as socialist property for 60 years, ostensibly falls under this claim. According to Title III of the Helms-Burton Act, United States nationals have the right "to file suits before U.S. courts against any alien who 'traffics' U.S. property that was nationalized in Cuba in the 1960s" (Cuba-MINREX, January 2019). As noted earlier, the nationalization process in Cuba was recognized by the Supreme Court of the United States and carried out by the Cuban government in full compliance with national law and international law. However, the U.S. had refused to accept the terms and chose instead to end diplomatic relations with Cuba.

Title III of the Helms-Burton Act is consistent with the aberrant U.S. blockade policy against Cuba and constitutes this law's dreadful and most unacceptable aspect. Among the most significant aberrations is the authorization to owners who were not citizens of the United States at the time of the nationalizations carried out in Cuba and, worse, to those alleged possessions yet uncertified. The Helms-Burton Act, also known as the Libertad Act, has been condemned by the Council of Europe, the European Union, Britain, Canada, Mexico, Brazil, Argentina, and other U.S. allies. In fact, the European Economic Community recently issued a statement citing its intention "to shield its companies in Cuba via WTO, blocking U.S. sanctions" (Emmort, Reuters, May 2, 2019).

Conclusion

Cultural genocide remains the nexus between residual neocolonial power and genocide in Cuba. According to Lemkin's *Axis Rule* (1944, p. 79), cultural genocide is at the center of the crime of genocide because it involves the subjugation, modification, destruction, etc. of group culture and identity. When the oppressor imposes its national pattern on the oppressed, the cultural values of the latter are modified or erased:

> … genocide does not necessarily mean the immediate destruction of a nation, except when accomplished by mass killings of all members of a nation. It is intended rather to signify a coordinated plan of different actions aiming at the destruction of essential foundations of the life of national groups, with the aim of annihilating the groups themselves. The objectives of such a plan would be the disintegration of the political and social institutions, of culture, language, national feelings, religion, and the economic existence of national groups, and the destruction of the personal security, liberty, health, dignity, and even the lives of the individuals belonging to such groups (Lemkin, 1944).

As a rising imperialist power during colonial times, the U.S. tried to impose its economic system and values on Cuba. This was evidenced by the many attempts to buy, annex, subjugate, rule, or otherwise dominate Cuba. A close look at the various policies for U.S. military or economic interventions in Cuba, either direct or indirect, imposed by the U.S. over the past century and a quarter constitute a long series of expressions of genocide. They constituted attempts at removing the Cuban right to self-determination by attempting to discredit the Cuban Revolution by tightening the blockade and interfering with Cuba's internal affairs, but the "[American] intent on mandating the regime and social ideology of capitalism is not the path that Cuba has deemed necessary for its development" (Perez, Jr., 2016).

The U.S. blockade limits the right of the Cuban people to self-determination, a right enshrined in the United Nations Charter, Declaration on Human Rights, International Treaty on Economic, Social and Cultural Rights, Treaty on Civil and Political Rights, and the Declaration on the Granting of Independence to Colonial Countries and Peoples (Radio Cadena, 2019). In so doing, the **blockade** against Cuba stands as an expression of genocidal conduct by the United States, aimed at crushing the will of the Cuban people by using brute economic force to break the medical and educational infrastructure and lower the standard of living of Cubans in order to weaken the popular Cuban resolve to live in a sovereign socialist nation.

As noted by the Minister of Foreign Affairs of Cuba in his address to the UN General Assembly before the 28th consecutive annual vote, on November 7, 2019, however: "[N]either threats nor coercion will extract a single political concession. Nor do we renounce our will to achieve a civilized relationship with the country [i.e., the U.S.] based on mutual respect and recognition of our profound differences" (Rodriguez Parrilla, November 8, 2019; Cuba Debate, 2019).

References

Acuña R. F. (2013, May 28). Letter from José Martí to Manuel Mercado, May 18, 1895. In Mexican History and Cutting Edge News. http://www.mexi-can.org/category/dr-rodolfo-f-acuna/.

Beckwith, R. T. (2016, March 22). Read President Obama's speech to the Cuban people (full transcript). *TIME* online. Politics. https://time.com/4267933/barack-obama-cuba-speech-transcript-full-text/

Black, H. C. (1995). *Black's law dictionary* (2nd ed.). Online. https://thelawdictionary.org/

Blum, W. (2004). *Killing hope: U.S. military and CIA interventions since World War I*. Monroe, ME: Common Courage Press.

Boca de Sama. (1971). Entry in *Cuban EcuRed Encyclopedia*. https://www.ecured.cu/Boca_de_Sam%C3%A1_(Banes)

Bohning, D. (2005, Summer) U.S. covert activities against Cuba: The untold tale of secret foreign policy. *ReVista: Harvard Review of Latin America*. http://revista.drclas.harvard.cu.

Cañedo, E. (2017, October 31). Fabricando el pretexto: una constante en la política de EE.UU. hacia Cuba. *Granma* Tabloid. Havana, Cuba. http://www.granma.cu/cuba/2017-10-31/fabricando-el-pretexto-una-constante-en-la-politica-de-eeuu-hacia-cuba-31-10-2017-22-10-12.

Capote, R. A. (2019, March 14). "Helms-Burton Act meant to re-colonize Cuba." *Granma* Tabloid.http://en.granma.cu/mundo/2019-03-14/helms-burton-act-meant-to-re-colonize-cuba.

Carothers, T. (1994, June 12). Backing the wrong tyrant. *New York Times*, Section 7, p. 34. [Book review of Thomas G. Paterson's book *Contesting Castro: The United States and the triumph of the Cuban revolution*]. https://www.nytimes.com/1994/06/12/books/backing-the-wrong-tyrant.html

Castro, Fidel. (1959). Castro denounces imperialism and colonialism at U.N. Assembly.

September 26, 1960. Castro Speech Database: Speeches, Interviews, Articles, 1959–1966. Latin American Network Information (LANIC). University of Texas. http://lanic.utexas.edu/project/castro/1959/.

-----. Speeches. Authors' comments appear in the chart's observation column. Lanic.utexas.edu>project>castro>1959.

-----, Miranda, O., and R. Ricardo (2016). *Guantanamo: Why the illegal US base should be returned to Cuba*. (2nd ed.) Melbourne, Australia: Ocean Press.

Chomsky, N. (2012, October 15). Cuban missile crisis: How the US played Russian roulette with nuclear war. *The Guardian*. https://www.theguardian.com/commentisfree/2012/oct/15/cuban-missile-crisis-russian-roulette.

"Chronology." Library of Congress. [1898] (n.d.). The world of 1898. The Spanish-American War. Chronology of Cuba in the Spanish-American War. https://www.loc.gov/rr/hispanic/1898/chronology.html.

Cuba-MINREX. (2019). Cuba categorically rejects the threat of activation of Title III of the Helms-Burton Act. Ministry of Foreign Affairs. Cuba. https://cubaminrex.cu/en/cubas-report-resolution-75289-united-nations-general-assembly-entitled-necessity-ending-economic

-----. (2018). Cuba's Report (2018) on Resolution 72/4 of the United Nations General Assembly entitled "Necessity of ending the economic, commercial and financial blockade imposed by the United States of America against Cuba." Ministry of Foreign Affairs. Cuba.

-----. [2024]. Editors' update: Cuban Foreign Minister once again condemns embargo as a crime of genocide. https://cubaminrex.cu/en/cubas-report-resolution-75289-united-nations-general-assembly-entitled-necessity-ending-economic#_Toc92704410.].

Cubadebate. (2013). Operation Mongoose: A Cuban History Lesson. www.cubadebate.cu.

Cuban Democracy Act ("CDA"). (1992). Foreign Relations and Intercourse. Codified in Title 22, Chapter 69, Section 6001, of the U.S. Code. United States Department of the Treasury. Congress. https://www.treasury.gov/resource-center/sanctions/Documents/cda.pdf.

Cuban Liberty and Democratic Solidarity (LIBERTAD) Act [Helms-Burton Act]. (1996). Codified in Title 22, Sections 6021-6091 of the U.S. Code. United States Department of the Treasury.

CubaMilitar [1898, December 10] (2019). Primera intervención norteamericana en Cuba. Havana: CubaMilitar, Enciclopedia Militar Cubana. www.cubamilitar.org.

Cubans seeking immigrant visas to USA must now go to Guyana. (2018, March 29). *Havana Times*. https://havanatimes.org/features/cubans-seeking-immigrant-visas-to-usa-must-now-go-to-guyana/.

Detzer, D. (1979). *The brink: Cuban missile crisis 1962*. New York: Thomas Y. Crowell Company.

Díaz, T. (1999). *La crisis de los misiles en Cuba*. Havana, Cuba: Editora Política.

Elfrink, T. (2008) Let terrorist Eduardo Arocena go. *Miami New Times*. www.miaminewtimes.com.

Emmort, R. (May 2, 2019). EU to shield its companies in Cuba via WTO blocking U.S. sanctions: Statement. Reuters. https://www.reuters.com/article/us-usa-cuba-eu/eu-to-shield-its-companies-in-cuba-via-wto-blocking-u-s-sanctions-statement-idUSKCN1S80DG.

English, T. J. (2009). *Havana nocturne: How the Mob owned Cuba and then lost it to the Revolution*. New York: William Morrow Paperbacks.

Escalante, A. (2006). *La guerra de la CIA contra Cuba*. Havana, Cuba: Editorial Capitán San Luis.

Fabry M. (2015, October 19). The U.S. trade Embargo on Cuba just hit 55 years. *Time Magazine*. Online newsletter. https://time.com/4076438/us-cuba-embargo-1960/.

Fernández, Arias F. (2018). Mafia, CIA y Narcotráfico: alianza estratégica contra Cuba. *Granma* Newspaper. http://www.granma.cu/mundo/2018-10-02/mafia-cia-y-narcotrafico-alianza-estrategica-contra-cuba-02-10-2018-20-10-57.

Foreign Assistance Act of 1961. Prohibition on assistance to governments supporting international terrorism. International Terrorism. [22 U.S.C. 2371] Section 620, p. 220. United States Congress.

Franklin, J. (1994, August 30). The politics behind Clinton's Cuba policy. *Baltimore Sun*. In Franklin, J. (2016) [1997]. *Cuba and the U.S. empire: A chronological history*. Foreword by Noam Chomsky. New York: Monthly Review Press.

Kimber, S. (2019). The Havana syndrome: An answer from science. *Cuba Business Report*. https://www.cubabusinessreport.com/the-havana-syndrome-an-answer-from-science/.

FIU-CRI. (2014). Chronology of U.S.–Cuba Relations. Florida International University Cuban Research Institute (FRI-CRI). https://cri.fiu.edu/us-cuba/chronology-of-us-cuba-relations/.

Fundamental Law of the Republic of Cuba [Ley Fundamental de la República]. (1959, February 7). Cuba. Available at Instituto de investigaciones jurídicas [http://biblio.juridicas.unam. mx/libros/6/2525/38.pdf]. English translation available in the World Constitutions Illustrated (WCI) database (William S. Hein & Co., Inc.).

GATT. (1994, April 15). General Agreement on Tariffs and Trade 1994, Marrakesh Agreement Establishing the World Trade Organization, Annex 1A, 1867 U.N.T.S. 187, 33 I.L.M. 1153 (1994).

Glass, A. J. (2013). Fidel Castro visits the U.S., April 15, 1959. https://www.politico.com/story/2013/04/this-day-in-politics-april-15-1959-090037.

González, A. (2018). Continua la Guerra Biológica contra Cuba. Wordpress. https://contrabloqueo.wordpress.com/2018/12/09/continua-la-guerra-biologica-contra-cuba/.

González Santamaría, A. (2017, December 18). Cuba y Estados Unidos: principales avances y retrocesos a tres años del 17 D. *Granma* Newspaper. Havana, Cuba. http://www.granma.cu/mundo/2017-12-18/cuba-y-estados-unidos-principales-avances-y-retrocesos-a-tres-anos-del-17-d-18-12-2017-00-12-48.

Government of Canada. (2019). Visa office in Havana, Cuba is closed. Immigration, Refugees and Citizenship Canada (IRCC). Visa Offices Outside Canada. https://www.canada.ca/en/immigration-refugees-citizenship/corporate/contact-ircc/offices/international-visa-offices/havana.html.

Granma (2019, September 23). Trading with the enemy: A U.S. law that only applies to Cuba. *Granma* Newspaper. http://en Havana, Cuba.granma.cu/mundo/2019-09-23/trading-with-the-enemy-a-us-law-that-only-applies-to-cuba.

Guerra Sánchez, R., [1927] (1976). *Azúcar y población en las Antillas*. Havana, Cuba: Editorial de Ciencias Sociales.

Guzmán, M.G. (2012, April). Thirty years after the Cuban hemorrhagic dengue epidemic of 1981. *SCielo MEDICC Review*, 14(2). [Translated from the Spanish and reprinted with permission from the *Revista Cubana de Medicina Tropical*, 64(1), 2012].

Helms-Burton Act. United States of America. (1996). Cuban Liberty and Democratic Solidarity (LIBERTAD) Act of 1996. Enacted by the 104th United States Congress. Pub.L. 104–114, 110 Stat. 785, 22 U.S.C. §§ 6021–6091). https://www.congress.gov/bill/104th-congress/house-bill/927/text.

Jefferson, T. (1823) [1898]. What Thomas Jefferson said about annexing Cuba. Letter to James Monroe seventy-five years ago. *San Francisco Call*, 83(131). (April 10, 1898). *California Digital Newspaper Collection*. Center for Bibliographical Studies and Research. https://cdnc.ucr.edu/?a=d&d=SFC18980410&e=-------en--20--1--txt-txIN--------1.

JFK Presidential Library and Museum. (2011). https://www.jfklibrary.org/events-and-awards/forums/past-forums/transcripts/50th-anniversary-of-the-bay-of-pigs-invasion?gclid=EAIaIQobChMI1qvLq5v-4QIVMhh9Ch0LdQzDEAAYASAAEgL3YfD_BwE.

Klepak, H., and Department of Foreign Affairs and International Trade Canada. (2000). *Confidence Building and the Cuba–United States Confrontation*. International Security Research and Outreach Programme International Security Bureau. Ottawa: Dept. of Foreign Affairs and International Trade. In archives at www.international.gc.ca/arms-armes/assets/pdfs/klepak2000a.pdf.

Law No. 851, Ley de Nacionalización [LN] [Nationalization Law]. (July 7, 1960). *Gaceta Oficial* [GO] [Cuba Official Gazette]. English translation at 55 AM. J. INT'L L. 822 (1960).

Lemkin, R. (1944). In Edward C. Luck's *Cultural genocide and the protection of cultural heritage*. J. Paul Getty Trust Occasional Papers in Cultural Heritage Policy. Number 2 (2018), p. 79.

Lemkin, R., and Carnegie Endowment for International Peace. (1944). *Axis rule in occupied Europe: Laws of occupation, analysis of government, proposals for redress*. Washington, D.C.: Carnegie Endowment for International Peace, Division of International Law.

Lemkin. R. (1958). "Totally unofficial man: The autobiography of Raphael Lemkin." In S. L. Jacobs and S. Totten (Eds.) (2002), *Pioneers of genocide studies*, pp. 365–399. New Brunswick, NJ: Transaction Publishers.

López Civeira, F. (2009) *Seis décadas de historia. Cuba 1899–1959*. Havana, Cuba: Editorial Félix Varela.

Maier, T. (2018). Inside the CIA's plot to kill Fidel Castro—with Mafia help. *Politico*. https://www.politico.com/magazine/story/2018/02/24/fidel-castro-cia-mafia-plot-216977.

Mallory, S. (1960). Memorandum from the Deputy Assistant Secretary of State for Inter-ter-American Affairs [Mallory] to the Assistant Secretary of State for Inter-American Affairs (Rubottom). Department of State, Central Files, 737.00/4–660. Secret. Drafted by Mallory. Washington, DC: Office of the Historian (Foreign Relations of the United States), 1958–1960, Cuba, Vol. VI, p. 886. https://history.state.gov/historicaldocuments/frus1958-60v06/d499.

McDonnell, M.A., and Moses, A.D. (2005). Ralph Lemkin as historian of genocide in the Americas. *Journal of Genocide Research*, 7(4): 501–29.

McKinley, W. (1898, April 11). Letter to U.S. Congress by President McKinley. United States, 55th Congress, Resolution 3699.

Martí, J. [1891, January 1] (2002). Letter to Manuel Mercado. *Our America* [Original Title: *Nuestra América*. (1891)]. In Esther Allen (Trans./Ed.), *José Martí: Selected writings*. (2002). New York: Penguin Books.

Miranda, O. (1996). *Nacionalizaciones y Bloqueo*. Havana: Editorial de Ciencias Sociales. eBook.

Monroe, J. (1823, December 2). The Monroe Doctrine: President Monroe's message at the commencement of the first session of the Eighteenth Congress. Boston, MA.

Newsday. (1977, January 10). CIA link to Cuban pig virus reported. https://www.cia.gov/readingroom/document/cia-rdp90-01208r000100220019-9

Nichols, M. (2018, November 1). U.N. urges end to U.S. embargo on Cuba, U.S. raises rights concerns. Reuters. https://www.reuters.com/article/us-usa-cuba-un/u-n-urges-end-to-u-s-embargo-on-cuba-u-s-raises-rights-concerns-idUSKCN1N65UX.

O'Connor, C. (2019). It's alive—Trump Administration resurrects Helms-Burton Title III. https://www.cozen.com/news-resources/publications/2019/it-s-alive-trump-admi nistration-resurrects-helm-burton-title-iii.

Ostend Manifesto. (1854). Aix-la-Chapelle, Prussia, and Ostend, Belgium. In "United States History," Britannica.com. http://www.britannica.com.

Paterson, T.G. (1994, January 1). *Contesting Castro: The United States and the triumph of the Cuban revolution*. New York: Oxford University Press. https://global.oup.com/aca demic/product/contesting-castro-9780195101201?cc=us&lang=en&.

Pérez, Jr., L. (2016). *Ser cubano. Identidad, nacionalidad y cultura*. Havana, Cuba: Editorial de Ciencias Sociales.

Pino Santos, O. (1960) *El imperialismo norteamericano en la economía de Cuba*. Cuba: Editorial Lex.

Randolph, C. (1901). The joint resolution of Congress respecting relations between the United States and Cuba. *Columbia Law Review*, 1(6).

Rennack, D., and Sullivan, M. (2018). CRS Report. Cuba Sanctions: Legislative Restrictions Limiting the Normalization of Relations. USA: Congressional Research Service. https://fas.org/sgp/crs/row/R43888.pdf.

Republic of Cuba. (2016). Cuba's Report on Resolution 70/5 of the United Nations General Assembly: Necessity of Ending the Economic, Commercial and Financial Blockade Imposed by the United States of America against Cuba. http://www.cubavsbloqueo.cu/sites/default/files/informebloqueo2016EN.pdf.

Rodríguez Álvarez, A. (2010, June 21). 1960: United States reduces Cuba sugar quota. Agencia Cubana de Noticias. Radio Rebelde. www.radiorebelde.cu.

Rodríguez Parilla, B. (2018, November 1). [Quoted in] "UN General Assembly renews long-standing call for end to US embargo against Cuba." Pre-vote speech by the Minister of Foreign Affairs of Cuba to the UN General Assembly. UN News. https://news.un.org/en/story/2018/11/1024672

-----. (2019, November 7). [Quoted in] "Cuba: UN Members overwhelmingly support end of US embargo, as Brazil backs Washington. Pre-vote speech by the Minister of Foreign Affairs of Cuba to the UN General Assembly. UN News. https://news.un.org/en/story/2019/11/1050891

-----. (2019, November 7). Full text of Rodríguez's speech delivered during the presentation of the UN resolution, "The necessity of ending the economic, commercial, and financial blockade imposed by the United States of America against Cuba" before the UN General Assembly.

Rodríguez, R. (2006). *Cuba: The masks and the shades*. Havana, Cuba: Editorial de Ciencias Sociales.

Roig de Leuchsenring, E. (1959*). Los Estados Unidos contra Cuba Libre*. Havana: Oficina del Historiador de la Ciudad/Office of the city historian. Vol. 1, pp 156–157.

Roosevelt, F. D. (1933). Good Neighbor Policy. Office of the Historian. The Office of the U.S. Department of State. www.history.state.gov.

Saco José A. (1978): *Contra la anexión*. Havana, Cuba: Editorial de Ciencias Sociales.

Salinger, P. (1992, Fall). Great moments: Kennedy, Cuba and cigars. *Cigar Aficionado*. http://www.cigaraficionado.com.

San Francisco Chronicle. (January 10, 1977). CIA link to Cuban pig virus reported. https://www.uky.edu/~rmfarl2/cubabio1.htm.

Sesin, C. (2019, June 3). Claims under Cuban seized-property law are fewer than expected. NBC News. https://www.nbcnews.com/news/latino/claims-under-cuban-seized-property-law-are-fewer-expected-n1010961.

Sesin, C. (2018, April 25). Sharp decline in US travel to Cuba spurs overall drop in tourism for the island." NBC News. https://www.nbcnews.com/news/latino/claims-under-cuban-seized-property-law-are-fewer-expected-n1010961

Smith, D. (2019, April 17). Trump's new Cuba crackdown puts US at odds with Canada and Europe. *The Guardian*.

Smitha, F. (1998–2018). "Castro and Eisenhower." Macrohistory: World History, 1945–21st century. Cold War 1953–60. http://www.fsmitha.com/h2/ch24t60.html.

Teller Amendment. United States Congress. (1898, April 16). H.R.J. Res. 233, 55th Congress., 2d Session, 30 Stat. 738 (April 16, 1898). https://www.visitthecapitol.gov/artifact/hj-res-233-teller-amendment-april-16-1898

Toledo, Y. (2019). *Diez preguntas y respuestas sobre la Ley Helms-Burton*. Havana, Cuba: Agencia Cubana de Noticias.

Trump, D. (2017, June). A new policy toward Cuba. Speech in Miami. http://www.whitehouse.gov.us. Trump unveils new Cuba trade and travel restrictions: US president says he is restoring some of the restrictions lifted after the Obama administration's détente with Cuba. See also https://www.aljazeera.com/news/2017/06/trump-unveils-cuba-trade-travel-restrictions-170616165127045.html.

TWEA. Trading with the Enemy Act of 1917. (1958). 50a U.S.C. Ch. 53, Sec. 4307. Library of Congress. https://www.loc.gov/item/uscode1958-010050a002/.

UN General Assembly, *Convention on the Prevention and Punishment of the Crime of Genocide*. (1948, December 9). United Nations, Treaty Series, vol. 78, p. 277. https://www.refworld.org/docid/3ae6b3ac0.html [accessed 29 October 2019]

UN News. (2019, November 7). Cuba: UN members overwhelmingly support end of US embargo, as Brazil backs Washington. Pre-vote speech by the Minister of Foreign Affairs of Cuba, Bruno Rodriguez Parrilla, to the UN General Assembly. UN News. https://news.un.org/en/story/2019/11/1050891

UN News. (2018, November 1). Cuba: UN members overwhelmingly support end of US embargo, as Brazil backs Washington. Economic Development. 74th General Assembly of the United Nations. https://news.un.org/en/story/2018/11/1024672

UN. (n/d). Office on Genocide Prevention and the Responsibility to Protect. United Nations. https://www.un.org/en/genocide-prevention/definition

U.S. Embassy in Cuba. Visas. Apply for a Visa [https://www.ustraveldocs.com/]. The Caribbean. Cuba (English). https://www.ustraveldocs.com/cu/index.html.

Valido, E. (2012) *La Crisis de octubre de 1962 o crisis del Caribe*. Minister of Foreign Affaires. Retrieved from: www.cubaminrex.cu.

Varela, F. (1826) [1997]. *El Habanero: papel político, científico y literario*. Miami, FL: Ediciones Universal.

Walters, R.S. (1966). Soviet economic aid to Cuba. 1959–1964. *International Affairs*, 42(1): 74–86.

Whitney, R. (2000). The architect of the Cuban state: Fulgencio Batista and populism in Cuba, 1937–1940. *Journal of Latin American Studies*, 32(2): 435–459.

Wiskari, W. (1960, July 6) U.S. embargo set on arms to Cuba; shipment halted. *New York Times*. www.latinamericanstudies.org.

World News. (2018, May 8). U.S. trade embargo has cost Cuba $130 billion, U.N. says. Reuters. https://www.reuters.com/article/us-cuba-economy-un-idUSKBN1IA00T.Xiqué Cutiño, D. (February 14, 2018). La independencia de Cuba se hundió con el Maine. *Granma* Tabloid. Havana, Cuba.

Yellow journalism. (2019). *Oxford English Dictionary*.

Zanetti, O. and A. García, A. (2017). *Caminos para el azúcar* (2nd ed.). Havana, Cuba: Ediciones Boloña. Oficina del historiador de la Habana/office of the historian. Havana, Cuba: Instituto Cubano del Libro.

CHAPTER FIVE

Guantanamo: A U.S. Thorn in Cuba's Side

Vilma Páez Pérez and Salvador Escalante Batista

One principle from the depths of a cave is more powerful than an army.
—José Martí (1894)

Abstract

Ever since President Thomas Jefferson in the early 1800s first set U.S. sights on obtaining Cuba "by hook or by crook," the United States has imposed on Cuba a series of unilateral actions with no validity under international law. These include various foreign policy measures, war measures, treaties, and so-called "permanent" lease agreements (among other codifications) aimed at buying, annexing, or otherwise controlling Cuba. Later measures stem from an 1898 war measure act authorizing the U.S. to militarily occupy Cuba at the end of its War of Independence against Spain, but only until Cuba achieved complete independence. A series of non-compliant actions by the U.S. commenced with Cuba's emergence from the Spanish-American War as a protectorate of the United States. Instead of withdrawing once Cuba had fulfilled the independence condition of the 1898 War Measures Act, the U.S. appended the Platt Amendment to the Army Appropriations Act (1901). It codified eight additional conditions for Cuba. Since the U.S. had no legal right to impose new conditions, this negated the validity of both the Platt Amendment (1901) and the later Treaty of Relations (1903; 1934) maintaining the U.S. right to operate its military base at Guantanamo. Moreover, the United States has violated the terms of the lease agreement for the Guantanamo Bay territory by carrying out numerous human rights abuses at the naval station and using it as a detention camp for U.S.-declared terrorists. Aside from putting Cuban national security at risk, such uses are other than those specified in the lease. This unilaterally imposed U.S. foreign policy contravenes international law and subjects the Cuban people and government to the will of a foreign power.

Keywords: Lease, Guantanamo Naval Base, United States, Cuba

Vilma Páez Pérez, Ph.D. in Pedagogical Sciences. Full Professor and Researcher at the Research Centre for Cultural and Identity Issues, Faculty of Social Sciences, University of Holguín, Cuba.

Salvador Escalante Batista, Consulting Professor, Department of English, University of Medical Sciences, Holguín, Cuba.

Introduction

This chapter presents an historical overview of how the U.S. came to occupy 45 square miles of territory at Guantanamo Bay and has perpetuated its occupation over time against the express sovereign will of Cuba and the Cuban people. The chapter has two sections and a conclusion. The first section recalls the consistent use of dubious tactics by the U.S. government against Cuba since the early 1800s aimed at the purchase, annexation, or control of Cuba. The measures adopted by the U.S. for its military occupation of Cuba during the so-called Spanish-American War are discussed: the Joint Resolution of Congress (1898, April 20) authorizing the U.S. to declare war on Spain; the Treaty of Paris (1898, December 10); the appendage as a rider bill of the Platt Amendment to the Army Appropriations Act (1901, March 2), which essentially dissolved the Teller Amendment's protections for Cuba concerning the conditions for U.S. military withdrawal; and codifications of U.S. rights within Cuba (see Platt, 1901-03), such as the right to establish a naval base or coaling station, signed by Cuba under coercive threat of continued military occupation by the United States. Lease agreements with no termination date would ensue, followed by the Treaty of Relations (1903 and 1934) leading directly to the establishment of the U.S.-controlled naval base at Guantanamo Bay (Elsea and Else, 2016). The second section of the chapter explores the illegalities of these actions and questions the validity of the oxymoronic "permanent-lease" agreement in light of violations of its terms and purposes by the U.S., including human rights violations and Guantanamo Bay's use as a detention camp for U.S.-declared terrorists. The authors will conclude with an overview of the collateral socio-economic damages for Cuba of the ongoing "occupation" of this portion of its national territory. They will posit the naval base as an affront to Cuban sovereignty and a violation of international law on the grounds that it subjects Cuba to the will of another power or state against the collective will of the Cuban people, something that has continued despite persistent appeals by the Cuban government, especially since the triumph of the Cuban Revolution in 1959.

Guantanamo Bay Naval Station: An Unwanted Foreign Presence in Cuba

The ongoing saga of the U.S.-held Guantanamo Bay Naval Base (GBNS) dates back to the formal instigation of the Spanish–American War on April 20, 1898, and President McKinley's signing of an Amendment to the U.S. Army Appropriations Act on March 2, 1901, which "acknowledged Cuban independence, demanded the Spanish government give up control of the island, forswore any intention on the part of the United States to annex Cuba, and authorized McKinley to use whatever military measures he deemed necessary to guarantee Cuban Independence" (U.S. Dept. of State, 2001–2009). The U.S. had authorized itself to intervene militarily, but with Teller's caveat of handing over "the government and control of the island of Cuba to its people so soon as a government shall have been established in said island under a constitution" (Army Appropriations Act, USA, 1901).

How the U.S. Maneuvered for Control over Guantanamo Bay

Starting in the early 1800s, a series of U.S. administrations used dubious tactics in various attempts to purchase, annex or otherwise dominate Cuba. The Spanish-American War was a last-ditch maneuver to gain control before Cuba won its hard-fought independence from the ever-weakening Spanish power. The United States claims that "[t]he long-held interest in ridding the western hemisphere of European colonial powers and American public outrage over brutal Spanish tactics created much sympathy for the Cuban revolutionaries" (Office of the Historian, n.d.) and that this was its motive for pre-empting the Cuban War of Independence; but the actions it took following the war tell a completely different story.

Almost immediately after the 1898 Joint Resolution of Congress gave President McKinley broad powers for military intervention against Spain in Cuba, the resolution was amended by the Teller Amendment (1898), which put a condition on the U.S. military interventions in Cuba. Under the Teller provisions, no more attempts at occupying or otherwise controlling Cuba could be made once it had achieved the condition of constitutional sovereignty. Despite this, the U.S. began disrespecting these conditions of its own War Measures Act almost immediately following the war (i.e., some two months later). It was under false premises that the bilateral (U.S.-Spain) signing of the Treaty of Paris (1898) craftily enshrined a new plan of "attack" against Cuba into international law. Moreover, since no termination date or conditions for the U.S. military occupation were specified, the withdrawal conditions of the preceding U.S. Army Appropriations

Act (1898) should have remained in effect. However, as history shows, that is not what happened.

What did happen helps explain the urgency with which new conditions were added to the U.S. Army Appropriations Act via the Platt Amendment in 1901. This urgency was likely motivated by the fact that three years had passed since the end of the war and Cuba was ready to establish its constitution as a sovereign nation. The Platt Amendment imposed eight new conditions for Cuba to satisfy before any "transfer of sovereignty" (U.S. Dept. of State, 2001–2009) would take place. The seventh condition authorized the ceding by Cuba to the United States of rights through sale or lease of "a segment of Cuban territory for the establishment of a coaling station or naval base in a location to be determined by the United States." The eighth and final condition called for ratification of a treaty to "make the Platt amendment legally binding." The U.S. then pressured Cuba—on threat of non-withdrawal—to codify the terms of the Platt Amendment in the 1901 Constitution of the Republic of Cuba; this was the only way the McKinley Administration could "shape Cuban affairs without violating the Teller Amendment" (U.S. Dept. of State, 1898).

The Constitution, enacted on February 21, 1901, proclaimed the country's sovereignty after centuries of colonization by Spain. However, the Cuban people would be rudely awakened from that dream for freedom. After more than 30 years of Cuba's freedom fighting, the imposition of the Platt Amendment converted the country into a neo-colony of the United States.

Guantanamo Bay and the So-Called Permanent Treaty of Relations (1903)

The Platt Amendment imposed by the U.S. on Cuba as seen in the Cuban press, 1901. Cartoonist unknown. Source: López, C. F. (2018, July 10). *Trabajadores* Newspaper, Havana, Cuba.

The Treaty, ordained by the eighth condition, enshrined into international law Cuba's responsibility under Article 7 of the Platt Amendment (1901) "to sell or lease to the United States land necessary for coaling or naval stations" (Permanent Treaty of Relations, 1903). By signing, Cuba agreed to lease a portion of its territory to the U.S. but also had to declare all *past* military acts carried out by the U.S. on Cuban territory as "holy" (i.e., lawful). Aside from getting around the Teller Amendment, this latter requirement at least symbolically demonstrates that the Platt Amendment was for all intent and purpose founded on the provisions of the Treaty of Paris. It should have given the Cuban people control over their nation as soon as Spain relinquished it by admitting defeat at the end of the war.

In addition, the U.S. claim, that it was helping Cuba attain or maintain independence under the original conditions imposed by the Joint Resolution (1898), was patently false. There had been no threat to U.S. or Cuban national security once Spain surrendered. The U.S. "violated international law by forcing Cuba to relinquish its territorial sovereignty," which "hypocritically ... posed a permanent threat to the sovereignty of the Republic of Cuba" (Castro, 2016). Cuba would not agree to the use of a portion of its territory as a buffer zone by another country, especially one that had "acquired" the use of said territory through coercion (Castro, 2016, p. 31) and refused to trade with Cuba. Subsequently established in 1903, the U.S. Naval Station at Guantanamo Bay (NSGB) occupies 45 square miles (177 square kilometres) of Cuban territory and is the U.S. government's closest and oldest overseas military base (Brown, M.H., 2003).

Guantanamo Bay and the U.S.-Cuba Treaty of Relations (1934)

U.S. foreign policy abruptly changed direction in 1934, moving from a model of military force to one of cooperation with the Caribbean and Latin America via President Roosevelt's Good Neighbour Policy. The Platt Amendment, which had formed the basis of the Permanent Treaty of 1903, ran contrary to this new policy. Therefore, the 1934 Treaty of Relations dispensed with all but one of Platt's conditions. It retained the provisions (article 3) for U.S. occupation related to coaling and/or naval stations at two Cuban territories, "Guantanamo Bay" and "Bahia Honda," but thanks to pressures from such Cuban patriots as Manuel Sanguily,* only the Guantanamo Naval Base was included in the new treaty. Ironically, because neither Cuba nor the U.S. was at risk of attack by Spain or any other country, this agreement also ran contrary to the prescriptions of the Treaty of

---

* Manuel Sanguily (1848–1906) was a colonel fighting against Spain in the Cuban War of Independence and opposed the Platt Amendment as a delegate to the Constituent Assembly in 1901. He served as Delegate to the Second International Peace Conference at The Hague in 1907, Secretary of State in the cabinet of President Gómez, Inspector General of the Armed Forces of Cuba, and Director of the Military Academy (Latin American Studies, n.d.). A lawyer, director of the Institute of Havana, a libertarian, magazine owner, editor, and journalist, Sanguily's work focused on the political process in Cuba, and as Senator of the Republic for the Province of Matanzas, he spoke out against "the passage of the country's natural resources in the hands of foreign companies"; a noted historian, Sanguily was a member of the Academy of Cuban History and editor of several publications (Radio26. CU-Matanzas, 2021).

Paris. The Treaty of Relations of 1934 also ambiguously revised the terms for termination of the lease (i.e., "the time required for coaling and naval stations"), to: "So long as the United States of America shall not abandon" or "the two Governments shall not agree to a modification of its present limits" (Treaty of Relations, 1934, art. 3)."

The Establishment of the Guantanamo Bay Naval Station (GBNS)
Article 56 of the Vienna Convention "addresses the repudiation of a treaty lacking provisions for its termination"). Since the determination of when the treaty expires (the lease will endure for "the time required") lies only with the United States, the 1934 Treaty does not allow for repudiation by Cuba (Miranda, 2016, p. 98). The lease and treaty were also established under (the threat of) coercion (Barbosa León, 2018), rendering them void under Article 52 of the Vienna Convention. In addition, the Treaty's designated purposes (i.e., "coaling or naval stations") are breached by the presence of U.S.-run terrorist detention facilities and associated structures, which include the Joint Task Force-Guantanamo and Office of Military Commissions–South Detachment (Military Commissions Act, 2006), established at Guantanamo Bay.

The Cuban Minister of Foreign Affairs Bruno Rodríguez Parilla cut to the heart of the matter recently in declaring the GBNB "an enclave that has long lost its strategic or military importance for the United States. Its permanence only pursues the political objective of trying to outrage Cuba's sovereign rights. Its practical usefulness in recent decades has been limited to operating as a center of detention, torture and systematic violation of the human rights of dozens of citizens from several countries" (MINREX, 2023). The existence of this U.S.-run prison camp, now occupying the entire southeast section of the GBNB territory, is grounds for termination under Article 60 of the Vienna Convention: "1. A material breach of a bilateral treaty by one of the parties entitles the other to invoke the breach as a ground for terminating the treaty or suspending its operation in whole or in part".

Cuba, however, has little recourse to contest this grievous assault on its sovereignty: neither the United States nor Cuba recognize the International Criminal Court; the principle of sovereign immunity dictates that a state must agree to being sued by another state; the "invalidity of treaties based on non-military coercion remains one of the biggest unresolved problems within the law of treaties" (Del Negro, 2017); and the Vienna Convention (Article 4) applies only to treaties concluded after 1969. Finally, the so-called Helms-Burton law of 1996 imposed a new condition that overrides the 1934 Treaty while attacking the democratic mechanisms of Cuban socialism. The fate of Guantanamo now depends "on whether Cuba has a government that Washington approves of" (Castro et al., 2011).

Guantanamo Bay Naval Station (GBNS): An Unwanted Foreign Presence in Cuba

The GBNS has always been an infringement on Cuban sovereignty, which is why the Cuban government demanded Washington end its occupation of Guantanamo Bay on March 5, 1959, but to no avail (Barbosa León, 2018). In an act of protest against the illegal occupation, "Cuba adopt[ed] "a policy of not cashing the yearly checks for lease of the territory" (Ricardo, 2016). The original annual rent of $2,000 in gold would become $4,085 in U.S. currency. Cuba, in non-recognition of the legality of the occupation, has not accepted payment since 1959 but the U.S. continues to deposit the amount—which has not been updated once in 115 years—of $4,085 per year into a Swiss bank (Ricardo, 2016).

Another act of resistance against the continued occupation of Guantanamo Bay appears in the Cuban Constitution (1976, Article 11) and the recently enacted 2019 Constitution (2019, Article 12), which was ratified in a national vote. Both state that "the Republic of Cuba repudiates and considers as null and illegal those treaties, pacts or concessions signed under conditions of inequality or which disregard or diminish her sovereignty and territorial integrity" (Cuban Constitution, 1976, 2019).

While Guantanamo is one of many "disputed borders or contested islands" around the globe, "the 45-square-mile American enclave at Guantanamo is something of a global geopolitical anomaly." In fact, "there is no other place in the world where the U.S. military forcefully occupies foreign land on an open-ended basis, against the wishes of its host nation" (Miroff, May 15, 2015).

Tensions at the Border—Violations of the Lease Agreement for Guantanamo Bay

As Professor Guillermo Paumier Labacena of Cuba's Universidad de Guantánamo has pointed out to Granma International (Barbosa León, 2018), it is difficult to put a number on the many bellicosities that originated at the base, mainly in the 1960s and '70s. Marines were known to make obscene gestures and shout vulgar words, even at our revolutionary leaders; GBNS personnel would set the vegetation on the Cuban side of the "border" on fire, throw rocks and Molotov cocktails at Cuban posts/

stations, among other unfortunate aggravations.

More serious attacks also took place, either from the base or involving it as a place of refuge for those having perpetrated what can only be considered terrorist attacks by the U.S. in and against Cuba. For example, on March 13, 1961, an armoured speedboat was used to attack the oil refinery at Santiago de Cuba, killing the Cuban sailor René Rodríguez and severely damaging the plant. The perpetrators sought refuge within the U.S. naval base at Guantanamo, where the Cuban government has no jurisdiction. Ten days later, a U.S. ship fired artillery at a Cuban plane near Imías, a small town in eastern Guantanamo, well beyond GBNS jurisdiction. GBNS was also used for an aerial and naval bombardment of Cuba, sabotage of Cuban crops and industry, occasional landings along the Cuban coast just outside the GBSC jurisdiction, and as a location from which to plan assassinations (Castro, 2016).

After the Cuban revolutionary militia's victory in the U.S. invasion of the Bay of Pigs on April 15, 1961, the CIA organized Operation Patty (Hevia Frasquieri, M., 2011), aka the Immediate Action Plan, which called for assassination attempts on Fidel and Raúl Castro (CAN, 2021). As shown in the images to the right, Cuban newspapers reported on the plans orchestrated by the CIA and the Pentagon to assassinate Fidel Castro (Mary Ferrell Foundation, n.d.) while he gave a speech at *Plaza de la Revolución* (Revolution Square) in Havana on July 26, 1961, and to kill Raúl on July 24 at the baseball stadium in Santiago de Cuba, where an activi-

Top: Facsimile, *Sierra Maestra* newspaper, August 19, 1961. Headline: *Attack on Raul and Simulated Attack on the Naval Base Planned by the CIA for July 26, 1961.* Source: M. Hevia (2011) in *Diario Granma*. Havana, Cuba. July 22, 2011. Año 15/ No. 203. **Bottom:** Facsimile of *Revolución* newspaper, August 17, 1961. Headline: *Cuba Denounces Yankee Plans for Radical Aggression at the Base.* Source: In M. Hevia (2011) in *Diario Granma*. Havana, Cuba. July 22, 2011. Año 15/ No. 203.

ty in celebration of the eighth anniversary of the attack on the Moncada Army Garrison would be taking place.

According to the Mexican professor/researcher Hassan Dalband (Autónoma University in Mexico City), an obsession with killing Fidel (Dalband, 2013) consumed Kennedy's administration, as evidenced by Operation Patty and many other operations of this kind. The failure of the Bay of Pigs Invasion made the U.S. Government worried about the cause of the defeat of its mercenary troops in less than 72 hours. As the Cuban historian, then a director with the Cuban Ministry of Internal Affairs (MININT), Hevia Frasquieri (2011) had reported, the plan also included an attack on the refinery in Santiago de Cuba and a fake self-attack on the base, serving as a pretext and (falsely) justifying an armed invasion of Cuba—a plan that was detected and foiled by the MININT through an operation called Candela.

The American general Maxwell Taylor was put in charge of analyzing the fiasco of the U.S. Bay of Pigs invasion. The sixth recommendation of the now declassified Taylor Commission report (1984) concluded that Fidel Castro's successful leadership of Cuba "constitute[d] a real menace capable of eventually overthrowing the elected governments in any one or more of weak Latin American republics" (CIA History Office and Pfeiffer, Vol. IV, 2011).

Cuban leaders have provided arguments and denounced the illegal character of the occupation since 1959; yet the U.S. authorities do not listen to reason:

> Since the triumph of the Revolution in January 1959, the revolutionary Government has denounced the illegal occupation of that part of our territory.... However, at the same time, the United States has transformed the occupied territory of the Guantanamo naval base into a permanent source of threats, provocations and violation of Cuba's sovereignty, with the aim of creating obstacles for the victorious revolutionary process. The base has always been part of the plans and operations conceived by Washington to overthrow the revolutionary Government. (Castro, 2016)

According to Ricardo (2016), it is evident that maintaining control over Guantanamo Bay in the face of refusals by the Cuban government constitutes a powerful symbol of U.S. domination of a portion of a sovereign land. In the authors' opinion, the base also represents a threat simply by its contested presence on Cuba's soil and its use as a tool to intimidate and threaten whenever necessary. Cuba's call for the occupied area's return is based on sovereignty, independence, and a people's right to self-determination.

Another reason, legally speaking, is that U.S. control over the Cuban territory at Guantanamo Bay is not derived from a sale but a lease, which means the leaseholder does not hold a perpetual right, and justice demands it be peacefully returned to Cuba (Bermúdez Cutiño, 2016). Also, the lease agreement stipulates that the area rented is to be exclusively used as a coaling station or naval base, but the U.S. Navy has used the Guantanamo base for other purposes, including as a detention camp for U.S.-declared terrorists since 2002.

International law is now clear regarding the legal terms of the lease for Guantanamo Bay. To lease means that the territory is ceded for a specified time. If a time frame is not specified in the lease, it is void. This agreement, signed in the first half of the 20th century, has a temporary nature, as indicated by the use of the word "lease," and the vague wording around duration can thus only be seen as intentional and devious.

For Cubans, the U.S. presence on Cuban soil at Guantanamo Bay is an age-old symbol of U.S. determination to keep its dream alive by seizing the "rebel island" in one way or another by hook or by crook. However, it is essential to remember that while Cuba may be the gateway to the Caribbean and Central and South America, it is also a sovereign nation. There have been other repercussions. While the base initially employed Cubans living in Caimanera, a small neighbouring town, it also brought in gambling and prostitution to satisfy the needs of the U.S. marines and soldiers stationed at the base (Rodríguez, 2016). No Cuban citizen is employed at this naval base on Cuban territory today.

Human Rights Abuses at the U.S.-Controlled Guantanamo Bay Naval Station (GBNS)

Guantanamo Bay Naval Station (GBNS) has been the site of numerous human rights abuses against Cuban citizens working at the base and young Cuban soldiers carrying out their functions near that part of the island under the Cuban border guard, known as the *Tropas Guardafronteras*, which operates in conjunction with the Cuban Army and Navy. Several horrendous acts are worthy of mention. As early as October 15, 1961, the body of a Cuban worker from the U.S. naval base, Ruben López Sabariego, arrested two weeks prior for allegedly being a revolutionary, was found in a ditch with signs of torture. Cuba accused the U.S. military at the base of torturing López Sabariego, but the U.S. authorities at the base steadily denied it (Castro, 2016).

Three other cases arose in June 1964. In one, a Cuban soldier named

José Ramírez Reyes was shot in the leg. In the same month, another Cuban border guard, Andrés Noel Larduet, was the victim of a similar incident. Both survived, but on July 19, another soldier, Ramón López Peña, was fatally wounded in another incident. In 1965, another Cuban, Berto Belén Ramírez, was seriously injured by gunfire. On February 23 of the same year, and again in May 1966, bullets fired from a truck transporting American soldiers to relief posts caused the death of another Cuban soldier, Luis Ramírez López, who also had been carrying out border-guard duty on Cuban territory (Barbosa León, 2018; Fole, 2019).

GBNS as a Detention Centre for U.S.-Declared Terrorists

On January 8, 2002, the Cuban authorities were officially informed that the U.S. government would be using the naval base at Guantanamo as a detention center for soldiers captured in Afghanistan. Three days later, hundreds of the prisoners arrived at the base, accompanied by even more U.S. soldiers (Castro, 2016). Fidel Castro was appalled:

> ... the Cuban Government issued a public declaration indicating its willingness to cooperate with medical assistance as required or any other useful, constructive and humane measures that might be needed. I was personally involved in detail concerning the note presented by the [Cuban] Ministry of Foreign Affairs in response to the U.S. note. We could have never imagined at that moment that the U.S. Government was preparing to create a horrendous torture center at that base." (Castro, January 11, 2016, p. 47)

In effect, the military operations in Afghanistan following the 9/11 attacks on the United States in 2001 required detention facilities to hold prisoners taken by U.S. Army. The U.S. decided to repurpose already existing migrant detention facilities at the base to create a prison for detainees in what they called the "war on terror" (CNN Library, 2008; Bond, 2005).

More than 700 detainees have been held at the Guantanamo "facility" since it opened in 2002, most from Afghanistan. The first 20 prisoners arrived at Guantanamo Bay on January 11, 2002. Within a couple of months after Bush's declaration of the war on terror, the U.S. military had captured 45 fighters from Al Qaeda and the Taliban in the Middle East and needed a place to hold them. Officials ruled out the Pacific Island of Guam—which is an unincorporated territory of the United States—after its citizens raised concerns about the presence of terrorism suspects. The U.S. settled on the naval base on Cuba's southeastern tip, calling it "the least-worst place we could have selected ... and a world-class operation," in the words of former U.S. Secretary of Defense Donald Rumsfeld. He then authorized, in December 2002, a list of 16 harsh interrogation tactics at the camp without showing any remorse (Sledge, 2013).

According to a writer and former officer in the U.S. Marine Corps, one of the key advantages to placing the detainees at Guantanamo Bay or anywhere except on U.S. soil was that it allowed the U.S. to ignore U.S. laws like "the right to legal representation, rights of prisoners, and rights to the American legal system" (Packard, 2013), not to mention presumption of innocence. President Bush argued that the four Geneva Conventions of 1949 do not apply to "unlawful enemy combatants," such as members of Al Qaeda and the Taliban (Seligson, 2013).

The Bush administration saw Guantanamo as ideal for use as a long-term detention facility, even though it had no legal right to do so. The base was initially capable of housing 100 detainees, with the first captives being held in steel-and-wire cages in June 2003 while the detention center was being expanded for a peak population of 684 detainees. The prison—and thus the Naval Station at Guantanamo Bay Cuba—became known as a place where torture and other violations of prisoners' human rights took place. Even though Cuba had absolutely no say or control over what went on at Guantanamo Bay, many foreigners who do not know this history may wrongly associate these goings on with Cuba. This represents yet another way that Cuba is disserved by the base.

Obama Wanted to Shut Down the Terrorist Prison but Keep the Naval Station

When Barack Obama ran for the White House in 2008, one of his promises was to shut down the prison (detention facility) for suspected terrorists at Guantanamo Bay. On January 22, 2009, two days after becoming President, he issued an executive order designed to "promptly close detention

Box 5.1

Ever since Guantanamo Bay Detention Camp at the U.S.-operated Naval Base at Guantanamo Bay opened on January 11, 2002, to hold terrorist suspects, the walls of its detention facilities have witnessed not only unlawful detention but torture, hunger strikes and deaths (CNN Library, 2008). Twenty years after the prison camp was opened at Guantanamo, the United Nations (2022) condemned the U.S.-run detention facility for "unrelenting human rights violations," calling it "a stain on the U.S. Government's commitment to the rule of law."

facilities at Guantanamo" (Lipman, 2008). The closing of that prison at the U.S. naval base at Cuba's Guantanamo Bay would, he said, take place no less than a year from that date. The many congressional restrictions, among other reasons, prevented this from happening. On the other hand, former President Donald Trump ordered the Guantanamo Bay "military prison" (née naval station) to remain open indefinitely since he intended "to load the prison up with some bad dudes" (Rosenberg, 2017). On January 30, 2018, Trump signed an executive order to keep the detention facility open and also allow for sending new prisoners there (CCN World, 2018). As shown below in Box 5.2, Trump used the nickname *Gitmo* to refer to the Spanish *Guantanamo* in a 2017 Tweet that caught the attention of Laura Pitter, deputy director of Human Rights Watch's U.S. program. According to Pitter, only 10 of the 59 men detained at Guantanamo "have been charged with a crime, most notably the five charged for their role in the September 11 attacks" (Pitter, 2017).

Box 5.2

Donald J. Trump
@realDonaldTrump
There should be no further releases from Gitmo. These are extremely dangerous people and should not be allowed back onto the battlefield.

Source: Laura Pitter, Human Rights Watch Deputy Director, US Program, anuary 4, 2017, 5:31 p.m.). Tweet by Donald J. Trump. (January 3, 2017, 1:20 p.m.). Humans Rights Watch. Headline: "Trump's Guantanamo Tweet was Uninformed and Ill-Advised: Keeping Facility Open Threatens US National Security."

Under international law, including the International Committee of the Red Cross (ICRC) regulations and provisions put in place by the Inter-American Commission on Human Rights and the U.N. Office of the High Commissioner for Human Rights, force-feeding hunger-striking detainees is a violation of Common Article 3 of the four Geneva Conventions, which prohibit cruel, inhuman, and degrading treatment. The World Medical Association (WMA) has condemned "feeding accompanied by threats, coercion, or physical restraint [as] a form of inhuman and degrading treatment" (Seligson, 2013) if applied to prisoners who are competent to decide on a hunger strike.

No one can deny that the use of a territory leased for use "as coaling or naval stations only and for no other purpose" and then converted into a prison is a violation of international law and complicates U.S.-Cuba relations. The Cuban government has insisted that human rights violations at Guantanamo are another reason to close the base and return the land to Cuban control. As the Cuban Foreign Minister Bruno Rodríguez pointed out at the United Nations in 2013, "One hundred and sixty-six persons have remained under detention for ten years now, without any guarantees, without being tried by a court or the right to legal defence.... That prison and military base should be shut down, and that territory should be returned to Cuba" (Rodríguez, 2013).

Conclusions: Why Should the Illegal U.S. Base at Guantanamo Bay Be Returned to Cuba? Let Us Count the Ways

Guantanamo Bay and the Paradox of the U.S. Nation
As the United Nations Deputy Special Envoy to Haiti Paul Farmer (2011) noted in his review of a book by the Harvard University historian Jonathan Hansen, *Guantanamo: An American History*, U.S. foreign policy has always been paradoxical:

> ... the United States' presence at Guantanamo Bay betrays the paradox that has shaped our history: the U.S. has been, since its inception, both a bastion of independence and an imperial nation. In this enthralling and meticulously researched narrative, the historian Jonathan M. Hansen lays bare the uncomfortable truths that precipitated our occupation of a small and fiercely independent neighbour. Guantanamo has been a stronghold of American influence over an independent Cuba, a holding pen for Haitian refugees living with HIV, and, more recently, the site of human rights atrocities at its notorious prison camp. Here, Hansen offers a clear-eyed and fearless examination of the place that remains a global theatre for the consequences of America's pursuit of power." (Farmer, 2011)

Since 1959, Cuban authorities have persistently denounced the illegality of the occupation of this portion of the country and demanded that the U.S. return to Cuba the area occupied by the Guantanamo Naval Base with no conditions. "Maintaining a military base in Cuba against the will of the people violates the most elemental principles of international law" and "not respecting Cuba's will is an arrogant act and an abuse of immense power against a little country" (Fidel Castro, 2009).

Except for the six-month duration of the Cuban Missile Crisis in 1962— when civilians were evacuated from the base, the number of U.S. troops increased to 16,000, and U.S. warships blockaded the island—there have been no threats from on or associated with the island of Cuba or Cuban national security since Spain relinquished control in 1898. Since the "time required for the purposes of coaling and naval stations" is long past, the terms of the 1934 Treaty or Relations should be discarded along with its termination clause, requiring mutual consent or a unilateral decision by the U.S., for the Guantanamo Bay lease, which should be dissolved.

From January to October 1962, in several diplomatic notes to the U.S. Government, Cuba protested hundreds of violations of its territory: 76 violations by planes from Guantanamo Base, provocations of soldiers from the base, occasional landings along the coast and assassinations. On June 12, 1964, the Cuban Armed Forces Minister Raúl Castro reported that U.S. troops at the Guantanamo Naval Base had been responsible for 1,651 acts of provocation since November 1962 (Castro et al., 2016). The human rights violations being carried out by the U.S. for the past 20 years at Guantanamo Bay (United Nations, 2022) also warrant the dissolution of the lease.

The damages to Cuba from having this foreign-controlled base on its territory range from economic to environmental. Construction at the base, for example, has hindered natural drainage and caused severe problems in the Caimanera area with frequent flooding from rainstorms or hurricanes. But Cuba has no say. How many world citizens may have thought that Cuba was responsible for the reported human rights abuses at Guantanamo Bay when the U.S. decided to use the facilities as a prison in 2002? However, Cuba had no say. At the dawn of the 21st century "during the conflict in the Balkans the U.S. agreed to put up 20,000 new refugees at Guantanamo, but that plan ended up scrapped for being too far from their European homelands" (Rothman, 2015).

More than 115 years old and created by U.S. foreign policy, maneuvering, and coercion, the U.S.-controlled Guantanamo Bay Naval Base stands as America's oldest military installation outside its territory. The United States is using Guantanamo Bay as a geostrategic harbour positioned to exert control over the Caribbean and Latin America.

Guantanamo is the only U.S. military base operating in a "socialist" country. It is an illegitimate base since it was leased under the auspices of the Platt Amendment, a humiliating settlement imposed after the so-called Spanish-American War, when it was believed that the base would be useful for local interventions and continental defence. The Cuban government has long criticized the U.S. presence at Guantanamo because Cuban control over the area where the base is located would have a positive political impact and critical economic and social advantages for Cuba, mainly regarding the economic development of the eastern part of our country.

Michael J. Strauss, an international relations professor at the Centre d´Études Diplomatiques et Stratégiques (diplomacy defence and international relations) in Paris, carried out a comprehensive analysis to identify the legal and political options and the practical implications for both Cuba and the United States regarding the possibility of full normalization of bilateral relations. In his article "Returning Guantanamo Bay to Cuban Control," Strauss (2016) points out that Cuba's deep-water port at Guantanamo Bay could be used for Cuban international trade. Being prevented from doing so by the U.S. occupation of Guantanamo reduces Cuba's competitiveness and the trade potential between it, Latin America and beyond. For example, Guantanamo Bay is closer to the Panama Canal than Cuba's other main ports.

In every possible international forum, Cuba continues to reiterate its position on the return of that portion of its territory to its real owners, the Cuban people. The international community has widely recognized the right of Cuba over that territory, but as Raúl Castro stated in an interview granted to the newspaper *El Sol de Mexico* (1993):

We will not act irresponsible on this matter, but we will not give up our absolutely firm stance demanding our sovereign right over that piece of our country's soil.... As I recently said at the city of Guantanamo, a few kilometres away from the U.S. facility, the U.S. military base is a dagger stuck in the side of our homeland. Also, we intend to draw it out peacefully and in a civilized manner. The demand for the return of the territory of the base is not only Cuba's unanimous claim, but also a clamour of world public opinion. (*El Sol de Mexico*, 1993. In Miranda, 2016)

The U.S.-run Naval Station at Guantanamo Bay is a 125-year-old thorn in Cuba's side. Rose thorns are peculiar in that they will not come to the surface; they burrow in and fester, causing significant damage to an organism. The same is true of a foreign thorn in a nation's side.

References

A CIA-Cuba Episode (2011). The Ill-fated Patty Operation—July 1961. Agencia Cubana de Noticias (ACN). Havana, Cuba: Radio Rebelde (digital). 2011.08.09-16:38:53/ACN. www.radiorebelde.cu>commentaries

Allen, T. (2012). "Mister President, the Navy Will Not Let You Down." *Naval History Magazine*. October. USNI News. USA. https://news.usni.org/tag/navy/page/15

Army Appropriations Act. (1901, March 2). Platt Amendment attached as a rider bill to the Army Appropriations Act. United States Congress. Vol. 1, No. 6, 1901, pp. 352–376. Platt Amendment rider bill. https://www.worldhistory.biz/modern-history/84759-army-act-1901.hml>Army Act (1901)</a>

Army Appropriations Act. (1898). United States Congress.

Army Appropriations Act. (1903). United States Congress.

Augustin, E. (2016). Welcome to paradise! Scanning Guantanamo. Portrait of the US military base in Cuba. Chapter 2. La Base. *On Cuba News*. https://oncubanews.com/en/special/scanning-guantanamo-en/.

Barbosa León, N. (2018, May 16). A close look at the Guantanamo Naval Base. *Granma Tabloid*. Havana, Cuba. https://en.granma.cu/cuba/2018-05-16/a-close-look-at-the-guantanamo-naval-base.

Benz, S. (2019, January 30). A brief history of Guantanamo Bay, America's "idyllic prison camp." A hundred years at the edge of Empire. Bunk via Literary Hub. https://www.bunkhistory.org/resources/a-brief-history-of-guantanamo-bay-americas-idyllic-prison-camp.

Bermúdez Cutiño, J. (2016, November 8). La Base Naval de Guantánamo. Ministerio de Relaciones Exteriores de Cuba [Ministry of Foreign Affairs (MINRIX)]. https://misiones.cubaminrex.cu/es/articulo/la-base-naval-de-guantanamo.

Bond, Jennifer. (2005). The language of war: A battle of words at Guantanamo Bay, 2005. *Appeal: Review of Current Law and Law Reform*, 70. CanLIIDocs 99. Canadian Legal Information Institute (CanLII). https://canlii.ca/t/2bzc.

Brown, M.H. (2003, December 22). Oldest U.S. base overseas harbors hometown feel. *The Orlando Sentinel*. https://www.orlandosentinel.com/2003/12/22/oldest-us-base-overseas-harbors-hometown-feel/.

Castro, F., O. Miranda, and R. Ricardo. (2016). *Guantanamo: Why the illegal U.S. base should be returned to Cuba*. 2nd. ed. Victoria, Australia: Ocean Press. www.oceanbooks.com.au.

CNN. (2021, April 17). "CIA planned to assassinate Raul Castro in 1960: Declassified documents." CNN News. CAN [English language Asian news network], Singapore. https://www.channelnewsasia.com/world/cia-plan-assassinate-raul-castro-1960-declassified-pilot-225366

CNN Library (2018, September 11). Guantanamo Bay Naval Station Fast Facts. CNN Editorial Research. https://edition.cnn.com/2013/09/09/world/guantanamo-bay-naval-station-fast-facts/index.html

Cohen, Jennie (2018, August 30). 6 Things you may not know about the Spanish-American War. *This Day in History*. https://www.history.com/news/6-things-you-may-not-know-about-the-spanish-american-war

Constitución de la República de Cuba. (1901). *Archivo*. Biblioteca Jurídica Virtual del Instituto de Investigaciones Jurídicas. México: UNAM. Constitution of the Republic of Cuba. https://archivos.juridicas.unam.mx/www/bjv/libros/6/2525/16.pdf

Constitución de la República de Cuba. (1976). Article 11. [*Asamblia nacional poder popular*—Cuban parliament]. *Gaceta Oficial de la República de Cuba* [Cuba official Gazette]. Constitution of the Republic of Cuba. Biblioteca Jurídica Virtual del Instituto de Investigaciones Jurídicas. Constitution of the Republic of Cuba. México: UNAM. https://archivos.juridicas.unam.mx/www/bjv/libros/6/2525/51.pdf

Constitución de la República de Cuba. (2019, April 10). [*Asamblia nacional poder popular*— Cuban parliament]. *Gaceta Oficial de la República de Cuba* (Cuba Official Gazette). No. 5. Constitution of the Republic of Cuba. http://www.cubahora.cu/uploads/documento/2019/04/11/goc-2019-ex5.pdf

Dalband, H. (2013, August 7). La obsesión de la CIA por asesinar a Fidel Castro: el fracaso estadounidense. *Rebelión*. https://rebelion.org/la-obsesion-de-la-cia-por-asesinar-a-

fidel-castro-el-fracaso-estadounidense/
Elsea, J.K. and Else, D.H. (2016, November 17). Naval station Guantanamo Bay: History and legal issues regarding its lease agreements. CRS Report [Prepared for Members and Committees of Congress] (R44137. V 7). Washington, DC: Congressional Research Service (CRS). https://crsreports.congress.gov/product/pdf/R/R44137/7
Farmer, P. (n.d.). Book review: *Guantanamo: An American History* by J. Hansen, 2011. New York: Hill & Wang.
Fole, A. (2019, May 21). Luis Ramírez López: Young man killed by marines from the Naval Base of Guantanamo. Canal Caribe. https://www.tvcubana.icrt.cu/cartel-era-de-la-tv-cubana/caribe.
Frank, M. (2009, January 29). Fidel Castro demands Obama return Guantanamo base. Reuters. http://www.reuters.com.
Goldman, J. (2015). *The Central Intelligence Agency: An encyclopedia of covert ops, intelligence gathering, and spies*. Santa Barbara, CA: ABC-CLIO.
Hevia Frasquieri M. (2011, July 21). La operación Patty de la CIA: a medio siglo de su derrota por Candela. Havana, Cuba: *Granma*. Tabloid, 15(203). Radio Santa Cruz, Latin America. https://www.radiosantacruz.icrt.cu/21374-recuerdan-cuba-fracaso-operacion-patty-cia/
Joint Resolution (1898). In Randolph, C. (1901, June). The joint resolution of Congress respecting relations between the United States and Cuba. *Columbia Law Review Association*, 1(6): 352–376. http://www.jstor.org/stable/1109239.
Latin American Studies. (n.d.). Manuel Sanguily (1845–1906). LatinAmericanStudies.org. http://www.latinamericanstudies.org/sanguily-bio.htm
Lipman, J. (2008). *Guantanamo: A working-class history between empire and Revolution*. Berkeley, CA: University of California Press.
-----. (2018, December 10). 5 things to know about Guantanamo Bay on its 115th birthday. *The Conversation*. Tulane University. https://theconversation.com/5-things-to-know-about-guantanamo-bay-on-its-115th-birthday-108301
López, C. F. (2018). 1901: Una constitución encadenada [an enchained constitution]. *Periódico Trabajadores* [Newspaper]. https://www.trabajadores.cu/20180710/1901-una-constitucion-encadenada/
Martí, J. (1894, July 14). El Día de Juárez. *Periódico Patria*. Portal José Martí. www.josemarti.cu/publicacion/el-dia-de-juarez/ English translation taken from AZQuotes.com. https://www.azquotes.com/quote/188501
Mary Ferrell Foundation. (n.d.). Preserving the legacy: PATTY. Ipswich, MA: Mary Ferrell Foundation. Cryptonym Database. https://www.maryferrell.org/search.html?q=patty.
Military Order of November 13, 2001. (2001). *Detention, Treatment, and Trial of Certain Non-Citizens in the War Against Terrorism*. Federal Register: Vol. 66, No. 222): Public Law 107-40. [Presidential document including Authorization for the use of military force]. Presidential Documents, pp 57831–57836. Federation of American Scientists (FAS). https://irp.fas.org/offdocs/eo/mo-111301.htm. Cited in Malcolm B. Savage (2015, January 12). "Guantanamo Bay and the United States military commissions: The perplexities of trial and punishment by the laws of war." https://papers.ssrn.com/sol3/papers.cfm?abstract_id=2583378 [PDF also available at http://www.lawyers.com].
MINREX. (2023). Cuba rejects presence of nuclear submarine in the Guantanamo Bay: Declaration of the Ministry of Foreign Affairs of Cuba. Havana, Cuba: MINREX [Ministry of Foreign Affairs]. https://cubaminrex.cu/en/cuba-rejects-presence-us-nuclear-submarine-guantanamo-bay-declaration-ministry-foreign-affairs-cuba
Miranda, O. (2016). How to end the Guantanamo Treaty. In Castro et al., *Guantanamo: Why the illegal U.S. base should be returned to Cuba* (pp. 91–108). Victoria, Australia: Ocean Press.
Miroff, N. (2015, May 15). Why the U.S. base at Cuba's Guantanamo Bay is probably

doomed. *The Washington Post.* https://www.washingtonpost.com/news/worldviews/wp/2015/05/15/why-the-u-s-base-at-cubas-guantanamo-bay-is-probably-doomed/

Office of the Historian. (n.d.). The Spanish-American War, 1898. *Foreign Relations of the United States* series, Milestones: 1866–1898. Foreign Service Institute. United States Department of State. https://history.state.gov/milestones/1866-1898/spanish-american-war

Packard, S. (2013, September 4). "How Guantanamo Bay became the place the U.S. keeps detainees." *The Atlantic.* http://www.theatlantic.com/national/archive/2013/09/how-guantanamo-bay-became-the-place-the-us-keeps-detainees/279308/

Pfeiffer, J. B. and CIA History Office and J. B. (2011). *CIA Official History of the Bay of Pigs Invasion.* Volume IV: *The Taylor Committee Investigation of the Bay of Pigs.* Approved for declassified release on July 25, 2011.

Pitter, Laura. (2017, January 4). Trump's Guantanamo Tweet was uninformed and ill-advised: Keeping facility open threatens US national security. Human Rights Watch. https://www.hrw.org/news/2017/01/04/trumps-guantanamo-tweet-was-uninformed-and-ill-advised

Platt Amendment. U.S. National Archives and Records Administration. https://www.ourdocuments.gov/doc.php?flash=true&doc=55

Radio26. CU-Matanzas and Mesa González, Tamara Caridad. (2021). Manuel Sanguily, writer and journalist. Radio. Cuban Press (Culture, Literature). Radio26.CU-Matanzas. https://www.cubanradio.cu/2018/06/19/feature-articles-about-radio/new-tecnologies-in-broadcasting/websites-directory-of-cuban-radio-stations/

Ricardo, R. (2016). "Guantanamo: A critical history." In Castro, F., et al., *Guantanamo: Why the illegal U.S. base should be returned to Cuba.* 2nd. ed. (pp. 51–90). Victoria, Australia: Ocean Books.

Rodríguez Milán, Y. (2016). Scanning Guantanamo. Portrait of the U.S. military base in Cuba. *Frontier Zone.* Chapter 1. https://oncubanews.com/en/special/scanning-guantanamo-en/

Rodríguez Parrilla, B. (2013, May 1). Exige Cuba cierre de cárcel y base naval de Guantánamo. CubaSi. https://humanrightsfirst.org/wp-content/uploads/2022/10/Guantanamo-Backgrounder.pdf and Human Rights First. (October, 2018). Background on Guantánamo Bay Prison. Fact Sheet. https://humanrightsfirst.org/wp-content/uploads/2022/10/Guantanamo-Backgrounder.pdf

Rosenberg, C. (2017, January 14). Why Obama failed to close Guantanamo. Interview conducted by A. Stewart. *PBS NewsHour Weekend.* https://www.pbs.org/newshour/show/obama-failed-close-guantanamo

Rothman, L. (2015, January 22). Why the United States controls Guantanamo Bay. *Time.* http://time.com/3672066/guantanamo-bay-history/

Seligson, S. (2013, May 28). Guantanamo: the legal mess behind the ethical mess. *B.U. Today.* http://www.bu.edu/today/2013/gitmo-the-legal-mess-behind-the-ethical-mess/

Sierra Maestra. (1961, July). Headline: Attack on Raul and simulated attack on the naval base planned by the CIA for July 26, 1961 [Partial picture of the cover page]. Newspaper. Santiago de Cuba: Sierra Maestra.

Sledge, M. (2013, September 4). Donald Rumsfeld confronted about Guantanamo at his summer house. *HuffPost.* http://m.huffpost.com

Strauss M. J. (2016). Returning Guantanamo Bay to Cuban control. *Cuba in Transition.* Annual Proceedings of the Association for the Study of the Cuban Economy, Vol. 26. https://ideas.repec.org

Teller Amendment. United States Congress. (1898, April 16). H.R.J. Res. 233, 55th Congress. 2d Session, 30 Stat. 738 (1898). https://www.visitthecapitol.gov/exhibitions/artifact/hj-res-233-teller-amendment-april-16-1898

Treaty of Paris. (1898). Treaty of Peace Between the United States and Spain; December 10,

1898. Lillian Goldman Law Library. Yale Law School. The Avalon Project: Documents in Law, History and Diplomacy. https://avalon.law.yale.edu/19th_century/sp1898.asp

Treaty of Relations. (1903). Treaty between the United States of America and Cuba. Lillian Goldman Law Library. Yale Law School. The Avalon Project: Documents in Law, History and Diplomacy. https://avalon.law.yale.edu/20th_century/dip_cuba002.asp

Treaty of Relations. (1934). Treaty between the United States of America and Cuba; May 29, 1934. Lillian Goldman Law Library. Yale Law School. The Avalon Project: Documents in Law, History and Diplomacy. https://avalon.law.yale.edu/20th_century/dip_cuba001.asp

CHAPTER SIX

Social Justice and Democracy in the Cuban Revolution

Vladimir Pita Simón, Julio Eduardo Ávila Pérez
and Violeta Rosa Mejías Rojas

Abstract

The fact that Cuba has developed what has been the most enduring and radical socialist experience in the western hemisphere implies model results and a high degree of authenticity regarding national social policies. Such policies were implemented under the challenging conditions of Third World underdevelopment and the enormous pressure exerted upon the island by the geopolitical dynamics of the Cold War. Transitional social policies, they were designed to improve living conditions, reduce inequality, and involve the vast majority of Cuban citizens in the political and nation-building process. By implementing these policies, the government made **Cuban socialist democracy** the linchpin of a political process aimed at ending direct economic domination and hegemony by our northern neighbour and favouring human development in Cuba. **Cuban socialism** is not a replica of orthodox Soviet socialism but stands as a *sui generis* political system characterized by Cuba's proprietary **socialist democracy** (i.e., the active participation of the people in politics and civic life) born through processes of political-legal transculturation and consolidated through a Cuban constitutionalist tradition aimed at the establishment of an egalitarian society. Uniquely, the revolutionary government initially implemented socialism and communism in unison. The **Cuban socialist democracy** aims to give all citizens a voice as part of their daily life and at election time. The self-determination of Cubans had first found expression through mass organizations such as the University Student Federation (FEU), the Federation of Cuban Workers, and many others that were instituted starting in 1960. Fidel Castro and other revolutionary leaders envisioned such organizations and they were enshrined in the 1976 Constitution as institutions of Cuban civil society. This mobilization for mass participation of the Cuban people—a phenomenon we continue to enjoy—represents a model of direct-indirect democracy characterized by the authors as the Organizations-Party-State triad. The Cuban network of social (mass) organizations comes together with the political (irrevocable socialism/public-not-private political architecture) and the state (i.e., legislative, constituent, and executive authorities) to become the mechanism for Cuban socialist democracy.

Keywords: social justice, National Liberation Movement, Fulgencio Batista, Fidel Castro, blockade, democracy, Cuban Socialism, Marxism

Dr. Vladimir Pita Simón is a María Zambrano postdoctoral researcher at the Universidad Rey Juan Carlos, Spain (2023). He received his law degree (2004) and doctorate in Juridical Sciences (2014) from the Universidad de Oriente, Santiago de Cuba. He is a former full professor of Philosophy of Law (2004-2023), dean of the Faculty of Social Sciences at the University of Holguín, researcher at the Research Centre for Culture and Identity (CECI) of the University of Holguín (2019-2023), as well as former dean of the Faculty of Social Sciences at the University of Holguín. Dr. Pita Simón has developed studies on Cuban legal philosophical thought, Latin American and Caribbean integrational law, the communication theory of law, and the rule of law in Cuba. He has published articles on these topics in Colombia, Mexico, Chile, the United Kingdom, and the United States of America. Email: vladimirpita@gmail.com.

Julio Eduardo Ávila Pérez holds a Master of Science of Law from the Faculty of Law at the University of Havana, Cuba (2015), and is professor of Legal Research Methodology and Democratic Theory at the University of Holguín. Email: j.avila00@nauta.cu.

Violeta Rosa Mejías Rojas holds a Master of Axiology and Social Sciences at the University of Holguín (2018), and is professor of History of the State and Law at the University of Holguín. Email: vrosamejias@gmail.com.

Introduction

This chapter aims to contextualize the characteristics of the Cuban political-legal system and illustrate how and why Cuba has been able to sustain its successes in human development through its *sui generis* political system established since 1959. The first section will outline the difficult conditions underlying Cuba's revolutionary social-change project, notably Third World underdevelopment and the geopolitical dynamics of the Cold

War, which remain a scourge for Cubans under the ongoing U.S. blockade against Cuba. This section will also explain how egalitarian social policies became the cornerstone of a political process aimed at ending direct economic domination and hegemony by our northern neighbour in favour of human development in Cuba.

The second section explains how the construction of **Cuban socialism** initially involved a rejection of the Soviet revolution-by-stages in favour of a combined socialist-communist distribution model that was later reverted to the principle of socialist distribution. The second section will explain **Cuban socialist democracy** within the little-understood framework of the Marxian dictatorship of the proletariat and the development of mass organizations as the institutions of Cuban civil society. Following this explanation, the authors will illustrate the mechanism that gives rise to the Cuban socialist democracy: the State-Party-Organizations triad. The third section will reference the vast social improvements engendered by the Cuban Revolution, such as increased living standards, reductions in inequality, priority attention to hitherto marginalized sectors, access to essential services, and equal opportunity in education and the workplace. Finally, we discuss how these core criteria are consolidated by the institutions of socialist civil society and their positioning vis-à-vis the state as a central element of the political system. The authors will also identify how various elements of classical, liberal, and socialist democracy and emancipatory economic structures came to be embodied in the public-not-private rationale and architecture of Cuba's *sui generis* political system.

Conditions at the Beginning of the Cuban Revolution

The Cuban Revolution was born in a socioeconomic context of underdevelopment of the country's productive forces, a situation linked not only to its role as an exporter of raw materials—mainly sugar and its derivatives, production of which occupied more than 50 percent of its labour force in 1958 (Del Toro, 1999, p. 18)—but also to associated development lags in the industrial sector. As part of this process, a profound neocolonial economic dependence on the United States had repercussions in all aspects of Cuban society.

The American "Legacy"

Sheltered by the Platt Amendment, the U.S. had long enjoyed *de facto* political and economic control over Cuba. By 1958, U.S. capital investment in Cuba topped $1 billion (all dollar figures are given in U.S. dollars) with more than 200 U.S. companies operating across all industries and sectors of Cuba's national economy. Of particular importance, given the dependence of the Cuban economy on sugar cane production, was the U.S. ownership of thirty-six "modern" sugar mills and the associated appropriation of Cuba's most arable lands.

The geostrategic interests in Cuba of the United States also included 100 percent ownership of three "oil companies [that] had continually bled the nation's economy [by] charging exorbitant monopoly prices" (Suárez Pérez et al., 2015), as well as a majority control of the island's electric utility and telephone monopolies providing basic services (Valdés García, 2007, p. 5) for which the Cuban people and government paid dearly. The social consequences of such structural problems rooted in the economy shaped a political system with many exigencies, a reality that reverberated in the new challenges faced by the Revolution after 1959.

Relations between Cuba and the United States were characterized by a long-standing history of U.S. domination and hegemony under various mechanisms and policies starting late in the 19th century and expanding throughout the following century until the triumph of the national liberation revolution in 1959. Upsetting the U.S. monopoly interests in Cuba would inevitably lead to conflict between the two nations. The impact on U.S. interests in Cuba and any animosity following the resounding and irreversible triumph against the U.S. invasion of the Cuban nation at the Bay of Pigs further conditioned a policy of U.S. hostility that continues to play out under its embargo against Cuba.

The political system being formed in Cuba after 1959 aimed at exponentially multiplying the number of citizens who could participate actively in the profound social transformations envisioned to ensure the inclusion of social sectors hitherto marginalized and disconnected by poverty. At the time, the masses—in both urban and rural spaces—had little access to the basic means of life, healthcare, or education, and were being charged monopoly prices for essential services such as electricity. The Revolution never swayed from the need to generate a framework of social justice that included, among other objectives, improved living conditions and the creation of direct mechanisms for popular intervention in public affairs. As part of this process, Cuba engaged in "a sustained advance towards a socialization of the means of production and national reproduction that gave emancipatory meaning to the economic forms implemented" (Valdés, 2017, pp. 136–140).

Social Justice at the Centre of Politics

The priority of the political platform created through the Cuban Revolution was to respond comprehensively to a set of expectations for social improvement ignited by the revolutionary discourse and fueled by the transformative action of the process itself. Beyond a doubt, this dynamic was the *sine qua non* of political consensus in revolutionary Cuba, far more than any institutional or political framework could ever have been. As this chapter attempts to show, the egalitarian policies and intense process of (re)socialization in Cuba have resulted in a broadening and deepening of the notion of citizen responsibility under the rubric of socialist civil society and as an essential element of the system's durability and stability.

The Cuban judge Manuel Urrutia Lleó arrived in Havana on January 5, 1959, to announce the necessary amendments to the 1940 Constitution in view of the new revolutionary process. He had been appointed provisional president of the Republic at a session held in the library of the Universidad de Oriente at Santiago de Cuba, which had been declared the provisional capital (Castro, January 3, 1959). Judge Urrutia began his interim presidency with the formal dismissal of then president Batista and his government and the dissolution of the Congress, Emergency Courts, and the Criminal Chamber of the Supreme Court.

José Miró Cardona, a prominent Cuban politician and lawyer who had opposed Batista, was named interim prime minister (Cantón Navarro and Duarte Hurtado, 2006). Cardona worked intently with the Council of Ministers, which had different powers at that time, adapting constitutional norms to the new political scenario through the constitutional reforms consolidated in the official adoption of the Fundamental Law on February 7, 1959 (Bohemia, 1959).*

The 1940 Constitution had been repealed by the Batista dictatorship, and Dr. Manuel Urrutia Lleó's provisional government passed the Fundamental Law (1959), which, among other things, transferred the constitutional authority (i.e., the legislative function) from the Congress of the Republic to the Council of Ministers and the executive function to the president of the Republic, thus elevating the role of prime minister to the most politically powerful entity of the revolutionary Cuban government (see Box 6.1). The precepts of the 1940 Constitution maintained their validity under this new structure but with significant changes regarding the structure and functions of the powers of the state, and with respect to the

---

* For a comprehensive description in English of Cuba's *Revista Bohemia* weekly magazine (1908–present), refer to O'Brien (2018), "When Cubans read *Bohemia*, they actively engaged with a tangible piece of Cuban democracy" (O'Brien, 2018, p. 3).

constitutional rules and relations for central and local government bodies. Various changes were made to these bodies through the 1976 and subsequent constitutions (see Chapter 7).

The "core" and most enduring of the transformations that took place in Cuban society at that time, transcending the political system and re-determining the vocation of each of its elements, were reflected in and consolidated through the revolutionary laws adopted. The initial set of laws (i.e., January–March 1959) focussed on the provision of essential services and the basic means of life, reflecting the revolutionary government's intention to redistribute the wealth initially through improved living conditions for the masses. Wealth distribution would engender an intense process of socialization and opportunities for human development in line with the revolutionary commitment to establish a social reality of a marked egalitarian nature.

> **Box 6.1**
> In the second month of the new government, the Fundamental Law of the Republic was enacted. Heir to the 1940 Cuban Constitution, this Act legally sanctioned the beginning of the formation of a new political system. The new government also marked the starting point for the creation of a socialist legal system in Cuba. Several regulations were enacted between January 3 and August 8, including the first Declaration of Havana, Agrarian Reform Law, Urban Reform Law, Nationalization of Education, and Nationalization of Industry (Suárez, 2015). Such radical changes were necessary given the abject failure of the predatory institutional schemes favoured by the U.S.-backed Batista dictatorship. Other regulations would be added to the Fundamental Law, marking a gradual radicalization of the revolutionary process and, consequently, an expansion of Cuba's social bases.

As the process became radicalized, however, political polarization and class struggles intensified. This led most of the middle- and upper-class Cubans to align themselves with a growing base of operations in the United States. Their numbers grew because of high levels of immigration occurring after the group's failure to garner effective resistance within Cuba. This opposition quickly adopted anti-communist fundamentalist positions in line with the dynamics of the Cold War, which was on the rise during that period.

The ongoing struggle for the survival of the revolution, which at times had warranted costly use of the armed forces, was divided by idealist conceptions and thwarted by the underdeveloped nature of the Cuban economy, which further weakened the system's capacity to maintain the economic sustainability of social benefits being implemented. The elements of the new political system had been focused on the transformation of the nation's productive and institutional bases, and this brought an essential contradiction to the fore: the incapacity of the economic base to guarantee social justice through equal (i.e., principle of communist) distribution of basic public goods and services by the state, regardless of the extent of individual contribution.

Orthodox Soviet Thought and Stalinism

Orthodox Soviet thought resolved this problem with the thesis of "revolution by stages": socialism first, then communism (see Box 6.2). For Fidel, the first phase of socialism—as per the orthodox socialist rationale of providing means according to individual ability—was unacceptable as it would offer no safeguards for those with no or lower-paying jobs; Cuban citizens did not yet have the skills for well-paid jobs or were otherwise unable to work (Plá León, 2008). Fidel's revolutionary ideal had been to dispense with the stages and build both processes (i.e., socialism and communism) in unison.

This ideal of social justice, which implied access for all Cuban citizens without exclusion to the basic means of life and equal pay, was integrated into the 1976 Constitution as a guiding principle of the political system. A period of gratuitous provision of numerous services and material means to the population began. This involved the elimination of collections and payments among companies, and the unlinking of salaries from performance, along with several similar measures. Before looking at this, however, an introduction to the ideological framework of **Cuban socialist democracy** is warranted.

> **Box 6.2: Orthodox Soviet Thought**
>
> The authors use the term **orthodox Soviet thought** to connote the political and social foundations of Stalin's vision of the communist system (Stalinism), which was a far cry from the reforms embraced by Lenin's New Economic Policy (NEP) or Nikita Sergeyevich Khrushchev's de-Stalinization.

Influence of the Marxian Doctrine on Cuban Socialist Democracy

At the core of Marxist theory lies the existence of a confrontation, irreconcilable over the long term, between the owners (i.e., bourgeoisie) or beneficiaries of the fundamental means of production and the proletarian majority who offer their work in exchange for a salary. According to Marx, there is an essential contradiction in capitalism (aka the free-market system). The production of goods and services is carried out with scarce resources but hinges on the participation of many workers, factors of production whose utility is appropriated over time by an ever-smaller number of people (i.e., capitalists).

In the same way that Cuba's Agrarian and Urban Reform laws implemented starting in 1959 recognized the social function of land (commercial) and housing (rental) as things that should not be commodified, neither can labour be commodified without resulting in exploitation according to Karl Marx. In his labour theory of value, price is given by the amount of labour time it takes to produce the product. This reduces labour to a form of property that the owner (worker) sells for a wage to the capitalist, to whom most of the profit then accrues. For Marx, therefore, profit can only occur when the wage (paid by capitalist entrepreneurs) is below the real value of the human labour. Thus, profit is derived from labour power but not shared with it.

The capitalist purchases (i.e., for a wage) the proletariat's labour power and gains exclusive ownership over the product and the accruing profits, which are largely regulated by the consumer's willingness to pay (i.e., the demand) for the product. According to Marx, this alienation of workers from products (i.e., lack of ownership) engenders inequality and associated social problems. This is further complicated by the fact that the various technologies introduced into production over time have reduced the need for labour power. The increasingly vast profits accrued by (few) owners are then turned over into capital investments requiring no labour power at all and, again, the profits do not reach the masses.

Such had been the case for Cubans starting in 1492 and again, starting in 1898. The first occurred under the Spanish colonization and the other through the neocolonial regime during which the U.S. took control of sugar production, electricity, and oil in Cuba. According to Marx, such exploitative states of affairs could only culminate in a revolution, whereby the dispossessed masses—most of the population—would begin the construction of the first stage of the communist system (i.e., socialism) through the "dictatorship of the proletariat."

Clarifications of the Term "Dictatorship of the Proletariat" in Marxist Literature

A few clarifications on the term "dictatorship of the proletariat" as used in Marxist literature are deemed necessary here. Although in disuse by most parties and intellectuals of the Left, largely because of Marx's understanding of the term as a means to true democracy, the term is important to this chapter because it refers to the initial means by which a capitalist state apparatus is dismantled and the construction of a socialist one begun.

As in the case of Cuba, the meaning of dictatorship of the proletariat in Marx (1850) is inextricably linked to the original etymology of the Roman word *dictatura*, which connotes an important Roman constitutional institution that lasted three centuries. This was necessary during the post-revolution period in Cuba because it allowed the immediate but temporary exercise of people's power by one citizen for the safeguarding of the public interest as a function of an emerging new class: the proletariat.

In Cuba, therefore, the term was never intended to be an antithesis to, or a rejection of, democracy as understood by liberalism, nor as a kind of tyranny, but instead as a means of expressing the temporary realization of the will of the oppressed majority. It was felt that for the new regime to prevail, quick action was needed because the political forces of the old (capitalist) state were still in place and capable of turning the situation using sheer economic force.

If, as Marx believed—and as was certainly the case in Cuba prior to 1959—the capitalist state constitutes a *de facto* dictatorship of a rich minority over a proletarian majority that is maintained through a country's legal system and institutions, then in keeping with Marx's views on the blight of capitalism, it is normal the minority would suffer a major blow when the state reverses things and hands the means of production and control of the state apparatus over from the rich minority to the proletarian majority.

Marxist theory thus situates antagonistic and anti-communal social classes in the inequality and social injustice created by the socio-economic forms (i.e., slavery, feudalism, and capitalism) imposed on people who had been living in a communal state (i.e., collectively owning the means of production: the land, capital and everything produced by society). The resocialization of the means of production (i.e., their return to the people) and consequent dismantling of social classes thus constitute a restorative process that ends the social exclusion and conflict that existed between and because of the social classes.

Given the extent to which petty theft and organized crime had developed in Cuba under the U.S.-backed Batista dictatorship (see Chapters 4 and 8), a belief in this process was among the Marxist claims held dearest by the Cuban Revolution and stands as a legitimizing factor of the construction of Cuban socialism.

Therefore, the originality of the Cuban Revolution hinged more on a vision of proper participation to avoid the pitfalls of the liberal-democratic tradition than on the application of the postulates of Marxism-Leninism. The Revolution also hinged on the capacity demonstrated by the new political power in 1959 to initiate the political transition from capitalism to socialism without a Communist Party to organize the process (Rafuls Pineda, 2015, p. 9). The Revolution took place amidst harsh popular global trepidation around the very mention of the word "socialism" and as noted above, in opposition to the establishment of a national democratic-liberal-bourgeois political power in Cuba. As prescribed by the classics of the Marxist-Leninist approach to power, the dictatorship of the proletariat emerged at the beginning, and this created the basis for the grassroots construction of a Cuban socialism embodying a national, popular-democratic, agrarian, and anti-imperialist power.

The development of Marxist theory is marked by the fact that the governments of several countries (e.g., Algeria, Nepal, India, and South Korea) follow a type of democratic socialism. Marxist theory has also been marked by its application at the state level in countries with little development of the national productive forces (e.g., China, Laos, and Vietnam).* Boosting the economic base would not be easy for Cuba, as there was no exception to the postulate advanced by Vladimir Lenin (1917) in his theory of the weakest link. In a surprising reversal, however, the U.S. was the weakest link in the Cuban economic sovereignty chain—as evidenced by the historical attempts at domination by the U.S. power. This is why the Fundamental Law of the Republic was the first order of business following the victory in 1959. Furthermore, it was the only means of severing the U.S.'s economic monopolies and restoring sovereignty to Cuba.

"History Will Absolve Me" (Fidel Castro, 1953)

In Fidel's famed "History Will Absolve Me" speech—a political manifesto delivered during his defence at the infamous Moncada Trial on October 16, 1953, in Santiago, Cuba—Fidel summarized this and subsequent revolutionary laws (Castro, 1953). Fidel implemented such laws starting in 1959 under what would become known as the Moncada Programme. Of those, the Agrarian Reform (1959; 1963) and the Urban Reform (1960) both recognized the social function of land and had constitutional power under the Fundamental Law of 1959. They became linchpins of the social change project by legalizing nationalization through expropriation where

---

* These countries are not Marxist-Leninist states, but their respective constitutions refer to socialist principles. For example, the Preamble to the Indian Constitution of 1949 states that "We, the people of India, hav[e] solemnly resolved to constitute India into a Sovereign Socialist Secular Democratic Republic and to secure to all its citizens."

warranted of large tracts of privately held land and certain urban residential properties (see Box 6.3).

> **Box 6.3: Impact of the Agrarian Law Reform**
>
> "The Agrarian Law damages an insignificant section of the people but even these persons are not entirely sacrificed, as they will keep a considerable amount of land; their standard of living will not be seriously affected, and at the same time thousands of poor families will be benefited. We can very conservatively estimate that two hundred thousand families will receive these benefits" (Castro, 1953).

In Cuba, such changes were necessary given the plundering institutional schemes that had characterized the U.S.-backed dictatorship of Fulgencio Batista. Thus, when "U.S. President Dwight D. Eisenhower's administration drastically and suddenly reduced Cuba's sugar quota" to zero in 1960, Fidel saw it as an attempt to "undermine our country's economy, defeat us with hunger, and subjugate our people" (Suárez Pérez et al., 2015) in an attempted act of genocide. The Cuban government responded under the powers vested in it by the 1959 Fundamental Law of the Republic (*Ley Fundamental*, 1959) and nationalized all U.S. interests (*Ley 851*, July 6, 1960), other foreign interests (*Ley 890*, October 13, 1960), and other small retail forms of commerce regardless of nationality (*Ley 1076*, December 5, 1962).

To paraphrase Julio Fernández Bulté, the renowned Cuban lawyer and University of Havana professor, the process of reconstruction of the legal system in Cuba coincided with a period of legal nihilism. The process of such reconstruction is generally the case in countries that carry out deep revolutions in the aim of creating changes that will affect the vast majority, such as improvements in living conditions to bring about reductions in crime and other anti-social behaviours through egalitarian policies. However, those years in Cuba were also characterized by ingenious and idealistic conceptions of how such social transformations would be wrought spontaneously through fundamental changes to the social relations of production (Bulté, 1998–99).

It is noteworthy that, some 15 years later, the United Nations General Assembly would adopt the Charter of Economic Rights and Duties of States, "by 115 votes to 6, with no abstentions" (UN Dec. 12, 1974) followed by the Declaration on the Establishment of a New International Economic Order promulgated at the Sixth Special Session, 2229th plenary meeting (UN, May 4, 1974). The Charter of Economic Rights and Duties of States extended to all states the right to nationalize properties, under the recognition that sovereignty is inextricably tied to a nation's ability to control and benefit from the wealth made possible by its resources (UN, 1974).

The Emergence of Cuba's Non-Orthodox Socialist Character

While Fidel had initially tried to build socialism and communism in unison, the country was still facing the consequences of trying to build a more equitable social system despite the inherited shortcomings of economic underdevelopment. Fidel soon realized that the transformative action of his policies was not having the expected outcome but instead had given rise to labour absenteeism and unproductiveness, excess money in circulation, and an ensuing lack of supply of goods and services (Toledo García, 2012). Given the underdevelopment of Cuba's productive forces, which included obsolete technology, widespread illiteracy, and lack of investment capital, the Cuban government was unable to deliver on its pledges of social improvements that included, among other factors, living conditions, access to essential services, and new rights regarding human development.

> *"Communism Cannot Be Established by Decree"*
> *(Castro, November 16, 1973)*

In effect, the growing needs of society could not be met and relational animosities among citizens and sectors were giving rise to social conflict. In his closing speech of the Thirteenth Congress of the Confederation of Cuban Workers (CTC, November 16, 1973) (see Box 6.4), Fidel explained the need to overcome these challenges by reverting from the Marxian principle of communist distribution "from each according to his ability, to each according to his needs" to the principle of socialist distribution, "of each according to his ability, of each according to his work". Pointing out that this "principle constitutes an inexorable law in the construction of socialism" and "distinguishes the socialist phase from the communist phase of the revolutionary process," Fidel highlighted the need to "courageously correct the idealistic errors" (Castro, November 16, 1973)

Box 6.4: Logo of the First Congress of the Communist Party of Cuba

The figures in black represent the unity of the Cuban people and our decision to fight for freedom (http://www.pcc.cu). The idea of social justice is expressed in the words of José Martí: "Con todos y para el bien de todos" ("With all and for the good of all").

IMAGE: 1975 CUBAN POSTAGE STAMP

As noted earlier in this chapter, these errors involved implementing the principle of communist distribution, paying the same wage for the same work regardless of output or quality. The more equalitarian approach of socialist compensation based on ability, competency, and skill was announced, and Cuban socialism officially separated itself from communism.

At the first Congress of the Communist Party of Cuba on December 17, 1975, Fidel explained "the importance to the country's political, institutional and juridical order of the next Constitution of the Republic, as the basis for the superior exercise of socialist legality, and highlighted the role of social and mass organizations, the Revolutionary Armed Forces, the Ministry of the Interior, the Young Communists League, and the Party" (Pedro, 2019). The principle of socialist development was subsequently enshrined in the Cuban Constitution of 1976 (see Chapter 7), which was approved by the majority (i.e., 97.7 percent) of Cubans in a national referendum. Throughout this and subsequent revisionary processes for the Cuban Constitution, the ideal of social justice, which means access by all Cuban citizens without exclusion to education, healthcare, the basic means of life, and opportunity, has remained the guiding principle of the Cuban political system.

The commitment to human development (i.e., humanism) reflected in the CRP Party slogan, "with all and for the good of all", was first uttered by Jose Martí on April 10, 1892, upon the founding of the Cuban Revolutionary Party, distributed in flyers by a co-founder, the Mexican Francisco Maria Gonzalez (Ecured, ([1892], 2019). It is well known in Cuba that Fidel used this slogan at the First Congress of the Communist Party, thereby reinforcing the notion that the Cuban Revolution had started on October 10, 1868, and also that the Cuban Revolutionary Party's ideas were based on Martí's same idea of social justice. It is enshrined as a constitutional value in Article 1 of the 1976 Constitution.

Che Guevara and the Development of a Cuban Democratic Socialism
As Fidel commonly made known, the seeds of his framework for the construction of **Cuban socialism** and **Cuban socialist democracy** were influenced by the work and thoughts of the Argentine Marxist revolutionary Che Guevara (1965). According to Guevara, who sought a solution to perceived limitations of the Soviet model applied in Eastern Europe, criticized Stalin for having depreciated communist education and instituted authoritarianism (see Guevara, 1967).

Guevara's rejection of the Stalinist version of Marxism at the core of Soviet socialism is personified in the figure of the *hombre nuevo* (i.e., new man) outlined in his 1965 letter, "Socialism and Man in Cuba," to Carlos

Quijano, editor of a weekly magazine, *Marcha*, published in Montevideo, Uruguay (Guevara, 1967). The letter outlined the process of building the "new man and woman" and the socio-economic conditions and relationships necessary for his/her emergence and development.

According to Guevara, appropriation had not put wealth within the reach of the masses in Eastern bloc countries (e.g., Estonia, Hungary, Latvia, Romania, Serbia, Poland, etc.) due to the pre-existing underdevelopment and the lack of capital creating a rocky road edged with sacrifice. For Guevara, the rise of consciousness—of the "new man and woman"—would hinge on this "initial period of the transition to communism, which is the construction of socialism" that takes "place in the midst of violent class struggles" (see Guevara, 1965).

Che Guevera (Alberto Korda photo/Wikimedia Commons)

Guevara's notion was a response to the combined need of overcoming the structural underdevelopment and jump-starting the process of decolonization in the Third World, where long-standing subordination by the colonial powers persisted. As the need for this in the mid-20th century had not been foreseen by Marxist theoreticians, new Marxists such as Guevara put revolution at the center of social transformation, departing from but ranking higher than the economist gradualism proper of classical Marxism. This new approach coincides in many ways with the more radical revolutionary universal thought of various historical time periods.

In Cuba, the state was thus ultimately assigned a predominantly assisting role providing basic means consistent with, first, the principle of communist distribution and then (and currently/exclusively) the principle of socialist distribution. This meant that the rest of the elements of the political system would be relied upon to bring about the greater material redistribution of wealth and social rights related to human development through accessible healthcare, housing, basic infrastructure for electricity and fuel distribution even in rural areas, and opportunities such as education for all:

> Formerly many industries, schools and even hospitals were managed by private owners. But times have changed. Once the most a

citizen could expect was that the state would set up a post or telegraph office. It never occurred to him that the state must take care of housing or other things. Today the citizen does expect the state to do that. And he is right. This is precisely a collectivist, a socialist mentality. Today the administrative apparatus, and above all the political apparatus representing it, is expected to take care of everything. People no longer rely on only their own strength and devices as in the past (Castro, 1970).

The commitment to ensuring fundamental means and services bears out in the tangible achievements of the economic policies implemented by the Cuban Revolution from 1959 to 1989, when average annual GDP growth was around 4.3 percent, growth in per capita GDP was 2.8 percent, and labor productivity increased annually by 2 percent. This placed the island on a path of accelerated growth thanks to the policy of centralized, solid planning carried out under the framework established by the Soviet Union's Council for Mutual Economic Assistance, of which Cuba became a member in 1972 (CMEA aka COMECON). This progress, however, was torn asunder with the fall of the Eastern bloc, then Cuba's main trading partner, in 1991, along with the reinforcement of the never-ending U.S. blockade against our country.

In the case of Cuba, socialism has been prioritized over Guevara's communism. What was never in doubt in Cuba, however, was the decisive role of the state and the people in the country's socio-economic and political transformation. In this sense, the window opened by Lenin's attempt to build socialism in a society characterized by underdevelopment constituted a significant pattern for the Cuban system. Marxist-Leninist theory thus accompanied the process as the main reference for the modelling and rationale behind the concentration of economic power in the hands of the state and the exercise of politics in Cuba. Cuban socialism is a composite, integrating elements of various political systems adopted through processes of political-legal *transculturation*—a term coined in 1940 by the Cuban anthropologist Fernando Ortiz. The term was/is used to describe the phenomenon of merging and converging cultures (see Chapter 9).

The Party-State-Organizations Triad: The Heart of Cuban Socialist Democracy

The self-determination of the Cuban people as evidenced by mass mobilization around the revolutionary leaders had already brought about significant transformations in the social sphere as early as 1959. The revolutionary dynamic of broad citizen inclusion was incorporated into the political process by creating and consolidating social and mass organizations. This process of democratic transformation added depth to the transformations brought about by the other revolutionary reforms, such as the shift from private to state ownership and concurrent disbanding of associated capitalist economic structures, the implementation of principles of socialist/communist distribution and housing frameworks, the institutionalization of health and education, and the elimination of bipartisan politics and lobbying.

Social and Mass Organizations: Instruments of Cuban Civil Society
Starting in 1960, several social and mass organizations were created by the revolutionary government; for example, Committees for the Defence of the Revolution (CDR), Federation of Cuban Women (FMC), Union of Pioneers of Cuba (UPC), Federation of High School Students (FEEM), National Association of Small Farmers (ANAP), and Young Communist League (UJC). Others were restructured—the University Student Federation (FEU) and the Confederation of Cuban Workers (CTC, 1973). Together, these organizations—the instruments of Cuban civil society—drove mass participation to an unprecedented level in Cuba. This network was designed to foster inclusion and community building while providing the structural means to mobilize citizens at local, regional, and national levels (Constitution of Cuba, 1976, Art. 7).

Constitutionally entrenched, this network of mass organizations and social organizations mobilizes the Cuban people—from the grassroots level to municipal, provincial, and national—by involving them indirectly in the national political and nation-building process. As shown in Figure 6.1 (page 134), the authors express this relational model of direct-indirect democracy as the **Organizations-Party-State triad**, where organizations come together with party (irrevocable socialist government/egalitarian access) and state (legislative, constituent, and executive authorities). The self-determination of Cubans that first found expression through mass organizations around the revolutionary leaders is today supported through the inherent relations of the elements in this triad. In this view, the Party-State-Organizations triad is the linchpin of **Cuban socialist democracy**.

Local, Municipal, Provincial, and National Assemblies of People's Power
The Assemblies of People's Power were formally established in the 1976 Constitution and have been supported at the municipal level by People's Councils since these latter were implemented starting in the 1990s. Cu-

ba's network of Municipal Assemblies is the central axis of the system. The Municipal Assemblies constitute grassroots legislative bodies run by local government representatives on two-and-a-half-year mandates elected through closed-ballot municipal elections. It is noteworthy that the Cuban legal framework prevents any formal involvement of the Communist Party of Cuba in municipal elections, and this is respected in practice.

The higher levels of centralization of the State administration have characterized the emergence and development of the Organs of People's Power (Law 54, 1985). The design of these organs at a local level departs from the provincial and municipal levels as the main government entities in the territories. The Municipal Assemblies are composed of delegates appointed and elected by the people in local-neighbourhood electoral districts and this remains the key to the Cuban electoral system.

The delegates of the Municipal Assemblies are supported in their functions "by People's Councils and [by] the initiative and the broad participation of the population and act in close coordination with the social and mass organizations" (Cuban Const., Ch. 2, §. 1, Art. 104). As their title might suggest, these councils "are constituted in cities, villages, neighborhoods, settlements, and rural zones," and "act in close coordination with the social and mass organizations" (CC 2019). These councils were instituted in the 1980s to enhance the participatory mechanisms of social and mass organizations and combat top-down centralism in decision-making. In Cuba, the access routes to public political power are thus defined through the various social and mass organizations and the mechanisms linking them to the state, which have been interrelatedly enshrined in the Cuban Constitution (Art. 7) since 1976. On the one hand, they act as extensions of the State, while on the other serve to integrate popular power at the state level.

As per its administrative divisions, Cuba has 169 municipal assemblies, including the special island municipality of Isla de la Juventud ("Isle of Youth"), across 15 provincial assemblies. Nominations for the Municipal Assemblies of People's Power are made by neighbourhood assemblies comprised of workers, youth, women, students and farmers, as well as members of the Committees for the Defence of the Revolution and other social and mass organizations (Constitution of Cuba, 2019, Art. 14). These local nomination assemblies then select the candidates through open ballot voting (i.e., show of hands). One-page profiles of each candidate are then produced and affixed in public places and outside polling stations approximately one month before the public municipal elections. The elections are closed ballot and occur every two and a half years. The votes are counted at each station, with multiple witnesses to the count and recording of the votes, lending the process a great deal of transparency (*Ley* 127).

The local Municipal Assemblies of People's Powers hold the highest power with their functions, which include planning and organizing production and services strategies and health care activities (*[B]*, March 11, 2014) with the relevant entities and approving and controlling provincial income, socio-economic plans and budget, among other functions.

Until 2019 when replaced by provincial governments, headed by a governor, the Provincial Assemblies carried out similar functions at the provincial level. The new Cuban Constitution (2019) changes the representative governmental structures of the Cuban government to empower the municipality as the democratic niche par excellence.

Provincial Assemblies of People's Power Replaced by a System of Provincial Governments

In the 2019 Constitution (Title VIII), the Provincial Assemblies of People's Power were replaced by Provincial Governments of People's Power composed of a Governor and council. "The Provincial Council is presided over by the Governor and is composed of the Deputy Governor, the presidents and vice presidents of the corresponding local assemblies of People's Power, and the municipal mayors" and "its decisions are adopted through a favourable vote of a simple majority of its members" (Cuban Const., S. 3). Working closely with the people for the social and economic development of the territory, each Provincial Government of People's Power is led by a Governor who is "the maximum executive-administrative authority within the province" (Art, 174).

This markedly executive structure serves as an interface between the national and territorial governments. Most importantly, these changes serve to expand the autonomy and capacities of the Municipal Assemblies of People's Power as the core territorial units directing the economic, social, and political life of the country. As such, this further consolidates the participatory element upon which the entire political system is rooted at the local level.

The Municipal Assembly also nominates the deputies of the National Assembly of People's Power (ANPP), which is the unicameral legislative parliament of the Republic of Cuba and has elected legislatures. It is the highest authority in Cuba, having the constituent authority to elect the executive branch of government, which is the President, Vice-President, Prime Minister, and the Council of Ministers. The ANPP is the only body to hold legislative and constituent authority and is supported in its functions by the 31-member Council of State.

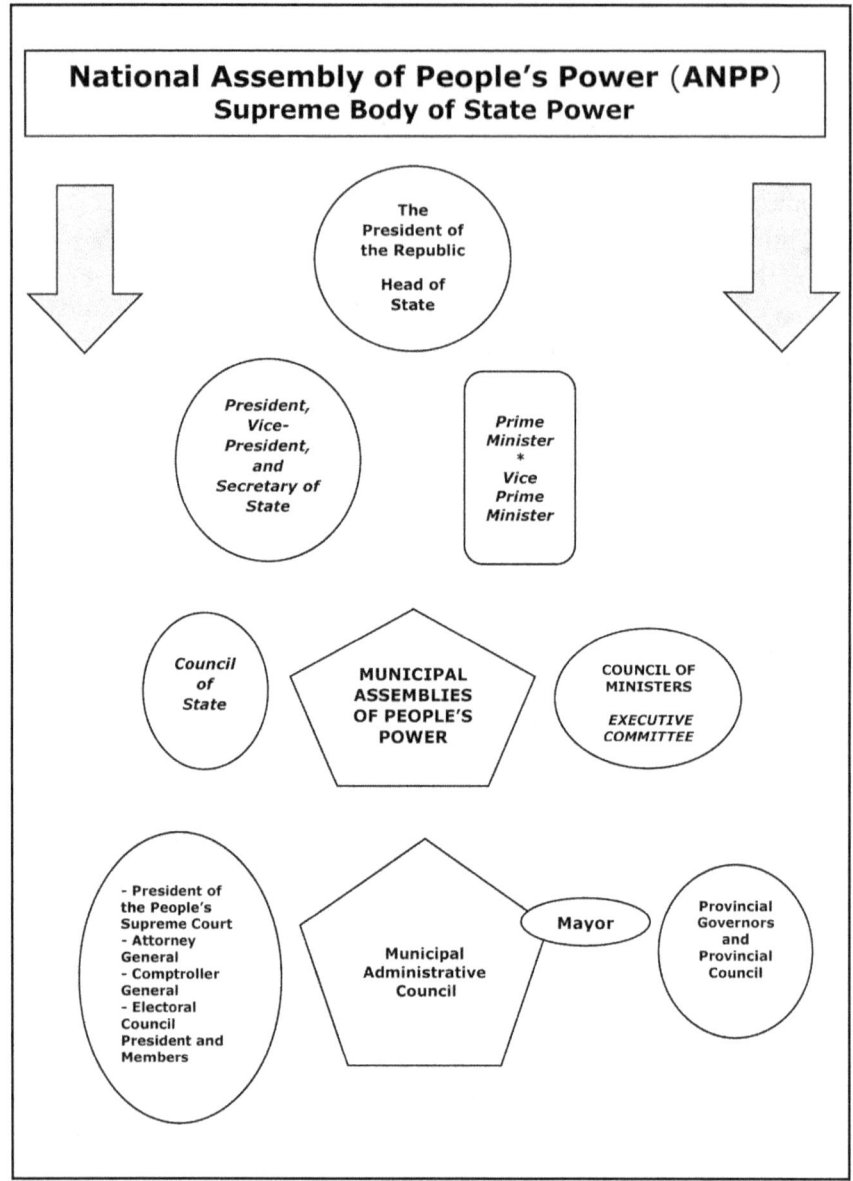

Figure 6.1. Organizations-Party-State triad, where organizations come together with the party (irrevocable socialist government/egalitarian access) and with the state (legislative, constituent, and executive authorities). Through the democratic mechanism of Cuban socialism, the power flows up through the Cuban people to the ANPP and back to the people through the structures of government. The legend to this figure is on the facing page.

Legend to Figure 6.1

The National Assembly of People's Power (ANPP) is the Supreme Body of State Power in Cuba and yields the legislative power. Half of the 470 ANPP deputies are representatives of social and mass organizations nominated and elected during plenary sessions. The other half of the ANPP deputies are elected at the local level by the municipal assemblies, whose deputies are elected by the people in secret direct votes. Candidates are not obligated to be members of the Communist Party of Cuba (PCC).

ANPP President, Vice-President, and Secretary—elected by the ANPP from among the Council of State members.

President of the Republic—appointed by the ANPP from among its deputies as the Head of State, representing the State and directing general policy; **Vice-President of the Republic**—appointed by the ANPP from its deputies.

Prime Minister is the Head of Government—appointed by the ANPP from among the 470 ANPP deputies and represents the government; the **Vice-Prime Minister**— also appointed by the ANPP from its deputies.

Council of State—elected by the ANPP to inter-sessionally represent and carry out decisions of the ANPP. Members of the Council of Ministers or the heads of the judicial, electoral, and state oversight authorities cannot be elected to the Council of State.

Council of Ministers—appointed by the ANPP as the highest executive and administrative body, constituting the Government of the Republic.

Executive Committee—appointed by the President of the Republic and comprising the Prime Minister, Deputy Prime Ministers, Secretary of State, and other members of the Council of Ministers.

Provincial Governors and Council— appointed by the ANPP. The Provincial Governor of each province represents the State in holding the highest administrative executive power.

President of the Supreme Court, Attorney General, Comptroller General, and Electoral Council President and Members—elected by the ANPP.

Municipal Assembly of People's Power—elected by public secret ballot election in each circumscription as the local body of state power.

Municipal Administrative Council—appointed by the Municipal Assembly of People's Power and presided over by the **Mayor**. Each Municipal Administrative Council oversees to ensure the economic, health, educational, cultural, sportive, and recreational needs of their jurisdiction.

All representative bodies of state/state power are renewed through elections. The people control state-body activities; deputies, delegates and/or officials are accountable for their actions and can be removed from office at any time (Art. 96).

Half of the ANPP deputies are representatives of social and mass organizations nominated and elected during their own plenary sessions. The other half of the ANPP deputies are elected from the delegates to the Municipal Assembly of People's Power. Candidates are not obligated to be members of the Communist Party of Cuba (PCC). The PCC is not a political party as traditionally conceived in the West; its role is to guide decision-makers in the direction, actions, and moral principles embraced by the Cuban nation. The other half of the nominations for ANPP deputies come from the municipal assemblies of people's power. The ANPP meets twice annually, and its Council of State, holding executive authority, represents the ANPP between sessions and elects the Cuban president from its ranks. The president of the Council of State is thus the head of state and the head of government. Figure 6.1 shows the flow of power/authority of the ANPP, including the positioning of the new Provincial Governments of People's Power, with the Municipal Assembly of People's Power at centre.

Through the reintroduction of the President of the Republic, the Prime Minister, and the Council of Ministers, the 2019 Constitution of the Republic of Cuba provides better separations of functions of government. The Council of the State remains a permanent organ of the ANPP, the President has a prominent role in the political sphere, whereas the Council of Ministers, under the leadership of the Prime Minister, guides the administrative functions of government.

The formation of mass organizations was one of the most complex tasks in the construction of the Cuban political system. These institutional structures include the Committees for the Defence of the Revolution (CDR), the Federation of Cuban Women (FMC), the Confederation of Cuban Workers (CTC), and the National Association of Small Farmers (ANAP). Appointing from within their own ranks one half of the ANPP delegates, the mass organizations can be consulted on and even bring new legislation forward. They are conceived to ensure inclusion of all Cubans in the revolutionary measures (laws) and process. The popular participation they guarantee serves multiple purposes for the government and the citizenry, such as providing a vehicle for the transmission of information to the population firsthand and ensuring that the voice of the people from the local, neighbourhood level reaches the highest levels of government.

The critical role played by social and mass organizations can be seen, for example, in the many achievements of the Federation of Cuban Women. The "FMC is recognized as both an official mechanism for the incorporation of women's issues into national politics and a non-governmental organization (NGO), because, while its membership includes the vast majority of Cuban women (85.2 percent over age 14), it is not government financed" (Cuba Platform, 2020). The FMC president is a member of the Council of State and directs the Commission for Attention to Women, Children and Youth of the National Assembly of Popular Power, which is constitutionally mandated to support the rights of mass organizations. "The [FMC also] coordinates the work of 81,260 volunteer social workers and 78,624 health brigade members who support mass vaccination campaigns and prevention against dengue fever, influenza AH1-N1 and HIV/AIDS at a neighborhood level."

The FMC has been effective in "mobilizing women and creating solidarity, and it has achieved significant change in Cuban society" (Cuba Platform, Report on the Federation of Cuban Women, 2020). Second only to Rwanda, the Cuban Parliament has the largest number of women in the world, accounting for 55.3 percent of the 470 ANPP lawmakers. Young people aged 18–35 years old represent 20 percent of all legislators, while 95.3 percent of all members of parliament have completed university studies.

In short, the mass organizations constitute a forum of political formation for the great revolutionary mass. At a core level, such revolutionary measures provide an effective means of interaction between people and state in the exercise of direct democracy and of the material relegitimization of public political power. This phenomenon legitimizes the Cuban political system, because civil society supports and relies on political organizations and institutions to fulfill its mandates. Cuba's social organizations include the Union of Writers and Artists (UNEAC) and the Union of Cuban Journalists (UPEC).

The institutional design of the Cuban political system enshrined in the 1976 Constitution formed a foundation for the functioning of the state by creating the unity of power or political action necessary for the construction of Cuban socialism (see Preamble, Articles 5, 6, 7, 8, and 66). This principle applied not only to the state, but to the rest of the elements of the system, such as the Communist Party of Cuba (PCC), Young Communist League (UYC), and the social and mass organizations. It is meaningless to speak of the complete autonomy of any element of a system that exists as the organic whole evidenced by the triad.

Where the Constitutional text of 1976 established Cuba's system of citizen associations to ensure mechanisms under the mass and social organizations for the guarantee of the rights of assembly, strike, and association (Constitution of the Republic of Cuba, 1976, Article 53), the dictatorship of the proletariat is explained as a conceptualization of this exercise of political power, for the creation of "socialist relations of production" (Art. 9); where the people are constituted by "workers, peasants and other manual and intellectual workers" (Art. 1), whose power is exercised through the Assemblies of People's Power and other organs of the State, indirectly or directly (see Art. 4).

Post-1959 Successes

The demographic diversification in Cuba after the Revolution made the establishment of social policies even more urgent. In 1960, medical services on the island were nationalized, making Cuba the first country in Latin American and the Caribbean to have universal health care. The Cuban Ministry of Health rolled out a program of regionalization reaching even the most remote communities. This was no easy task, given that some 50 percent of the country's doctors had emigrated to the U.S. during the exodus of 1959 (Toro-Morn and Alicea, 2004).

The social right of all Cubans to universal health care was subsequently enshrined in the Constitution of Cuba in 1976 under Article 50. Cuba's health care system is recognized the world over and is one of the major successes of the Cuban Revolution. It is no small irony that the American Public Health Association has looked to Cuba for answers to why the United States "is lagging behind other industrialized nations in population health outcomes" while "the Cuban health system is celebrated as an example of a national integrated approach resulting in improved health status" (Keck and Reed, 2012).

The nationalization of health care also engendered progressive increases in purchasing power—through savings on medical costs and an enhanced capacity for work—of families for goods or services not provided by the state. Exponential decreases in unemployment, the shift to ownership over rent, and the institutionalization of education also contributed to the significant improvements in living conditions brought about almost immediately following the rise to power of the Cuban Revolutionary government under Fidel Castro. In 2014, there were 8.2 physicians per 1,000 people in Cuba, compared to 2.6 per 1000 in North America, thanks to the Cuban "community-based polyclinic" (World Bank, 2019). Cuba's total expenditure on health was 11.1 percent of GDP in 2016 (PAHA, 2019). The 2019 state budget allocated 27.5 percent of the national budget to public healthcare and social assistance (CubaDebate, 21 December 2018).

When Fidel's revolutionary government rose to power, it nationalized all educational institutions. Fidel's Literacy Campaign of 1961 made Cuba the first country in Latin America and the Caribbean to be free of illiteracy and have a universal education system offering higher education. This not only helped ensure a greater quality of education but also minimized the differences between urban and rural access. Scholarships served to eliminate all costs associated with higher education, such as room and board, and thus make associated opportunities in the labor market accessible to the masses. The Cuban government also invested heavily in emergency services, relative to available resources, creating the need for graduates from specialties in technology in the pharmaceutical industry and in biotechnology and illustrating the productive forces of human knowledge.

In 2014, public expenditure on education in Cuba was 13 percent of GDP and the nation went into "2015 with a world class level of attainment in the six Education for All (EFA) goals" (UNESCO, 2014). Cuba's commitment to human development thus remains strong, despite the impact of the great economic challenges imposed through the U.S. embargo against Cuba, which—curiously—has become even more restrictive since the fall of the Soviet bloc in 1991 (Griswold, 2015).

The Cuban Revolution also favoured women's rights and liberated them from traditional roles that had prevented their access to full socio-economic inclusion. The achievement of a greater degree of autonomy in planning various aspects of their lives, such as marriage and motherhood, allowed a significant number of women to enter the country's labour force. Women were given equal access to different levels of education and favoured in higher education. Today, women make up almost 50 percent of enrollment in the many university majors representing 67.2 percent of professionals and technicians in the country. Cuba is one of three countries "with more women in parliament (i.e., 53.2 percent) than men" (World Economic Forum, 2019). Such trends have drastically changed the proportion of the qualified workforce in favour of women, and policies were implemented to reconfigure the allocation of management positions (Garcia Elizalde, *Granma*, March 5, 2019).

Another central element of Cuban social policies has been the welfare and care of children. The transformative action of social policy of the Cuban Revolution can be seen most clearly in this sector of the population. The exponential reduction in the infant mortality rate from 1963 to the present (see Table 6.1) is a sign of the priority given to children and evidences the wide-ranging health and education coverage that guarantees their healthy development.

Table 6.1.
Infant Mortality Rates: Cuba and Selected Countries (per 1,000 live births)

Year	CUBA*	CANADA*	USA*	WORLD‡
2022	6.2	4.3	5.4	26.7
2021	5.9	4.4	5.4	27.3
2020	5.6	4.5	5.5	28.0
2019	5.4	4.5	5.5	28.6
2018	5.2	4.5	5.6	29.3
2017	5.0	4.4	5.6	30.2
2015	4.8	4.6	5.8	32.1
2007	5.3	5.1	6.6	42.6
1997	7.8	5.5	7.5	58.1
1991	10.3	6.6	9.1	64.5
1985	14.0	8.0	10.6	71.9
1976	22.7	13.3	15.2	88.5
1963	36.8	25.0	24.4	120.4

*Source: Infant mortality rate per 1,000 live births, World Bank Group, https://data.worldbank.org/indicator/SP.DYN.IMRT.IN. Estimates developed by the UN Inter-agency Group for Child Mortality Estimation (UNICEF, WHO, World Bank, UN DESA Population Division) at childmortality.org. Retrieved 2024-12-04.
‡United Nations—World Population Prospects, via https://www.macrotrends.net/global-metrics/countries/WLD/world/infant-mortality-rate'>World Infant Mortality Rate 1950-2024</a>. www.macrotrends.net. Retrieved 2024-12-04.

As shown in Table 6.1 above, Cuba steadily lowered the infant mortality rate, as well as protecting education and healthcare, despite the extreme poverty of the Special Period following the fall of the eastern European bloc and in spite of the United States tightening its blockade. The measures taken by the revolutionary government since 1959 were successful in turning the situation around in Cuba. This commitment to human development despite the U.S. trade embargo and the crash of the economy in the early 1990s is evidenced by successes in education, health, sports, and the cultural sector. The revolutionary government also acted to overcome institutionalized racism in the workplace and cultural sphere. Education bolstered by anti-racism campaigns against the pre-revolutionary cultural and racial norms that had brought about this phenomenon represented a fundamental step forward. Culturally, recognition of African heritage was implicit in the construction of the Cuban national identity. Racial discrimination continues to be surveyed and guarded against in state policies, especially in terms of access to essential services, education, and the job market, including the government sector.

On November 21, 2019, the President of the Republic, Miguel Diaz-Canel Bermúdez, reiterated that Cuba would never stop working towards its goals, and he listed the upcoming priorities of the Cuban government (Martinez, 2019). Also, at a Council of Ministers meeting, the Cuban Vice Minister of Culture, Fernando Rojas Gutierrez, announced a national program against racism conceived to combat and permanently eliminate any vestiges of racism, racial prejudice and racial discrimination that remain in Cuba. Gutierrez pointed out that traces of racial discrimination remain, not at a policy or institutional level but in the culture of individuals and some groups of people, and that silence is not the answer. It is hoped that the creation of a National Program against Racism and Racial Discrimination will eliminate the traces of racism, racial prejudices, and racial discrimination still found in Cuba (Martinez, 2019).

The Cuban President himself will preside over a governmental commission that will coordinate tasks and aim to identify the causes of the propagation of discriminatory practices based on race and to prescribe potential actions to be taken by each territory, locality, branch of the economy and society. In addition, the historical-cultural legacy of Cuba's indigenous peoples and other non-white peoples within a framework of Cuban cultural diversity will be broadly disseminated, and public debate on racial issues within political, mass, and social organizations and in the media will be encouraged (Fowler, 2019).

Cuba has ranked consistently high on the Human Development Index (HDI). In 2021, Cuba ranked 83rd among 191 countries, falling into "the high human development category." (By comparison, Switzerland ranked first, Canada 15th, and the United States 21st.) The HDI is based on measures of life expectancy, education, and income (United Nations Development Programme, 2022). Cuba's strong HDI ranking despite a relatively low GDP has much to do with the fact that Cuba currently allocates more than 80 percent of its national budget to such services as health, education and social security, while 12 percent goes to business financing (ECLAC, 2022). The political will to maintain margins of equality, universal coverage of basic services, and gratuities that may cushion a process of impoverishment initiated by the loss of Cuba's main trading partner in the early 1990s is in line with the principles of the Cuban revolutionary process.

Cuba: A *Sui Generis* Democracy: Institutionalization of the Revolutionary Political System

The extraterritoriality of the U.S. embargo reduces Cuba's economic decision-making capacity. The process of institutionalizing a form of collective state management in Cuba started in the 1970s and was also conditioned by its adaptation to the civic scheme of Soviet socialism and an increasing reliance on Soviet markets, perpetuating local agrarian underdevelopment in Cuba. On the other hand, the alliance included military protection deemed necessary following the costly Bay of Pigs invasion by the U.S. on April 17, 1961, and made it possible for Cuba to purchase fuel and sell its sugar production, yields for which were improved using Soviet agricultural techniques. It also opened the door to enhanced national development via the Soviet Union Council for Mutual Economic Assistance (COMECOM, 1972).

The political system enshrined in the Constitution thus presented a set of peculiarities; it fused features of Soviet socialist constitutionalism with original contributions accumulated through 17 years of provisionality under the Fundamental Law of the Republic (1959) and entrenched in a historical-political constitutional framework that supports human development through a range of social rights, policies, and institutions. The singularity of **Cuban socialism** and the **Cuban socialist democracy** has thus emerged through an arduous process of political-legal transculturation:

> The decade of the 70s represented an inflection for the Cuban Revolution. Until then, perhaps, its most distinctive feature had been the impossibility of it fitting the cast of East European socialism. Both in its internal dynamics and in its international projection, it was perceived as something different, ungraspable in the concepts and categories of real socialism. The Cuban leadership had distanced itself from the general methods and approaches of [orthodox Soviet] socialism. The non-institutionalized Revolution maintained a fluid communication between its vanguard and the people and international positions characterized by their independence. The tradition of unity forged in the previous decade had had an essentially political, non-doctrinaire, or predominantly ideological basis. In the mid-70s, and with the new Constitution, as the culmination of a rapid process of change, that situation changed. (Azcuy, 2000, p. 133)

In Cuba, a perennial tension between the national and international poles is related to dominating forms of global power and privileged local elites alongside Cuba's efforts regarding national and social emancipation of subordinate classes. The Revolution radicalized this dialectic process by focusing on the emancipatory pole, solving the imperatives of self-government—the effective exercise of sovereignty—by adopting an institutional scheme that guaranteed maximum social mobilization in favour of transformative human development according to the revolutionary program. The result was the articulation of power united enough to address, at the same time, the internal challenges and the external confrontations that characterize one of the most intense and prolonged campaigns of aggression by the U.S. in the western hemisphere.

Democracy in Cuba is seen as an essential factor in forming revolutionary leadership and the primary mechanism for population mobilization. The content and form of Cuban socialist democracy are innovations resulting from processes of political-legal transculturation in which aspects of different models are adopted and amalgamated to meet the contextual challenges surrounding our development. As shown in Table 6.2, Cuban socialist democracy results from a fusion of various elements of classical democracy, representative democracy, socialist democracy, and the autochthonous constitutional tradition.

Table 6.2. Cuban Socialist Democracy

Classical (Athenian) Democracy	Liberal Democracy	Cuban Social 'People' Democracy
• Developed in ancient Greece. • Introduced the ideal of civic virtue. • Participation in public affairs by a (relatively small) segment of the citizenry through election of the ordinary magistrates.	• Ordinary citizens are the representatives (principle of representivity). • Separation of powers imposes limits on the authority of government. • Human rights becomes the framework upholding individual and personal development. • Elections become synonymous with the expression of popular will. • Political parties become the key element of the electoral and political system. • Freedom emerges as a constitutional right.	• Embracing a principle of popular sovereignty. • Emphasizing social participation through citizen's assemblies. • Implementing equality as the fundamental constitutional norm. • Egalitarianism in all spaces, from economics to politics to social. • No separation of powers. • The principle of unity is invoked through specialized bodies that reach the local level to ensure popular representation. • One party responsible only for guiding the social totality.
Forged through processes of political-legal transculturation, the Cuban socialist democracy embodies elements of classical (Athenian) democracy and liberal democracy. *Source: Authors.*		

Summary and Conclusions

As noted in the introduction to this chapter, the fact that Cuba has developed the most enduring and radical socialist experience in the western hemisphere implies model results and a high degree of authenticity regarding applied social policies. Much foreign literature denounces Cuba for not being a "democracy"; but as we have tried to explain in this chapter, we feel that we do have one—it is just different. Cuba has a single-party system and bicameral parliament because we believe in the humanity and egalitarianism of sharing the wealth, a concept we fondly refer to as "Cuban socialism." As also explained earlier in this chapter, the Government-Party-Organizations triad illustrates how the people hold the power through what we call "Cuban socialist democracy." The processes of political transculturation continue to evolve Cuban socialism and the Cuban socialist democracy. For example, there has been (at the time of preparing this chapter) some discussion of a move to infuse the Cuban system with a more traditionally democratic presidential electoral process, but the exact form this would take should it ever happen is unknown.

Again, as discussed in this chapter, Cuba holds elections to choose the members of the National Assemblies of People's Power, and it is they who elect the members of the Council of State. Discussions of Cuba reverberate ad nauseum in Cold War rhetoric now driven by the continued existence of the U.S. embargo, which is the vehicle still being used to define Cuba. Since this blockade restricts other nations from trading with Cuba, it also has an evident influence on Western discourse, which has traditionally failed to reflect on the particular historical factors and ideologies of humanism that produced the dynamics informing one of the most radical and complex quests for individual freedom and development in contemporary history.

The resilience and successes of the Cuban socialist project embrace the dynamics of transculturation which is characterized by its keen ability for adaptation of government processes needed to counter an extremely aggressive international environment characterized by the U.S. embargo. These variables are complicit in articulating civic-political participation in constructing a new social order that breaks from the canons of Western liberalism and the orthodoxy of failed Eastern European socialism. Mobilization of popular power via Cuba's social and mass organizations combines with the guarantees of basic needs, commitment to human development, and a remuneration protocol based on the principle of socialist distribution to become the sustaining mechanism of the social and political system born through the Cuban Revolution (1953–1959).

The Cuban revolutionary process has been influenced by the aggressions of the various U.S. administrations with which it has co-existed. These aggressions range from military intervention, state terrorism, and economic blockades to forms of cultural aggression. The situation was greatly exacerbated by the collapse of the Eastern European socialist bloc, which deprived Cuba of its main source of foreign trade (some 85 percent) and political support (see Chapter 3).

The Cuban Revolution inverts the logic of Western capitalist-democracy discourse characteristic of modernity, which puts the institutional sphere and capitalistic processes of modernity ahead of the recognition of basic human and social rights of underdeveloped countries. The Cuban experience has made the construction of the political sphere a function of social justice. Here, equality is a premise for the realization of human dignity through development and creating a civil society in defence of a new social order.

The Cuban Revolution has fostered an inclusive political participation centred on the equitable distribution of wealth and based on an ethics of work and education as the means to individual and group opportunities. Services such as education, health, full employment, paid leisure and vacation destinations, and a universal social security system were recognized as rights strongly supported by both legal and material guarantees. These social rights, as the core content of the social justice agenda of the Cuban Revolution, became the basis of the enormous legitimacy and popular support upon which the revolutionary government has counted over the decades.

The Cuban people passionately embrace their right to self-determination, which first found expression in mass mobilization around the revolutionary leaders and continues to find expression through Cuba's network of social and mass organizations and the National Assembly of People's Power. The organizations function within the State-Party-Organizations triad, the linchpin of Cuban socialist democracy. Cuban socialism defends a broad notion of social justice mobilized through the state provision of the formal and material means of life, affording first-, second-, third-, and fourth- (i.e., future) generation human rights. A commitment to this was reflected in the Fundamental Law (1959) and consolidated in the 1976 constitutional project, which also modified certain social, economic, and cultural rights in support of the transition from a principle of distribution based on complete equality (according to ability/need) to equity (according to ability/work).

While Cuba has the right to self-determination, as does any other country, it continues to be misjudged, misconstrued, and undermined not only by the U.S. but by the governments of other countries and especially in relation to the U.S. embargo. The resulting economic pressure on Cuba clearly imposes limits on Cuba's right to self-determination, and this deplorable positioning of so many countries against Cuba wrongly posits Cubans as victims of a dictatorship that does not allow the people to choose.

The updated Constitution of the Republic of Cuba (2019) gives more autonomy to the municipal level, thereby diminishing administrative workloads at the provincial level. There are changes in the titles of the leading representatives of the (local) government at the provincial level, with the Provincial Assembly now the Provincial Council (Const., 2019, Art. 170). The Provincial Councils exist and function as mediators between the associated municipality and the central administration of the state (Const., 2019, Art. 171). The Municipal Assembly of People's Power maintains its authority as the main body of state power in each area/district (Cuban Const., Ch. II, §1, 2019,) and its members are delegated by direct vote in public elections by Cuban citizens (see Chapter 7 for details on the new Constitution).

The irrevocability of Cuban socialism was implemented by Fidel on June 26, 2002 (Cuban Const. Reform, 2002 Amend.) and reaffirmed by the national referendum (Cuban Const. Title XI, Art's. 4, 16, 229, 2019) on our 2019 constitution. Cuba constitutes a concrete historical example of the confrontation between liberal democracy and social justice, within the context of the construction of a socialist society under conditions of Third World underdevelopment and Cold War economic exclusion. Sixty years after the triumph of the Cuban Revolution, its political model of Cuban socialism and socialist democracy remains at the antipodes of capitalism and capitalist democracy.

The constitution and legal system underlying the political and institutional framework of Cuban socialism and Cuban socialist democracy contain elements derived from multiple legal traditions forged through political-legal transculturation. The mass organizations of social inclusion and democratic power erected following the Cuban Revolution continue to ensure involvement and participation by most Cubans, a democratic process that continues to this day.

Finally, the 2019 Constitution continues proclaiming the Communist Party as having the guiding role in Cuban society and also the irreversibility of socialism. This new constitution contains structural changes legalizing certain capitalistic mechanisms, such as entrepreneurship. Some may see this market-oriented approach as a failure of the Cuban Revolution to transcend individual wealth accumulation; however, the egalitarian aims of the Cuban Revolution are safeguarded through the irrevocability of Cuban socialism twice ratified by the vast majority of the Cuban people in secret, direct ballot, open-election referenda.

References

Azcuy, H. (2000). Análisis de la Constitución Cubana. In *Papeles de la FIM 14* (p. 133). Creative Commons. SciELO. https://www.scielo.org.ar/pdf/rhd/n61/1853-1784-rhd-61-111.pdf

Bohemia (Revista). Online weekly magazine. www.bohemia.cu

Bulté, F. J. (1999). Tras las pistas de la Revolución en cuarenta años de Derecho. In *Temas*, October 1998 and June 1999. Special Issues.

Cantón, Navarro J., and Duarte Hurtado, M. (2006). *Cuba 42 años de Revolución: Cronología histórica 1959–1982*. Tome I. Havana, Cuba: Editorial Ciencias Sociales.

Carmona Tamayo, E. (2018, August 29). Reforma constitucional: Propuesta de nueva estructura del Estado (Infografía). *Ahora*. http://www.ahora.cu/images/stories/infografia/infog-estructura-estado2.jpg

Castro, R. F. [October 16, 1953] (1968). *History will absolve me: The Moncada trial defence speech, Santiago de Cuba*. London: Cape.

‑‑‑‑‑. (1959, January 3). *Castro speaks to citizens of Santiago*. Castro Speech Data Base: Speeches, Interviews, Articles 1959–1966. USA: University of Texas at Austin: Latin American Network Information Center (LANIC). http://lanic.utexas.edu/project/castro/1959 /

‑‑‑‑‑. (1959, May 17). *On the promulgation of the Agrarian Law: Two million Cubans will find their income increased*. Speech. Castro Speech Data Base: Speeches, Interviews, Articles 1959–1966. Austin, Texas: LANIC. http://lanic.utexas.edu/project/castro/db/1959/19590517.html.

‑‑‑‑‑. Castro, R. F. (1970, July 26). *Discurso pronunciado 26 de julio de 1970*. [Speech delivered by Fidel Castro on the 17th anniversary of the Moncada assault]. LANIC. Abridged version (1970, July 27) published in *Granma* Newspaper. Havana, Cuba. http://lanic.utexas.edu/project/castro/db/1970/19700726.html.

‑‑‑‑‑. (1973, November 16). *Fidel Castro addresses Cuban workers Congress*. Speech at the 13th Congress of the CTC. Castro Speech Data Base: Austin, Texas: LANIC. http://lanic.utexas.edu/project/castro/db/1970/19700726.html.

[Cuban Constitution (2019, April 10).] (2019, April 10). *Constitución de la República de Cuba*. Title VI, Ch. 1: The Structure of the State. Cuba *Gaceta* [Gazette] *Oficial 2019-406-EX5*. Havana, Cuba. Available in English at Oxford Constitutions of the World. https://global.oup.com/academic/product/oxford-constitutions-of-the-world-9780199799848?cc=us&lang=en&].

[Cuban Constitution (1976). (1976, February 24).] *Constitución de la República de Cuba*. (February 24, 1976): Ch. 1, Art. 1 [adoption of Cuba as a socialist State of workers]; Ch. 1, Art.7 [recognition of social and mass organizations]; Art. 14 [adoption of the principle of socialist distribution. Trans. © DESOFT 2019]. *Gaceta* [Gazette] Oficial. Havana, Cuba.

[Cuban Const. Reform. (2002, June 26).]. *Constitución de la República de Cuba*. (2002). Amend. [The National Assembly approved amendments making socialism irrevocable in Cuba]. *Palacio de las Convenciones*. Havana, Cuba.

[Cuban Const. (2019, April 10).] *Constitución de la República de Cuba*. (2019). Title XI, Arts. 4, 16, 229. [Irrevocability of Cuban socialism]. 2019, April 10. *Gaceta* [Gazette] *Oficial 5* (GOC-2019-406-EX5). Havana, Cuba.

[Cuban Const. (2019).] *Constitución de la República de Cuba*. (2019). Title VIII, S. 3. [the

Provincial Council]. *Gaceta* [Gazette] *Oficial* 5 (GOC-2019-406-EX5). Havana, Cuba.
[Cuban Const. (2019, April 10).] *Constitución de la República de Cuba* (2019, April 10). Ch. 1, Art. 14. [Recognition of social and mass organizations]. *Gaceta* [Gazette] *Oficial* 5 (GOC-2019-406-EX5). Havana, Cuba.
[Cuban Const. (2019, April 10).] *Constitución de la República de Cuba* (2019, April 10). Ch. 3, § 1, Art. 104. [The People's Councils]. *Gaceta* [Gazette] *Oficial* 5 (GOC-2019-406-EX5). Havana, Cuba.
CTC, XIII Congress. (1973). Resolution to adopt the socialist system of distribution. Havana, Cuba.
CubaDebate. Reinaldo, O.F., Concepción, J.R., Guerrero D. D., Tamayo, E.C., and Terrero, A. (2018, December 21). ¿Cuál es el Presupuesto del Estado cubano para 2019? Havana, Cuba: CubaDebate. http://www.cubadebate.cu/especiales/2018/12/21/cual-es-el-presu puesto-del-estado-cubano-para-2019-infografias/
Cuba Platform. The Federation of Cuban Women. (2020). https://cubaplatform.org/federation-cuban-women
Del Toro González, C. (1998–1999). *Antecedentes socioeconómicos de la Revolución de 1959*. (p. 18) No. 16–17. Havana, Cuba.
ECLAC. (2022, December). Preliminary overview of the economies of Latin America and the Caribbean 2022. Economic Commission for Latin America and the Caribbean (ECLAC). https://repositorio.cepal.org/server/api/core/bitstreams/d2de9809-2c37-41 56-a9d4-6edcb7b3573f/content
Fowler, V. (2019, December 26). Pensando en clave de "raza" [Cuba, Discriminación, Racismo]. Cubadebate. http://www.cubadebate.cu/especiales/2019/12/26/pensando-en-clave-de-raza/
Engels, Friedrich. [1884]. (1942). *The Origin of the family, private property, and the state*. New York: International Publishers.
Fundamental Law of the Republic of Cuba [Ley Fundamental de la República]. (1959, February 7). Cuba. English translation retrieved from the World Constitutions Illustrated (WCI) database (William S. Hein & Co., Inc.).
Garcia Elizalde, A. (2019, March 5). No descuidar las brechas que nos quedan, ni los desafíos que tenemos por delante [interview with the General Secretary of the Cuban Women's Federation, Teresa Amarelle Boué]. Havana, Cuba: *Granma* Newspaper. http://www.granma.cu/cuba/2019-03-05/no-descuidar-las-brechas-que-nos-quedan-ni-los-desafios-que-tenemos-por-delante-05-03-2019-20-03-12
Granma. (2014, March 11). Elecciones en Cuba: "El poder del pueblo" [The People's Power]. Havana: *Granma* Newspaper 18(70). http://www.granma.cu/granmad/secciones/ele cciones/112.html
Griswold, D. (2005). *Four decades of failure: The U.S. embargo against Cuba*. Speech. Presented at the James A. Baker III Institute Program, Cuba and the United States in the 21st Century at Rice University, Houston, Texas. https://www.cato.org/publications/speeches/four-decades-failure-us-embargo-against-cuba
Guevara, C. E. (1967). *Man and socialism in Cuba* (Trans. Margarita Zimmermann). Havana, Cuba: Guairas Book Institute [El socialismo y el hombre: Havana, Cuba: Ediciones Revolucionarias. 1965].
Keck, C.W., and Reed, G.A. (2012). The curious case of Cuba: Lessons from Cuba's national health system. *American Journal of Public Health*. https://www.ncbi.nlm.nih.gov/pmc/articles/PMC3464859/
Lenin, V. I. (1917 [1964]). *Lenin Collected Works*. Pravda 67. Russian Tabloid. [Trans. Bernard Isaacs]. Moscow: Progress Publishers, vol. 24, pp. 519–20]. https://www.marxists.org/archive/lenin/works/1917/may/27.htm
Ley 54 de asociaciones [Law No. 54, Associations law]. 1985. Ley No. 54 [National Assembly of People's Power (legislative parliament of the Republic of Cuba)]. Asamblea Nacional

del Poder Popular. Havana: Parlamento Cubano. http://www.parlamentocubano.gobcu/index.php/documento/ley-de-asociaciones/
Ley 127 Electoral de la República de Cuba [Law No. 127, Electoral Law]. (2019, August 19). [National Assembly of People's Power (legislative parliament of the Republic of Cuba)]. Asamblea Nacional del Poder Popular (parlamento Cubano). *Gaceta* [Gazette] Oficial 60: 1271. (GOC-2019-735-060). Havana: Cuba. https://www.gacetaoficial.gob.cu/sites/default/files/goc-2019-060_0.pdf
Ley 851 de nacionalización [Law No. 851, Nationalization Law]. Ley No. 851. (1959, July 6). *Gaceta* [Gazette] *Oficial*. Havana, Cuba.
Ley de Reforma Agraria. [Agrarian Reform Law]. (1959, June 3). *Gaceta* [Gazette] *Oficial*. Havana, Cuba.
Ley de Reforma Agraria. [Agrarian Reform Law]. (1959, June 3). Enacted in October, 1960, *Gaceta* [Gazette] *Oficial*, October 15, 1963. Havana: Cuba.
Ley de Reforma Urbana [Urban Reform Law]. (1959, June 3). *Gaceta* [Gazette] *Oficial*. Havana, Cuba.
Ley No. 890 [Law No. 890]. (1960, October 15). *Gaceta* [Gazette] *Oficial Extraordinaria* 24, 1960. Havana, Cuba.
Ley No. 1076. [Law No. 1076]. (1962, December 4). *Gaceta Oficial*. Havana, Cuba.
Ley Fundamental de la República de Cuba. [Fundamental Law of the Republic]. (1959, February 7). Havana, Cuba. https://archivos.juridicas.unam.mx/www/bjv/libros/6/2525/38.pdf
Martinez Hernandez, L. (2019, November 21). Díaz-Canel en el Consejo de Ministros: "No vamos a renunciar las conquistas y los sueños por realizar" [We are not giving up on our dreams]. Havana, Cuba: *Granma* Tabloid. http://www.granma.cu/cuba/2019-11-21/diaz-canel-en-el-consejo-de-ministros-no-vamos-a-renunciar-a-las-conquistas-y-los-suenos-por-realizar-21-11-2019-22-11-18.
Marx, K. [1850] (1945). Dictatorship of the proletariat [In Marx's *The class struggles in France 1848–1850*]. London: Lawrence and Wishart.
-----. [1859] (1965). *Pre-capitalist economic formations*, ed. Eric J. Hobsbawm, trans. Jack Cohen. New York: International Publishers.
Marx, K. and Engels, F. [1948] (1996). *The communist manifesto*. Pamphlet. London and Chicago: Pluto Press.
Nohlen, D. (2005). *Elections in the Americas: A data handbook 1*: 197. Germany.
O'Brien, J. E. (2018). *Percepción y periodismo: Bohemia in 1950s Cuba* (Master's Thesis). Department of History. Louisiana State University and Agricultural and Mechanical College. LSU Digital Commons. https://digitalcommons.lsu.edu/cgi/viewcontent.cgi?article=5666&context=gradschool_theses.
PAHA. (2019). Cuba statistics. Pan American Health Organization. https://www.who.int/countries/cub/en/.
Pedro, R. (2019). The First Congress of the Communist Party of Cuba. Havana, Cuba: *Granma* Newspaper. Communist Party of Cuba (CPC). http://www.fidelcastro.cu/en/articles/first-congress-communist-party-cuba.
Plá León, R. (2008, June 27–29). *La tesis cubana de la construcción paralela del socialismo y el comunismo*. Las Villas, Cuba: XI Internacional de Pensamiento Symposium. Latin America. Central "Marta Abreu" University.
Rafuls Pineda, D. (2015). *The beginnings of the political transition to socialism in Cuba: The dilemma between the formal power and the real one.* Universidad de la Habana. UH no. 279 la Habana ene.-jun.2015 Online versión: scielo.sld.cu_ISSN: 0253-9276
Referendum. (2019, February 24). Constitución de la República de Cuba. (2019, April 10). Constitutional amendments approved by national referendum on February 24, 2019. Havana, Cuba.
Res. 53. 14 July 1986. [Resolution 53 dictating the rules of Law No. 54, 1985]. Havana: Cu-

ban Department of Justice.

Suárez Pérez, Eugenio et al. (2015, August 10). Fifty-five years ago: Cuba nationalizes U.S. companies in defense of the country's economy and sovereignty. Havana, Cuba: *Granma* Tabloid. http://en.granma.cu/cuba/2015-08-10/cuba-nationalizes-us-companies

Toledo García, J. (2012). Prologue. *Cuba: Propiedad social y Construcción socialista*. Collected Edition. Havana, Cuba: Editorial Ciencias Sociales.

Toro-Morn, M.I., Alicea, M. (2004). *Migration and Immigration: A Global View*. Westport, CT: Greenwood Press.

UN Development Programme. (2022, September 8). Human Development Report 2021–2022. https://hdr.undp.org/content/human-development-report-2021-22

UN General Assembly, 3281. (1974, December 12). Charter of Economic Rights and Duties of States. United Nations. 1974.

UN General Assembly, 3201 (S-VI). (1974, May 1) Declaration on the Establishment of a New International Economic Order. Adopted during the Sixth Special Session of the United Nations General Assembly. United Nations. 1974.

UNESCO. (2014). Cuba rates the highest EFA Development Index in Latin America and the Caribbean. http://www.unesco.org/new/en/santiago/press-room/newsletters/e-newsletter-education-for-all-in-latin-america-and-the-caribbean/no16-may-2014/nota-habana-03/

Valdés, G. O. (2007). *La Revolución Cubana. Premisas económicas y sociales*. Havana, Cuba: Editorial de Ciencias Sociales.

Valdés Gutiérrez, G. (2017). *Pensar y soñar en Cuba*. Havana, Cuba: Editorial Filosofía. In Luis Suárez Salazar et al. (2019). *Cuba en revolución: Miradas en torno a sus sesenta aniversarios*. Buenos Aires: CLACSO. http://biblioteca.clacso.edu.ar/clacso/se/20191017033409/Cuba_en_revolucion.pdf

World Economic Forum. (2019, February 12). These countries have the most women in parliament. Geneva: International Organization for Public-Private Cooperation. https://www.weforum.org/agenda/2019/02/chart-of-the-day-these-countries-have-the-most-women-in-parliament/

CHAPTER SEVEN

The Cuban Socialist Constitution and Legal System

José Augusto Ochoa del Río

Abstract

The history of Cuba's legal system has been characterized by processes of national liberation, legal-political transculturation, and informal innovation designed to weather rough international tides. This history is reflected in our eight constitutions, and the result is a unique socialist legality underlying an equally unique Cuban socialism. Since the 19th century, the Cuban legal system has fluxed and been molded by various processes of legal transculturation, first theorized by the Cuban anthropologist Fernando Ortiz in 1940. In terms of legal-political transculturation, various structures of Romano-French law, such as the Code, typify our system; but when it comes to safeguarding the sanctity of constitutional norms, the National Assembly of People's Power is at the top of the state hierarchy. The formal sources of law are not laid out in the Cuban constitution, but the normative legal act (interpreted in the courts) is considered to be the main formal source of law, which means the legislative act is the ultimate source. Cuban law experts argue that the influence of the Cuban Supreme Court's Governing Council at times makes the jurisprudence function of our civil systems operate—albeit informally—as another formal source of law. In 2019, the Cuban people approved the 2019 Constitution and several regulatory trends given by constitutional amendments have been analyzed within a framework of their impact on the country's legal phenomena. The 2019 Constitution reaffirms Cuba's commitment to socialism and introduces changes to the economic, political, and social model that will require associated changes in law, such as legalizing certain forms of capitalist activities such as small business and self-employment and enacting a new electoral law and amendments to the Family Code. As well, references to the goal of communism found in the previous constitution have been deleted. The legalization of same sex marriage in the Family Code was approved by national referendum in 2022.

Keywords: legal-political, transculturation, constitution, insurrection, referendum

José Augusto Ochoa del Río holds a Ph.D. in Pedagogical Sciences (University of Holguín, Cuba, 2014) and an LL.B. (University of Camagüey, Cuba 2001). He is Researcher and Professor of General Theory of Law at the Centre for Culture and Identity Studies (CECI), Faculty of Social Sciences, University of Holguín, Cuba.

Introduction

Cuba is an enigma in many ways, but the situation is particularly complex from a legal standpoint. Like other nations, Cuba's history, mistakes, and virtues are reflected in its legal system. The Cuban judicial system is unique, presenting influences formed through legal transculturation processes identified and first theorized by the Cuban anthropologist Fernando Ortiz in 1940. This chapter will present the historical dynamics that influenced and led to the creation of the current Cuban legal system. The basic principles underpinning the lawmaking process and the courts will also be outlined, with a summary focusing on changes implemented in the past 11 years. This chapter has three sections. The first discusses Cuba's eight constitutions, four of which are known as *Mambisa* constitutions. They were proclaimed by Cuban patriots fighting against Spanish colonization throughout the second half of the 19th century. The other four are the formal constitutions of 1901, 1940, 1976, and 2019. As part of this overview and within a context of what could be considered legal-political transculturation, the influences of Romano-French law and Anglo-Saxon law will be explored along with those of Cuban socialist law upon which our legal and national identity are premised and our idea of nation legitimized. The second section will explain the process of law creation and enactment by the National Assembly of People's Power (i.e., Cuba's legislative parliament) and the executive power, respectively, and will also present the guiding principles of the Cuban judiciary. The third section will assess current regulatory trends given by amendments to the Cuban Constitution (2019) within a framework of their impact on the country's legal phenomena. The conclusion will present several issues likely to be addressed in a future reform.

The Expression of Roman-French and Socialist Legal Systems in Cuba: A Brief Summary

Legal phenomena are a product of the historical moment in which they arise and an expression of the political conditions that give rise to them. The Cuban legal system and Constitution are no exception. Both have undergone changes, albeit dissimilar, from the colonial era through to the triumph and concrete materialization of the Cuban Revolution and beyond. These changes reflect various influences that include reformist, independentist, annexationist, humanist (José Martí), nationalist, and Marxist-Leninist. The evolution of Cuba's socio-political ideology—which is reflected in the various constitutions that have governed our nation—has been informed by ongoing processes of socio-economic and legal-political transculturation.

The Cuban homeland has had eight constitutions, with four corresponding to the colonial period, two to the republican period, and two to the Revolution in power. From the legal standpoint of a democratic constituent movement, however, there are only four: the U.S.-tinged 1901 Constitution, the progressive 1940 Constitution, the Socialist Constitution of 1976, and today's unique Magna Carta of 2019. The four that emerged during the colonial stage are *Mambisa* ("In Arms"/insurgents) constitutions created by groups of Cuban dissidents and insurgents through the second half of the 19th century. The *Mambisa* liberated small villas and farms in rural areas and created constitutions in the free areas. Cuba's *Mambisa* constitutions were unofficial but contributed significantly to shaping thought around a nationalist and humanistic dogma.

The Cuban socialist legal system, a product of Fernando Ortiz's legal transculturation, is supported by legal norms that reflect the ideology and system of values of Cuban socialist democracy. Simply put, Cuban law gives expression to our unique culture, Cubanness, and outside Cuba our not necessarily well understood socio-economic and political system. Organized under a largely civil law system, the formal source of Cuban law is the normative act. It is interpreted in the courts by magistrates, professional judges, and lay judges. Laws, decrees with the force of laws, presidential decrees, decrees, resolutions, and other provisions by the relevant organs must be published in the Official Bulletin of the Republic (Art. 165, Const. 2019).

In form, Cuba's legal system remains heavily influenced by the Spanish Civil Code (1889), which was replaced in 1987 by the Cuban Civil Code (Law 59) to meet the needs of (1) full national sovereignty and independence achieved through the Cuban Revolution and (2) the requirements of a society building a new and unique brand of socialist legality. The Cuban Revolutionary Government entrusted the legislative function to the National Assembly of People's Power, reorganized the judicial system in 1973 (and the Criminal Code in 1973/1977/1987) and replaced the Civil Code the same year. The institutionalization of the Revolution commenced in 1973 with the Judicial Organization Law and was reaffirmed in the 1976 Constitution.

Characteristics of the Cuban Legal System and its Constitutions
Colonial Stage

The Cuban socialist legal system has a rich and interesting history. Roughly speaking, in terms of beginnings, we can talk about a major influence from the Romano-French tradition that has been maintained although with significant variation. On the other hand, this is little more than an historical nuance since Spain brought its laws proper to the colonies and overseas lands without enacting any local constitutions. That is what Antonio Prudencio López (1884) meant when he said the Laws of the Indies* were always those of the metropolis, modified for the special conditions under which the Spaniards residing in the various colonies found themselves. Many of the "new" institutions were copies of counterparts in Spain, while the codes sanctioned by the Kingdom of Castile were considered the supplemental right of the Law of the Indies (Lopez, 1864).

For example, the Spanish Civil Code was extended to Spain's colonies by royal decree in July 1889. It remained in force† in Cuba until 1987, which means it coexisted with Cuban socialism or, according to some, through the ongoing construction of this latter. The Spanish metropolis had simply exported the legal system prevailing in Europe to its colonies in the Americas. The Code, born of the French Revolution's promulgation of the Napoleonic Code (1804), brought the best of Roman and modern codified law together into a legal heritage that has lasted to this day.

Characteristics of the Roman-French Tradition of Civil Law Systems
Unlike Anglo-Saxon (i.e., common law) systems, the **legislative act** is by far the most important formal source in civil (civilian) law systems, as highlighted in Box 7.1. In Cuba, judges base their decisions on what is written in the codes rather than on precedent derived from the rulings of past cases. The term **jurisprudence** also has a different connotation in civil and common law systems. In civil systems, a body of written rules, aptly named a code, lies at the foundation of all laws—but other laws may be created to complement it or make exceptions. The court uses jurisprudence to regulate interpretations, but a ruling never establishes a legal precedent

---

* The Laws of the Indies was a system of royal decrees compiling the entire body of law devised, enacted, and enforced by Spain for the governance of its colonies from the 1500s to the 1700s and culminating in the *Recopilación de las leyes de los reinos de Indias*, 1680.

† The Civil Code was extended to overseas by the royal decree of July 31, 1889 (De Bustamante y Montoro, Antonio Sánchez, *Jurisprudence in the Hierarchy of the Sources of Cuban Positive Law*).

> **Box 7.1: Civil Law Systems**
>
> The legislative act is the ultimate formal source of the law, making other sources, such as custom and jurisprudence, secondary. In essence, legislative acts create the law, while normative acts implement and operationalize the law. The main formal source of the law is the normative legal act. There is a tendency toward positive law; both emanate similarly from a higher power, are based on a written code stemming from the XII Tables of the Napoleonic Code, and aim specifically to protect against class-based discrimination.

that will function as a law, as under common law. Under common law systems, judges use precedent (aka jurisprudence) to regulate legal relationships and conduct but also to ensure translation into judicial practice. Civil law systems give legislators (i.e., publicly elected officials) more influence in shaping the law than judges. In short, the court applies legal norms, it does not create new ones. However, aside from the normative act, many see the Supreme Court's Governing Council's role in guiding interpretations as an indirect precedent and thus an unrecognized formal source of law (Bruzón Viltres and Tamayo Blanco, 2014).

Accordingly, the Cuban system regulates all legal relationships through the direct application of statutes and other legal codes establishing procedure. Where common law uses precedent, or case law, established by judges in past rulings of similar cases, these sources of law (e.g., custom and precedent) rank second in civil law systems; judges use jurisprudence to ensure uniform interpretation of the laws. In Cuba, the system of lay judges bridges a gap between the abstract reality of a law and the inevitable evolution of social norms at the local level. Like professional judges, Cuban lay judges are elected by the ANPP, which is the Cuban parliament.

It is argued that civil law systems offer more legal certainty and security than common law systems. Because the Code's abstractions of real-life occurrences are organized into a single legal body (i.e., known as legislation or statutory law), they can be systematically updated as new laws or constitutional amendments are passed. Under civil law systems, judges act as arbitrators for those appearing in court and are inquisitorial, determining the facts of a case and establishing rulings based on what is written in the codes. The codification characteristic of civil law systems emerged with Rome's Twelve Tables, was extended to France's Napoleonic Code, and reflects the desire to end class struggle.

It is argued that codification offers greater legal certainty in a national legal and political tradition formerly dependent on the law of a foreign power. Aside from ensuring stability and transparency, codification performs a social-ethical pedagogical function supporting legitimate social progress and transitional demands and reflects the guiding principles that underlie and sustain the entire political structure (San Miguel, 2006).

The Written-Constitution Movement of the 19th Century

The forging of a constitutional will in Cuba began early in the 19th century under the influence of the **written constitution movement** emerging through the bourgeois revolution of the thirteen colonies in North America in 1776, the French Revolution's declarations of rights and constitutional texts circa 1789, and the application in Cuba of Spain's Cortes de Cádiz Constitution in 1812. Several draft constitutions, however, had been drawn up in Cuba but never enacted. The precursors to the regulatory norms and standards on power and public freedoms enjoyed in Cuba today can be found in those early texts. Examples include the philosopher and Priest José Augustín Caballero's 1811 charter for autonomist government in Cuba, a regional project against oligarchy; Joaquín Infante's Draft Constitution of 1812, the first to contemplate Independence; the Narciso López Constitution of 1851, falsely labeled annexionist; and the *El Ave Maria* (i.e., Hail Mary) Constitution of 1858, proposing independence and abolition of slavery.

The first constitutional law extended to Cuba was the famous Spanish Constitution of 1812 issued by the Cortes de Cádiz (i.e., Cadiz Courts). It had two periods of validity: 1812–1814 and 1820–1823. Its 389 articles covered everything from the nation, the territory, the courts, the King, the military, and public education to constitutional reform. Embodying some of the liberal dogma of the Napoleonic Code, the Cádiz Constitution instituted what was a progressive effort for its day by the Spanish bourgeoisie to transform Spain's regime of absolute monarchy. It referred expressly to the civil and political rights of citizens: sovereignty resides essentially within the nation and, for the same reason, the state's exclusive right to establish its fundamental laws (Cádiz 1812, Art. 3).

The 1812 Constitution was abolished in 1814 but restored in 1820 under the same liberal political pressures that had helped bring it into being. In 1823, Spain again reverted to absolutism until passing the Royal Statute of 1834. Informed by the testimonials of attorneys and solicitors, this granted constitution shaped the first bicameral organization of parliament but bestowed it relatively little power. It was not seen as a true constitution but as a summons to the 1812 Cádiz.

The 1834 statute was succeeded by the constitution of 1837, a revised version of the 1812 document. It remained in place until a new conservative constitution emerged in 1845, which augmented absolutism by returning control over the Senate to the monarchy, restricting entry to congress, and omitting any reference to national sovereignty. This constitution remained in effect until the June 30, 1876, when King Alfonso XII of Spain convened the General Courts of the Spanish kingdom to promulgate the constitution that was in force during the Spanish Bourbon dynasty, and which introduced guidelines for civil and political rights.

On November 25, 1897, the Autonomic Constitution emerged, coming into effect on January 1, 1898. Among its main guidelines was the idea that all Spaniards are equal under the law, whether from or in Spain or its colonies (Cuba and Puerto Rico). This constitution was a last-ditch effort by Spain to thwart Cuba's War of Independence. The Autonomic Constitution recalled the Cuban liberal constitutionalist Félix Varela's petitioning of Spain in 1811. It remained in force until the signing of the peace treaty between the United States and Spain in 1898.

Four Cuba-In-Arms Mambisa Constitutions: 1867–1897

The first constitution created by Cubans emerged from 1869 through 1897 and ruled only in the areas where the rebels opposing Spain had gained control. It was the first of four constitutions, called *Mambisa* constitutions in Cuba but known more formally as the Constitución de Guáimaro (April 10, 1869). It came into being when Cuban revolutionary hero Captain General Carlos Manuel de Céspedes was president of the Republic of Cuba in Arms and leader of the Ten Years' War (1868–1878). This marks the first official phase of the Cuban independence movement. Carlos M. de Céspedes wanted a free and independent Cuba, but the proposed constitution had some similarities with the U.S. Constitution that not all the rebels liked. The Guáimaro Constitution supported the insurgency against Spanish rule and was followed by three more *Mambisa* constitutions: Baraguá (1878), Jimaguayú (1895), and La Yaya (1897).

The Guáimaro Constitution was the outcome of insurgency against Spanish rule, yet one of the main problems de Céspedes faced was division among rebels living in different areas of the country. With the Guáimaro, therefore, the insurgents adopted a text that would link the various groups of resistance forces and establish a steering apparatus for the free areas. This first Cuban constitution, said to be "in arms," contained 29 articles organizing a single chamber called the Chamber of Representatives as the legislative body and power centre. This body appointed, and could depose, the president of the Republic and the commander in chief of the army. Still, its powers were limited by Article 28, which upheld inalienable rights such as people's right to freedom of worship, peaceful assembly, access to education, etc., and declared all inhabitants of the Republic equal (Article 24). It should nonetheless be noted that the Guáimaro consisted simply of statements guiding the enforcement of regulations and introduced no tenets.

On March 15, 1878, the second *Mambisa* constitution was drafted at Mangos de Baraguá, Cuba. A far cry from a formal Magna Carta, the Baraguá Constitution contained just six articles, laying out rules for organizing the dissident groups and giving a legal purpose to the ongoing revolution; it contained no tenets or guidelines other than independence. The Baraguá Constitution remained in force until the start of the next acute phase of the war on February 24, 1895, and the associated need for legalization and institutionalization of the revolution. Such factors motivated the third *Mambisa*, the Constitution of Jimaguayú (September 16, 1895). It consisted of 24 articles and is recognized for the unique structure it gave government.

The Jimaguayú Constitution organized a government council as the administrative and legislative authority. The council consisted of a president, vice-president, and structured four secretary of state offices to deal with war and social, foreign, and home affairs. It had a reform clause, self-imposing a two-year provisional duration under which—even if independence had not yet been obtained—the Assembly of Representatives would have to extend the constitution or approve a new one.

The fourth *Mambisa* constitution was signed and promulgated at La Yaya on October 29, 1897. Consisting of 48 articles, the La Yaya Constitution was enriched by the legal and political experience of the previous three *Mambisa* constitutions. It was the first to contain a dogmatic part embodying a set of precepts for citizen rights. The La Yaya gave all powers to an Assembly of Representatives located at Santa Cruz del Sur. Although this assembly never ruled on the validity (or not) of the La Yaya Constitution, its abrogation was given by changes to the form and structure of the state management mechanism and apparatus, which were made with no reference to the La Yaya Constitution. This constitution was somewhat surreptitiously terminated on November 25, 1897, less than three months before the notorious sinking of the battleship *Maine*.

The ensuing U.S. intervention in the Cuban War of Independence had other impacts on the Cuban legal system. Since Cuba was under Spanish sovereignty, Spain's Autonomic Constitution (1897) governed the Cuban territory except for the areas occupied by the Mambí army, which was ruled by the Constitution of La Yaya. Meanwhile, the government in Havana was directed by U.S. military leaders stationed in Cuba and by U.S. president

McKinley. At the same time, Santiago de Cuba was under the constitution of a U.S. Army major general, Leonard Wood. Its validity stretched from October 20 to December 31, 1898.

Known as the Wood or Santiago Constitution, it can hardly be considered a constitution. It was an instrument to safeguard personal rights during the U.S. occupation through guarantees. The Wood constitution at Santiago contained 10 sections organizing a body of laws to regulate certain rights, such as the right to peaceful assembly, to religious freedom, to be equal under the law, to a fair trial, to not be forced to testify against oneself, to a bail hearing, and to the privilege of habeas corpus, along with protections for private property, business, and freedom of speech (Wood, 1898).

Republican/Neo-colonial Phase (1901–1959)

Later, during the Republican or Neo-colonial phase (1901–1959), features of common law, the predominant system in the United States, were transferred and incorporated into Cuba under U.S. power in the archipelago. Some of the first norms introduced during this phase were of U.S. origin. For example, the Platt Amendment granted but also became the condition for U.S. military withdrawal from the island. With the Platt Amendment, the U.S. circumvented its war resolution, as per the Teller Amendment (1898), which had been passed before the Spanish-American War, to preclude any potential "disposition of intention to exercise sovereignty, jurisdiction, or control over said island except for pacification thereof" and to guarantee Cuban rights to self determination won through sovereignty. In other words, "to leave the government and control of the island to its people" (Teller Amendment, 1898). Despite this, Guantánamo Bay has remained under U.S. control against Cuba's sovereign wishes since 1903.

It was under these new conditions and through Military Order No. 181—issued by the Military Government of the Island of Cuba on May 20, 1902—that the Constitution of the Republic of Cuba was proclaimed, along with its constitutional appendix. The date of the 1901 Constitution's coming into force was banned from post-revolutionary Cuban historical writings, unnecessarily in the author's opinion. It was decided that the proscription of this date would constitute an act of resistance against U.S. coercion during the creation of Cuba's first constitution as a sovereign nation. The Platt Amendment was also designed to wipe the U.S. slate clean, so to speak, with its provision for a sweeping retroactive approval of any military interventions undertaken in Cuba by the U.S. during the Spanish-American War.

The Platt Amendment gave the U.S. neocolonial power and domination over the Republic of Cuba. The amendment contained eight articles, all with direct bearing on Cuban sovereignty, but the first was subtly ironic and richly contradictory to the United States' own purposes. It prohibited the Government of Cuba from entering into any treaty or other agreement with a foreign power that could undermine or tend to undermine the independence of Cuba or in any way authorize or allow any foreign power or powers to obtain by colonization or for military or naval purposes or otherwise, settlement in or control over any portion of the island.

The terms of the Platt Amendment obliged the Cuban government to authorize continued U.S. intervention for the preservation of Cuban independence, as well as the maintenance of an adequate government for the protection of lives, property, and individual liberty (Art. 3). Among its other impacts, the Platt Amendment set the formal stage for continued "occupation" of Guantanamo Bay following the war: "the Government of Cuba will sell or lease to the United States the necessary lands for coal bunkers or naval stations in certain determined points that will be agreed with the President of the United States" (Platt, Art. 7, 1903).

In other ways, the 1901 Constitution was quite progressive for the day. It established a mechanism for defending the constitution and enforcing citizen rights by giving the Supreme Court (par. 4, article 83) authority to rule on the constitutionality of laws, decrees, and regulations. It formulated broad civic freedoms in a section of guaranteed rights divided into three sections: individual rights taking minorities into account, right to suffrage (all males over 21 years of age), and the suspension of certain constitutional guarantees for people in prison. However, Gerardo Machado managed a constitutional reform in 1928 amending the 1901 Constitution to lengthen the presidential term up to a total of six years, clearly in the aim of extending his tyrannical power. Machado favoured a policy of U.S. investment, which brought about the age-old outcome of foreign success on the island at the expense of the Cuban masses. Subsequent constitutional reforms were enacted in 1934 and 1935, the most significant being the right to female suffrage under Decree 13 (January 2, 1934).

The mass resistance to Machado's tyranny and to ongoing U.S. political and economic power in Cuba stirred feelings of nationalism among Cubans, orienting thought even further away from the U.S. "free"-market system. The wealthy Machado ruled until 1933 when he was deposed through a general strike led by then U.S. Assistant Secretary of State Sumner Welles. Machado fled the island, seeking refuge in the United States. Welles supported the election of Carlos Manuel de Céspedes (junior) and himself ended up wielding much of the power in the country. This period of Cuban history exemplifies the paradox between the idealism of Roosevelt's Good Neighbour Policy, which brought about the abrogation of the Platt Amendment, and the well-entrenched effects of U.S. hegemony in Cuba. During this period the Spanish Civil Code was in effect, with the influence of Anglo-Saxon law seen in supreme court judgments especially in civil and family matters. The precepts and provisions of the 1901 Constitution were restored under Decree-Law 1298 in 1933 (August 24). While this constitutional law put a theoretical spotlight on civics and mechanisms for the guarantee and defence of rights, it also supported continued domination by the U.S. power in Cuba.

The Constitution of 1940 and the Recognition of Cubanness

At a celebrated convening of the Constituent Assembly, a new constitutional text was adopted in the Republic of Cuba on July 1, 1940. Enacted on October 10, one of its most progressive innovations was the human rights provisions contained in Titles IV to VII. Under Fundamental Rights (Title IV), the first section regulates individual or civil as well as political rights and the right to suffrage (Title VII). It includes the same civil and political rights as the 1901 Constitution but with greater guarantees through criminal sanctions for offenders.

The 1940 Constitution also recognized a new number of so-called second-generation (i.e., economic, social, and cultural) rights by regulating the right to work and defending workers' rights, social security, social assistance, and paid vacations, among others. It provided education and protection for women and children as well as limiting foreign ownership. It was imbued with the spirit of nationalism and influenced by the ideology espoused by Fernando Ortiz's theory of transculturation and the idea of Cubanness. These factors, more than any constitution or legal system, are what made national unity possible in Cuba. The 1940 Constitution also instituted a court of constitutional and social guarantees (aka the Constitutional Court), which coincided with the thoughts of the day but dealt a harsh blow to the nation by ruling in favour of constitutional statutes promulgated by the tyrant Fulgencio Batista following his military coup of March 10, 1952.

From that moment until the triumph of the Revolution in 1959, Cuba suffered one of the bloodiest tyrannies in its history under the U.S.-backed Batista. While the extent to which even the most basic of human rights were trampled under the Batista dictatorship will never be fully known, it is true to say the social guarantees under the 1940 Constitution were disregarded and violated by the Batista government, proving it insufficient to protect the rights of the Cuban masses.

Revolutionary Phase: 1959–Present

With the triumph of the Revolution in 1959, a sovereign Cuba still faced U.S. hegemony and was in dire need of strategic international alliances to guarantee national sovereignty while forging the envisioned humanist state model. With the Cuban economy still dependent on sugar sales in the immediate post-Revolution period, the U.S reneged at the last minute on the purchase of its annual sugar quota. When the Soviet Union agreed to assume the quota, Cuba became progressively more inclined to adopt a political system compatible with that of its new strategic international ally. Hence, the adoption of a socialist legal system that presumed state ownership of property was in line with the envisioned political system and other legislative changes supporting socio-economic equity that would ultimately transform the entire Cuban social reality after 1959.

During this time, many legal practices were eliminated or fell into disuse for the simple and naïve reason that they belonged to what is commonly known as **bourgeois law**, which went against the humanistic bent of Cuban ideology by prioritizing and privileging bourgeois rights. Roman law was eradicated from university curricula, and even law career training was not offered for two consecutive school years in the first half of the 1960s, along with many other university subjects such as commercial law, financial law, and the study of jurisprudence as a source of law. The wealthy Spanish and Italian tradition of doctrine was also rejected. In other words, history, philosophy, and everything related to the private law of the market system were considered futile areas of study by those interested in the rise of a socialist legal system. In the author's opinion, such studies would have been fruitful and of comparative value to law students.

The fall of the socialist bloc in the early 1990s opened the door to a new era for the Cuban legal system, which has expanded in different directions ever since, including certain pro-market economic reforms related to corporations, joint ventures, small businesses, independent workers, and foreign investment. The result is the **Cuban socialist legal system**—an authentic and flexible legal model of Cuban heritage greatly influenced by the Roman-French tradition within the normative framework of a socialist legality.

Cuban Socialist Law

The Cuban legal system has long been cast simply as "socialist," but a more accurate term for it would be **Cuban socialist legality** because its approach is markedly different from all preceding historical "socialist" models (Zhidkov, Chirkin and Yudin, 1980). The Cuban socialist legality offers an indispensable instrument with which to restrict private capitalistic forms.

Taking into account that socialist law is transformative because it translates human values into legal norms that reflect the sovereign will of the people, democratism, equal rights of citizens—and that stress the relation between citizen rights and responsibilities, legality and humanist ideology—the Cuban socialist legal model can be articulated along the following guidelines: the law is a fundamental (ideological) principle of the state; the democratic and legislative functions are carried out via mass social organizations; there is no theoretical division between public law and private law, between the rule of law and individual social relations, as in the sense of bourgeois law (e.g., freedom of contract). The Cuban legal system, as compared with other legal systems, is thus less independent from and greatly influenced by the political system. In Cuba, the political system underlies the social system and interacts with the economic system and other non-political elements of the sociopolitical state structure differently that in most other Western nations.

The socialist legal model developed by the Soviets rejected everything related to bourgeois law, without realizing that many legal institutions have more to do with relations between private persons than with the political system. The no-private-only-public concept of law kept them from seeing that the relations between natural persons, whether patrimonial, family, or other, necessarily belong to the category of private law, since the state is not involved except in fulfilling specific functions, such as protecting a minor through the Office of the Prosecutor or upholding individual rights. No matter how you look at it, the fundamental characteristic of all socialist law remains the same: the normative act is the main formal source of the law, but Cuban-derived precepts regarding social relations are what underlie and fortify the Cuban socialist legality.

Thus, the Cuban socialist legal system gradually took shape, pushing aside earlier Cuban legal processes derived from the Spanish tradition. Over the years, and because of the fall of European socialism, some aspects of our legal system have been modified. The unique and mysterious feature of the Cuban legal system lies in its embodiment of the legal-technical basis of the Roman-French system but within the transformative, socio-political mechanism of socialist law.

January 3, 1959: Prioritizing Human Rights in Cuba

When the Cuban Revolution triumphed on January 1, 1959, it became imperative to re-establish constitutional order, the rule of law, and address the human rights issues created by the 1952 coup d'état. To such ends, on January 3, 1959, a provisional government was established at a session held in the library of the Universidad de Oriente at Santiago de Cuba, with the Cuban judge Manuel Urrutia Lleó being declared President of the Council of Ministers. On January 5, President Urrutia Lleó arrived in Havana to announce the necessary amendments to the 1940 Constitution considering the revolutionary process, starting with the departure of Batista and the dissolution of his government, congress, emergency courts, and the Criminal Chamber of the Supreme Court. This provisional text transferred constitutional authority (i.e., the legislative function) from the Congress of the Republic to the Council of Ministers and the executive function to the president of the Republic.

A new prime minister was appointed on January 5, 1959. José Miró Cardona worked intently with the Council of Ministers, adapting constitutional norms to the new political scenario through reforms to the 1940 constitutional texts that became law through the official adoption of the republic's Fundamental Law on February 7, 1959. The precepts of the 1940 Constitution maintained their actual validity under this new structure but with major modifications regarding the structure and fundamental functions of the state's powers and concerning the constitutional relations of central and local authorities. Fidel Castro would come to rule by decree as prime minister under this law from February 16, 1959, until adoption of the 1976 Cuban Constitution.

The Fundamental Law of 1959 restored the 1940 Constitution, amended to meet the socioeconomic and political agenda of the Cuban Revolution. In the first section, Chapter IV maintained the fundamental rights designation under the progressiveness principle recognized in the 1901 and again in the 1940 Constitution and dedicated its first section to individual or civil and political rights. The validity of the Court of Constitutional and Social Guarantees, instituted thereby in 1940, to hear and decide on questions of constitutionality, was maintained in principle until subsequent amendments to the Fundamental Law of 1959 modified constitutional control. The law of constitutional reform (LRC 1960) then eliminated the Court of Constitutional and Social Guarantees as an independent chamber and made it a chamber of the Supreme Court. This new structure was maintained until the coming into force of Law 1250, June 1973, approved by the Council of Ministers, which created Cuba's single system of courts and definitively eliminated the constitutional-jurisdictional control model.

Nevertheless, in the present Constitution of 2019, this constitutional-jurisdictional control model is included in the court law being revised for its approval and implementation by the ANPP.

During the provisional period the right to vote was not put into practice since elections were neither held nor needed. Given the popular nature of the Cuban Revolution, the people accepted this along with other limitations deemed necessary given the circumstances under which the country was preparing to build a new state machine. On February 24, 1976, Cuba's socialist constitution, approved in the days preceding through a democratic popular referendum, was proclaimed. A commission appointed by the Revolutionary Government's higher governing bodies and the Communist Party of Cuba (PCC), articulated the social organization's basic postulates and drew up the preliminary drafts. This constitution's developmental process was characterized by broad popular participation, from discussions over the first draft leading to proposed amendments to various articles, through to the final version ratified by national referendum. It was approved by 97.7 percent of the 98 percent of the Cuban population of voting age who voted.

The Constitution of 1976 recognized a broad set of individual rights and freedoms that guaranteed first-generation rights and second-generation rights. The constitutional text was amended in 1978 to rename Isla de Pinos (i.e., Isle of Pines) Isla de la Juventud (i.e., Isle of Youth) when the XI World Festival of Youth and Students was held in Havana that same year. The 1976 Constitution was reformed in 1992 (LRC 1992) due to changes in the international sphere related to the fall of the Soviet and eastern European blocs. The amendments formed part of a constitutional reform law approved earlier by the National Assembly of People's Power. This expanded the democratic character of the Cuban state, made it secular, and introduced socio-economic and political transformations making certain corporations and joint ventures legal.

These socio-economic and political changes formed part of the measures adopted to overcome the economic crisis of the Special Period. After all, the Soviet socialist bloc had long accounted for most of Cuba's trade. These changes, made during the Special Period in Times of Peace, aimed to enable Cuba to continue fulfilling its social and economic goals and reinsert itself once again into world market relations in compliance with recommendations of the IV Congress of the Communist Party of Cuba. In Cuba, the country's development, and setbacks are analyzed at the annual Congress of the Communist Party, which then makes recommendations to guide the state to take the necessary measures. The National Assembly of People's Power is the body that approves the constitution, laws, decrees, etc.

Due in part to persistent hostility by the United States towards Cuba and the real threat of subsequent attempts at economic domination, the constitution was again amended in 2002. Key amendments impacted business by broadening the scope of foreign investment in Cuba and legalization of joint ventures involving foreign parties. The 1992 amendments also gave citizens the right to fight, including with arms, any acts being against the political, economic and social order of Cuba. To this same end, Cuban socialism was made irrevocable, having "demonstrated its ability to transform the country and create an entirely new and just society" (Art. 3). While these amendments were not subject to a vote or referendum, public consultations demonstrated an almost unanimous widespread acceptance. The democratic nature of the People's Power Assemblies must not be underestimated and Cuba certainly passes the test of an informed citizenry.

Cuban Law Today

Based on the above, the Cuban legal system has been acquiring greater independence and has proven capable of theoretically separating private law from public law. As highlighted in Box 7.2, the Cuban legal system is a product of Fernando Ortiz's legal transculturation. The laws created by the ANPP remain the primary formal source of the Law. Still, regulatory branches for private international law and commercial law have been reinstated, consequently allowing for the creation of corporations. An important first step in this direction was the constitutional acceptance of joint ventures and the entry into force in 2014 of a foreign investment law (Law 118), which ensures investor guarantees and dedicated tax schemes, as well as procedures to resolve disputes.

Box 7.2: Processes of Fernando Ortiz's Legal Transculturation

As noted in the Preamble to the 2019 Constitution, the Cuban nation is guided by the most advanced revolutionary, anti-imperialist, Cuban-Marxist, Latin American, and universal thought, by the ideal and example of Martí and Fidel, as well as by the social emancipation ideas of Marx, Engels, and Lenin.

The state substantiates its political decisions under the law by the principles that underlie Cuban socialist legality. This means that before making a political decision, the Cuban state verifies its legality with respect to our public law and this regulates the functioning of the state. The Cuban legal system is constantly in flux but governed by certain features of the Romano-French system within the broader fundamental principles of a socialist legality adapted to our unique political system and social characteristics and goals. In Cuba, popular debates are encouraged and take place at the local level as well as provincially and nationally, such as leading up to the national referendum for the 2019 Constitution and the subsequent Family Code reform for examples.

Law Formation and the Cuban Judicial System

Cuban law, in general, contains various legal branches regulating specific aspects of social life. To understand the meaning and objectives of a nation's law, one must look to the underlying legal system and its formal sources. The notion of formal sources of law is complex and increasingly the subject of debate. The legal doctrine of Emilio Biasco (2012), a Uruguayan law professor at the University of Montevideo, refers to **formal sources of law**, those from which the law derives its source and validity, as the "set of rules that make up the legal system and that are applied to the specific cases that occur in the legally relevant social sectors." This means that both the conflict (Marxist) and consensus (Western) models of justice play out in tandem in Cuba. In Cuba, professionals and non-professionals work together to apply the law, with lay judges weighing the facts and professional judges applying the law.

Cuban law professor Julio Fernández Bulté (2005, p. 44) identifies the formal sources of law as the procedures, methods, mechanisms, etc., that give rise to the law or legitimize it if they are recognized and empowered by the rules of recognition, adjudication, and change. For Bulté, the formal sources of Cuban law do not include jurisprudence or legal doctrine; rather, they are as follows:

- Custom.
- Judicial precedent (either the jurisprudence of the Roman-French (civil) system, or the precedent of the Anglo-Saxon common/case law precedent).
- Normative act.

The legal doctrine of the eminent Chilean law professor Jorge Hübner (1976), however, characterized formal sources as forms or channels that embody positive law and allow it to manifest in the social sphere. In this case, formal sources are simply the forms of expression of the law: legislation, custom, sentence, and, according to some, the opinions of certain writers and international treaties.

As constitutional law expert Professor Martha Prieto Valdés (1999) has long pointed out in Cuba, opinions and agreements of the Governing Council of the Supreme People's Court represent mandatory regulations arising from certain interpretive guidelines to which all courts in the country must integrate and adapt (Valdés, 1999). Therefore, while jurisprudence is not theoretically recognized as a source of law in Cuban legal practice, it is used informally within a framework of the interpretive guidelines emitted by the Council of Government of the People's Supreme Court, which create peremptory or mandatory norms. Such judicial interpretation ultimately manifests in jurisprudence while setting legal guidelines (Bruzón Viltres and Tamayo Blanco, 2014). Through the Council of the Supreme Court, the Council of State "gives instructions of a general character to the courts" (art. 122, m, Const. 2019) and this, according to many, constitutes a formal source of law.

Going back through Cuban law experts Biasco and Valdés to Hübner, we see different theoretical takes on the formal sources of law. The perspectives range from considering only the normative act, as per normative-legal theory, to considering all aspects of legal creation including academic legal doctrine. Examples in Cuba include the laws created by the National Assembly of People's Power (i.e., the Cuban parliament), the decree-laws of the Council of State, or the decrees of the Council of Ministers, which have force of law under the Constitution.

The Cubans working in the criminal law branch of our legal system consider neither precedent (aka jurisprudence in common law systems) nor legal doctrine as formal sources of law (Quiróz Pírez, 1999). This is why we say that judges have less authority to shape the law in civil systems than under common law. Civil law systems give ultimate power to State statutes. It bears repeating that, in Cuba, the normative act is the only formal source of the law. It signifies the set of steps, procedures, mechanisms and authorities or bodies that create legal norms and establish legal precepts as a conscious transformative action of the Cuban state apparatus.

Interpreted in the courts, the normative act is the law par excellence, the formal source of Cuban socialist legality. Normative acts issued by the ANPP constitute primary source legislation or statutory law in Cuba. The constitution, however, is the supreme norm of the state, the highest legal norm, because it defines and limits who makes the law (ANPP, the legislative authority), who enforces the law (executive authority), who interprets the law and how (judicial authority), and establishes the rights and freedoms of Cuban citizens, as shown in Box 7.3. The normative act itself embodies creation phases that arose from the 19th century's trend toward

> **Box 7.3: Cuban Parliament (National Assembly of People's Power [ANPP])**
>
> Central to the socio-legal and political apparatus, the ANPP, in the exercise of its power:
>
> - Elects the President and Vice President of the Republic;
> - Elects its own President, Vice President, and Secretary;
> - Elects the members of the Council of State;
> - Designates, at the proposal of the President of the Republic, the Prime Minister as well as the Deputy Prime Minister and other members of the Council of Ministers, which is the supreme power of the State;
> - Chooses the President of the People's Supreme Court, the Attorney General of the Republic, and the Comptroller General of the Republic;
> - Chooses the President and the other members of the National Electoral Council;
> - Chooses the vice presidents and the magistrates of the People's Supreme Court as well as the lay judges of this body;
> - Chooses the deputy attorneys general and deputy comptrollers general of the Republic; and
> - Revokes or substitutes the people it has chosen or designated (Paraphrase, Article 109, Constitution of the Republic of Cuba (2019).

constitutional establishment of the essential lawmaking steps in greater or lesser detail. In other words, the procedure required to ensure the legitimacy of the legislative function is a testimonial to the democratic aspect of the Cuban legislative process and the popular participation guarantees to which it must respond.

It is thus fair to point out that all these creation phases are manifest in the law as the highest normative act of the state, but this also requires explanation. In Cuba, the democratic mechanism is embodied in the network of Assemblies of People's Power and based on the unity of power principle (see *Basic Principles* below). It manifests through the top tier of this network, the National Assembly of People's Power, which is Cuba's unicameral legislative parliament.

The six essential phases in the Cuban Parliament's lawmaking process are as follows (Fernández Bulté, p. 65):

- A legislative initiative is presented to the Cuban Parliament;
- Discussion of the proposed law;
- Voting and approval;
- Promulgation;
- Publication; and
- Entry into force.

A nation's legislative bodies have different forms and titles worldwide, such as congress, chamber, assembly, diet, or courts. In Cuba, the legislative body (i.e., the parliament) is the National Assembly of People's Power (ANPP). As in other nations, before being proposed as an act, a law is just an idea circulating in Cuban society and/or government until it is enacted by parliament.

As under the constitutional laws of most countries, popular legislative initiative is possible in Cuba, based on a petition signed by at least 10,000 citizens of legal voting age and status (k). The judicial initiative is adjudicated in section (g) to the Council of Government of the People's Supreme Court's in matters related to the administration of justice (g) and the Attorney General for issues within its competence. The Constitution (2019) also grants the executive initiative (d) to the Council of Ministers, which is "the maximum executive and administrative organ and it constitutes the Government of the Republic" (Art. 133).

Once the proposed act has been initiated within the legislative body, a period of debate, analysis, and discussion commences. The approval phase of a law, of course, derives from a favourable vote by a relevant number of legislators deemed necessary for each initiative. The proposed act then changes from a projected law into a written law as recognized by the legislative body.

Legislative voting takes several forms in Cuba: with a show of legislator hands, normally with credentials in sight; by calling legislators one by one to voice their stand; and finally, under certain circumstances, by secret ballot on which legislators explain their positions. All legislators are asked to exercise their right to vote. But they also have the right to abstain. It is worth mentioning that legislative voting is one of the least publicized aspects of the functioning of the sessions of the assemblies of People's Power at the municipal and national levels, but the results are always made public.

In Cuba, the promulgation mechanism is a function of the president of the National Assembly of People's Power, under article 111(f), which gives him the responsibility of signing decrees having the force of law and agreements adopted by the National Assembly of People's Power and the Council of State, as required, and to issue the publication of decrees having the force of law and agreements from both organs in the *Official Gazette of the Republic*.

The publication phase of the normative act after promulgation by the executive power or, as in Cuba, by the same legislative body or its president, must be made public to ensure that the population and national depositaries have full knowledge of the new normative act, which enters into force the day it is published in the official *Gazette*. There is also a requirement for

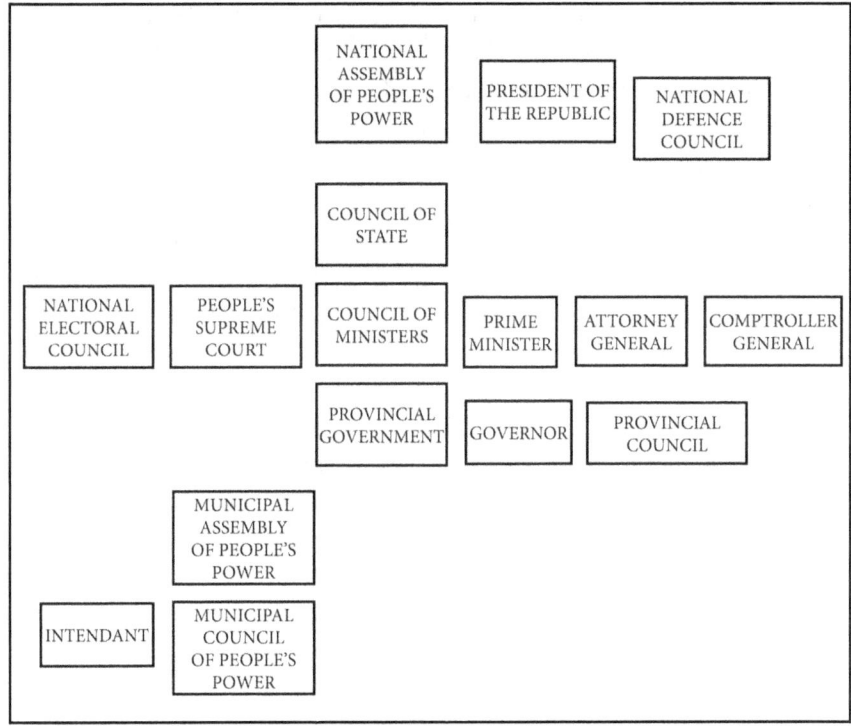

Figure 7.1. Structure of the State
Source: Based on a graphic prepared by the National Assembly of People's Power (ANPP) of the Republic of Cuba (the Cuban parliament).

the date of entry into force to be stipulated in each act (Article 165).

The Cuba Constitution sets out no remedy for any omission of the date of entry into force; however, it is generally accepted that entry into force would be the day after its publication in the *Gazette*. Under the constitution of the Republic of Cuba, the laws, decrees having the force of laws, executive decrees, resolutions, and other general interest provisions to all citizens and stakeholders must be made public through publication in the *Official Gazette of the Republic*. Once a law has been published in the *Gazette*, ignorance does not excuse noncompliance (Civil Code, Art. 2).

It is also noteworthy that the ANPP is responsible for ensuring the constitutionality of the law. The National Assembly of People's Power has the authority to revoke any laws, presidential decrees, decrees, agreements, general provisions, etc., found to contradict the Constitution (Art. 108, Constitution, 2019), even if dictated by an organ hierarchically superior (Art. 108, g). As shown in Figure 7.1 above, in terms of safeguarding the sanctity of the constitutional norms, the National Assembly of People's Power is the top of the state hierarchy.

As shown in Figure 7.1, the elected bodies are the ANPP (National Assembly of People's Power) and the AMPP (Municipal Assembly of People's Power). The ANPP is elected for a period of five years and is the body that elects, from its members, the Council of State, the organ that represents the ANPP between sessions, executes its agreements, and performs the other functions that the Constitution and the law attributes to it (Article 107, Const. 2019). As an administrative body and representing the government of the republic, the ANPP also elects the president and the vice-president of the republic, the Council of Ministers, and at the proposal of the president of the republic, designates the prime minister, a position added after 1976 (Article 109, Const. 2019).

Among its duties, the ANPP chooses the president of the People's Supreme Court, the attorney general and the comptroller general of the republic, the National Electoral Council, and the National Defence Council (Art. 109 Const. 2019), among other important organs of the state. These superior state bodies issue different regulatory acts: the National Assembly issues laws (normative acts), the Council of State issues decree-laws, the Council of Ministers issues decrees, and the president of the republic issues decrees that have the force of law. The other state bodies issue lower regulatory provisions, namely resolutions, agreements, opinions, instructions, etc.

Basic Principles of the Cuban Court System Today

As is quite well known, Cuba prides itself on extremely low rates of illiteracy and infant mortality but also on measures of public safety. One of the mainstays of public safety has been the Cuban court system, which has not been affected by the tendency toward corruption seen in other sectors of the country, such as the popular gastronomy and currency collector shops.

Cuba remains faithful, theoretically, to the retributive justice model and has adopted very few elements of the consensus model (aka restorative justice), although alternatives do exist in relation to youth justice and also find expression through the overall emphasis on educational and work-related options in general. As Cuban constitutional law expert Dr. Martha Prieto Valdés (2020) has pointed out, the 2019 Constitution offers several new guarantees, two of which bear on the justice model. The first guarantee is the right for people to settle their disputes using alternate methods of conflict resolution (Art. 93) and the second is the right to access and request corrections and non-disclosure of personal information stored in public registries, archives, or other databases (Art. 97). As Dr. Valdés accurately suggests, however, such guarantees will be fully implemented once further legal development has bee carried out, including a review of the appropriate mechanisms to settle a dispute and the effectiveness of such procedures.

Cuban citizens also now enjoy constitutional rights against undue harm, prejudice, and any rights violation, and can make a complaint with the court to obtain restitution, including redress or indemnity related to individual harm or prejudice by organs of the State (Arts., 98 and 99). Dr. Valdés (2020), who has taught several generations of jurists at the University of Havana, received the Carlos Manuel de Céspedes National Law Award in 2019 in recognition of a lifetime dedicated to developing the legal sciences in Cuba.

The 2019 constitution defines the function of imparting justice as stemming from the Cuban people and exercised on their behalf by the People's Supreme Court and other courts established by the legal system (Art. 147). As with all the courts, the primary formal source of law for the Supreme Court is the normative act. The Supreme Court does not exercise legislative initiative or regulatory power but, through its Governing Council, makes decisions and dictates norms with which all lower courts must comply; this is to standardize interpretation of the written laws (Art 148, 2019). Supreme Court decisions handed down in the form of sentences are final; they cannot be revoked by any state organ, except following the Council of State's mandatory review of any death penalty sanction. Box 7.4 lists the sources of law in Cuba.

Constitutional law establishes the objective principles of the judiciary's activity and regulates the organization of courts: supreme, provincial, and municipal courts and the civil and administrative tribunals and the extent of their jurisdiction, competence, and powers (and how to exercise them); requirements for judges, including the participation of lay judges and how they are elected, and the causes and procedures for revocation or cessation of practice.

Another essential element of the court system is its functional independence from any other organization, such as the local organs of people's power at the municipal levels, and its hierarchical subordination to the National Assembly of People's Power and the Council of State. It is worth noting that one of the cornerstone principles of the organization of the Cuban state is the unity of power, as opposed to the three-fold separation of government power exercised in most other states.

While the Cuban state does have the same three branches (i.e., legislative, executive, and the judiciary), the line between executive and regulatory power may seem blurred. This may make the division of powers between these government branches unclear; however, there is no division of powers under the Cuban socialist legality. As Dr. Valdés (2020) so appropriately argued during the 2018 debates around the constitutional

> **Box 7.4: Sources of Law in Cuba**
>
>
>
> Constitution (2019)
>
> ANPP – LAW
>
> COUNCIL OF STATE – Decree-Laws
>
> PRESIDENT OF THE REPUBLIC – Presidential Decrees
>
> COUNCIL OF MINISTERS – Decrees
>
> MINISTERS AND INSTITUTIONS – Resolutions
>
> The "law" regulates the procedure to make these duties effective (Paraphrase, Article 9, Constitution 2019).
>
>

reform project, Cuba has a division of *functions*, not a division of powers. These functions are embedded in the state bodies because there is only one power in Cuba—the people's power.

As discussed earlier, one of the gaps in the Cuban judicial system is the lack of reference to the formal sources of law in the Constitution. It simply states that we must follow the "law" (aka normative act). But Cuban law is also more than the normative act. Other competent bodies deliver decrees with the force of law, or decree-laws, and resolutions, etc. All told, however, legislative initiative and regulatory authority are exercised through the ANPP's Governing Council; and magistrates and judges in their function of imparting justice are independent and do not owe obedience except to the law (Art. 150, Const. 2019).

Renowned University of Havana professor Dr. Andry Matilla Correa (2004) attributes the Cuban legal system's unique nature to the lack of a legal rule or precept that expressly establishes the sources of national law and, in turn, the hierarchy between them. Indeed, a question as central and necessary as the system of legal sources, on which the juridical construction of a country is based, is not resolved positively in the Cuban case, bringing serious upheavals and difficulties to attempts at theoretical and practical systematization.

Likewise, Cuba's highest judicial branch of government, and court of last resort, the People's Supreme Court, ruled that vitally important legal norms such as the constitution or the substantive law itself are limited to establishing the bodies with normative powers. There is no precept in our legal system that lists their sources or their hierarchical relation (Supreme court ruling, 2006, No. 219). Yes, the normative act (i.e., the "law") is considered the only official formal source of law in Cuba, but this is not always the case: for example, under the Cuban Civil Code (Art. 322), goods subject to the sale must comply with quality and quantity, size, and weight to the provisions laid out in the legal regulations or, failing that, to custom generally or in relation to the location. Whenever parties are in conflict about what law is applicable, the arbitral tribunal determines it by applying the rules of international private law forum and, where appropriate, according to the rules, principles and custom of international trade and commerce (Decree-Law 250, Art. 30).*

The limitation posed by constitutional Article 150 (formerly Art. 122 in the 1976/2002 constitutions) mandating judges to follow the law†may, in this author's opinion, have come about through a misnomer. In effect, this principle was originated by the European bourgeoisie in the 18th century in making a general reference to the law. This means it was not referring specifically to the written legal norm but to the law overall, which would include previous court judgments, legal custom and, in many countries, legal doctrine as a supplementary but equally formal source.

Regardless, Cuba decided to base rulings on the written law, the legal norm alone; and, no matter how Marxist we may be, we still basically have a normative practice. More clearly, decision-making for the Cuban jurist is to follow the "law" or normative act to the exclusion of other sources that exist and might contribute positively to certain cases. Of course, being philosophically Marxist in theory, we still have a positivist legal practice; however, philosophically, we are against this.

Let us look to the Spanish Civil Code (Art. 117:1) for clarity. Justice emanates from the people and is administered on their behalf by judges and magistrates. It is independent, irremovable, and liable and subject only to the rule of law. But this does not stop the Spanish Civil Code from regulating the sources of law (Art. 1) as follows: Where the sources of the Spanish legal system are statutes, custom, and general legal principles, case law shall complement the legal system by means of the doctrine repeatedly

---

* Just to mention two, article 322 of the Civil Code: The goods that are subject to sale must be adjusted, both in their quality and in their quantity, size, and weight, to the provisions of the legal regulations or, failing that, to the custom or use of the location; and article 30 of Decree-Law 250: When the parties, in their case, have not agreed on the applicable law, the arbitral tribunal applies the law determined by the rules of Private International Law of the place of the forum, as well as, where appropriate, the uses and principles of international trade.

†Article 122: Judges, in their function of imparting justice, are independent and owe obedience only to the law.

upheld by the Supreme Court in its interpretation and application of statutes, custom and general legal principles.

In other words, no duty of obedience to the law can disqualify the rest of the sources. For example, any decision by the Cuban Supreme Court high forum (2006) determining that the Constitution's vitally important normative force or the substantive law itself is limited to establishing the bodies having normative powers. Since there is no precept to list their sources, a material and indirect source of general principles of law is a binding force and does not infringe upon the principle of formal legality. Considering the general principles of law as a binding force does not violate the duty of obedience to the law, because those principles are part of the law, not brought about by political authority or by individual judicial discretion. Cuba's Supreme Court is correct, in our opinion, but unfortunately, this ruling is not a rule but an exception.

Other regulated principles concerning the work of the courts are related to the fact that compliance with verdicts is unavoidable by state organisms, economic and social entities, and the citizens; the collegiate form and upheld also by the accountability of the courts before the Assembly of People's Power.

Current Reform Trends

Since 2018, Cuban society has experienced significant transformations driven by changes in the legal order, which was long regarded as immutable. These transformations emerged in response to evolving social, political, and historical contexts. Allowing non-regulated economic activities resulted in the emergence of a petty bourgeoisie, which, although limited in almost all its mechanisms of development and consolidation, has had consequences that must be considered.

In good faith, Article 14 of the 1976 constitutional text declared that the economic system based on the socialist ownership of the means of production by all the people will prevail and that it suppresses phenomena related to man's exploitation by man. The principle of socialist distribution "of each according to his capacity, to each according to his work" was also in effect. This same sentiment is addressed in the preamble to the 2019 constitution. However, while the principle is not found in any of the articles, the absolute irrevocability of the socialist system is as re-affirmed in Article 229 of the 2019 constitutional law.

Similarly, certain autonomy is given to individuals, such as engaging in contracts, creating private documents to serve as evidence, and having the right to go to court to settle differences/conflicts. Mechanisms for these have been established but are not yet in wide use by citizens due to lack of knowledge, non-exigency, or permissibility issues in work centers. An example will help explain what I am saying. Today in Cuba, a worker hired by a private individual—let's say in a private restaurant—can sue his/her employer for violating certain rights; this was not previously allowed.

Some processes have also been democratized, and some bans eliminated, such as the sale of some properties (homes, cars, cell phones, etc.) and other bans related to migration. In other words, due to the imperative economic changes being carried out in Cuba, the Cuban legal sphere has expanded and is open to accommodating change.

These recent transformations have placed the Cuban state in the difficult position of anticipating previously unthinkable behavior, say people travelling abroad to import minor goods for local sale, especially clothing and footwear (a practice that has created an appealing black-market alternative to stores), unsanctioned economic activities such as cell phone recharges designed to allow transfer of minutes for cash, commissions from tenants and private taxi drivers for tourists, tips in all areas of the service industry, all of which had all been taking place for decades with no regulation.

In 2018, a process called constitutional reform began, ending with a new constitution's promulgation in 2019 following its ratification via referendum. A document outlining the details of the reform was made available to all citizens across the country, prompting local discussions and debates across the country and various media. The reform amounts to a legal revolution wrought through important changes, with transcendental implications for the citizens and society in general. The 2019 constitutional project initially eliminated all references to communism, except those appearing in the names of the party and youth political organization. However, when the point became the topic of lively public debate, the term was re-incorporated in precepts. The word "politics" was also incorporated (Art. 5) to define the Communist Party as the supreme political force in Cuban society and the state. This was in response to requests by several Cuban scholars to eliminate perceived confusion between political and administrative functions.

In the realm of property, the inclusion of private property (this always had existed but was limited to personal property) means it encompasses "certain means of production" and there was also an extension of the definition of cooperative property, which was previously allowed only for agricultural goods.

Other changes regarding rights include an acceptance of dual citizenship, of same sex marriage (a controversial article was eliminated; the regulation of marriage (Article 37) no longer states it as a union between a man and a woman, as was the case in Article 36 (1976/2002)). These issues were widely discussed by all Cuban citizens as part of debates on final approval of the new Family Code. As well, the constitution set out a series of previously unidentified rights, namely to information, to honour, to life, to water, and to claim before the courts the restitution of rights violated by any branch of the government structure and obtain compensation.

Finally, the state structure will undergo complete change, with the creation of the positions of President of the Republic, Vice President, and Prime Minister at the national level; and of Governor, Provincial Council, and Mayor at the local level. This reflects influences of ancient traditions of the Spanish era and the neo-colonial era (i.e., the *Mambisa* constitutions) in some cases and of contemporary theories about the separation of the positions of head of state and head of government in others. Under the former constitution (1976; 2002 amend.), the President of the Council of State was both head of state and head of government. Under the new constitutional law, the Prime Minister is head of government, and the President of the Republic is head of state. The power structure is also changing significantly, with the removal of the Provincial Assembly of People's Power and the establishment of the Provincial Government of People's Power along with the position of Governor, who will be the executive administrative officer at the provincial level subject to controls by the National Assembly, the Council of State, the President of the Republic, the Council of Ministers, and its Prime Minister (Prieto Valdés, April 25, 2020).

Perhaps most significantly, a challenge can be foreseen in transitional provisions for the creation of a new electoral law, law of the courts, and modification of the rules of civil procedure and criminal proceedings, as well as a popular consultation for revisions to the 2002 statute of the Family Code (see Chapters 8; 10).

Conclusion

The process of legal transculturation continues to be recognized and celebrated by the Cuban population. This is evidenced by the numerous ground-breaking changes in the 2019 Constitution. These modifications were accompanied by changes to the Cuban socialist legality, making the Cuban legal system more unique and mysterious than ever. The new constitution reaffirms the 1976 Constitution's irrevocability provision safeguarding socialism, but excludes any mention of a future communist society. The Cuban socialist legality underlies a unique brand of socialism that will continue to be sustainable. This decision was ratified democratically through the extensive publication of the constitutional texts and public secret voting by most Cubans.

In sum, since 2010, the Cuban government has carried out a series of necessary reforms that generally represent a democratization of processes and services. These reforms collided with basic principles of the system, generating a constitutional anomaly resolved in part with the enactment of the 2019 Constitution. The process of constitutional reform initiated in 2018 resulted in changes in the sphere of citizen rights and to state organization. Still, the real challenge will be the development of complementary laws, and the adequacy of the Cuban socialist legality with respect to this genuinely revolutionary constitutional text.

These reforms have culminated in several changes at the economic, political, and state levels. Major changes to the structure of People's Power will be brought about by provisions in the constitutional law, such as eliminating the Provincial Assembly of People's Power in favour of Provincial Governments of People's Power and establishing the roles of Governor and Mayor. Another significant change is the creation of President of the Republic's position as head of state and the ensuing elimination of its dual personality in the past when the head of government and head of state were the same. The new constitution does not address important informal changes to the judicial system, such as some use of jurisprudence as precedent; however, this is a reality in Cuba that will likely be explored in years to come.

While the blurriness of the line between executive and regulatory power may make the division of powers between these government branches unclear to foreigners, it is important to note that ultimately there is no division of powers under the Cuban socialist legality. As the Cuban professor Pietra Valdes (2020) so appropriately argued during the 2018 debates around the constitutional reform project, Cuba has a division of functions, not a division of powers. These functions are deposited in the state bodies because there is only one power in Cuba, the people's power.

In terms of the Cuban judiciary, our dynamic has historically been subject to abrupt changes in the international sphere beyond the country's control that impact how we see and apply national law. In today's Cuba, the Romano-French and socialist systems are reflected in the different relationships and legal norms that sustain the state apparatus and citizens' actions. However, common law's influence within the current statutory law system in Cuba is another area for future investigation. Cuba's embrace of legal-political transculturation and innovation is one of the reasons our system continues to seem somewhat peculiar to the rest of the world.

In Cuba, our view of the normative act as the only formal source of law is an informal one, since there is no formal consensus on the sources of Cuban law. However, the increasing evidentiary use of jurisprudence and legal custom in Cuba has shaken up the old socialist design and is establishing a new, more complex, and more complete system to meet new needs. In Cuba, the basic principles behind the passing of laws are reflected in the regulations, adapting them to the particularities of a sovereign, socialist, and besieged nation. The Cuban socialist legal system aims to grant José Martí's wish, as expressed by Fidel at the end of the preamble to the Cuban Constitution of 1976: "I wish that the first law of our Republic be the devotion of the Cubans to the full dignity of man." With this wish, 150 years after our first *Mambisa* constitution was approved in Guáimaro on April 10, 1869, the Cuban people adopted the 2019 constitution through a popular referendum by public secret vote.

References

ANPP [National Assembly of People's Power]. (2021). Asamblea nacional del poder popular República de Cuba. ANPP Website. https://www.parlamentocubano.gob.cu/index.php/estadocubano/

Abreu Fernández, Alberto. (2009). *El derecho en el transporte marítimo*. 2nd ed. Havana, Cuba: Editorial Félix Varela.

Benessaieh, A. (2010). Multiculturalism, interculturality, transculturality. In Benessaieh, A. (ed.), *Amériques transculturelles–Transcultural Americas* (pp. 11–38). Ottawa: University of Ottawa Press.

Biasco, Emilio. (2012). *Apuntes sobre las fuentes del derecho*. Course materials for Public Law and Law 1. Montevideo, Uruguay: Universidad de la República.

Bruzón Viltres, C. J., and Tamayo Blanco, I. R. (2014). La jurisprudencia en Cuba: Reconocimiento dentro del sistema de fuentes del derecho y posibles consecuencias. *Boletín Mexicano De Derecho Comparado*, 47 (139): 251–83. https://doi.org/10.1016/S0041-8633(14)70506-X

Bulté, Fernando. 2005. *Teoría del derecho*. Havana, Cuba: Editorial Félix Varela.

–––––. (1989). *Colectivo de autores. Teoría socialista del estado y el derecho*. Havana, Cuba: Editorial Félix Varela.

Bustamante, V., and A.S. de Montoro. (1937). *La jurisprudencia en la jerarquía de las fuentes del derecho positivo cubano* [Jurisprudence in the hierarchy of the sources of Cuban positive law]. 2nd ed. Havana, Cuba: Jesús Montero.

Civil Code of Spain, Amended [Código Civil Modificado]. (1889, July 25). Spain. *Gazette*.

[Civil Code of Spain]. Código civil español. 24th ed. (1888, October 6). Resolution 32 (2005). Madrid, Spain: Editorial Tecnos.

Constitución de la República de Cuba. (1940, July 5). Promulgated by Gustavo Gutiérrez Sánchez, Lex at Havana, Cuba, 1941.

Giralt San Miguel Johannes. (2006, January/July). Derecho Romano-francés. ¡A escena! *Revista Cubana de derecho*, 27: 77–101 [Cuban law review].

Correa, A.M. (2004). Comentarios sobre las fuentes del Derecho Administrativo cubano. In *Temas de derecho administrativo Cubano*. Havana, Cuba: Félix Varela.

Côté, J. (2010). From transculturation to hybridization: Redefining culture in the Americas. In A. Benessaieh (Ed.), *Amériques transculturelles–Transcultural Americas* (pp.

121–148). Ottawa: University of Ottawa Press.
Decree [Decreto Nº] 13. (1934, January 2). El voto a la mujer [women's suffrage]. Havana, Cuba: Gaceta Oficial de la República de Cuba [GO – Official Gazette].
Decreto-Ley No. 250. [DLCACI 250] (2007, July 31). De la Corte de arbitraje comercial internacional" [Decree-Law No. 250. Of the international commercial arbitration court]. Gaceta Oficial Extraordinaria [GOE] No. 3. Havana, Cuba: Félix Varela.
Fernández Bulté, J. (2005). *Teoría del estado y el derecho.* Part II. Havana, Cuba: Editorial Félix Varela.
Hübner Gallo, Jorge Iván. (1976). Fuentes y formas de expresión del derecho. In *Introducción al derecho.* Chili: Editorial Jurídica de Chile.
Legaz Lacambra, L. (1980). Introducción al estudio del derecho (p. 345). Cited in García Maynez, E. Mexico: Editorial Porrúa.
[LRC 1960] Ley de reforma constitucional. (1960, June 29). [Law of constitutional reform]. (1960, December 20). National Autonomous University of Mexico (UNAM). https://archivos.juridicas.unam.mx
[LRC 1992] Ley de reforma constitucional. (1992, July 12). [Law of constitutional reform]. Gaceta Oficial de la República de Cuba [GO –Official Gazette]. www.gacetaoficial.gob.cu
[LIE 2014] Ley No. 118. (2014, April 16). Ley de la inversión extranjera. [Law on foreign investment]. Gaceta Oficial Extraordinaria de la República de Cuba [GO – Cuba Extraordinary Official Gazette]. www.gacetaoficial.gob.cu
López, A.P. (1984). *Reseña histórica del derecho de ultramar.* Havana, Cuba: Imprenta La Antilla.
Mantilla, A. (2004). "Comentarios sobre las fuentes del derecho administrativo cubano." En *Temas de derecho administrativo Cubano.* Cuba: Universidad de la Habana [University of Havana]. Havana: Cuba
Pérez Gallardo, L.B. (2014). [Civil Code] Código civil de la República de Cuba: ley no. 59/1987 de 16 de Julio: anotado y concordado. (1987, July 16). Havana, Cuba: Félix Varela.
Platt Amendment. (1901, March 2). Amendment to the Army Appropriations Act of 1901 (31 Stat. 895). 31 Stat. 897 (1901). [Proposed by Senator Orville Platt, Conn.].
Teller Amendment. (1898, April 20). Amendment to the U.S. joint resolution of the United States Congress. [Proposed by Senator Henry M. Teller, Colorado]. 55th U.S. Congress.
Prieto Valdés, Martha (2020, April 25). *La Constitución cubana de 2019: Nuevos contenidos y necesidades/2019 Cuban constitution 2019: new contents and necessities.* No. 289. Cuba: University of Havana. Epub. http://scielo.sld.cu/scielo.php?script=sci_arttext&pid=S0253-92762020000100003&lng=es&nrm=iso
San Miguel Giralt, J. (2006). Derecho Romano-French y Common Law ¡A escena!, *Revista Cubana de Derecho* 27: 79–102 [Cuban law review]. [English (translation) paraphrase]. https://cuba.vlex.com/vid/derecho-romano-frances-common-law-escena-50172127
Quiróz Pírez, R. (1999). *Manual de Derecho Penal.* Parte I. Havana, Cuba: Editorial Félix Varela.
Tribunal Supremo [Cuba Supreme Court]. (2006, March 31). Sala de lo Civil y de lo Administrativo, Sentencia No. 219. Segundo Considerando. Ponente Arredondo Suárez.
Wood, L. (1898, October 20). Constitución provisional de Santiago de Cuba. [Provisional constitution]. Mexico: Biblioteca Jurídica Virtual del Instituto de Investigaciones Jurídicas de la UNAM. www.juridicas.unam.mx
Zhidkov O., Chirkin V y Yudin Yu. (1980). *Fundamentos de la teoría socialista del Estado y el derecho.* Moscow: Editorial Progreso.

CHAPTER EIGHT

The Cuban Criminal Justice System: A Social Reintegration Model

Manuel Alberto Leyva Estupiñán, Larisbel Lugo Arteaga, and Luis Manuel Probance Labrada

Abstract

The Cuban criminal justice system differs from and shares elements with other Western nations. This diversity evidences the process of transculturation as a factor in developing the Cuban criminal justice system. Cuba's criminal legal system blends Spain's more modern legal norms with various external influences. Given the country's current situation, it faces contradictions, successes, and challenges. Nevertheless, due to the political, economic, and social system created by the Cuban Revolution, Cuba enjoys the highest levels of public safety in Latin America. A transformative approach to criminal justice, transitional and regular, dates to the period immediately following the Cuban Revolution when the country confronted the need to repair the harm done under the U.S.-controlled Batista dictatorship. Extending from the establishment of the People's Popular Courts in the 1960s and the Family Code in 1975 to the current judicial system and Criminal Code (1979; 1987), the ongoing application of Fidel's "Battle of Ideas" and the concept of "confidence tasks" aim to counter recidivism. As evidenced by the proliferation of work and study centers for convicts, the Cuban criminal justice system's goal is re-education and social reintegration, not retribution. As in most Western nations, the treatment of young offenders has been evolving in recent decades. Young offenders are not housed in adult prisons, numerous re-educative incarceration facilities embodying transformative, restorative rehabilitation models have been implemented, and there are calls to extend the differential treatment accorded young offenders from age 16 to 18. Community policing characterizes the pivotal role of the Cuban police in crime prevention and social reintegration.

Keywords: criminal justice system, penal system, sentencing, youth justice, transformative justice, re-education, social reintegration.

Manuel Alberto Leyva Estupiñán is Associate Professor of Criminal Law and Dean of the Faculty of Social Sciences (University of Holguín, Cuba). A specialist in Criminal Law, he is a member of the National Union of Jurists of Cuba. Email: mleyvae@uho.edu.cu.

Larisbel Lugo Arteaga is Associate Professor of Criminal Law, Faculty of Social Sciences (University of Holguín, Cuba) and a member of the National Union of Jurists of Cuba. Email: llugo@uho.edu.cu.

Luis Manuel Probance Labrada is Associate Professor of Criminal Law, Faculty of Social Sciences (University of Holguín, Cuba) and a member of the National Union of Jurists of Cuba. Email: lprovance@uho.edu.cu.

Introduction

From a historical point of view, Cuba's criminal justice model has undergone three significant stages and reforms since the late 1400s. Although each stage can be separated into time intervals with specific characteristics, the 400 years of Spanish colonization, 1492–1898, is the first historical period for the purposes of this chapter. The second stage, 1902–1959, is characterized by the Republic of Cuba's emergence (i.e., independence from Spain). The third period extends from the 1959 Cuban Revolution to the present day. The Cuban criminal justice system (CJS) is a composite of these three essential stages.

This chapter will describe the characteristics and functioning of the Cuban penal system from a criminal justice perspective and emphasize re-educative rehabilitation and social reintegration service delivery within an evolutive framework. The chapter includes four sections and a conclusion. The first section outlines Cuba's CJS, extending from a brief historical purview to the present day, including transitional transformative justice measures implemented immediately following the Cuban Revolution to redress human rights abuses under the Batista dictatorship. The second section describes the purposes and sentencing principles of the Cuban Criminal Code (1987) and their application in the criminal justice system, including post-release. The third section explores Cuba's approach to juvenile offenders, and the fourth discusses the pivotal role of the police in crime prevention at a community level. A conclusion situates these elements within the broader Cuban social justice framework.

The Cuban Criminal Justice System: Major Stages and Reforms—1492 to Present

From the second half of the 19th century, as the rise of capitalism was ushering in the industrial revolutions in Europe, countries like France, Germany, and Spain began introducing modern laws to meet the new needs. Until then, criminal justice in Cuba had been local, patriarchal and solidly rooted in religion, mainly Catholicism. The Spanish Criminal Code (1870) and Code of Criminal Procedure (1889) consolidated a mishmash of criminal laws accrued over the first three centuries of Spanish colonization. Spain's more modern legal norms and principles of law laid the foundation of Cuba's legal system.

The fact that all other Latin American countries had obtained their independence several decades before the colonizing countries of Europe began reforming their laws made our country's experience superior at the time. The oral and public trials that would form the basis of reforms of the criminal justice systems across Latin America in the late twentieth century had existed in Cuba since the 19th century.

During the Republican period, which ran from 1902 to 1959 and coincided with two occupations of the island by the U.S., the prison system was harsh and chaotic. The panoptic *Presidio Modelo* or "model prison" (shown below) was constructed between 1926 and 1928 on the Cuban *Isla de Pinos* (Isle of Pines), which was renamed *Isla de la Juventud* (Isle of Youth) under the Constitutional Reform Act (1978, Art. 10). The prison is an extreme example of how severe overcrowding and deteriorating infrastructures characterized the prison system of the day. The situation of inmates was horrible. The prison populations were often mixed, and the portrayals of misery, decay and corruption suggest that the inmates were seen and treated as dispensable commodities (De la Torriente Brau, 1975, p. 15), with forced labour translating into a supply of cheap labour not only for the construction of public works but also for companies and on private estates.

Inmates were neither classified according to their crimes or sentences nor separated by gender, which favoured promiscuity and abuse. The prisoners' treatment was not only repressive, but they were malnourished and also punished and taunted in many other ways. For example, unless a family could provide one, an inmate had to

The "Presidio Modelo" prison on the *Isla de la Juventud* [Isle of Youth] (Cuba), where Fidel Castro was held prisoner in 1953. (Photo: Friman/Wikimedia Commons)

pay ten to fifteen U.S. dollars to get a bed or would be forced to sleep on the floor. Alcohol and marijuana were routinely smuggled into the corrupt penal institutions, and the guards had de facto control inside—with internal orders being issued by the heads of cell sections and certain prisoners acting as wardens. In contrast, actual wardens never entered the prison (Centeno, 2002, p. 15). This situation was eliminated after 1959.

Following the successful conclusion of the Cuban Revolution in 1959, the Spanish Social Defence Code of Cuba (1936) was kept in place for almost two decades. It upheld the principles of the reformed Spanish Code (1870) extended to Cuba by royal decree in 1879 but was infused with strong influences from the Italian Criminal Code and the spirit of positivism, gaining momentum from the early 20th century onward. It is noteworthy, however, that the "*Mambisa* criminal code" of 1898, which had been introduced between the third and fourth *Mambisa* Constitutions, was applied across the rebel territory during the war of national liberation (i.e., the Cuban Revolution) from December 1956 to January 1959.

The Cuban Criminal Justice System: Preliminary Ideas

Concerning positive law and doctrine, Cuban scholars agree that the country's Criminal Code has been shaped gradually through various fusions of "transcultural" elements and influences. Several examples include the concept of dangerousness from the Italian positivist school of criminology, the four centuries of old-colonial Spanish criminal rule, the United States' judicial system, and, from the second half of the 20th century, the socialist legal system of Eastern Europe. The authors further submit that the structure and organization of Cuban criminal law, both substantive and procedural, is heir to Spanish doctrine modified by provisions and amendments from other foreign systems over time through transculturation processes. Thus, the Cuban criminal legal system has long comprised a mixed criminal justice system inherited mainly from Spain but with other external and internal humanistic influences. The resulting criminal justice system is richly infused with an informal but evolving restorative and transformative—humanistic—approach that has been emblematic of the Cuban Revolution in all its spheres, and imbued with elements of other systems, including the Cuban socialist legal philosophy, mainly incorporated starting in the 1970s.

A transitional justice phase for the judiciary characterized the years immediately following the Cuban Revolution's triumph in 1959. Prime Minister Fidel Castro introduced a provisional system of Revolutionary Courts. Not infringing on the civilian courts' jurisdiction, these courts were established in 1959 to hear trials for military criminals and assassins from the Batista government. Ernesto (Che) Guevara supervised the entire judicial system, including the prosecution and other processes, on behalf of the Revolutionary Government. At the same time, Miguel A. Duque de Estrada Ramos, a jurist who had graduated in 1955, was assigned to organize the Revolutionary Courts.

Cuba's People's Popular Courts were created in 1963 for offences carrying sentences of less than 180 days, and the judges were elected in the people's power assemblies. Evidencing a restorative approach to criminal justice, Cuba's system of People's Popular Courts (PPC) was transformative and designed to deal with certain criminal activities—such as prostitution—deemed symptomatic of the inequity, widespread poverty, and social exclusion experienced by the majority of the Cuban people under the Batista dictatorship. The jurists were ordinary Cuban citizens with no legal training, and the court aimed to "influence" offenders out of prior anti-social behaviour rather than act through criminal sanctions.

In use across the country through the 1960s, the People's Popular Courts shared certain principles with what is recognized in many Western jurisdictions as courts based on the idea of an independent judiciary as opposed to an elected one, found mainly in the United States (Firschein, B. 2018). Two thousand transformative courts were introduced across Cuba through the 1960s.

In 1973, the Cuban Council of Ministers dismantled these transitional structures by promulgating the Judicial Organization Law (Law 1249). This statute replaced the court system based on the following four levels of jurisdiction: People's Basic Courts, People's Regional Courts, People's Provincial Courts, and People's Supreme Courts. Private law practice on the island became obsolete through the 1973 reforms, making membership in law collectives mandatory for all practicing lawyers. Cuba's unique system of lay judges was also established. Serving on panels alongside professional judges, lay judges add an independent judicial presence to all tribunals at all levels of the Cuban judicial system, which does not recognize trial by jury.

The 1973 reforms also saw the promulgation of a new Criminal Procedure Law, which supplanted the Law of Criminal Procedure for Cuba and Puerto Rico (1901). The new Law revolutionized the Cuban criminal justice system by outlawing private legal practices on the island in favour of collective law firms (i.e., *bufètes colectivos*), the first of which had been created in 1964 (Resolution 18, 1965) and fell under the jurisdiction of the Cuban Bar Association.

The 1973 changes ensured affordable legal services, direct citizen involvement in court and crime prevention/control, and restorative alternatives to formal court mechanisms, among other innovations. In 1977, a new Organization of the Judicial System Law (Law 4, August 10, 1977) and a Criminal Procedure Law (Law 5, August 13, 1977) amalgamated the two lower courts into the People's Municipal Courts and established Cuba's current three-tier jurisdictional judicial framework. A Military Procedure Law with criminal or disciplinary military jurisdiction and a Criminal Procedure Law with ordinary (i.e., civilian) jurisdiction were also established.

The principles of socialism were introduced under a new Constitution in 1976, and those based on the statute and custom of earlier civil and common-law traditions were modified because the injustices of the pre-Revolution era tainted their integrity. The 1936 Social Defence Code remained in force until 1979 (Criminal Code, Law No. 21, 1978), when its failure to correspond to the reality of our economic, social, and political development was recognized. The 1979 Code better reflected the belief that eradicating exploitation and oppression would prevent crime. The Cuban people voiced concerns over sentence severity, which led to an extensive 1985 review of sentencing in past cases during which many were deleted. This sentiment was then codified through reforms introduced into the 1987 Code, which was also imbued with Cuba's humanistic vision; it emphasized re-educative rehabilitation and social reinsertion within a trend toward decriminalizing certain offences, reducing sentences in general, and focusing on alternatives to prison including for more serious offences. The 1987 Code also outlawed the death penalty for most cases (Art. 28). Subsequent reforms through the 1990s made the judiciary autonomous from the Ministry of Justice, making the Governing Council of the People's Supreme Court the court authority, and also introduced governing councils for the provincial courts (Law No. 82, Law of the People's Courts). As per the tenth transitory provision in the 2019 Constitution, a new Law of the Courts will soon be proposed by the Council of Government of the People's Supreme Court to the National Assembly of People's Power.

The Cuban Court System Today

The Cuban judicial system has three tiers. The People's Supreme Court is the highest judicial authority (Art. 148) and has six chambers (criminal, civil and administrative, labour, state security, economic, and military). The People's Provincial Court has five chambers (i.e., criminal, civil and administrative, labour, state security, and economic). The Provincial Court uses three-judge (two professional and one lay) panels and five-judge panels (three professional, two lay). The People's Municipal

Court, the lowest court, has three-judge panels. Lay judges are domestic engineers (i.e., parents), professionals, workers, peasants, and university students who serve one month a year. They are nominated in workplace assemblies, and the Minister of Justice reviews their suitability. Lay judges have renewable mandates (if ratified) and can serve in the courts for years.

The Cuban Criminal Code (Law 62, 1987) remains in force today, along with the Cuban Criminal Procedure Law (Law 5, 1977) as amended by Decree-Law 310 (June 25, 2013). A new Cuban Criminal Code, a significant step in Cuba's commitment to human rights, is currently under discussion and is expected to be enacted in October 2021.* The reforms aimed to promote leniency in court rulings involving offenders who pose no danger to society. Along with this trend toward leniency came legislative changes emphasizing alternatives to incarceration (Cuban Criminal Procedure Law, 1977; 2013).

The Criminal Code was amended in the 1990s during the Special Period to liberalize foreign currency/investment (Decree Law 151, June 10, 1994). This amendment was brought on by the fall of the Soviet bloc, after which Cuba lost its primary trading partners since most other nations fell (and today continue to fall) under restrictions of the U.S. embargo against Cuba. The Code consists of two books, defining and regulating criminal law, crimes and their corresponding sanctions (Book 1) and listing all criminal offences (Book 2).

The Cuban Criminal Code (1987) has a dual character; it regulates crimes, sanctions, and dangerous states against the common good of society and associated security measures. Criminal defence is provided by lawyers chosen by the defendant or designated by the state who belong, in either case, to the Cuban National Organization of Collective Law Firms (ONBC) (Minjus, 1965). The Cuban National Organization of Collective Law Firms (ONBC) is an autonomous, non-state organization of social interest and professional character; it is self-financed and has a legal personality given by an extensive network of law firms nationwide. It has a

---

* Editors' note: The new Criminal Code, Ley 151/2022 "Código Penal," was enacted in September 2022, after the writing of this chapter, and became effective on November 29, 2022. The main penalties are the deprivation of liberty, correctional work with internment, correctional work without internment, home confinement, restrictions on liberty, community service, fines, and reprimand. The new regulation maintains the death penalty sanction for some of the most serious crimes. The main modification is the introduction of other types of penalties not contained in the previous Law No. 62/1987, such as home confinement and community service, in addition to the fact that such main penalties may be autonomous and alternative penalties.

Provincial Directorate and representation in each municipality. Lawyers of great professional prestige belong to these firms and offer services across the diverse legal landscape (Cubadebate, 2015).

The Criminal Procedure Law (1977) embodies three main phases for the administration of criminal justice: the Preparatory (pretrial) Phase, carried out by a criminal investigator supervised by the prosecutor; the Intermediate Phase (questioning the accused and investigation by the prosecutor to determine sufficient grounds); and the Oral Trial Phase (characterized by debate between the two parties).

The Cuban Revolution's success is partly evidenced by the decline in violence since 1959. One confronts two very different realities if one compares today's Cuban criminal justice landscape with the earlier panorama (circa 1948–1958). The criminal activity in the decade before the Revolution was characterized by a high percentage of violent crimes (approximately 700 incidents and 30 homicides per 100,000 inhabitants) that constituted 30 percent of known crime, according to the police statistics. It ranked among the highest of the day in Latin America. By 1973, homicides had fallen to 10 per 100,000 (De la Cruz Ochoa, 2001, p. 73) and the trend has continued according to the Statista (2019) data for Latin America and the Caribbean (Pasquali, 2020).

In his 2018 report to the United Nations Human Rights Council, the Cuban Minister of Foreign Affairs Bruno Rodríguez Parrilla (UNHRC, 2018) affirmed that protecting the right to life remains the highest priority. The protection is ensured by legal recognition of the right to physical integrity and inviolability through the guarantees of due process, preventing anyone from being deprived of freedom except under the law (CC, arts. 261, 263, 1987).

Cuba has continued to strengthen its participation and cooperation with the United Nations and is currently party to 44 of the 61 international human rights proclamations, including the following (Rodríguez Parrilla, 2018):

- Universal Declaration of Human Rights (1948);
- Code of Conduct for Law Enforcement Officials (1979);
- International Covenant on Civil and Political Rights (1976);
- Declaration on the Protection of all Persons from Being Subjected to Torture and Other Cruel, Inhuman or Degrading Treatment or Punishment (1976);
- Declaration on the Elimination of All Forms of Racial Discrimination (1963);

- Body of Principles for the Protection of All Persons under Any Form of Detention or Imprisonment (1988);
- Standard Minimum Rules for the Treatment of Prisoners (adopted by the United Nations in 1955 and by the UN Economic and Social Council in 1957), rev. 2015 (Nelson Mandela Rules);
- International Convention on the Suppression and Punishment of the Crime of Apartheid (1976);
- Convention for the Prevention and Punishment of the Crime of Genocide (1948); and
- Vienna Convention on Consular Relations (1967)

Purposes and Sentencing Principles of the Cuban Criminal Code (CCC) and their Application through the Prison System and Post-Release

The system of sanctions in Cuba (Law 62, 1987) is based on principal sanctions; subsidiary sanctions (Ch. II, Art. 28.1), which depend on whether the principal sanction has been imposed (namely the sanction of deprivation of freedom (Arts. 32, 33) for less than 5 years); and additional sanctions (Art. 34.1).

> **Box 8.1: Sanctions regulated by the Cuban Criminal Code**
>
> **Principal:** Death, deprivation of freedom, and fine.
> **Subsidiary:** Correctional work with internment, correctional work without internment, restriction of freedom).
> **Accessory:** Deprivation of rights, suspension of driver's license, confiscation, among others).

In Cuba, the death penalty is exceptional, cannot be imposed on offenders under 20 years of age (Art. 29, 1–2), and is only applicable to offences against the security of the state and in aggravated cases (for example, murder or rape) as identified in the various articles of our Criminal Code. On April 28, 2008, Cuba announced this way of administering the death penalty to the World Council of Human Rights (Resolution, 2006). A People's (popular) Provincial Court can issue the death penalty, but it is automatically sent on appeal to the Supreme Court to acquit, maintain, or commute. A decision to keep the sentence must be ratified by the Council of State, which is the country's highest executive body and holds the supreme power of the State between sessions of the Cuban Parliament, the National Assembly of People's Power (ANPP).

As part of this process, sentences for crimes committed before 1999 were commuted to the maximum punishment, 30 years of deprivation of freedom (Art. 30.1), a provision introduced by Law 87 in 1999. The sanction of deprivation of freedom can be thus both temporary and perpetual. Inmates serving such sentences have rights established in the Criminal Code (1987) and the Penitentiary Regulations (Order 7) issued by the Vice-Minister of the Cuba Ministry of the Interior (December 1, 2016). Cuban prison policy has been developed by taking international standards into account in both legislation and prison practice. The death penalty has not been applied in the country since 2003.

The Cuban Penitentiary System

In June 1965, Prime Minister Fidel Castro said of crime and criminals, "We will be more revolutionary not once we know how to fight that delinquent enemy but as soon as we can know how to re-educate or rehabilitate them" (Castro, 1965). In 1968, the first re-educative/rehabilitative course was given in Havana. In compliance with the Minimum Rules for the Treatment of Inmates (OHCHR, 1985), since 1959, the Cuban government has worked on improving penitentiary legislation and its regulatory base in the development of a profoundly humane prison system based on respect and rigorous control over the application of laws, regulations, and policies taking into account the precepts of the International Minimum Rules for the Treatment of Prisoners approved at the First Congress on the Prevention of Crime and the Treatment of Offenders in 1955. Successive international updates to these standards have also been assimilated and applied to the Cuban system (Gómez, May 22, 2012).

Since 1959, the policies implemented in Cuban prisons have been based on precepts of re-education and rehabilitation for detained persons and post-release support for their full social reintegration (Gómez, 2012; Ecured, n.d.; *Granma*). Terminology changes were even made to prevent social stigmatization and potential self-degradation of sanctioned persons; for example, the terms "inmate," "offender," and "prisoner" have been discarded in favour of "intern" (Order 7, 2016). Most recently, the 2019 Constitution gives rights related to the correctional system a constitutional character, the elements of which will be discussed later in this chapter.

Several laws were enacted early on to make alternatives to prison available. Worthy of mention here is Law 548 of September 15, 1959, regulating the custody of minors, and Law 653 (1959), reducing the sanctions for common crimes. Two more laws, 592 and 593, were introduced in 1961, establishing a good behaviour parole option. Parole is carried out by the police together with social and mass organizations (Criminal Code, Title VII, Art. 58.6) and depends on a positive evolution of behaviour by the intern (see below). Finally, on April 25, 1964, the first set of comprehensive regulations enforcing the principle of protection and re-education of interns, such as work/study re-education centres, was inaugurated. Such regulations were considered a leap forward in facilitating coherence of actions as they established a classification system for inmates based on attitude and behaviour.

Cuban Regulation of the Progressive Regime of Re-Education of 1967

In 1967, the Regulation of the Progressive Regime of Re-education began to be applied. This regulation grouped Cuban prisons into two categories: semi-open regime prisons and higher-security prisons. Its objectives included individualizing prison treatment, re-education through fair constitutional treatment, life skill/work development and respect for human dignity, and post-release follow-up and assistance. This system empowers the transition into probation for those who have accomplished various things in the preparatory phase. Periodic conduct evaluations determine the evolution of intern behaviour to regulate benefits and introduce new stimuli. Inmates are given the options of work or study programs to reduce their sentence and obtain certain privileges as incentives. The availability of such opportunities is not automatic or guaranteed but determined as a function of the crime's nature and the inmate's regime and progress.

Education is prioritized throughout the Cuban prison system (MINREX, 2005) and includes training for socially helpful labour, academic education, technical training for the trades, civic and patriotic education, and artistic, sporting, and recreational activities. This broad and humane focus on rehabilitation aims to change behavioural habits, create a sense of respect for the law, and prepare the interns for reintegration into society.

From the dawn of the triumph of the Cuban Revolution, starting in 1959 with the Ministry of Education (MINED) as lead, many new schools were opened to the prison populations, providing all the facilities and conditions needed to facilitate their rehabilitation and reintegration into society through a successful teaching-learning process emphasizing a holistic, re-educative approach (MINREX, 2005). An intern sentenced to less than a year, over 45 years of age, or a non-permanent resident cannot opt for these programs. Interns determined to have a high risk of dangerous behaviour or a physical disability are placed in higher security institutions.

Work programs are prioritized in the Cuban prison system for all other interns. Those who opt for a work regime are given a job and earn the same salary as workers from the general population. The intern who chooses to join a study and/or work program receives special privileges in prison, such as permits for additional family members' visits and reduced sentences. Technical education and occupations are prioritized for those under 27 years of age. Interns who had previously attended university can continue to do so, although not all degree programs are available in the prison setting. Socio-cultural Studies and Psychology were the first degrees made available to interns.

The Confidence Task System

The confidence task system, a restorative notion, iterated in Fidel's Battle of Ideas (Castro, 2004), discussed more fully later in this chapter, envisions social justice as a means of preventing crime and recidivism and is the core of the work-program rationale (García Santos, 2007). Activities within the confidence task system of alternatives to conventional prison can allow young people and, depending on their behaviour and availability of services, those not so young, to be gainfully employed while serving their sentence. The confidence task conceptualizes social justice as a means of preventing crime and recidivism and is premised on the belief that people who commit a crime have the right to opportunities for social reintegration.

Alternatives to prison are also available to those who have committed non-violent offences and been sentenced to or are already serving in a minimum-security prison. A multidisciplinary group confidentially evaluates those newly sentenced and those closest to release and is involved in their progress through the system, which is much akin to an apprenticeship. Instead of serving their sentences in a regular prison, such interns live at the centres. The interns are afforded an environment and living conditions often superior to their homes. They can work in the community while acquiring higher-level education, life skills and/or an essential trade if they do not already have one. The recidivism rate in this system for traditional crimes, such as theft, is low (Barroso González, 2014), which demonstrates its effectiveness in terms of prevention and social reintegration.

The benefits of the confidence system include the following:

- Guaranteed economic support for the intern's family.
- Instills confidence in the intern, who will not feel like a burden to society.
- Availability of a significant labour force available to the nation under fair and beneficial terms and conditions.

- Social inclusion for the intern via a housing environment is better than conventional prison and often nicer and more sociable than their home environment.
- Social contacts and exchanges as a worker and increased communication with family favours successful post-release social reintegration.
- Sentence reductions such as probation are possible but require additional justifications.

Depending on the demand in the given employment sector, a prison intern may keep their jobs post-release. An intern who commits another crime or otherwise breaches any confidence-task system conditions is returned to a conventional prison.

Principles and Purpose of Cuban Prison Policy

The principles and purpose of the prison policy are defined in the Constitution and the Criminal Code and supported in the Regulations (Order 7, 2016) dealing with the prison system:

- Lawfulness (recourse to the justice system).
- Proportionality (the punishment should fit the crime and be the same for any who commit it).
- Re-socialization (restoration of social values through education, work and other interventions aimed at rehabilitation).
- Independent judiciary (fairness of court proceedings).
- Presumption of innocence (innocent until proven guilty).
- Humanism (primary health services include universal access to medical care, provision of family doctors and nurses and mental health professionals, clinical testing, and prison hospitals).
- Provision of an adequate standard of living: Interns receive three meals per day as per Ministry of Health regulations regarding caloric intake and a balanced diet.

In sum, the Cuban CJS accords interns the following rights:

- Physical integrity, dignity, and individual rights.
- Medical, hospital, and dental care as required.
- Library services at the institution and nearby areas if there is no public safety risk, study materials, and sufficient information to understand the process.
- Visits from family and friends and intimate relations with the spouse.

- Employment with fair compensation. The interns earn such salaries to help with family expenses, pay any civil liability resulting from the crime, pay personal loans, and make alimony payments.
- Continuing education (academic and vocational training) programs (see Gálvez Puebla, 2004, p. 6).
- Alternative to prison options (for interns who pose no risk to public safety).

Prisons Around the World in Crisis

It is becoming increasingly clear to people around the world that modern prison systems now face crises related to overcrowding. At the same time, there is no shortage of reports on the over-representation of certain ethnic groups, such as Black Muslims and Indigenous people, across the continents of Australia, Europe, and North America. Many nations worldwide are responding to this crisis in corrections by embracing restorative justice and other alternatives to the traditional court and prison system.

In the U.S., the issue is further complicated by prison privatization, which arose in the 1980s, and "quickly grew into a multibillion-dollar industry." This disturbing trend was seen by some to be fueling the U.S. economy, even as the U.S. was "beginning a nationwide push to decrease its incarcerated population, leading to a growth industry in exporting corporate prison knowhow" (Biron, August 20, 2013). Currently, "less than 10% percent of [U.S.] state and federal inmates are in the care of private prisons" (Greene and Hadavi, January 2, 2020).

During the Obama administration, the detention of Central American migrants took off. With that, so did the federal funding of private detention centres. In addition, "Two of the biggest companies, CoreCivic and the Geo Group, are publicly traded ... and have been the target of scandals and lawsuits.... In the wake of the zero-tolerance policy at the U.S.-Mexico border, the U.S. public became increasingly vocal against the separation of families and the conditions in which migrants were detained" (Green and Hadavi, January 2, 2020).

Pressures from the "Families Belong Together" coalition, which "collected over one million signatures urging J.P. Morgan Chase and other banks to separate themselves from CoreCivic and The GO Group" in 2019, have had the following impact:

> In March, J.P. Morgan announced that it would no longer finance private operators of prisons and detention centers. Seven other [U.S.] banks followed suit. In June, Democrat Elizabeth Warren said

she would abolish the industry if elected president. Other candidates have espoused similar intentions. The largest pension fund in the country is divesting, and several states are passing laws to phase out private prisons. The stocks of the GEO Group and CoreCivic have fallen by 30 percent since June (Green and Hadavi, 2020).

According to research into the complex relationship between criminology and criminal justice policies such as incarceration, the reputed author and Argentine judge of the Inter-American Court of Human Rights Raul Zaffaroni declared privatization and the involvement of private enterprise in prisons as utopias of the liberal state that will not work in Latin America. Moreover, many countries' movement from an economy of production to a service economy is hypertrophying the prison system by generating an incredible demand for services, meaning that almost one out of every 25 people walking down the street "lives off" the prison system (Zaffaroni, 1993).

Prisons in Latin America and the Caribbean are also "in crisis," with "deplorable and inhumane conditions that make [inmate populations] vulnerable to coercion and recruitment by the most sophisticated criminal gangs" (Dudley and Bargent, 2017). Also, "prison guards, as well as police officers and members of the military, often abuse their power vis-à-vis prisoners and participate in corruption networks that enable the generation of more crime. Prisons have also become incubators for criminal activity" (Dudley and Bargent, 2017). The prison system in Latin America and the Caribbean has taken a beating in recent years because "rather than thinking of prisons as an integral part of the justice system, they are often viewed as criminal repositories—a place where policymakers simply bottle up their problems and ignore the consequences" (Dudley and Bargent, 2017).

The deplorable situation of prisons in Cuba under the U.S.-controlled Batista dictatorship before the Cuban Revolution's triumph in 1959 gave Cuban citizens and revolutionary leaders an early understanding of how over-representation of certain groups due to ethnicity and poverty both signals and is a root cause of social problems. Notably, the Cuban confidence-task approach, often fortified through continuing education, as discussed above, has consistently rejected the notion of profiteering on detention since the 1959 triumph of the Cuban Revolution.

The Dual Purpose of Deprivation of Freedom as a Sentencing Tool in Cuba

In line with modern trends in criminology and criminal law, the Cuban law specialist, former Attorney General of the Republic of Cuba (1959–

2001), and legal director of UNECA Santiago Cuba Fernández (Fernández, 2009) pointed out in a 2009 interview with the Imery Urdaneta law firm of Venezuela that the sentence of deprivation of freedom does not constitute revenge or retribution against individuals having violated the law. Instead, it isolates offenders from the social environment in which they committed a crime to re-educate and reintegrate them into their community as active, law-abiding citizens.

A fine is considered an impersonal sentence because it indirectly punishes someone other than the offender and thus violates a basic sentencing principle. Generally, the person who pays the fine is not the one who has been sentenced; instead, it is usually paid by a relative. Fines are called "quotas" in Cuban, and the judge determines the amount, which can range from 1.00 to 50.00 Cuban pesos (Law 62, Art. 35, 1987).

Accessory sanctions in Cuba include deprivation of certain personal rights (e.g., running for public office), confiscation of goods, and deprivation of parental/filial rights. The sentence depends on the crime. The court's discretion considers the characteristics of the act and the offender's profile.

According to the underlying assumption of afflictive penalties in the Cuban Criminal Code, the punishment aspect of sentencing is inevitable, given the deprivation of access to one's property and individual freedom (Quirós Pírez, 2009, p. 29). However, as regulated by Article 27 of the Cuban Criminal Code (Law 62, 1987), the purpose of sentencing is not only punishment but also to re-educate those who have been sanctioned as to the principles of an honest attitude about work, strict compliance with the law, and respect for the norms and values of socialist coexistence. This is in line with the practical objectives set out by Cuban society regarding education methods: to prepare citizens for regular and healthy lives.

Re-education establishes the primary purpose and the underlying basis of crime prevention in Cuba. The adaptation of an intern towards positive social relations is developed throughout the sentence. This is carried out in various ways and considers the individual's educational and life-skill base. When a sentence is handed down in Cuba, the main objective is not to punish but to re-educate, rehabilitate, reinsert, and reintegrate to prevent recidivism and eradicate the particular type of crime at a social level. A program called Educate Your Child aims to allow women who have violated the law to spend time with their children, which helps stem the tide of secondary social problems from the justice system.

Figure 8.1 shows how the social reintegration of interns is ensured by the participation of several state institutions, such as the Ministries of Education and/or Health, the National Institute for Sports and Recreation, and mass organizations like the FMC, CDR, and Cuban Trade Union, among others, which are involved with police for post-release services aimed at helping achieve successful social re-insertion of an intern.

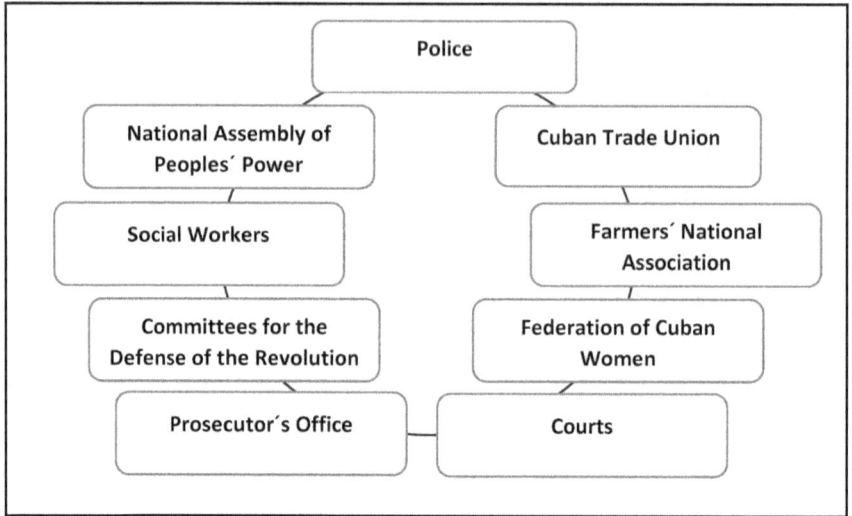

Figure 8.1. State Institutions and Mass Organizations Participating in the Social Reintegration of Inmates in Cuba. (Source: Authors)

Another characteristic of the Cuban criminal justice system is that former interns are presented to their community by the presiding judge following release. This lets neighbours and other community members know they have served their sentences and are ready to be reintegrated into society. Social reintegration is also incorporated into the constitutional text approved on February 24 and enacted on April 11, 2019 (Cuban Constitution, 2019).

Among post-release options is a regular job related to the ex-intern's field of expertise, a license to work as an independent (i.e., self-employed) worker or to receive a piece of land in usufruct. This latter provision guarantees a decent livelihood for the former intern while boosting food production, perhaps one of the country's primary challenges in the current circumstances (Cuban Constitution, 2019, Art. 77).

Age of Criminal Responsibility and Youth Justice in Cuba

Children are still in the formative phases of development, which means they need help and guidance rather than punishment to correct their behaviour. The minor's responsibility in a crime is deemed minimal. The age of criminal responsibility in Cuba was established under Cuba's first socialist Criminal Code (Law 21, 1979) and is maintained under the current Criminal Code (Law 62, 1987), which came into force on April 30, 1988. According to the Cuban legal expert Quirós Pírez (2009), this was likely related to the fact that 16 is the age of majority under Cuba's Electoral Law (Law 72, 1992). Multiple legal pundits say the age limit should be increased to 18 as prescribed by the United Nations Convention on the Rights of the Child (1989), which Cuba ratified in 1991.

The Ministry of the Interior created the Cuban Department of Prevention and Social Security to oversee juvenile crime prevention under Resolution No. 1001 in March 1962 (Art. 1.). By 1964, hearings for under-age offenders were being held in a special room of the then Havana Audiencia and, in 1966, the first Centre for Evaluation, Analysis, and Guidance of Minors of Havana (CEAOM) Resolution No. 1001 (March 27, 1962), discussed more fully below, was created. Equipped with a multidisciplinary commission comprised of medical doctors, psychiatrists, psychologists, pedagogues, and other specially trained personnel, the Centre's objective was to improve minors' custodial treatment and rehabilitation. It is noteworthy that the Federation of Cuban Women not only plays an essential and active role in social re-insertion but also in preventing criminal behaviour and recidivism among underage youth living in each community.

Subsequent measures tempered the law to better meet minor offenders' needs. Law No. 1249 (1973) amended section B of Article 37 of the Social Defence Code concerning a young person over 12 years but under 16 years of age. As noted earlier, the threshold age of criminal liability stipulated in of the Criminal Code (Title V, 1987) is 16 years, but the court is empowered to cut sentences in half for individuals who were between 16 and 18 years old when they committed the crime (Art. 17.1). Similarly, the court can reduce by a third the sentences of those aged 18 to 20 years at the time of the crime (Art. 17.1), and the same is true when the individual is 60 years old or older at time of trial (Art. 18). Also, offenders under 20 years of age do not serve time in adult prisons and cannot be sentenced to the death penalty in Cuba.

Finally, children's constitutional protections and rights have been carried over from the 1976/2002 Constitution into the new Cuban Constitution (2019). Children are protected against all forms of violence and have specific rights related to their exceptional particular condition(s) as a developing person (Arts. 66 and 86, 2019). The national education system also guarantees the inclusion of teaching and practicing physical education and sports as an integral part of childhood, adolescent, and teenage education (Article 74). Mothers and fathers or other relatives by blood or marriage who perform the roles of guardianship and caretakers must feed children and adolescents, respect and guarantee the full exercise of their rights, protect them from all types of violence, and contribute actively to the holistic development of their personality (Article 84, 2019 CC). The 2019 Constitution also provides against child labour (Art. 66).

International Protections on the Rights of Children

In 1989, world leaders decided that a Convention devoted exclusively to children was needed, since persons under age 18 need special and developmental care protection. The goal was to ensure world recognition of children's intrinsic rights to just treatment and exercise their rights in all capacities as social, economic, political, civil, and cultural actors. On November 20, 1989, the United Nations General Assembly adopted the Convention, which acknowledged the care of children and adolescents as a shared responsibility of family and society. The state also plays an active role in ensuring their welfare:

> Two postulates must be observed in doing so: the absolute priority of children and adolescents in the formulation of public policies, the allocation of budgetary resources and the provision of services, and the respect for the special condition of persons in development, which demands services that are tailored to their needs and contribute to their psychological and social development (Yamamoto et al., 2015, p. 95).

The first juvenile courts emerged in Chicago, Illinois, in 1899 to prevent children from being judged as and incarcerated with adults. The minor's responsibility was considered minimal, reformatories were prioritized, and youth were obliged to learn a trade while in detention. Since children are still in the formative phases of development, as noted earlier, they need help and guidance (i.e., *parens patriae*) rather than punishment to help them correct their behaviour.

The Cuban Doctrine of Integral Protection (1989)

In the same year, Cuba created a new and comprehensive ideological, philosophical, legal, and social concept for its juvenile courts that transcends and transforms traditional precepts about childhood and crime (Doctrine of Integral Protection, 1989). Since the advent of the International Convention on the Rights of the Child (CRC) (1989), children could no longer be considered objects but as subjects with rights. In Cuba, the government's and adults' understanding and responsibility towards children have been strengthened by this doctrine.

Several international legal instruments protect the rights and guarantees of minors. The normative concerns that served as the background to the Convention on the Rights of the Child go back many years to several international accords, such as the Universal Declaration of Human Rights of 1948, the Declarations of the Rights of the Child of 1923 and 1959, and the International Covenant on Economic, Social, and Cultural Rights of 1966. More recent agreements include the United Nations Standard Minimum Rules for the Administration of Juvenile Justice (Beijing Rules adopted in 1985), United Nations Standard Minimum Rules for the Protection of Young People Deprived of Liberty, Guidelines of the United Nations for the Prevention of Juvenile Delinquency (Riyadh Guidelines—signed in 1990), and the International Convention on the Rights of the Child, which Cuba ratified on January 26, 1990. The accession document was received at the United Nations on August 21, 1991, and came into force on September 20, 1991.

At the Third International Conference on Child Protection held in Havana on May 24–26, 2017, supported by UNICEF (Rodriguez Guerrero, 2017), then Cuban Deputy Minister of Justice Rosa Charro Ruiz (Cubadebate, 2017) addressed the issues during the inauguration ceremonies and emphasized the relational impact of Cuban social policies and programs on its legal system. Ruiz noted that the Cuban legal system is also a function of the design, implementation, and evaluation of social policies and programs in the areas of health, education, arts, culture, sport, recreation, and social security, with the broadest possible participation of different agencies, social organizations and civil society.

The Cuban Childhood and Youth Code—Cuba's special law on the protection of children and adolescents—supports and develops principles contained in the UN Convention on the Rights of the Child, such as equality and non-discrimination, and also includes premises and characteristics in line with the island's own social and legal system, such as comprehensive participation and education (Ruiz [in Rodríguez Guerrero], May 25, 2017).

Cuba's policies toward child protection are widely recognized, and UNICEF has supported the island in holding Cuba's important 2017 conference noted above and contributed to an important group of projects for children (Rodriguez Guerrero, 2017). Decree-Law 64 (1982) regulates the treatment of minors whose severe disciplinary or permanent behavioural disorders, and/or any unsocial or anti-social behaviours not considered to be significant indicators of social deviation and/or dangerousness, have impeded their progress in the national education system and contributed to their breaking the law. Within the context of available resources in Cuba, these young people are housed in special schools equipped with all the resources needed, including the qualified personnel required to look after them and give them the confidence and assistance needed for successful integration back into society.

The Cuban Family Code (1975 [2022])

The Cuban Family Code* (*Codigo de Familia*) was Cuba's way of fathoming the normativity of age-related to child offenders for the first time. Passed by the Council of Ministers on February 14, 1975, Law 1289, modified by Law 8 in 1977, the first draft of the Family Code, adopted in 1975, embodies the principal institutions of Cuban family law.

Box 8.2: The Cuban Family Code (1975)

The legal concern over minors was addressed in the 1976 Constitution of the Republic of Cuba, amended in 1992 to include the Family Code (Law No. 1289, February 14, 1975). This Code dispensed with outmoded norms on illegitimacy and issued legal obligations for issues relating to child welfare, including equality, education, rights during divorce of parents, and basic care. At a procedural level, the rights legislated under the Family Code are not enforceable under the law but provide a framework of reference for the Superior Court. Most importantly, however, the statute codified the rights of children and women as societal norms, and associated legislation (i.e., which was enforceable) was subsequently introduced into the legal system. The Code also brought about substantive changes for Cuban women regarding education and employment by promoting equitable family relations, such as sharing household duties and childcare (Clause 28) (see Chapter 10).

In Cuba, the family is recognized as the giver of care and guidance, instructors of the conscience of children and young people to help develop their self-awareness and agency within a framework of positive social en-

---

* Editors' note: The new Family Code (Law 156/2022) was voted on and approved in a national referendum in September 2022, after the writing of this chapter. Experts have considered it as one of the most advanced in the world. It takes affection as the fundamental axis of family relationships, and follows Cuban policy towards international commitments such as the Convention on the Rights of the Child, the Convention on the Rights of Persons with Disabilities, and the Convention on Violence and Harassment. This new code legalizes equal marriage and adoption rights regardless of sexual orientation, recognizes the rights of surrogate mothers, recognizes a parent-guardian's work in the household, and recognizes the role of grandparents in the family, among many more progressive victories (Peoples Dispatch (2022).

gagement and inclusion. In fulfilling a social mandate, schools must also provide specialized attention to students who present discipline or other behaviour problems and make whatever efforts necessary for healthy development. In the criminal justice sphere, this system outlines the measures that can be adopted, from reinforcement of the educative role of parents and the community to internment in specialized schools directed by the Ministry of Education's Ministerial Council on Attention to Minors: Behaviour Schools, Diagnostic and Guidance Centers (CDO).

As well, the Ministry of the Interior's Directorate for Minors guided by its Ministerial Council on Attention to Minors offers Prevention Activities for Minors, Protection Centers for Girls, Boys and Adolescents (CPNNA); Centers for Evaluation, Analysis and Guidance of Minors (CEAOM); and Comprehensive Development Schools (EFI) (Fariñas Acosta/*Granma*, 2013). Again, there are no children's prisons in Cuba (Fariñas Acosta, Granma, November 28, 2013).

Twelve Comprehensive Development Schools (EFI) exist in Cuba. The socio-psycho-pedagogical basis of the associated educative program is recognized by UNICEF and based on the understanding that such young people need help, counselling, and guidance to become upstanding individuals and successfully reintegrate into society (Fariñas/*Granma*, 2013). There are no bars, perimeter guards, mistreatment, or criminal records. These schools' educative/conduct program is based on love and understanding. The students are enrolled in courses corresponding to their level of education, learn a craft, or prepare to move forward with their studies. Again, the idea is that children and youngsters who have had severe behavioural disorders or any criminal behaviour can be socially reintegrated (Jimenez, 2013).

The decision to send a youth to a conduct school requires an administrative procedure, independent of the judiciary and separate from criminal law. The Ministries of Education and the Interior set the minors' pedagogical goals and social therapy needs. Given the interdisciplinary needs of wayward youth, the framework extends into many domains. "These centres have multidisciplinary teams composed of psychologists, educators and legal experts. Individualized guidance is afforded to families during the process of evaluation via parents' classes and group or family therapy" and is considered one of the essential functions of these innovative centers (Fariñas/*Granma*, 2013).

Again, such measures, institutions and programs are governed jointly by the Ministry of Education and the Ministry of the Interior, each having councils composed of specialists in the field and across different branches of associated knowledge: psychologists, lawyers, pedagogues, etc. Such professionals are responsible for adopting relevant measures for troubled youth. A comprehensive assessment is produced by multidisciplinary teams at the Centre for Diagnosis, Analysis, and Guidance of Minors to provide them with in-depth knowledge of each child's personality. This information is then available for review by the same council and plays a role in its recommendations.

Possible intervention measures related to youth crime in Cuba include the following:

- Internment or compulsory attendance at a school for students with severe conduct behaviour (Conduct Schools) governed by the Ministry of Education or internment in a Re-education Centre run by the Ministry of the Interior.
- Mandatory hospitalization in a center run by the Ministry of Public Health.
- Obligatory ambulatory medical treatment.
- Surveillance and attention by the Ministry of the Interior.
- Reinforced surveillance of parents or guardians or those in charge of the minor.
- Individual attention in the regular schools of the National Education System aimed at correcting behaviour without the need for internment in specialized schools.
- Placement of the child as a trainee in a work unit respecting current labour laws.
- Involvement with social workers from the Federation of Cuban Women.

Parents, guardians or other persons taking care of children who have broken the law must adhere to obligations laid out in the Family Code and elsewhere in the law related to minors' care, maintenance, nutrition, education, etc. Failure to meet these obligations first results in warnings but can lead to criminal proceedings.

In sum, Cuban minors (i.e., under the age of 16) with behavioural problems attend specialized schools, effectively removing them from the realm of criminal law and criminal procedure. Once over 16 years of age, a provincial council for the care of minors (Decree-Law 64, 1982) can decide to extend their attendance until age 18 if deemed necessary for successful re-education/rehabilitation and social reintegration. Any minor having participated in an intentional act constituting a crime and who is deemed a high risk for recidivism upon turning 18, combined with a high index of social dangerousness, can be transferred to an adult facility for up to five years. The prosecutor's participation in the Cuban legal system is particularly significant in youth criminal justice since minors are not considered criminals. Prosecutors represent the interests of the youth, primarily those who are victims of crime.

The Role of Community Policing in Crime Prevention in Cuba since 1959

Before 1959, the police had generated an atmosphere of terror among the Cuban population. More than 10,000 people are said to have been killed or otherwise disappeared during the final period of the U.S.-backed Fulgencio Batista's dictatorship in 1956–1958. Places like the Ninth Police Station in Havana were synonymous with terror and death. Officers from both the army and the Batista police received training in military academies in the United States, which supported Batista logistically, militarily, and financially from his first reign of power from 1933 to 1944, through his military coup starting in 1952 (History.com, 2009). This explains the generalized rejection by Cuban society of the use of the armed forces prior to 1959.

Box 8.3: Impact of Batista Regime

President John F. Kennedy, in an interview on October 24, 1963 with journalist Jean Daniel Bensaid for the French daily newspaper *L'Express*, said the economic colonization, humiliation, and exploitation in Cuba was greater than any colonized country owing in part to the U.S. policies during the Batista regime (*Granma International*, 2013; Riversong, n.d.).

Defence has been the purpose of the National Revolutionary Police (PNR) since its founding on January 5, 1959, as an organ of the Ministry of the Interior (MININT). Fidel himself recognized at the time that the strength of the MININT was inseparable from the power of the people. On this basis, a phenomenon similar to what is referred to elsewhere as community policing is alive in Cuba. Police sector chiefs must live within the community they serve. Such sector chiefs intervene in the control of criminals, play a prominent role in crime prevention, and ensure community reception of interns in their community free of any discrimination or stigma that might negatively impact reintegration. Reintegration can sometimes be hindered in Cuba because the family rejects members who have committed a crime.

In Cuba, police officers are typically normally assigned to serve in the same general area where they live and are expected to be exemplary neighbours and community members. This allows the police to be familiar with and accepted by the community, which is also the officer's family's community. Working in the community where they live ensures that police are familiar with and accepted by the community. This permanent presence within the community not only affords the Cuban police a unique opportunity to talk, exchange, and observe but also be able to circumvent crime at the local level and ensure that those serving time can be reintegrated into and subsequently maintain a normal life in their community.

Police are present on the main public roads, provide security at parties and mass events, and help anyone in need. This public service is carried out professionally, and the police enjoy the population's support. Among the particulars of Cuba's community policing ethos is that the police participate and offer post-release follow-up and assistance, including helping with the job hunt and a smooth transition back into society. Since the beginning of the Revolution, the police's public service and professionalism have also helped ensure people's identification of those who have tried to oppose the ideas underlying the purpose of the Cuban Revolution, which Cuban citizens support.

The Cuban police do not have independent structures in the municipalities or provinces. The central Ministry of the Interior administers all. Having a single body at the national level has avoided possible conflicts of competence and helped eliminate jurisdictional issues for police between states or regions across the country. There are provincial and municipal military facilities, but these do not have autonomy levels or subordination to municipal or provincial governments. Nevertheless, these armed institutions can play a role in maintaining public safety and crime investigation and participate actively in civil defence actions. Any violations of the rights or values of the people of Cuba by the police are dealt with through internal control mechanisms and are subject to military court jurisdiction. The military prosecutor's office is the oversight body that investigates citizens' complaints and presents them to the courts.

There are different ways of joining the Cuban police forces. In addition to mandatory (and demanding) physical requirements and psychometric tests, potential police officers receive comprehensive multidisciplinary training in legal matters and psychology, general cultural relations, and martial arts. In the years following the Cuban Revolution's triumph in 1959, police schools, institutes, and academies were also created to provide officers with sufficient educational levels to attain the degree of Doctor of

Science. Officer training also allows them to specialize in areas such as the prison system, public safety, and criminology, among others. Likewise, the police engage at schools and community education centers to motivate students to join "circles of interest" related to various professions.

Circles of interest are adopted as early as primary school and aim to familiarize groups of children with the police's work and duties or other fields and encourage them to consider their vocation. Professionals from various fields visit schools to illustrate their careers, and then interested students are brought into the workplace.

Policing and Cuban Enforcement Judges

In addition to the authority and powers afforded the Cuban police, the Popular People's Supreme Court and the Provincial and Municipal Courts are responsible for enforcing the police's charges, provided there is sufficient and compelling evidence. Hence, for the system to work effectively, enforcement judges and judicial assistants play an essential role in the justice process. Representatives of the courts accompany the sector chief in presenting the former intern to the community. They are also empowered to revoke benefits such as early conditional release and assist police by issuing orders forcing companies and institutions to admit interns returned to the community. Since their adoption in the new millennium, enforcement judges have gained significant experience in social reintegration.

Fidel Castro's "Battle of Ideas"

At the dawn of the 21st century, following a proposal made by Fidel Castro himself, a vast social movement called "Batalla de ideas" ("Battle of Ideas") that included transformations in different sectors of Cuban society reached the Cuban penitentiary system. These transformations affected not only the treatment of prison interns but also dealt with crime prevention. This process aimed to determine the social factors underlying crime, including family and community issues such as economic situation and educational levels, among others, as well as the inherent social exclusion and vulnerability induced by being in prison. Such ideas of fairness would prove unstoppable.

Box 8.4: Unstoppable

Like stones rolling down hills, fair ideas reach their objectives despite all obstacles and barriers. It may be possible to speed or hinder them, but it is impossible to stop them. —José Martí (1853–1895), cited by Ripoll (1994).

The Battle of Ideas constituted a comprehensive set of measures and public policies aimed at rescuing diverse social sectors, which, having suffered the consequences of the severe economic crisis of the 1990s, had been left vulnerable amid a deterioration of values across society. This process evidenced the existing gaps within society, the vulnerable social state in which those already in prison had been formed or deformed, the type of family, economic situation, and schooling levels, among others. This analysis fostered new social programs generated through increases in the number of social workers, including programs aiming to integrate young people neither working nor studying by ensuring such things as a stipend and television and video rooms in their neighborhoods.

The Battle of Ideas had a favourable impact on Cuban society. It constituted a means of socially reintegrating thousands of people left in an unfavourable situation. Following the Revolution's humanistic underpinnings, approximately 170 programs were carried out during the immediate post-Revolution period and focused mainly on delivering education, cultural awareness, public health, and information to the Cuban people.

The search for new practices and methods led to the opening of the San Francisco de Paula Center in Havana to look for new ways for the social reintegration of interns. Starting in October 2001, a social re-insertion program studied the in-prison behaviour of one hundred young interns (serving for non-violent crimes) and the family's socio-cultural background. This was the precursor to what was later coined "Tarea confianza" (confidence task) (Palenzuela, 2015). Several task centers exist in Cuba offering work-study programs in an open prison regime, providing education and training for work in the construction of public facilities such as schools, parks, buildings, etc. After serving their terms, the interns are ready and able to enter the construction sector's labour force. In some cases, their employment under the program is continued post-release. These paid apprenticeships have a considerable impact on the social reintegration of offenders. The housing and living conditions afforded by this semi-open regime are sometimes better than the intern has ever known. As noted earlier, they are sent back to traditional prison if they commit a new crime or violate any conditions.

On the eve of Pope Benedict's visit, the Council of State granted a pardon of more than 2,900 sanctions. As of May 2012, there were 57,337 interns in the country (31,494 in closed conditions and 25,843 in open facilities) according to information published in the government newspaper *Granma* and reported by the digital site *La pupila insomne* (Gómez, 2012). Although maximum-security prisons do exist in Cuba, most correctional centres operate under open or semi-open regimes according to the sentences imposed and the crimes committed. Men and women are separated in the prison facilities and interns are grouped by age.

The government newspaper *Granma* (September 15, 2015) reports that 27,095 interns were receiving schooling, with 24,531 also involved in on-the-job training and programs or specialized courses, all of which has a positive impact on intern-guard relations. In 2012, 23,113 interns were working and earning the same rates as other workers (Gómez, *Pupila Insomne*, May 22, 2012).

Raising the cultural level of incarcerated persons is another Cuban prison policy priority. Starting in 2008, an initiative organized by singer-songwriter Silvio Rodriguez has carried out several concerts under the banner "Cultural Expedition for Human Improvement" among other activities to bring interns together with artists, writers, filmmakers, painters, etc. The Cuban National Council of Fine Arts conducts activities and art exhibitions in prisons. Various Cuban organizations have brought art and cultural activities into the prison domain since 2009 (Granma, September 15, 2015).

Conclusion

The authors submit that the structure and organization of Cuban criminal law, both substantive and procedural, is heir to Spanish doctrine but modified by provisions and amendments from other foreign systems through transculturation processes unique to Cuba. Social justice has always been a top priority for the Cuban revolutionaries. Through social justice promotion, public safety in Cuba is among the highest in Latin America and the Caribbean. This is considered one of Cuba's most significant achievements since the Cuban political project was consolidated by the Cuban Revolution in 1959.

Today in Cuba, there is considerable debate over the age of criminal responsibility. Most such discussions align with the various international conventions and treaties, to all of which Cuba is a signatory member. In all cases, interns (i.e., inmates) receive humane treatment in Cuba, with the objective of transformation away from criminal behaviour by instilling confidence through enhanced life skills and academic levels and/or the obtention of a trade. This fosters successful reintegration into the community society post-release. The Cuban police play a vital role in the follow-up and control of those serving terms of deprivation of freedom. The police's mandate is focused on crime prevention.

The 2019 Constitution grants the Cuban correctional policy its constitutional character, with provisions for rights in relation to social reintegration section and norms for how interns are treated both in prison and after release. Other rights related to the criminal justice system include alternate methods of conflict resolution (Art. 93), protection from false imprisonment (Art. 94), victims' rights (Art. 95i), guarantees of due process such as habeas corpus (Art. 96) and the right to access one's personal information (Art. 97), legal assistance in the exercise of their rights (Art. 95b), and the retroactivity of penal laws (Art. 100).

In the future, other significant changes are envisioned. Specifically, these include greater rights and guarantees to defendants in the criminal process. The legal reforms also include establishing new laws, including the right of victims to participate in the judicial process and eliminating certain crimes from the Criminal Code. Also, new laws regarding the courts and the prosecutor's office will lead these institutions toward more efficient and modern operations.

Since 1959, the Revolution's ideals have influenced Cuba's social and political system. While the ideals have served the country well and been seen as a model of what the principles of Cuban socialism can achieve, six decades later there are signs that reforms are strengthening the criminal justice sector's existing social justice character.

References

Barroso González, J. L. (2014). Historia y actualidad de la resocialización en Cuba. https://dspace.uclv.edu.cu/handle/123456789/12289

Biron Carey, L., and IPS News Agency. (2013, August 20). More countries turn to faltering U.S. prison privatisation model. http://www.ipsnews.net/2013/08/more-countries-turn-to-faltering-u-s-prison-privatisation-model/

Bodes Torres, J. (2001). Sistema de Justicia y procedimiento penal en Cuba. Havana, Cuba. *Editorial ciencias sociales.*

Body of Principles for the Protection of All Persons under Any Form of Detention or Imprisonment. (1988). 43/173 of December 1988. *Resolution.* United Nations. https://digitallibrary.un.org/search?ln=zh_CN&as=0&p=subjectheading:[Body+of+Principles+for+the+Protection+of+All+Persons+under+Any+Form+of+Detention+or+Imprisonment+%281988%29]

Bufetes colectivos [Collective law firms]. (1984, June 8). [Decree-Law No. 81, "On the legal profession and the national organization of collective law firms". English translation in *Guide to Cuban Law and Legal Research.* I2017). Online. Cambridge University Press. doi:10.1017/jli.2017.22] "*Sobre el Ejercicio de la Abogacía y la Organización Nacional de*" [DLEAONBC]. *Gaceta Oficial* [Official Gazette], 12, Art. 3(a).

Castro Ruz, F. (1965). Speech [on the] 4th Anniversary of the Interior Ministry. Chaplin Theater. http://lanic.utexas.edu/project/castro/db/1965/19650617.html. Havana.

Castro Ruz, F. (2004, December 5). Speech given at the closing session of the Young Communists League 8th Congress, held in the Havana Convention Centre, Havana, Cuba. http://www.cuba.cu/gobierno/discursos/2004/ing/f051204i.html

Centro, U. C. (2016, November). Observatorio de libertad religiosa de America Latina y El Caribe. Boletín jurídico. *Derecho y Religíon. Chili: Pontifical Catholic University of Chile. Law Faculty.* http://derechoyreligion.uc.cl/es/docman/boletin-jurid

ico/2016/989-noviembre-2016/file
[Constitution of the republico of Cuba] [Constitución de la República de Cuba]. (April 2019). [Official Gazette] *Gaceta* Oficial No. 5 Extraordinaria. [National Assembly of People's Power] Asamblea Nacional del Poder Popular. *Havana (GOC-2019-406-EX5)*. http://media.cubadebate.cu/wp-content/uploads/2019/04/Constituci%C3%B3n-de-la-Rep%C3%BAblica-de-Cuba.pdf
[Constitutional Reform Act]. (1978). *Ley de Reforma Constitucional*, Article 10, amended changing the name "Isle of the Pines" to "Isle of Youth."
Convention for the Prevention and Punishment of the Crime of Genocide. (1948). United Nations. https://www.un.org/en/genocideprevention/doc
[Criminal Code of the Republic of Cuba]. *Ley 21*. (1979). [Law 21] http://www.files.sld.cu/prevemi/files/2013/03/ley-21-codigo-penal-19791.pdf
[Criminal Code of the Republic of Cuba]. *Código Penal. Ley 62.* (1987). [Law 62] http://www.parlamentocubano.gob.cu. Also Retrieved from https://www.gacetaoficial.gob.cu/html/codigo_penal.html. Cuba: Havana, 62. [National Assembly of People's Power] Asamblea Nacional del Poder Popular. [Law 62].
[*Criminal procedure Law.* 1977]. Ley de procedimiento penal (1977). Asamblea nacional del poder popular. Republic de Cuba. http://www.parlamentocubano.gob.cu/index.php/documento/
Cubadebate. (2014). Cuba entre los países con menos homicidios en América Latina. http://www.cubadebate.cu/noticias/2014/04/12/cuba-entre-los-paises-con-menos-homicidios-de-america-latina
Cubadebate. (2015). [Collective law firms] [Bufetes colectivos]. http://www.cubadebate.cu/etiqueta/bufetes-colectivos/
Cubadebate. (2017). http://en.cubadebate.cu/news/2017/05/25/cuba-calls-for-comprehensive-protection-childhood-and-adolescence/
Cuba Fernández, S. (1929–2001). Santiago Cuba Fernández. https://www.ecured.cu/Santiago_Cuba_Fern%C3%A1ndez. Havana: Ecured.
Cuba's national report to the third cycle of the Universal Periodic Review (UPR) of the Human Rights Council. (2018, May 16). http://www.minrex.gob.cu. Geneva.
Declaration on the Protection of all people from torture and other cruel, inhuman or degrading criminal treatment. UN Resolution 2200A (XXI) of 16 December 1966. (March 1976). https://www.ohchr.org/EN/ProfessionalInterest/Pages/CAT.aspx, article 49.
De Armas Fonticoba, T. (Coord.). (2015). El problema de la edad en el derecho penal cubano. Cited in Mejías, C. A. (Coord.). *Temas de derecho penal parte general, libro homenaje al profesor Renén Quirós Pírez.* Havana, Cuba: Editorial del Ministerio de Justicia I. Agramonte y Loynaz.
[Decree law 151] [de 10 de junio de 1994]. (1994). *Gaceta Oficial Extraordinaria* [Official Gazette], 6: 151. https://www.parlamentocubano.gob.cu/sites/default/files/documento/2022-09/goc-2022-o93_0.pdf
De la Cruz Ochoa, R. (2001). El delito, la criminología y el derecho penal en Cuba después de 1959. *Criminología*. Havana, Cuba: Editorial Félix Varela.
De la Torriente Brau, P. (1975). *El Presidio Modelo.* Havana, Cuba: Editorial ciencias sociales.
Dudley, S., and Bargent, J. (2017, January 19). The prison dilemma: Latin America's incubators of organized crime. https://www.insightcrime.org/investigations/prison-dilemma-latin-america-incubators-organized-crime/
ECURED. (n.d.). Reeducación penitenciaria en Cuba. https://www.ecured.cu/Reeducaci%C3%B3n_Penitenciaria_en_Cuba
[Electoral Law]. (1992). *Ley Electoral vigente.* http://www.parlamentocubano.cu/wp-content/.../LEY-ELECTORAL.pdf
[Family Code] [Código de familia]. [Law] Ley 1289. (1975). [Under Cuban legislation, Law

59] Legislación Cubana, Ley [Law] 59. Havana: *Gaceta Oficial* [Official Gazette].
[Family Code] [Código de familia]. [Law] Ley 156. (2022). [Under Cuban legislation, Law 59] Legislación Cubana, Ley [Law] 59. Havana: *Gaceta Oficial* [Official Gazette].
Fariñas Acosta, L. (2013, November 28). Education and love for juvenile offenders. *Granma* Newspaper. http://www.granma.cu/idiomas/ingles/cuba-i/28noviembre-escuela.html
Firschein, B. (2018). Judicial Independence in the United States. Sistemas Judiciales. https://sistemasjudiciales.org/wp-content/uploads/2018/08/temacentral_bfirschein.pdf
Gaceta Oficial de la República de Cuba–Publicación Digital. *Legislación Cubana* [*Cuban Legislation*]. Havana: Gaceta Oficial [Official Gazette, Digital Edition]. https://www.gacetaoficial.gob.cu/html/legislacion_cubana.html
Gaceta Oficial de la República de Cuba. ANPP: *Ley No. 140*/2021. De los tribunales de Justicia (Law of the Courts of Justice). *Gaceta Oficial* [Official Gazette] GOC-2021-1070-O137. https://www.parlamentocubano.gob.cu/sites/default/files/documento/2022-09/goc-2022-o93_0.pdf and https://cuba.vlex.com/vid/ley-no-140-2021-878842507
Gálvez Puebla, I. (2004): Evolución y Desarrollo del sistema penitenciario. In *Criminología*. Havana, Cuba: Editorial Félix Varela.
García Santos, N. (2007, September 25). Inauguran centro para la Tarea Confianza. *Periódico Juventud Rebelde*. http://www.juventudrebelde.cu/cuba/2007-09-25/inauguran-centro-para-la-tarea-confianza. http://www.cubadebate.cu/especiales/2012/05/22/sistema-penitenciario-cubano-protege-derechos-de-los-reclusos/
Gilna, D. (2019). GEO Group CoreCivic face class actions alleging prisoner "slave labor." *Prison Legal News*. http://www.prisonlegalnews.org
Goite Pierre, M., and Cuenca, A. M. (2017). Interrogantes, alternativas y desafíos en clave de derecho penal y criminología. Libro homenaje Prof. Dr. Miguel Olmedo Cardenete. Havana, Cuba: Editorial UNIJURIS.
Gómez Castellón, H. (2012). Arquitectura penitenciaria cubana en regímenes abiertos. Los centros de trabajo y Estudio. *Revista Legalidad Socialista* No. 35, Año 2012. Revista de la Fiscalía General de la República de Cuba.
Gómez, S. A. (2012). Granma informa sobre las prisiones y los reclusos en Cuba. De la pupila insomne. *Granma* Newspaper. https://lapupilainsomne.wordpress.com/2012/05/22/granma-informa-sobre-las-prisiones-y-los-reclusos-en-cuba/
Granma, D. [Editorial]. *Granma*. (2016, November 14). Concede el Consejo de Estado Indulto a 787 sancionados. *Granma* Newspaper. Reprinted in Havana on January 27, 2021. http://www.granma.cu/cuba/2016-11-14/concede-el-consejo-de-estado-indulto-a-787-sancionados-14-11-2016-23-11-43
Green, D., Hadavi, T., and CNBC. (2020, January 2). Why big banks could be killing private prisons. CNBC online. https://www.cnbc.com/2020/01/02/why-private-prisons-geo-group-and-corecivic-are-struggling-under-trump.html
History.com. (2009). Batista was forced out by Castro-led revolution. A&E television networks. Originally published October 22, 2009. https://www.history.com/this-day-in-history/batista-forced-out-by-castro-led-revolution
International Convention on the Suppression and Punishment of the Crime of Apartheid; adopted by the United Nations General Assembly on December 19, 1966. Came into force on March 23, 1976. https://www.un.org/en/genocideprevention/documents/atrocity-crimes/Doc.10_International%20Convention%20on%20the%20Suppression%20and%20Punishment%20of%20the%20Crime%20of%20Apartheid.pdf
International Convention on the Suppression and Punishment of the Crime of Apartheid. G.A. res. 3068 (XXVIII), 28 U.N. GAOR Supp. (No. 30) at 75, U.N. Doc. A/9030 (1974), 1015 U.N.T.S. 243, entered into force July 18, 1976. https://www.un.org/en/genocideprevention/documents/atrocity-crimes/Doc.10_International%20Convention%20on%20the%20Suppression%20and%20Punishment%20of%20the%20Crime%20of%20Apartheid.pdf

International Covenant on Civil and Political Rights; UN Resolution, 2200a (XXI). Approved on December 16, 1966, and in force from March 23, 1976. https://www.ohchr.org/sites/default/files/Documents/ProfessionalInterest/ccpr.pdf?ref=tftc.io

Jimenez, E. A. (2013). Escuelas de formación integral: Educar en sensibilidad. *Cubadebate*. http://www.cubadebate.cu/opinión/2013/11/20/la-bondad-de-las-escuelas-de-las-escuelas-de-formacion-integral

Kann, D. (2019, April 21). 5 facts behind America's high incarceration rate. CNN. http://www.cnn.com

Ley [Law] 21. (1979). Approved by the National Assembly of People's Power in its 2nd session, December 1978. Havana: [Official Gazette of the Republic of Cuba] *Graceta Oficial*.

Ley [Law] 62. Approved by the National Assembly of People's Power. (1987). [Criminal Code of the Republic of Cuba]. [Ley de procedimiento penal]. *Código Penal*. http://www.parlamentocubano.gob.cu/index.php/documentos/

[Law] Ley 653. (1959). [Laws] Leys 592 and 593. (1961). https://www.unicef-irc.org/portfolios/documents/372_cuba.htm. United Nations Children's Fund, 592 and 593.

[Law of Judicial Organization Act] [Organización del sistema judicial]. (1973, June 23). Ley [Law]1249. Approved by the National Assembly of People's Power in its first session. http://www.parlamentocubano.gov.cu/index.php/documento/ley-de-organizacion-del-sistema-judicial

[Law of the Judicial Courts] [Ley de los Tribunales de Justicia]. December 2021, Law 140. Approved by the National Assembly of People's Power. Gaceta Oficial [Official Gazette]. GO 221-1070-0137. https://www.gacetaoficial.gob.cu/es/gaceta-oficial-no-137-ordinaria-de-2021

[Law No. 5] *Ley 5*. Criminal Procedure Law] [Ley de procedimiento penal [LPP 1977]. (August 13, 1977). *Art.* 8, as amended in 2013 by [Decree-Law] Decreto-Ley 310. *Gaceta Oficial Extraordinaria* [GOE]. June 25, 2013.

[Law 87] *Ley 87*. (1999). [Perpetual Deprivation of Freedom]. [National Assembly of People's Power] Asamblea Nacional del Poder Popular. Cuba.

[Law 151] *Ley 151*, (September 2022). *Gaceta Oficial* [Official Gazette] *de la República de Cuba 93*.

Llobet Rodríguez, J. (1998). *Proceso penal comentado*. Costa Rica: Universidad para la Cooperación Internacional.

Magro Servet, V. (2005). La victimización secundaria de los menores en el proceso penal. *Diario La Ley*, 6282, 27 June 2005, Ref. D-160.

Maier, J. B. (1997). El Ministerio Público en el proceso de Reforma en América Latina. In Pena and Estado (Eds.). *Revista Latinoamericana de política criminal*, Argentina: Ministerio Público. *Editores del puerto-número*, 2(2).

Martínez Dalmau, R. (1999). *Aspectos constitucionales del ministerio fiscal*. Tirant lo blanch. Spain.

Informativa, M. R. La Batalla de Ideas, el trabajo social y las transformaciones en el sistema penitenciario. *Televisión cubana. Canal Cubavisión*. March 23, 2024, 7 p.m. Cuban Radio and Television.

Michalowski, R. *World Factbook of Criminal Justice Systems*. Cuba. https://www.bjs.gov/content/pub/pdf/wfbcjsc.pdf

[Ministry of External Relations]. MINREX. (2005). Converting prisons into real centres for education and human enhancement. [Minister of External relations] Ministerio de relaciones exteriores. http://cubaminrex.cu/Derechos%20Humanos/Articulos/Archivo/2005/LibroBlanco2005/English/3_6.html

[Ministry of the Interior]. (1962, March 27). Resolution No. 1001. Havana, Cuba: Ministerio del interior.

――――. (2016, December 1) Order 7. Viceministro Primero del Ministerio del Interior.

[Penitentiary System Regulation] Reglamento del Sistema penitenciario. Ministerio del interior. https://cubalex.org/wp-content/uploads/2018/10/D.16.pdf

Ministry of Justice. [MINJUS]. (January 22, 1965). Resolution No. 18. Havana. http://www.cubadebate.cu/especiales/2015/02/12/de-puerto-principe-a-hoy-la-historia-de-la-abogacia-cubana/. Cuba.

Montero, J. (1938). Código de defensa social. Havana, Cuba: Editorial económica.

Morais, Y. (2015). A guide to legal research in Cuba. https://www.nyulawglobal.org/globalex/Cuba.html

Palenzuela Paez, L. (2015). La ejecución penal en Cuba. *Legalidad, derecho y sociedad. Revista de la Fiscalía General de la República de Cuba*. http://www.fgr.gob.cu/sites/default/files/20160420/Publicaciones/leg_der_y_soc_no.2.pdf, 2.

Pasquali, M. (2020, March 24). Homicide rate in Cuba. https://www.statista.com/statistics/1002695/homicide. Statista.

Peoples Dispatch (2022). Cubans just ratified the world's most progressive Family Code. https://peoplesdispatch.org/2022/09/26/cubans-just-ratified-the-worlds-most-progressive-family-code/

Pérez, C. J. (2001, July–September). El Sistema Judicial cubano desde 1959 hasta la actualidad. *Revista Jurídica Cajamarca*, 2(4). Cajamarca, Peru. http://www.derechoycambiosocial.com/RJC/Revista4/cuba.htm

President Kennedy recognized U.S. responsibility for the Batista dictatorship and Cuba's underdevelopment in the 1950s. (2013, May 13). Havana, Cuba: Granma International. http://www.granma.cu/idiomas/ingles/international-i/30may-Kennedy.html, 143

Prieto Morales, A. (1982). Derecho procesal penal. *Ministerio de educación superior*. Havana, Cuba: Ediciones ENSPES.

Quirós Pírez, R. (2009). *Manual de Derecho penal*, IV. Havana, Cuba: Editorial Félix Varela.

Radeska, T. (2017, May 18). Fulgencio Batista: One of the worst and most cowardly dictators in history. *Vintage News*. https://www.thevintagenews.com/2017/05/18/fulgencio-batista-one-of-the-worst-and-most-cowardly-dictators-in-history/

Raposo Fernández, J. M. (2019, May 3). Estudio crítico del proceso contra menores delincuentes. Aspectos necesitados de reforma. *La Ley: Revista jurídica española de doctrina, jurisprudencia y bibliografía* (1997), 6, pp. 1599–1613. https://dialnet.unirioja.es/servlet/articulo?codigo=74971

[Resolution No. 18, of the Ministry of Justice] Resolución No. 18. (1965, January 22). *Del Ministerio de Justicia [RMJ]*. Havana: Gaceta Oficial [Official Gazette of the Republic of Cuba].

Ripoll, C. (1994). Martí: Thoughts/pensamientos. https://www.azquotes.com/author/9523-Jose_Marti?p=2

Riversong, R. (2011, May 14). *Fidel Castro and JFK: Shifting the paradigm of human culture. Turning the tide*. Riversong blog. https://riversong.wordpress.com/jfk-fidel-castro/

Rodríguez Guerrero, L. (2017, May 25). Cuba calls for the comprehensive protection of childhood and adolescence. *Granma* Newspaper. http://en.granma.cu/cuba/2017-05-25/cuba-calls-for-the-comprehensive-protection-of-childhood-and-adolescence

Rodríguez Parrilla, B. (UNHRC). (2019). Informe De Cuba Sobre La Resolución 73/8 De La Asamblea General De Las Naciones Unidas. Necesidad De Poner Fin Al Bloqueo Económico, Comercial Y Financiero Impuesto Por Los Estados Unidos De América Contra Cuba [Cuban Report. United Nations human rights council to the human rights council]. https://cubaminrex.cu/sites/default/files/2019-09/Cuba%20vs%20Bloqueo.pdf

Rondón Centeno, A. D. (2002). *La reinserción social de los egresados de prisiones como continuidad del tratamiento reeducativo. Dificultades actuales en la provincia de Camagüey*. Cuba: Camagüey: Editorial Universitaria.

[Social Defence Code] [Código de defensa social]. (1936), 24. Havana, Cuba: Biblioteca

Jurídica de Autores Cubanos y Extranjeros.

Standard minimum rules for the administration of juvenile Justice (Beijing Rules). (1985, November 28). (UN Resolution 40/33.) http://www.cidh.org/ninez/pdf%20files/Reglas%20de%20Beijing.pdf

Statista. (2019). Latin America and the Caribbean (Pasquali, M., 2020). https://www.statista.com/statistics/1223144/latin-america-contact-centers-country/

UN Standard Minimum Rules for the Treatment of Prisoners (Nelson Mandela rules). (2015) (rev. version). https://www.penalreform.org/resource/standard-minimum-rules-treatment-prisoners-smr/

UN Declaration on the Elimination of All Forms of Racial Discrimination. (1963). https://www.oas.org/dil/1963%20United%20Nations%20Declaration%20on%20the%20Elimination%20of%20All%20Forms%20of%20Racial%20Discrimination,%20proclaimed%20by%20the%20General%20Assembly%20of%20the%20United%20Nations%20on%20November%2020,%201963,%20resolution%201904%20%28XVIII%29.pdf

United Nations. (1948). Universal Declaration of Human Rights. https://www.un.org/es/documents/udhr/UDHR_booklet_SP_web.pdf

United Nations. (2006). World Council of Human Rights (Resolution 60/251, 2006). https://www2.ohchr.org/english/bodies/hrcouncil/docs/a.res.60.251_en.pdf

United Nations. (1955). Standard Minimum Rules for the Treatment of Prisoners. Adopted by the First United Nations Congress on the Prevention of Crime and the Treatment of Offenders, held at Geneva in 1955, and approved by the Economic and Social Council by its Resolutions 663C (24) of July 31, 1957. https://www.ohchr.org/Documents/ProfessionalInterest/treatmentprisoners.pdf

Vienna Convention on Consular Relations. (1967). Done at Vienna on 24 April 1963. https://legal.un.org/ilc/texts/instruments/english/conventions/9_2_1963.pdf. Entered into Force on 19 March 1967. *United Nations Treaty Series*, 596: p. 261.

Yamamoto, A. et al. (2015), p. 95). Administration of juvenile justice in Brazil: Recent advances and remaining challenges. In J. A. Winterdyk (ed.), *Juvenile justice: International perspectives, models and trends* (pp. 89–106). Boca Raton, FL: CRC Press.

Zaffaroni, E. R., and Oliveira, E. (2013). *Criminology and criminal policy movements*. Lanham, MD: University Press of America.

Zaffaroni, E. R. (1993, July 26 and 27). ["The Contemporary Penitentiary Experience: contributions and experiences." Mexico City. Paper presented at the Congress held under the coordination of the General Directorate of Prisons and Social Rehabilitation Centers of the Department of the Federal District and the II Assembly of Representatives of the Federal District.] La Experiencia del penitenciario contemporáneo: Aportes y experiencias. Ponencia presentada en el Congreso celebrado bajo la coordinación de la Dirección General de Reclusorios y Centros de Readaptación Social del Departamento Del Distrito Federal y la II Asamblea de Representantes del Distrito Federal.

CHAPTER NINE

Sociocultural Anthropology in Cuba: Historical Overview*

José Vega Suñol

Abstract

This chapter deals with the origin and development of Cuban anthropology in its sociocultural dimension. Applied in the context of nation, anthropology has allowed us to study, explain, and understand the process of the ethnic formation of the Cuban people. In Cuba, this scientific discipline recognizes three fundamental historical stages of national formation: the colonial period, from Christopher Columbus's *Journal of Navigation* (1493) and Dominican Fray Bartolomé de las Casas' *History of the Indies* (1527) to the founding in Havana for scientific pursuits of the Anthropological Society of Cuba in 1877 along the lines of its Madrid counterpart; the republican period, from 1902 to 1958, during which the symbolic figure of Fernando Ortiz and his indisputable contributions to this science would emerge; and the revolutionary period, when anthropological studies would inform a cultural policy oriented to the rescue and popular expression of endogenous values. A process of institutionalization of the field also began during this period, having a corresponding impact on social and cultural research on the island. The descriptive analysis in this chapter thus offers an anthropological perspective on the critical historical periods of the Cuban nation.

Keywords: anthropology, history, sociocultural policymaking, transculturation, cultural theory, ethnology, Indigenous values.

José Vega Suñol holds a PhD in Historical Sciences (University of Havana, Cuba) and is Full Professor at the Research Centre for Culture and Identity Issues (University of Holguín, Cuba). A member of the Cuban Academy

---

* This is a revised version of a paper originally published in Spanish in 2017 and copyright © 2017 by Lea Carvalho Rodrigues Isabelle Braz Peixoto da Silva. Full details for the original paper are found in the reference section of this chapter.

of Sciences; the National Union of Cuban Artists and Writers (UNEAC), and the Cuban Union of Historians, Dr. Vega is President of the Cultural Anthropology Centre at University of Holguín. Email: jvega@uho.edu.cu

Introduction

This chapter presents a synthesis of the historical journey of Cuban anthropological studies from a sociocultural point of view and shows how it helped forge an understanding of the basic principles underlying the Cuban nation and nationality. The first section tackles the origins of anthropological discourse on the island during the colonial period; the second is devoted to the figure of Fernando Ortiz and the foundation of Cuban sociocultural anthropology; and the third depicts the subsequent rise of Cuban sociocultural anthropology as one of the most prolific disciplines in the field of social sciences in Cuba during the revolutionary period.

Colonial Origins of Anthropology in Cuba

The Cuban archipelago, located in the Caribbean Sea, is one of the pristine territories of America found by European man upon his arrival on this continent. From the moment Admiral Christopher Columbus set foot on its coast on October 27, 1492, Cuba became part of the historical perspective of European expansionism. The Columbian *Journal of Navigation* is the first documentary reference written about Cuba. Describing the geography and insular flora and fauna, it draws a literary portrait of the island's first inhabitants, which is why it is considered indispensable ethnographic material for any study of Cuba and the Caribbean.

One of the most emblematic figures of the Chroniclers of the Indies was Dominican Fray Bartolomé de las Casas, whose prolific work contemplates the Cuban island scene of the day. *History of the Indies** includes descriptions of his witnessing, written and compiled through his voyages (1527–1552). It abounds with stories about Cuba's Indigenous communities. De las Casas gave us the first texts written from a European perspective and taking a humanistic view of American man, based on eyewitness accounts and testimonials—his work would become a prototype for the recognition of cultural difference and the rights of the Other (de las Casas, 1995).

The origins of West Indian proto-anthropology come into view in that first narrative on the encounter between European man and the American Indigenous peoples in the Caribbean, at a time when Cuba and *Quisqueya*, the Indigenous name given by the Arawak to the island territory

---

* This work remained unpublished for more than three centuries, with the first edition coming to light in Spain circa 1875–1876. It is available in English.

now known as Dominican Republic and Haiti, were renamed Juana and Española respectively by the conquerors. De las Casas' is the first of many relevant descriptions by chroniclers and remains the most important of all the chronicles. This account, nonetheless, would be incomplete without the French Monk Ramón Pané* and his *Account of the Antiquities of the Indians* (1498), the first text about the Americas written *in situ* by a European.

Early European cartographers, draftsmen and engravers, mainly Dutch, English and French, also warrant mention here. Using the techniques and graphic supports of the day (16th, 17th, and 18th centuries) as well as the new printing technologies, which by the fifteenth century included the printing press, they could record descriptions of what they saw as they passed through the Caribbean. Their contribution is considerable because such representations today constitute a visual heritage for the study of the Indigenous peoples, Europeans, and Africans who came together in the agonizing saga of the conquest and colonization of the New World.

Throughout the long colonial period endured by Cuba—one of Spain's last colonies to gain independence—the island was visited by dozens of travelers, mainly of European, North American, and Latin American origins. Travel books (Olivera, 1998) are primary sources for social studies because they provide data on population, race, customs, fashion, and other topics of interest from a foreign perspective on Cuba and Cubans. Among the many travel accounts and books, those by German scholar Alexander von Humboldt are relevant. Cubans consider Humboldt the "second discoverer" of Cuba for his detailed descriptions of its inhabitants, the flora and fauna, the socio-cultural and economic realities of the insular society, and his condemnation of slavery. Humboldt visited Cuba twice, in 1800 and 1804, and subsequently published one of the key critical antislavery texts of the first half of the 19th century, *Political Essay on the Island of Cuba* (1827). It is loaded with data of interest to any anthropological study of the period and of particular value to historical anthropology related to the Caribbean.

At the end of the 1820s, Reverend Abiel Abbot of the Congregational Church visited the island from the U.S. In his book *Letters from Cuba (1828)*, Abbot recounts his several-month stay in the Matanzas and Havana regions and his work remains relevant to Cuba's anthropological history. In the 1850s, one of the founders of cultural evolutionary anthro-

---

* Fray Ramón Pané of the Order of San Gerónimo arrived in America on Columbus' second voyage, lived with the Indians in Española, learned the Arawak language, and left a written record of his cultural experience: *Relación de las Antigüedades de los Indios*. The text was found in the Archives of Seville and was published (and translated) in the twentieth century.

pology, Edward B. Tylor, was in Cuba and left written impressions that provide valuable information. Another visitor of interest to the history of anthropology on the island is the French Doctor Henri Dumont (Rivero de la Calle, 1978), whose anthropometric measurements of African slaves in the early 1860s can be considered the first examples of such work in Cuba. The books and notes left by these foreign visitors, generally written in a descriptive style, contain dense ethnographic material about Cuba and its people and are required sources for an understanding of the social trajectory of the Cubans. Contemporary researchers have not sufficiently examined these materials, so an in-depth analysis of these works and their contributions to the field of anthropology remains to be done.

The Rise of Cuban Scientific Thought in Anthropology

The event that stands out the most in the history of insular anthropology is the founding of the Anthropological Society of the Island of Cuba, which took place in Havana in 1877 as an extension of a similar body in Spain created in the previous decade. Comprising mainly Cuban professionals, some of whom were Europe-trained doctors such as Luis Montané Dardé (1849–1936), its first director was the Cuban intellectual and naturalist Felipe Poey Aloy (1799–1891). This society laid the foundations of an anthropology that embraced the Darwinian-evolutionist and positivist paradigms. It was relatively short-lived, however, dissolving in 1895 with the resumption of the fight for independence.

In reality, the early Anthropology Society was one of the few settings in which the emerging Cuban scientific thought could be debated and challenged along with the ideas of the international scientific community. Some of its members, such as Fermín Valdés Domínguez and Enrique José Varona, were known public figures affiliated with independence. The depth and scope of the debates and use of scientific methods then in vogue are evidenced in the minutes, which were later published (*Actas*, 1966). The topics addressed in the working sessions mainly concerned the formation of the Cuban being and the biological or cultural material located on the island. Their discussions took up various interpretations of Indigenous remains uncovered in archaeological excavations, such as through the analysis of fragments and objects, or the rich controversy over the race question, the recurring focus of which defines a good part of the thematic and conceptual course of such debates during the eighteen-year existence of Cuba's first anthropological society (1877–1895).

Fernando Ortiz and the Foundation of Sociocultural Anthropology in Cuba

Towards the beginning of the twentieth century, when the Neocolonial Republic (1902–1958) was underway, several scientific authorities made contributions to the different fields of anthropological work that would distinguish them in their respective areas of knowledge.* However, the basic foundations of sociocultural anthropology are owing to the prolific work of Don Fernando Ortiz (1881–1969), the reputed Cuban sociologist, anthropologist and historian. Both his scientific thinking and approaches diverged from the presuppositions and objectives of European and North American social and cultural anthropology; Ortiz's sociocultural studies are constructed and supported within the framework of an anthropology of decolonization decentred from Eurocentric models and set in a context of the Third World.

The magnitude of his work and focus on the African roots of Cuban culture are key to a comprehensive understanding of what Ortiz coined as *Cubanness*. His legal training in Spain and encounter with the eminent Italian criminologist Césare Lombroso (1835–1909), whose studies, albeit racist, at the dawn of criminal anthropology afforded Ortiz the tools for taking a scientific look at the culture and behaviour of Africans and their descendants by studying their customs, beliefs, music and dances, which until then had been excluded from the scientific debate due to the economic, social and cultural marginality of the *Negro*.

Ortiz's written works include more than twenty books as well as several hundred pamphlets and articles. His early books include *Hampa afro-cubana: Los negros brujos* (1906) [*Afro-Cuban Underworld: Black Wizards*], and *Los negros esclavos* (1916) [*Black Slaves*], while those produced at the height of his intellectual and anthropological maturity include *Contrapunteo cubano del tabaco y el azúcar* (1940) [*Cuban Counterpoint: Tobacco and Sugar*, 1947], *El engaño de las razas* (1946) [*Deception of Race*], and *Historia de una lucha cubana contra los demonios* (1959) [*History of a Cuban Struggle against the Demons*], to mention only a few of his best-known titles, allow us to place him at the vanguard of scientific Cuban anthropology in the first half of the twentieth century.

A forerunner in the field of Indigenous archeology, Ortiz's comprehensive research moved from extensive accounts of black and white witchcraft,

---

* In terms of biological anthropology (then classified as physics), the indispensable Aristides Mestre Hevia (1865–1952) stands out as a propagater of the legacy of Luis Montané Dardé and the two worked worked together as university professors and as practicing anthropologists.

Catholicism and the Cuban cult of the Virgen de la Caridad del Cobre (El Cobre Virgin of Charity), and African ethnic groups, to critical explorations of the economics of tobacco and sugar production and its role in the formation of national culture. The theoretical dimension of Ortiz's work and scope of his proposals and concepts are also relevant. Ortiz drank from every available source, as any man of science would do, but there is no evidence of a blind reception to such Western currents and schools of thought as positivism, evolutionism, diffusionism, or functionalism. Although he took advantage of these models, his critical orientations were very original, and his work was in no way overshadowed by Eurocentric thought. With Ortiz, an anthropological current from an endogenous source began to flow and take shape in Cuba, marked by a desire to fathom the diverse aspects of Cuban cultural identity.

Ortiz was the main bastion of the initial process of decolonization in the branch of knowledge that would become peripheral anthropology and signaled the emergence of a Cuban thought emancipating itself from the entropic processes of the classical currents that had characterized the science of anthropology (Cardoso de Oliveira, 1987). But Ortiz did not act alone. From the beginning of the twentieth century, and even before, a Latin American anthropological discourse had begun to be glimpsed, and its precursory voices are those of the Haitian thinker and anthropologist Anténor Firmin and his antiracist work, *The Equality of the Human Races* (1885), which was published in France and responded to the racist theories of Gobineau (France, 1816–1882); the publication of the first texts by the Mexican anthropologist Manuel Gamio (1883–1960), founder of the indigenismo movement; and the works of anthropologists Gilberto Freyre, such as *The Masters and the Slaves* (1933), and Arthur Ramos, such as *The Peoples of Brazil* (1940). These works formed a primary *avant-garde* core that would lead to the decolonization of anthropological thought in Latin America. This group, geographically dispersed and disconnected from each other, gave shape to an emerging Latin American anthropology with its own perspective, supported by voices from the respective national communities whose research was oriented to studying their own cultural beings. From then on, a movement—first of emancipation and then decolonization—would take place and lead simultaneously to the founding of national and Latin American anthropology.

In this context, Ortiz proposed the neologism *transculturación* (transculturation) in 1940, the acceptance of which contributed to the move away from the use in Spanish of the United States' assimilatory term *acculturation* to describe the process of cultural change experienced by subjects acquiring a new culture in a context other than colonization. Ortiz defended the need to replace this anglicism because it fathomed cultural change from a strictly colonial perspective. For Ortiz, decolonization was devoted to the development of new terminologies for mapping theoretical and methodological paths that would lead to a better explanation of who we are:

> We have chosen the term transculturation to express the very varied phenomena that originate in Cuba due to the complex transmutations of cultures that take place here; without knowing them it is impossible to understand the evolution of the Cuban people, both economically and institutionally, legally, ethically, religiously, artistically, linguistically, psychological, sexual and in all the other aspects of life (Ortiz, 1963).

Ortiz proposed this conceptual definition of what he understood by transculturation because he felt his neologism better expressed the transit from one culture to another, which is not only about one culture assimilating another through contact, as implied by acculturation, but also involves "the loss or uprooting of a previous culture" ("deculturation") and the "consequent creation of new cultural phenomena" ("neoculturation") (Ortiz, 1963).

The fact that Ortiz introduced the concept of transculturation in 1940 puts the Cuban scientist several decades ahead of the debate about the current process of cultural change through intercultural encounters being generated by contemporary migrations. Despite the multiple interpretations of transculturation, it always retains its anti-racist connotation and attachment to social justice/humanism assigned by Ortiz. His inclusion of black people and the dispossessed layers of society as equal and integral components of the formation of Cuban culture have not been sufficiently fathomed outside Cuban anthropology. In Ortiz, the lines of humanism and social justice fuse into a transversal that runs through all of his work. This evidences an interactive ecumenical spirit between the different parts of the seed of nationality in Cuba: whites, blacks, mulattoes, Indigenous (*Indians*), Chinese, and mestizos (*half-breeds*); all anthropological groups fused through this transcultural experience, making way for the emergence of a new historical figure: the Cuban people.

"Cuban is More than White, More than Mulatto, More than Black"

Of course, Jose Martí's maxim "Cuban is more than white, more than mulatto, more than black" (1893) had already established an emphasis on natural origin over racial difference in the foundations of Cuban thought; Martí felt that placing the emphasis on the racial issue would be a mistake that would end with the social and ethnic balkanization of Cuba, which was to be avoided in favour of the unity needed for the fight for independence. Martí's legacy echoes and finds continuity in the work of Ortiz, who devoted much of his anthropological efforts in the first half of the twentieth century to the vindication of the black as an object of discrimination and socio-political exclusion. In Martí and Ortiz, the same sentiments of justice and liberation include the underprivileged classes of the Cuban people, whose omission in the social discourse of the nation defiled the integrationist notion that national culture was found on heterogeneous roots.

Finally, Lydia Cabrera (1899–1991) also bears mention in relation to Ortiz. Cabrera entered into Cuban anthropology with a seminal work devoted entirely to syncretic cults of African origin. Her best-known work, *El Monte* (1954), was a scholarly text about the beliefs, myths, and rituals of Afro-descendants and included an oral repertoire of key figures from whom she learned about practices hitherto secret and thus unknown to researchers. Her work is also highly relevant to understanding and interpretating socio-religious manifestations. Over the first five decades of the 20th century, progress was made in the study of the Cuban people thanks to the dedication of the above-mentioned researchers, who emphasized that the African element had been excluded from social and cultural analysis. In this sense, Fernando Ortiz and Lydia Cabrera laid an important part of the foundations and lines of work that would find continuity in the Cuban anthropology of the second half of the twentieth century.

Sociocultural Anthropology and the 1959 Revolution

In relation to 1959, it is crucial to recognize the considerable heritage left by these predecessors who fostered a relationship of validity and continuity in their own work and that of their students and colleagues. A cultural policy outlined from the beginning of the revolutionary process made its debut in Fidel Castro's 1961 speech entitled "Words to Intellectuals" where it set the stage for the establishment of strategic bases, at conceptual and institutional levels, for the future sociocultural reality envisioned for the island:

> Our fundamental concern will always be the great majority of the people, that is, the oppressed and exploited classes of the people. ...

[F]or us what will be good for them will be good for us; whatever is noble, useful and beautiful for them will be noble, beautiful and useful for us (Fidel Castro, 1961).

This premise, intended to rescue the popular foundations of national culture, was at the heart of a series of new institutions established for the study, evaluation and identification of the cultural specificities of the Cuban ethnos: these included the Institute of Ethnology and Folklore (1961) within the Cuban Academy of Sciences (1961), an institution overseeing national research projects and playing a leading role in the diverse and infinite field of popular culture. The Cuban music researcher and professor Argeliers León (1918–1991), a former student of Ortiz and head of the Institute of Ethnomusicology at the University of Havana, which was founded in 1728, played a major role in the development of the academy together with María Teresa Linares and an enthusiastic group of volunteers. The institute approached much of the anthropological work with an ethnographic emphasis on the folklore and culture of the Cuban people. Some of León's findings were published in *Proceedings of Folklore* (1961), which would become the first serialized anthropological journal in Cuba created after 1959. The journal featured articles by such Cuban anthropologists as Rogelio A. Martínez Furé and Romulo Lachatañeré, among others, alongside that of its founder and director, Argeliers León.

In the second half of the sixties a new literary genre, "testimonial literature," was born in Cuba with the publication of the young Cuban poet, writer, and ethnologist Miguel Barnet's *Biography of a Runaway Slave* (1966) and *Rachel's Song* (1969). With these first testimonial novels, Barnet introduces the new genre, an anthropological storytelling narrative form imbued with the authenticating voice of lived experience. Barnet elaborated the novel *Runaway Slave* and its main protagonist from real-life interviews he taped years prior with the then 103-year-old Esteban Mesa Montejo—a maroon, a *Mambí*, and a witness to the U.S. occupation of Cuba following the so-called Spanish-American War. *Rachel's Song* is a testimonial novel about the life of a cabaret dancer named Amalia Sorg, who Barnet also interviewed, and depicts the disillusionments of life in Havana in the 1920s and 1930s. The young anthropologist-writer Barnet used testimonial witnessing, including quotes, to give a voice to those not heard by creating main protagonists and turning them into vibrant literary characters on the stage.

In the 1960s–70s, the systematic acceptance of Marxist theory opened the door to methodologies and concepts of socio-cultural discourse that had only circulated narrowly among small groups of specialists who applied them in specific scientific papers. Its incorporation immediately impacted the social sciences in Cuba, lending a new approach and authority to both theory and practice. It was considered an epistemic resource for unraveling and understanding issues in social and cultural discourse. Around the same time, publications such as *Structural Anthropology* (1970) by Claude Levi-Strauss and *Culture, Society and Development* (1973), an anthology by John Dumoulin with Euro/Western authors (Soviet, American, and Latin American, including Mexican Gonzalo Aguirre Beltran and Peruvian Augusto Salazar Bondy), also proved helpful. In a way, the authors above and their published works also contributed to the plural matrices of Cuban anthropological science by enlightening an important group of young researchers who are recognized participants in the ensuing development of this discipline in Cuba.

Institutionalization in Cuba of Anthropological Studies in Recent Decades
The creation of the Cuban Culture Ministry and the Science, Technology and Environment Ministry in the second half of the 1970s opened up a range of possibilities to help accelerate the development of national anthropological work via cultural and scientific policies aimed at the recognition, promotion, and preservation of heritage and environmental values embodied in the Cuban cultural identity. One of the priorities of Cuban cultural policy in the late 1970s and throughout the 1980s was to rescue traditional popular culture and promote a national set of cultural and scientific institutions that radiated out to the local levels. In this same period, characterized by the institutionalization of culture and the sciences, the Cuban Ministry of Higher Education was also created to focus exclusively on matters of university education, which resulted in research autonomy and allowed the state to better target its research funding. Such conditions fostered cultural and historical research of a national, regional or local scope and gave rise to new research projects for anthropological studies on the island.

In the early 1980s, a cultural research institution, Casa del Caribe (Caribe house), was founded in the city of Santiago de Cuba by the Cuban scholar, writer, historian and researcher Aníbal Joel James Figarola (1940–2006) who also served as its director. Casa del Caribe published two important journals: *Caribe* (*Revista del Caribe*) and the *Journal of Caribbean Archaeology* (*Caribe Arqueológico*), and also developed the Caribbean Festival (*del Caribe*), which made Santiago de Cuba the annual anthropological meeting point for this whole cultural area. The subsequent emergence of a body of institutions supporting a qualitative turn in sociocultural studies is also worth mentioning. The creation of the Centro Juan Marinello (renamed the Cuban Institute of Cultural Investigation—ICIC—in 1995) to promote and develop Cuban culture was a significant force in this turn. The Centro would become a thought and research hub able to ensure the systematic publication of important works thanks to its publishing arm, which continues to make a major contribution across many research areas.

In 1995 came the creation of the Fernando Ortiz Foundation, chaired by Miguel Barnet and with a mandate to disseminate the work of the eminent Cuban scholar and to support the promotion of anthropology in Cuba as an instrument for the study of national identity following the legacy of Ortiz. The foundation created the *La Fuente Viva* collection for publishing findings from the field across the country, and *Catauro (Journal of Caribbean Anthropology)* (1999), the most important anthropology journal to emerge in Cuba in recent decades. Featuring Cuban and foreign authors, it disseminates anthropological research findings and updates. Also worth mentioning in this group of institutions responsible for the promotion of cultural studies are the Centre for Research and Development of Cuban Music (CIDMC); Cuban Institute of Anthropology, attached to the Academy of Sciences of Cuba in 1978; and House of Africa (Casa de Africa, 1986), which promotes national and international events in the field. The fact that the national set of cultural and scientific institutions radiated out to the local levels allowed a vertical approach to racial problems on the island.

The Institutional Framework of Sociocultural Anthropology in Cuba in Recent Decades

This network of institutions has become the backbone of current Cuban anthropology. The planning, design, and first fieldwork that culminated in the *Ethnographic Atlas of Cuba* (CIDCC, 1999) began in the 1980s. This digital publication presented the findings of Cuba's most complete national census on the make up of its population and traditional popular culture. The ICIC (formerly Juan Marinello CIDCC) mobilized dozens of local experts and researchers in every province for data collection involving advanced ethnographic data collection techniques, computerized statistical procedures, and cultural mapping; it is one of the most complex multidisciplinary research projects ever undertaken in Cuba. The CIDCC had also been involved with an earlier atlas, *Folkloric and Popular Musical Instruments in Cuba* (CIDMUC, 1997). The first cultural research departments at the provincial level came into being during this period, and commissions of inquiry into patrimonial conservation were also established across the country's territories.

The existence of an institutional network of research centres dedicated and committed either directly or indirectly to anthropological studies and the emergence of associated print or digital journals and collections is a testament to the growing profusion of topics related to this science. It also speaks to a copious number of professionals, most having scientific degrees, supporting a prolific body of work as authors in the field of national anthropology. A wave of young people—mainly sociologists, historians, and philosophers, "doing" anthropology from within their respective disciplines—were attending events and workshops, taking postgraduate courses, master's degrees, and doctorates, and contributing to the journals and scientific literature. Although there is no "career" in anthropology in Cuba and the establishment of a scientific board of examiners for the field is far away, anthropological research in dissertations at the doctoral level are defended before the examining boards of other disciplines such as biology, history, sociology, philosophy, psychology, or linguistic sciences. This approach has allowed the inclusion of anthropology and a means of channeling of the multiple contributions being made in this area of knowledge.

The only master's degree program in anthropology in Cuba was established at the University of Havana at the beginning of the 21st century, but the creation of postgraduate options in anthropology (such as at the University of Holguín) are signs that steps are being taken toward a necessary academic institutionalization of this branch of knowledge in the domain of the Ministry of Higher Education. More anthropology content is being added to curricula for sociology at the bachelor's, master's, and doctoral levels. At the undergraduate level, a degree in sociocultural studies, created experimentally at the University of Cienfuegos in 1999 and extended to several Cuban universities since 2000, includes cultural anthropology in its syllabus; prior to this the syllabus of the history major offered similar programming.

Significant Achievements in Cuban Anthropology in the 21st Century

It would be amiss to not mention a number of remarkable achievements in anthropology at the beginning of this century. The *Archeological Census of Cuba* (2013) was conducted by the Cuban Institute of Anthropology and is the most comprehensive scientific survey conducted so far in Cuba. It records previously undiscovered Indigenous settlement sites, some hypothetically dating back over 8,000 years, and archaeological sites in Cuba from before and after the arrival of Europeans (Peláez, December 10, 2013). Importantly, this gives us the contact and transculturation sites at different stages of development, evidentiary signs of the multiple and diverse communities that inhabited the island and left the remains of their cultural heritage. Studies on racialism, racism, and racial prejudice in Cuba have advanced logically, with research in recent years pursued by a group of researchers at the Cuban Institute of Anthropology (2006) (formerly named the Centre for Anthropology) and the University of Havana whose findings may help clarify the differences between racial discrimination and racial prejudice, with the latter focusing on individual mindsets and social psychology.

The field of religious anthropology has also been of interest to Cuban cultural anthropology and there have been several doctoral theses on the subject. With findings firmly backed by fieldwork, they enrich our knowledge of religious figures, eschatological sects, Pentecostalism, and the transformations that have taken place in the religious practices of African origin, traditionally seen as syncretic cults. Another of the substantial advances in anthropological studies in Cuba in recent decades has resulted from a focus on ethnological and racial perspectives *vis-à-vis* the ethnic composition of the Cuban people. The work of the renowned Cuban anthropologist Jésus Guanche focusing on ethnohistorical processes in Cuba stands out in this sphere of activity (Guanche, 2008). Aside from his research into cultural identity and "being" Cuban, Guanche has broached topics related to the characterization, evaluation, and preservation of tangible and intangible heritage, such as traditional popular culture, African imagery, the oral tradition, and the slave route (Guanche, 2008).

When it comes to anthropological linguistics, Cuba's foremost central authority is the renowned philologist Sergio Valdés Bernal, senior researcher at the Cuban Institute of Literature and Linguistics and later at the Fernando Ortiz Foundation. His meritorious works include one on linguistic anthropology (Bernal, 2000) and another on national language and cultural identity in Cuba (Bernal, 1998). Linguistics is among the processes of transculturation elaborated by Ortiz (1940). Bernal's texts deepen our understanding of the relational connections between anthropology and language and how the Cuban variant of the Spanish language in Latin America is enriched by Indigenous languages and words of African, Caribbean, or Anglo-Saxon origin. Several innovative findings in anthropological linguistics were made in in Cuba at the beginning of the 21st century, including the Cuban scholar Avelina V. Couceiro's investigations into an urban anthropology in Cuba (Couceiro, 2009). Couceiro focuses on Havana but offers a methodological framework for its application in other Cuban cities. For the first time we are seeing anthropological studies related to marginality, urban tribes, and gay culture, topics previously absent from Cuban publications.

Another broad area of national anthropological inquiry is tourism. Both the study of the type of tourist that visits the island and evaluations of potential cultural exchanges fall within the scope of interest for the first time as Cuba's tourism represents an agent of economic change and has a dynamic relationship to sociocultural processes in Cuba (Basail and Dávalos, 2003). Another benchmark of interest across the regional and local levels are the archeological excavations at *El Chorro de Maíta** Cemetery site, in the province of Holguín, Cuba, where biological and cultural anthropology have come together to unravel the complexity and multiplicity of the findings, making it a favoured Cuban destination for studying the first contacts between American man and Europeans in the New World (Valcárcel, 2012).

Psychology represents yet another critical area of anthropological science in Cuba. An excellent example of this is found in the work of the Cuban psychologist Carolina de la Torre Molina, whose prolific research centres on the Cuban psychosocial identity. De la Torre worked and directed a project on national identity at the Juan Marinello Cuban Culture Research and Development Centre, has teaching links with the University of Havana's School of Psychology and today's JM Cuban Institute of Cultural Research, and has been the recipient of a number of awards for scientific research, including the Catauro Award for her contributions to the study of Cuban cultural identity (Ruth Casa, 2019). The weight of patriarchal culture in corresponding manifestations of machismo and its implications for gender relations is one aspect, among others, of her work (de la Torre, 2001).

The creation of cultural research departments within provincial and municipal sectors of the Ministry of Culture has opened up a range of opportunities for local and regional research. This has led to in-depth examination of such topics as the presence of the culture of Haitian immigrants and their descendants in locations in eastern Cuba today, or the Arab footprint in cities and populations in the interior of the country and the presence of the different Hispanic migratory components in cities such as Gibara or in the sugar settlements of eastern Cuba. Similarly, the creation of MA and PhD programs in the humanities in the Cuban university network has allowed us to regionalize some of the scientific materials obtained

---

* Chorro de Maita is an Indigenous cemetery located in the province of Holguín, not far from Guardalavaca beach, that dates back to Hindi-Hispanic transculturation processes in the Caribbean and an "encomienda" site in the 16th century.

from the field samples. This has helped expand the findings and decentralize areas of scientific and academic anthropological development in Cuba, which has had the support of a vast network of provincial publishers and territorial literary production.

Numerous Cuban publishing houses, such as Editorial de Ciencias Sociales, Editorial Félix Varela, Editorial Oriente, Ediciones Holguín, and Editorial Capiro in Santa Clara, among others, have also contributed to the publication of historical works, fiction and essays, some of which relate to anthropology. Digital editions have been becoming available in addition to print. Such is the case of Batey (2010), presenting a peer-reviewed Cuban quarterly electronic journal specializing in cultural anthropology, which has been operating since 2010 and has a wealth of articles on its website thanks to the dedication of young professionals pursuing anthropological studies at a regional, national, and international level.

Conclusions

This brief expedition through the insular evolution of Cuban anthropology demonstrates just how important this latter is in explaining and understanding the basic foundations and tenets underlying and sustaining Cuban culture. Our island continues to play a referential function in modern anthropological studies, since part of the first Indo-Hispanic contact in the history of America took place here. Cuba was also the first country described by the Chroniclers of the Indies, the forebears of a pre-scientific anthropology, whose works remain of great ethnographic value due to their highly descriptive accounts of peoples, customs, cultures, and events. With the passage of time, these accounts opened the pathways in modern anthropology for the dedicated study of the Other.

Anthropology as a scientific discipline emerged in Cuba as a metropolitan strategy aimed at recognizing elements of modernity in the agonizing saga of the colonial system. The Anthropological Society of the Island of Cuba was born in the light of such precepts, and it brought together an important group of Cuban scientists who knew how to defend their ideas and thoughts oriented to the study of society and the emerging national culture.

The legitimacy of the anthropological discourse in Cuba crystallized in the figure of Don Fernando Ortiz, father of the sociocultural, folkloric, and ethnographic dimensions of Cuban anthropology. His work has been the most influential and speaks to the maturity of this science on the island. The most relevant event in the history of the Caribbean during the second half of the twentieth century, the 1959 Cuban Revolution, prioritized the cultural values of social groups until then excluded and stimulated the rescue of popular culture in both urban and rural settings. One of the indisputable achievements of anthropology in Cuba in recent decades has been the creation of an institutional network based on a body of scientific-cultural centres dedicated to the research, preservation and promotion of the nation's identity through specialized publications, seminars, and conferences, and in an ever-increasing number of academic spaces.

The new Cuban anthropology scene offers a broad spectrum of rich and multithemed findings, from studies on the components of the Cuban people to that of our popular culture, among many other. The biggest challenge for this field today in Cuba is to increase the awareness of anthropology's continued importance as a critical scientific instrument for understanding the social and cultural transformations that are continually in flux in nation, an area of investigation in which much work remains to be done.

References

Abbot, A. (1829) [1965]. Cartas escritas en el interior de Cuba: entre las montañas de Arcana, en el este, y las de Cusco, al oeste, en los meses de febrero, marzo, abril y mayo de 1828 (J. Vander Gucht, Trad.). Havana, Cuba: Consejo Nacional de Cultura. [*Letters written in the interior of Cuba, vetween the mountains of Arcana, to the east, and of Cusco, to the west, in the months of February, March, April, and May 1828*. Boston: Bowles and Dearborn.]

Actas de la Sociedad Antropológica de la Isla de Cuba. (1966). Havana, Cuba: Proceedings of the Anthropological Society of the Island of Cuba.

Atlas Etnográfico de Cuba. (2000). CD-ROM. [Ethnographic atlas. Havana, Cuba: CIDCC.

Barnet, M. (1966) [1994]. *Biography of a runaway slave*. Trans, W. Nick Hill. Connecticut: Curbstone Press.

----- (1969) [1991]. *Rachel's song*. Trans. W. Nick Hill. Connecticut: Curbstone Press.

Basail, A. Rodríguez, and Dávalos, D.R. (2003). *Materiales de antropología sociocultural*. Havana, Cuba: Editorial Félix Varela.

Batey. (2010–2019). *Revista Cubana de Antropología Sociocultural* [Cuban sociocultural anthropology journal]. http://www.revista-batey.com/index.php/batey

Cardoso de Oliveira, Roberto. (1987). *Identidade e diferença entre Antropologías Periféricas*. Brazil: Pan-American Institute of Geography and History.

Casa, Ruth. (2019). Profile of Roberto Valcárcel Rojas, Roberto. (2012). Interacción colonial en un pueblo de indios encomendados. El Chorro de Maita, Cuba: Unpublished doctoral thesis. Available in PDF format.

Casas, Bartolomé de las. (1876) [1971]. *Historia de las Indias*. [History of the Indies]. Trans./ed. Andrée Collard. New York: Harper & Row.

Castro, Fidel. (1961). *Palabras a los intelectuales* [Fidel Castro's Speech to Intellectuals]. Latin American Network Information Centre (LANIC). http://lanic.utexas.edu/project/castro/db/1961/19610630.html

Catauro: Revista Cubana de Antropología [Cuban journal of anthropology]. Havana, Cuba: Fundación Fernando Ortiz [Fernando Ortiz Foundation]. http://www.ffo.cult.cu/index.php?option=com_content&view=article&id=71&Itemid=66

CIDMC. (1997). *Instrumentos de la música folklórica-popular de Cuba*. [musical instruments]. 2 vols. Atlas. Havana: Centro de Investigación y Desarrollo de la Música Cubana [Centre for research and development of Cuban music]. *Los estudios antropológicos en Cuba*. Mimeograph booklet. Havana, Cuba: Academy of Cuban Sciences.

CIDCC. (1999). Centro de Antropología Centro de Investigación y Desarrollo de la Cultura Cubana. Juan Marinello. (CIDCC) [Juan Marinello anthropological research centre for Cuban cultural development.

Couceiro Rodríguez, Avelino. (2009). *Hacia una antropología urbana en Cuba*. Coll *La Fuente Viva 32*. Havana, Cuba: Fernando Ortiz Foundation.

Dávalos Dominguez, R. and Basail Rodriguez, A. (Eds). (1997). *Desarrollo urbano: proyectos y experiencias de trabajo*. Havana, Cuba: Sociology Department, University of Havana.

De la Torre Molina, C. [coedited with CIDCC]. (2001). *Las identidades: Una mirada desde la psicología*. Havana, Cuba: Juan Marinello Cuban Institute of Cultural Investigation (CICC).

Firmin, Anténor (1885) [2002]. *De l'égalité des races humaines*. Paris : F. Pichon. [The equality of the human races. Trans. Charles Asselin. Reprinted by arrangement with Garland Publishing, Inc.].

-----. (1835–1855) [1915]. *The inequality of human races*. Trans. Adrian Collin. London: Heinemann.

Gamio, M. (1916) [2010]. *Forjando patria. Mexicano: Librería de Porrúa Hermanos*. [Forging a nation. Trans. Fernando Armstrong-Fumero. *Journal of the Society for Latin American Studies*. Boulder, CO: University Press of Colorado, 2010].

-----. (1942). Calificación de características culturales de los grupos Indigenas. *America Indígena* 4(2): 17–22.

Freyre, G. (1933) [1956]. *Casa grande y senzala*. Rio de Janeiro: Maia & Schmidt. [*The masters and the slaves: A study in the development of Brazilian civilization*. Trans. Samuel Putnam. New York: Knopf].

Guanche, Jesús. (1983) [2008]. Componentes étnicos de la nación cubana. Coll. *La Fuente Viva 3*. Revised and expanded edition. Havana, Cuba: Fernando Ortiz Foundation.

-----. (1983) [2016]. *Componentes étnicos de la nación cubana*. Kindle Edition. Panama: Ruth Casa Editorial.

Humboldt, A. von (1827). *Ensayo político sobre la Isla de Cuba*. Paris: J. Renouard [*Essai politique sur l'ile de Cuba*. Paris: Librairie de Gide Fils & Paris: J. Smith. (1826)] [*Political essay on the island of Cuba* (Trans. V. Kutzinski and O. Otte. 2010. Chicago: University of Chicago Press.].

León, A. (1961) [2005]. "La expresión del pueblo en el TNC." *Actas del Folklore* 1(1): 13–16. Havana: Fernando Ortiz Foundation.

Martí, J. (1893) [2002]. *Mi raza*. [My race. In Esther Allen (Ed. and Trans.). *José Martí: Selected Writings* (New York: Penguin Books]. (Originally published in Cuba in *Patria* magazine, 1871).

Olivera, O. (1829, January 1). Viajeros en Cuba (1800–1850). Coll. Cubay Sus Jueces. Miami: Ediciones Universales. English versión available at Amazon.ca.

Ortiz, F. (1906). *Hampa afro-cubana: Los negros brujos*. Madrid: Librería de Fernando Fé.

-----. (1916). *Los negros esclavos*. Havana, Cuba: Revista Bimestre Cubana.

-----. (1940) [1947]. *Contrapunteo cubano del tabaco y el azúcar*. Havana: J. Montero. [*Cuban counterpoint: Tobacco and sugar*. Trans. H. de Onis. New York: Knopf, [1947].

-----. (1945) *El engaño de las razas*. Havana: Editorial Páginas [1946].

-----. (1959). *Historia de una pelea cubana contra los demonios*. Havana, Cuba: Cultural Relations Department, Universidad Central de Las Villas.

Pané, R. (1988) [1999]. *Relación de las antigüedades de los indios*. Mexico: XXI century. [*An account of the antiquities of the Indians: Chronicles of the New World encounter*. Trans. J. Arrom and S. Griswold. Durham, NC: Duke University Press].

Peláez, O. (2013, December 10). *Más de 3 mil sitios arqueológicos aborígenes en Cuba*. Granma Newspaper, Havana, Cuba. http://www.granma.cu/ciencia/2019-03-15/como-

eran-nuestros-aborigenes-15-03-2019-21-03-14
Ramos, A. (1940) [1951]. *Los pueblos de Brasil.* Sao Paulo. [*The Negro in Brazil.* Trans. Richard Pattee. Washington, DC: Associated Publishers, Inc., 1951].
Rangel Rivero, Armando. (2004). Los orígenes de la antropología, su desarrollo desde lo biológico. Anthropology. PDF. Havana, Cuba.
Valdés Bernal, S. (1998). *Lengua nacional e identidad cultural del cubano.* Havana, Cuba: Editorial de Ciencias Sociales (Madrid).
-----. (2000). *Antropología Lingüística.* Coll. La Fuente Viva. Havana, Cuba: Fernando Ortiz Foundation.
Vega Suñol, J. G. (2017). La antropología en Cuba: Esbozo histórico y perspectivas actuales. In *Saberes locales, experiencias transnacionais* (pp. 119–135). Brasilia, Brazil: ABA (Associação Brasileira de Antropología).

CHAPTER TEN

Education in Cuba:
A Model of Justice and Social Equity

Yohannia Ochoa Ardite
and Vilma Páez Pérez

Abstract

There has long been a global consensus that quality education is essential to national development and, more importantly, to the development of humanity itself. The objectives and goals established at each phase of a country's development reveal transformations required to bring about an effective renewal of education. The Cuban social project embodies this concept of education as a necessary mechanism for building a free and robust society. This notion was first advanced by the most universal of all Cubans, José Martí, and has remained a mainstay of the Cuban social and political reality since the Revolution. The Cuban education system's infrastructure, rationale, and methods have been shaped by four main historical periods: Colonial; Republican, aka pseudo-republican or neo-colonial; pre-Revolution; and Revolution up to the present day, as well as by the tenets of the Cuban Family Code (Law 1289, 1975; 2022).

Following the Cuban Revolution (1959), public funding was used to develop all education levels, from primary-secondary and higher academic learning to vocations and trades. Despite the strength and quality of our national education sector (recognized worldwide), today the Cuban education sector faces various limitations and challenges. The challenges are primarily related to the increasingly difficult economic conditions imposed by the now-intensifying United States embargo against Cuba, which has been steadfastly maintained since 1962.

Keywords: education, Cuban educational system, Cuban model of education, José Martí, Cuban Family Code, embargo.

Yohannia Ochoa Ardite, PhD in Pedagogical Sciences. Dean of the Faculty of Letters and Communication, Universidad de Holguín, Cuba.

Vilma Imilce Páez Pérez, PhD in Pedagogical Sciences. Full Professor and Researcher at the Centre for Culture and Identity, Faculty of Social Sciences (Universidad de Holguín). Director of the Canadian Studies Department (*Centre*), Universidad de Holguín, Holguín, Cuba.

Introduction

Education represents one of the Cuban state's fundamental pillars and is supported politically and socially within the nation's legal bases. Education is embodied in national laws, regulations, norms, and standards established through policy and legal custom. Education is mentioned in several articles of the Constitution of the Republic of Cuba; for example, "The State guides, sponsors and promotes education, science, culture" (Title 3, article 32 p. 4); "Everyone has the right to education" (Chapter II, article 46, p. 5); and, "In education, society and families have responsibilities" (Chapter II, article 73, p. 6). The Cuban Family Code (1975, 2022*) also lays out citizen rights and responsibilities related to education (art. 1) for "the most effective fulfillment by parents of their obligations regarding the protection, moral upbringing and education of their children" (art. 85) and by the Childhood and Youth Code (Law 16/1978 art. 17), which puts young people first in terms of education, employment, and health. At the writing of this chapter, these codes are being modified to meet upcoming generations' needs *vis-à-vis* transformations within Cuban society brought about by changes to our Constitution (2019) and through implementing the country's social and economic development action plans for 2011–2036.

The Cuban Family Code (Law 1289) was first passed in 1975 and enacted on International Women's Day, March 8 of that year. It recognized the family as a focal hub of the Cuban social institution (i.e., society), an integral part of the Cuban people's ongoing mobilization of Cuban society, and an essential part of the Cuban people's ongoing mobilization of the nation's development. It was drafted by the Judicial Committee of the Communist Party of Cuba (PCC). The PCC is the organized vanguard—Martí's thought, Fidelista, Marxist and Leninist—of the Cuban nation supported by its democratic character and permanent ties to the people; it is the leading driving force of the society and the state (Art. 5, 2019 Constitution). The role of the PCC is to guide and supervise. As with other codes, laws, and regulations, the Family Code was drafted by a committee representing all sectors of Cuban Society.

The Cuban emphasis on education implies an unwavering commitment

---

* Editors' note: The new Family Code (Law 156/2022) was voted and approved on September 2022, after the writing of this chapter (see Chapter 8).

to the people and recognizes that only an effective national education policy can maintain an education system that meets social needs. José Martí considered the updating of education as a quantum factor in national development, and viewed the divorce between the education provided in a given era and the needs of that era itself as criminal (Martí, 1975, vol. 8, p. 281). Education today also prepares people to understand global economic, cultural, political, social, and scientific-technological changes. For these reasons, now more than ever, educational programs must be continually adapted and fine-tuned to ensure they successfully prepare new generations to face the complex realities within and beyond the nation.

> **Box 10.1**
>
> To educate is to give man the keys to the world, which are independence and love, and to give him strength to journey on his own, light of step, a spontaneous and free being.
> —Martí, 1889, pp. 290-91

This chapter proposes a socio-historic approach to Cuban education. The first section reviews the main events that characterize essential periods of change in the education sector and briefly describes how education has evolved over four historical periods: Colonial, Republican (often called pseudo-republican or neo-colonial), the pre-Revolution, and the Revolution (1959) to present. The second section describes the principles of Cuban education as a central component of Jose Martí's conceptualization of civic education, which naturally affects people's beliefs, commitments, capabilities, and actions as community members and fosters a sense of national pride, belonging, security, and identity. The third section examines the quality of education related to international ratings and assessments by various national and international organizations. The final section considers the limitations and challenges facing education today but celebrates Cuba's enthusiastic willingness to maintain the high standards attained thus far, despite the difficult financial conditions imposed by the U.S. embargo.

Historical Panorama of Education in Cuba
Colonial Stage

In colonial Cuba, primary education schools were available only in the private sector. Keep in mind, public schools in Spain only came into being with the mid-19th century Reform period. Therefore, for almost two centuries, learning in Cuba was limited primarily to private tutoring accessible only to the wealthy. Alternatively, a limited curriculum and poorly trained teachers characterized the little schooling made available by the Catholic Church and even this was inaccessible to the poor masses. The situation began to change somewhat with the founding of the Royal Economic Society (Havana, 1792) and Sociedad Económica Amigos del País (1793), which sponsored education in Cuba through various venues and promoted changes that allowed the country to reach a certain level of development. Certain religious orders, such as the Ursulines, whose nuns arrived in Havana in 1803, also helped increase educational opportunities.

In the 19th century, the concept of public education was broadened and strengthened by the wise philosophical-pedagogical reflections of eminent compatriots—for example, two priests, José Augustin Caballero (1762–1835) and Félix Varela (1788–1853), a teacher, José de la Luz y Caballero (1800–1862), the afore-mentioned José Martí (1853–1895), and the philosopher and pedagogue Enrique José Varona (1849–1933). Their thought imbued the education system with its national character and sense of national identity attained through the Cuban War of Independence. José de la Luz y Caballero was among the prominent minds of his time, a teacher *par excellence* who constructed a transcendent awareness that humanistic morality can be imparted through education. This sentiment is reflected in many ways in the liberating actions that would unfold in Cuba over time. The importance of Varela and Luz y Caballero's contributions lies in the ground they broke to open Cuban education up to the methods of modernity within a framework of the Hispanic tradition.

Neocolonial or Pseudo-republican Stage

The Neocolonial Republic, established in 1902, was characterized by a growing abandonment of the school system. The neglect of educational services was characteristic of successive governments operating under the United States' domination mechanisms after its appropriation of the Cuban War of Independence (i.e., the so-called Spanish-American War between Cuba and Spain). The island's U.S. occupation following Spain's retreat had a direct and vigorous influence on all areas of national life in Cuba. This would interrupt and distort the above Cuban thinkers' advanced pedagogical legacy for education and other sectors.

National development was hindered during this phase of U.S. intervention in Cuba. Reproductive learning, which emphasizes memorization, was popular in the day; students were seen as empty vessels to be filled with existing knowledge, which played a role in maintaining the status quo. However, the eminent Cuban pedagogue Enrique José Varona* (1849–1933) would continue to advocate an alternative education model in which the development of minds like sponges was rejected in favour of open minds capable of embedding and transforming ideas (Martínez O'Farrill, 2018).

Pre-revolutionary Stage

When dictator Fulgencio Batista took power in the 1950s, almost 50 percent of Cuba's school-aged population did not attend school, and half the adult population was illiterate. In 1953, a group of young Cubans led by Fidel Castro took up arms to transform this terrible reality. After the well-known attack on the Moncada Garrison in Santiago de Cuba on July 26 of that year, Fidel and a small group of his supporters were taken prisoner.

In the ensuing trial, this young Cuban lawyer and revolutionary uttered words in his self-defence that would go down in history: *History will absolve me.*† Fidel characterized the problem with public education as one of the primary evils to be fought, condemning a system in which thousands of schools were without teachers when more than 200,000 teachers were unemployed. Other pressing problems were also at hand, including the following iniquities (*Granma*, July 29, 2020):

- Approximately 30 percent illiteracy;
- Primary school accessible to just over half of children (56.4 percent);
- Secondary school education accessible to barely 28 percent of those aged 13 to 19;
- Only six schools for teacher training, with limited enrolment;
- Lack of agricultural and technical-professional education opportunities;
- Only three public universities serving the entire country: the University of Havana (1728), the University of Oriente (1947), and the Central University of Las Villas (1952);
- Most official and private "university" colleges centres of corruption, favouritism, and privilege;
- Despite receiving a large share of the national budget, public education languishing while new private schools emerged, making education inaccessible to the poor majority.

---

* For more on Enrique José Varona, see J.G. Wilson and J. Fiske, eds. (1889), *Appleton's Cyclopedia of American Biography*, a six-volume collection of biographies of notable figures in the history of the New World.

† Fidel Castro's self-defence speech delivered during his trial for having commanded the attacks on the Moncada (Santiago de Cuba) and the Carlos Manuel de Cespedes Garrisons on July 26, 1953. For more in English on these attacks and their ideological ties to Martí and Céspedes, see *Granma*, July 29, 2020.

Box 10.2: The Cuban Revolution in Education: Excerpts from Fidel Castro's famous Moncada speech, *History Will Absolve Me* (1975)

In terms of struggle, when we talk about people we're talking about the six hundred thousand Cubans without work, who want to earn their daily bread honestly without having to emigrate from their homeland in search of a livelihood; the five hundred thousand farm laborers who live in miserable shacks, who work four months of the year and starve the rest, sharing their misery with their children, who don't have an inch of land to till and whose existence would move any heart not made of stone; the four hundred thousand industrial workers and laborers whose retirement funds have been embezzled, whose benefits are being taken away, whose homes are wretched quarters, whose salaries pass from the hands of the boss to those of the moneylender, whose future is a pay reduction and dismissal, whose life is endless work and whose only rest is the tomb; the one hundred thousand small farmers who live and die working land that is not theirs, looking at it with the sadness of Moses gazing at the promised land, to die without ever owning it, who like feudal serfs have to pay for the use of their parcel of land by giving up a portion of its produce, who cannot love it, improve it, beautify it nor plant a cedar or an orange tree on it because they never know when a sheriff will come with the rural guard to evict them from it; the thirty thousand teachers and professors who are so devoted, dedicated and so necessary to the better destiny of future generations and who are so badly treated and paid; the twenty thousand small business men weighed down by debts, ruined by the crisis and harangued by a plague of grafting and venal officials; the ten thousand young professional people: doctors, engineers, lawyers, veterinarians, school teachers, dentists, pharmacists, newspapermen, painters, sculptors, etc., who finished school with their degrees anxious to work and full of hope, only to find themselves at a dead end, all doors closed to them, and where no ears hear their clamour or supplication. These are the people, the ones who know misfortune and, therefore, are capable of fighting with limitless courage! To these people whose desperate roads through life have been paved with the bricks of betrayal and false promises, we were not going to say: "We will give you..." but rather: "Here it is, now fight for it with everything you have, so that liberty and happiness may be yours!"...

Our educational system is perfectly compatible with everything I've just mentioned. Where the peasant doesn't own the land, what need is there for agricultural schools? Where there is no industry, what need is there for technical or vocational schools? Everything follows the same absurd logic; if we don't have one thing we can't have the other. In any small European country there are more than 200 technological and vocational schools; in Cuba only six such schools exist, and their graduates have no jobs for their skills. The little rural schoolhouses are attended by a mere half of the school age children—barefooted, half-naked and undernourished—and frequently the teacher must buy necessary school materials from his salary. Is this the way to make a nation great?

Source: Castro, Fidel. (1953). *History Will Absolve Me*. Pedro Alvarez Tablo (Trans.) and Andrew Paul Booth. Retrieved from www.marxists.org/history/cuba/archive/castro/1953/10/16.htm

At the dawn of the Cuban Revolution, radical socioeconomic transformation was needed. This helped set the stage for dual-goal educational reforms to make education available and accessible to all and align education with the nation's socioeconomic demands.

The Revolution Stage

In 1959, the newly recognized Cuban State and Revolutionary Government immediately made great efforts to bring improvements to all sectors, including rural areas, and guarantee the right to education and other infrastructure development, such as equitable access to the associated work opportunities. To set this in motion, the new Revolutionary Government aimed its social policies at human improvement by providing care and protection for children and adolescents. Cuba's continued success in this regard has been recognized worldwide.

Primary educational services were extended to the masses on December 26, 1959, under Decree-Law 680. They consolidated the head of the revolutionary government's vision of universal formal education, which Fidel had voiced as early as 1953 as the only vehicle to ensure the ability of workers and all citizens to successfully contribute to the new society envisioned in his Moncada speech. More than 10,000 classrooms were opened in a single day with the enactment of the decree-law. Given this historical context, the transformation of 69 of Batista's soldier barracks into schools was of great political and moral significance. Schooling was soon accessible to almost 90 percent of children under 12 years of age. These first steps quickly flowed into subsequent changes to the Cuban education system (Box 10.3).

Scientific research has been at the core of Cuban medicine and was embraced during the 1960s, focusing on scientific research, academic medicine, and the revolutionary government's public healthcare strategy. The 1965 establishment of the first scientific centre founded by the Revolution, the National Centre for Scientific Research (CNIC),* would lead to the creation of the Medical University of Havana in 1976, among others.

Cuban Engineering and Biotechnology Centre (1986+): COVID Vaccine

In 1986, Fidel Castro inaugurated two important educational institutions and initiated a third that has been key to national development. First, on July 1, he inaugurated the Engineering and Biotechnology Centre at Hava-

---

* For more information on the more than 50 scientific institutions seeded by the CNIC, see López Mola et al. (2002, September 27), "Development of Cuban biotechnology," *Journal of Commercial Biotechnology*.

Box 10.3: Summary of Significant Transformations brought about by Changes to the Cuban Education System during the Revolutionary Stage

1960
Constitution of the Volunteer Teacher Contingent
Three thousand young people marched to the mountains in celebration of the opening of classrooms throughout the country for all school-aged children. Intensive teacher training courses were also created to ensure a sufficient and effective supply of teachers at all levels in a short period of time.

Constitution of the "Frank País" Vanguard Teachers' Brigade
A total of 707,212 illiterate people learned to read and write in one year, reducing illiteracy from 23.6 percent to 3.9 percent. Follow-up plans were organized for literacy and worker improvement programs for the under-educated to ensure primary-level education of all adults (Worker and Peasant Education) through the "Battle for the Sixth Grade" program.

1961
Educational Program for Girls Living in the Countryside
More than 150,000 girls from remote rural areas received sewing and other cultural classes in the "Ana Betancourt" school in Havana. The initial steps for the training of art instructors were taken. Work of volunteer teachers and literacy brigades commenced, and a teaching law suppressing private education and changing old teaching methods was nationalized.

Literacy Campaign
While illiteracy generally affects the poorer segments of a society and makes them vulnerable in a variety of ways, education affords the means to escape poverty. Fidel Castro's successful Literacy Campaign laid the foundations for popular support for this credo underlying Cuban education. Attention was focused on one million illiterates, and the 250,000 teachers and thousands of youth brigades mobilized were able to make it all happen in a year.

1962
University Reform
The reform addressed the aims of university in the academic and social spheres, teaching and research services, and established a comprehensive system of scholarships, among other major changes. A pedagogical principle of study-work programs was initiated, and new syllabi consolidated and implemented at a national level.

1963
Vocational Training. Relations between Ministries
Vocational interest circles and the monitors movement began. The INDER-MINED Plan was organized. The INDER (Institute of National Sports and Physical Education, since its constitution (February 23, 1961) affirms that sports, education, and physical recreation must be seen as integrated, key elements for the healthy development of the human being. With the motto "healthy mind →

CONTINUED FROM PREVIOUS PAGE
in healthy body," physical education is taught from early childhood education up to university level.

1970
Diversification of Training and Creation of New Infrastructures
Teacher training schools were created and would later become faculties of higher pedagogical institutes to train graduates of university education programs in primary education.

1971
First National Congress on Education and Culture (Castro, April 30, 1971)
First stage of teacher preparation through the perfection process of the national education system: content, curricula, programs, and texts. Secondary schools were opened in the countryside to meet the demand of graduates and make the study-work model accessible beyond the urban cores.

1972
Creation of the "Manuel Ascunce Domenech"
The fulfillment of Fidel's idea on how to guarantee continuity of studies for the  large numbers of graduates from the primary education system he had extended to the masses. An advanced group of senior high students was trained through this newly created detachment. They had volunteered to become teachers rather than opting for other more profitable specialties. This detachment celebrated 45 years in December 2019 and today trains students who opt to serve as teachers in remote areas (Parra, 2019).

1975
First Perfection Process of the Education System
Adaptations of schools' organization; the family's and community's role are defined in the Family Code Law (1975; 2022). In Cuba, education is recognized as a system organized into subsystems that include the family, mass and social organizations, and community.

1985
Second Perfection Process of the Education System
A more flexible and contextualized education model. Fewer hours in the syllabi and curricula. Major emphasis on teacher training.

2012
Third Perfection Process of the Education System
Rooted in the Guidelines of the Economic and Social Policy of the Party and Revolution introduced during the 6th Congress of the Communist Party of Cuba (see Chapter 2), the third stage of the perfection process of our national education system began with the 2019/2020 school year (CMHW, 2019). It aims for a qualitative leap in the education system with better results in all spheres. The training of teachers and professors is key.

SOURCE: AUTHORS

na (CIGB).* Then, the day after the annual July 26 celebrations of Moncada (Ojito/Cubadebate, November 27, 2019), he launched the Faculty of Medical Sciences (FCM) at the University of Havana (Ojito/Cubadebate, 2019; CIGB, 2021), and announced his plan to install a smaller centre at Sancti Spiritus. The new centre would be headed by a female Cuban scientist, Dr. Ada Triguero, founder of the Espirituan CIGB in 1990, who served as director until her retirement in 2001. At the inauguration, Triguero thanked Fidel, recognizing him for conceiving and initiating the idea of a scientific pole in the remote community of Sancti Spíritus (Ojito/Cubadebate, November 26, 2019).

According to Dr. Enrique Perez Cruz, head of the Research and Development Department of the provincial CIGB in Sancti Spíritus, Fidel trusted in the talent of the country people and the whole nation enough to create small centres in various provinces (Ojito/Cubadebate, November 26, 2019). The fruits of this labour are evidenced by the success of past research into dengue fever and HIV, but it also represented a saving grace for Cubans in relation to COVID-19.

The research into a vaccine for COVID-19, "common in clinical-epidemiological analysis, included a total of 150,000 [volunteer] subjects, more than 70,000 of whom worked in healthcare and the biotechnology and pharmaceutical industries, while another 124,000 citizens [who] volunteered in Havana, Guantánamo, Granma, Santiago de Cuba, and Sancti Spíritus have received the Abdala candidate" (*Granma*, April 21, 2021). Employing Cuba's well-trained university graduates while keeping our nation on the cutting edge of engineering and biotechnology, the CIGB (2021) tested three successful COVID-19 vaccines on its premises in Cuba.

The COVID vaccines Abdala (CIGB-66) and Soberana 02 developed by the Cuban Centre for Genetic Engineering and Biotechnology showed 92.2 percent and 91.2 percent efficacy, respectively, after three doses (Finlay, July 9, 2021). Cuba fully vaccinated its entire population over two years of age with at least one dose, as required, in 2021 on a completely voluntary basis. Cuba's Centre for State Control of Medicines, Equipment and Medical Devices granted emergency-use authorization and allowed massive vaccination across the country and for export to other countries—Viet-

---

* Fidel Castro speech at the founding of the Engineering and Biotechnology Centre at Havana (in Spanish) on July 1, 1986. By the end of the 20th century, the Centre had already created some 30 products, mainly to combat serious diseases such as dengue or HIV (Cubadebate, August 8, 2016). For more information on the Cuban CIBG, go to https://biomed.cigb.edu.cu/

> **Box 10.4: Cuba's COVID-19 Vaccines**
>
> Cuba's first approved vaccine was named **Abdala**, reminding us of the epic poem Martí wrote when he was just a teenager. While these days the word Abdala conjures great joy, it also evokes the memory of Martí, who at just 15 years of age dedicated this poem to the homeland. In the verse, the young hero, Abdala, heads to war to defend his fatherland, full of patriotic fervour no matter how strong and powerful the enemy. The logo for the Abdala vaccine is the monument to José Martí in Havana. Equal devotion to Cuban sovereignty motivated our scientists to create one of the five vaccine candidates celebrated throughout the island.
>
> We are very proud of the sole star in our national flag. It symbolizes our independence and sovereignty. We are not another star to be added to the U.S. flag. **Soberana** translates into sovereignty, and its very existence illustrates the decision not to depend on others but develop human and technical resources to fulfill the needs of our country. We could do more, but the blockade prevents us from doing so.
>
> Another vaccine, **Mambisa**, is named for the revolutionary soldiers (*mambises*) who fought against Spanish rule in the first Cuban war of independence.
>
>
>
>
> From left: Abdala logo; José Martí memorial; Mambisa logo, which features the Cuban national flower, the "butterfly," pictured immediately below; and Soberana 02 vaccine, featuring our single star.
>
> IMAGES: FLOWER—TONY HISGETT (WIKIMEDIA COMMONS); OTHERS—AUTHORS.

nam, Saint Vincent and the Grenadines, Nicaragua, Venezuela, Syria and Mexico*—that decided to use Cuban vaccines.

Miguel Díaz-Canel Bermúdez, President and First Secretary of the Communist Party of Cuba affirms that the country has made successful advances in biotechnology. Despite the harsh conditions imposed by the tightening of the blockade† in the past three years, "Hit by two pandemics [COVID-19 and the U.S. blockade], our scientists at the Finlay Institute and the Centre for Genetic Engineering and Biology [CIGB] have … giv-

---

* See (in English), *The Conversation* (March 16, 2022).

† Cuba refers to the U.S. embargo against Cuba as a blockade.

en us two very effective vaccines: #Soberana02 and #Abdala" (TeleSUR[HD] 2021, Miguel Diaz-Canel on Twitter).*†

Cuba has historically considered education the key to national development and has consistently put its money where its mouth is. Despite the severe economic restrictions facing Cuba today, the Cuban Ministry of Education has made all possible efforts toward continuous improvements in education. Besides education being a primary right for all Cuban citizens, the policy directing it is recognized as the most important means of guaranteeing the continuity of the humanistic social goals pursued by the Cuban society to ensure equality and public safety for new generations.

Education during the Special Period in Times of Peace: An Interval of Social and Economic Complexity

At the end of the 1990s and the dawn of the 21st century, the difficult socio-economic situation known as the Special Period in Times of Peace forced Cuba to make significant changes in all sectors of the economy and society. Education, however, remained a steadfast priority.

All possible efforts have since been made to maintain the developments achieved in education, health care, and other social sectors. This process, which had a political and ideological framework that came to be known as the Battle of Ideas,‡ fostered the following changes:

1. **Emergent teacher-training model (2000+):** for faster teacher training and to limit the student-teacher ratio to 20:1 per classroom at the primary level.
2. **Comprehensive teacher training (2000+):** to raise the quality of secondary education through comprehensive teacher preparation for all subjects (i.e., humanities and sciences) and reduce the student-teacher ratio to 1:15 at the basic secondary level.
3. **Educational TV (2000+):** The *Canal Educativo* (Educational Channel)

---

* Cuban president highlights success of COVID-19 vaccine candidates on Twitter.

† Note: Since the writing of this chapter, Cuba has approved additional COVID-19 vaccines and is recognized as having "one of the highest national dose rates of any country worldwide" (Statista, March 2023). Cuba may be a developing country with a very poor economy, but its investments in education and research show that the health and wellbeing of the population are the highest priority.

‡ **Batalla de Ideas:** The Cuban Battle of Ideas (Ecured, 1999) was a political action by the Cuban Revolution arising from the kidnapping of the child, Elián González, by a Cuban American said by some to be a mafia resident of Miami. The Battle of Ideas encompasses a set of educational and social programs carried out in different spheres of society and offers an ethical debate in defence of the advances of the Revolution in social justice, national integrity, and internationalism.

1 of Cuban TV, inaugurated on May 9, 2002, and Educational Channel 2, which followed in 2004, were used by the Ministry of Education as delivery vehicles for general education to the Cuban people. Both channels continue to offer various educational courses and programs for all educational levels. The educational programming on Channel 1 includes tutoring in various subjects such as foreign languages (i.e., English, French, Portuguese), science, civic education, history, arts and crafts, and manual labour, as well as training in matters of civic, historical, scientific, and ethical import as a complement to training received in the school system. These subjects are available on television within the University for All Program framework inaugurated on October 2, 2000, as an essential component of the Battle of Ideas to provide broad accessibility to higher knowledge. During the COVID-19 pandemic, the two educational TV channels and other Cuban TV channels were used as necessary by the Ministry of Education to keep students from all levels of education active with their classes while learning at home. This was followed by just a few weeks of contact with their teachers and end-of-the-year exams.

4. **Community Computer Clubs (2002+):** Opened nationwide to computerize the entire society by teaching computer literacy and programming.
5. **"Freedom" Publishing Program (2000+):** School libraries became equipped with a comprehensive collection of encyclopedias, atlases, and dictionaries, as well as numerous volumes containing world literature classics.
6. **Comprehensive Improvement Courses (2002+):** Available to young people who had had to leave their studies or jobs during the difficult years of the Special Period in Times of Peace.
7. **Schools of Social Work (2000+):** Affording opportunities to those who had left school and were jobless, former interns (i.e., inmates) who were not working, and other vulnerable groups, with the aim of educating them so they could become active agents in the social transformation of their communities. Such measures constituted an inclusive way of taking care of the most vulnerable citizens' needs; and this, during the catastrophic economic crisis in the Special Period in Times of Peace.

The seven programs mentioned above would not have been possible without the country's mass, social, and non-governmental organizations. Thousands of young people returned to school and became social workers, initially working across different socio-economic sectors and then given part-time university education to produce more humanities and social sciences professionals.

The Cuban Education Rationale

The Cuban education approach is rooted in a mass systemic approach having philosophical, sociological, medical, psychological, pedagogical, and legal foundations. This multidisciplinary, integrative approach heightens the scope and quality of education. It is a holistic system with built-in mechanisms to ensure no child or youth falls through the cracks. Cuban educators seek to identify and resolve any sensory, intellectual, or physical deficiencies that may hinder a student's performance and thus take a preventive approach to the risk of disassociation from dropping out of school. In short, children whose risk or emotional factors affect learning and/or personal relationships are provided the extra services they need to succeed.

The preventive nature of education thus constitutes a system of actions aimed at guaranteeing the educational and socio-environmental rights and needs of all Cuban children, adolescents and young people. This means that educators are always involved in research, knowledge-building, reflection, planning, and creating comprehensive psycho-pedagogical evaluations with the participation of the family, mass organizations, people in the workplace, educational administrators, and fellow teachers. This educational project meets the individual needs of the troubled student at all levels of schooling. Cuban educational policy stresses the need for the early identification of learners' needs. The centre conducts this process for diagnosis and orientation, and it is a specialized institution based in each municipality of the country. Every elementary school has a psycho-pedagogical commission working in conjunction with the diagnostic support commissions from special schools.

Such special educational supports include comprehensive psychological-pedagogical evaluations carried out by multidisciplinary teams at diagnostic and orientation centers run by the Ministry of Education at all regions' municipal and provincial levels. These teams are composed of specialists (a psychologist, a psychopedagogue, a pedagogue, a speech therapist, a psychometrist, and a social worker) whose mission is to guarantee the quality of the diagnostic process and the preventive approach of education. This encompasses giving specialized guidance and monitoring and evaluating the needs of each child to provide the necessary input and assistance to the methodological teams at the various educational levels, and guiding families. Student needs can be physical, sensory, mental, or behavioural; permanent or transitory. For those with physical disabilities, the Cuban government opened several special education schools staffed by recent graduates in September 2019.

In Cuba, special education refers "not only to special schools or institutions, because we offer other specialized orientation services as well, including at Diagnosis and Orientation Centres, with specialists who advise teachers, families, and the population whenever there is a concern related to attention provided a given child" (Silva Correa, 2019, September 3). Multidisciplinary teams provide necessary care for students with behavioural problems and advise parents, teachers, and community members on actions. Children are guaranteed special treatment under the law when legal disciplinary measures are needed.

A group of social or community work programs directed by the Ministry of Education also helps ensure the preventive nature of Cuban education (Ortega Rodríguez et al., 2011 p. 4), such as the following:

- Curricula and syllabuses for the entire national education system.
- National action program to respond to the agreements of the World Summit on Children.
- *"For Life"* Community Education Program.
- *"Educate your Child"* Program, aimed at raising awareness on the importance of the first years of life and the need for parental-education programs by parents whose pre-school children do not attend the Daycare centres.
- Comprehensive preventive care programs at the local level for socially disadvantaged minors are directed at preventing adverse conduct and behaviour of a minor in part by fostering the knowledge of the risks those misconducts may imply and the danger they entail for the minor, their family, and society.
- Integral program of medical-psycho-pedagogical attention for children and adolescents, as well as workers in educational centres, including regular schools of all levels. Such educational programs are also instituted in hospitals for school-age children requiring extended periods of hospitalization or whose physical and mental conditions preclude attendance at a school centre. In January 1985, a Resolution (No. 13) was issued by the Ministry of Education for the inclusion of psycho-pedagogical care at home by mobile teachers for children, adolescents, and young people who, due to limitations related to physical or disabling conditions of different natures and degrees of seriousness, are unable to attend regular school.
- Master Guidance Program for health promotion and education includes

personal and collective hygiene, sexual education, nutritional education and food hygiene, accident prevention and roadway education, natural and traditional medicine, education against the use of tobacco, alcohol and drugs, and rules of coexistence and communication.
- "Life Task" (*Tarea Vida*) programs help students and communities develop a love for nature and care of the environment, among other moral values.
- *Yo sí puedo* (Yes, I can) and *Yo sí puedo seguir* (Yes, I can continue) are two Cuban literacy programs contributing to the eradication of illiteracy in other countries.

Many of the above-mentioned above social or community work programs are included in school-year activities and, in most cases, associated with the circles-of-interest career process explained later in this chapter or with extra-curricular activities planned by student organizations at all levels, such as the Young Pioneers Organization (OPC), the Federation of High School Students (FEEM), the Federation of University Students (FEU), among others.

Yo sí puedo/Yes, I Can:
Cuba's Contribution to the Eradication of Illiteracy in Other Countries

It is worth mentioning that the Cuban program *Yo sí puedo* (Yes, I Can) (2001) is currently in use in multiple countries around the world (Cubadebate, 2015). It has been translated into several languages, including Indigenous languages, and is adaptable to meet the needs of each country that applies the method. The *Yes, I Can* program was created by the celebrated Cuban pedagogue Leonela Relys. Up to July 31, 2019, this unique program has helped more than 10 million people in more than 30 countries learn to read and write. A group of Cuban specialists is updating the program to make it available from the cloud in digital form (Mined, 2019). Cuba's *Yes, I Can* program enjoys broad international recognition:

> In 2006, the Youth and Adult Literacy and Education Chair of the Latin American and Caribbean Pedagogical Institute of the Republic of Cuba (IPLAC) was awarded the UNESCO King Sejong Literacy Prize to celebrate the adaptation and replication of the program around the world: The *YSP* [*Yo, sí Puedo*] is more than a method. It would be more appropriate to understand it as a literacy training model that goes beyond processes, materials, strategies, etc., by including, both explicitly and implicitly, concepts of literacy training,

learning, life skills and social mobilization involving a wide range of actors with varied roles—from the beneficiaries of the literacy training to other stakeholders such as state entities and other concerned institutions. (UNESCO, 2006, p. 4)

Table 10.1. *Yo, Sí Puedo* Campaigns by Country

COUNTRY	SOURCE
Latin America and the Caribbean (n = 17)	
Argentina	Fundación UMMEP (2013)
Bolivia	Artaraz (2012); Lamrani (2012)
Brazil	Documents and Exhibits of Cuba's International Literacy Missions (n.d.)
Colombia	UNESCO (2006)
Dominican Republic	Canfux Gutteres et al. (2006)
Ecuador	Artarz (2012)
Grenada	Grenada's "Yes I Can" Adult Literacy Program (2008); "Yes I Can" DVDs, held by authors on license from IPLAC
El Salvador	Canfux Gutteres et al. (2006)
Haiti	Canfux Gutteres et al. (2006)
Honduras	Alvarado (2008)
Mexico	UNESCO (2006)
Nicaragua	Canfux Gutteres et al (2006); Parra (2009); Muhr (2013)
Panama	Torres (2009)
Paraguay	UNESCO (2006)
Peru	Canfux Gutteres et al. (2006)
Uruguay	Canfux Gutteres et al (2006)
Venezuela	Wagner (2005); Reyes (2011); Artaraz (2012); Lamrani (2012)
North America (n = 2)	
Canada	ArrowMight Canada and IPLAC (n.d.)
U.S. (New Mexico)	LALA (n.d.)
Europe (n = 1)	
Spain	Artaraz (2012)
Asia-Pacific (n = 3)	
Australia	Boughton et al. (2013)
New Zealand	Canfux Gutteres et al. (2005); Documents and Exhibits of Cuba's International Literacy Missions (n.d.)
Timor-Leste	Boughton (2010; 2012)
Africa (n = 6)	
Angola	Cuban News Agency 20/5/13
Guinéa Bissau	Lopez and Herrera (2012)
Mozambique	UNESCO (2006)

COUNTRY	SOURCE
Namibia	Mwaala, E. (Pers. comm. 8/2/13)
Nigeria	Documents and Exhibits of Cuba's International Literacy Missions (n.d)
South Africa	Mlotshwa (2009)

NOTE: Saint Kitts and Nevis, Santa Lucia and Jamaica have also implemented the *Yo sí puedo* program (Cubadebate.cu, October 17, 2019).
SOURCE OF TABLE: Based on Table 1 (335–336) in Boughton, B., and Durnan, D. (2014). Cuba's Yo, Si Puedo. A global literacy movement? *Postcolonial Directions in Education*, 3(2): 325–359. https://www.um.edu.mt/library/oar/handle/123456789/19932

ArrowMight Learning for Life Project: A Cuba-Canada Collaboration

In Canada, the ArrowMight Learning for Life Project was designed in collaboration with Cuba (Cubadebate, 2008). Given previous Cuban experience with literacy in different countries, such as New Zealand, a team of Cuban literacy specialists spent two years researching the Canadian context to adapt the ArrowMight Program methodology (Patterson et al., 2010). Participation in the different stages of the program—diagnosis, elaboration, pilot trial and implementation—helped the Cuban professors learn about Canada in various ways and include Canadian content within the program (ArrowMight, n.d.).

A Few Words on Canada-Cuba Cooperation in Higher Education

Cuba-Canada relations go back to the late 18th century when the codfish trade for sugar and rum began. In 1903, the first economic offices in Havana and Nova Scotia were opened, followed in 1945 by diplomatic relations. Cuba was the first Latin-American country with which Canada initiated diplomatic ties. These have been steadily maintained over the years, even after the Revolution's triumph when the U.S. declared the blockade against Cuba. The Organization of American States (OAS) broke relations with Cuba. Canada and Mexico were the only two countries that did not follow suit.

The two countries have developed a sound and respectful relationship favouring cooperation across many fields. Education is one of the areas solidly included in the many collaborative-action projects over the years:

> Canada's history, geography, policies, and programs are also promoted through Canadian Studies Centres located in six universities across Cuba. Academic cooperation represents one of the most important aspects of the relationship between Canada and Cuba, with expanding networks of academics and researchers from both countries working together in various disciplines. (Embassy of Canada in Cuba, April 25, 2020)

Canadian Studies Programs in Cuba and Conferences

The University of Holguín is one of the six Cuban universities having a Canadian Studies program. Collaboration between the University of Holguín with Canadian scholars and their institutions dates back to 1998. One of the main activities in which this collaboration has been evident is the participation of Canadian academics, students, and officials in the University of Holguín's scientific events—for example, the annual International Conference on Foreign Languages, Communication and Culture (WEFLA, since 1998) and the International Canadian Studies Seminar (SECAN, since 2006). Since 2006, this latter has allowed new institutions and personalities in the scientific and academic exchanges between the Universidad de Holguín and its Canadian counterparts. The WEFLA-SECAN event represents a collaboration with several notable Canadian universities and one in Mexico and support in Cuba from the Canadian embassy and the Hotel Club Amigo Atlántico-Guardalavaca.

Over the years, this collaboration has expanded into signing memoranda of understanding regarding potential student exchanges and four official agreements with Canadian universities for second-language programs at the University of Holguín in Cuba. Professors and academics from several Canadian universities have come to the University of Holguín during sabbaticals to teach courses to our students and faculty. Professors from this university have also been to Canadian universities as visiting scholars or on scholarships granted to complete MA or PhD programs.

The WEFLA-SECAN events are most popular among Canadians. Although participants also hail from many other countries, more than 500 academics from more than 70 Canadian universities and other educational institutions have participated over the years. The University of Western Ontario (now known as Western University) became a conference co-sponsor with the 2002 edition. Other universities that have been co-sponsors include Calgary, Guelph, Ottawa, McGill, Alberta, Waterloo, St. Thomas, the University of Toronto/Mississauga, Université de Sherbrooke, and Université de Québec à Trois Rivières, among others who have supported the organization and development of the annual conference in various ways.

Structure of the Cuban Education System

The Cuban national education system is organized through organically articulated subsystems covering all levels and types of education ranging from daycare centres to universities:

Preschool or early childhood: This is the initial part of the system. It is not mandatory but accepts children from six months to five years old. It is linked to the "Educate Your Child Program" for those who are not already attending daycare centres.

Primary education: Six compulsory grades divided into two cycles: grades one to four, and grades five and six.

Secondary education: Compulsory for grades seven to nine. Once the students have completed this basic secondary education, they are supported in choosing how best to proceed with their education from several options.

Pre-university education: Grades ten and twelve are otherwise not compulsory. The main objective is to prepare students for university. There are also specialized centres in every province, such as the Vocational Pre-University (High School) of Exact Sciences and the Military Vocational Pre-University (i.e., the Camilo military school at Cienfuegos *Escuela Militar Camilo*), among others that serve the same purpose.

Technical and professional education: Options after high school for students who wish to become skilled workers or mid-level technicians (with a basic professional level equivalent to twelfth grade). Upon completing their studies, graduates can also then access university and complete a major in their knowledge area, such as computer programming or tourism, among many others. This subsystem also includes **Professional trade schools** to train qualified workers as intermediate level technicians in regions experiencing the most significant demand for labour. Adolescents who opt for skilled worker programs can choose from the following programs, among others: Cigar Rolling, Fishing Boat Sailor, Industrial Chemistry, Glass Working, and Non-ferrous Metalworking.

Adult education: Seeks to ensure a high educational level for adults who are under-schooled. It also includes language schools both public (university) and private where individuals or students in various fields at various levels of their studies may decide to enroll to learn English.

Special education: Conceived as a subsystem that caters to students with special (or transitory special) educational needs due to, for example, intellectual and developmental disabilities, vision, or hearing impairment, and/or behavioural disorders.

Higher education: Several regimes are in place to ensure the accessibility of higher education: regular daytime courses for high school graduates or equivalent; part-time courses; and distance courses for workers or others interested in pursuing higher education. Candidates must pass three entrance exams: Mathematics, Spanish, and Cuban History. Every education level is free in Cuba (i.e., classes, training, workshops, diploma courses, masters, and doctoral programs), including residence support for those living outside the urban centres.

For the 2019–20 school year, Cuba welcomed more than 1.7 million students into its many levels and education subsystems. At the university level, about 257,347 students were enrolled in higher education. Currently, 50 universities offer 113 specialties, and several short-cycle higher education programs have been added (Alonso, 2020). These condensed-cycle programs respond to the demand for a skillful workforce in priority areas, such as certain roles in secondary school teaching, nursing, health care technicians in several specialties, customs workers, network administrators, and computer security technicians. This new approach ensures professional training of graduates at a level surpassing that of a mid-level technician but lower than that of the complete university diploma, which can be completed in later years if so desired.

Principles, Purposes, and Functions of Cuban Education

All of Cuba's educational institutions and programs are holistically guided by fulfilling the preventive, transitory, and integrative functions of education. Cuba supports its educational policy by applying organizational and theoretical-methodological principles that guide and structure the basic concepts and educational practices to form a broad psychological understanding of the needs of the inherent diversity of children, adolescents and young people being educated.

Several principles can be considered distinct features of education in our country. These principles constitute the starting governing positions that define the general aspects of the Cuban education system's theory, methodology, and organization.

(a) **Mass and equitable character of education:** Education is both a right and a duty for the Cuban people. All citizens have access to education without discrimination regarding age, gender, race, religion, or place of residence.

(b) **Study-work combination:** Linking theory with practice, school with life and teaching with production, the Cuban study-work approach pursues the formative objective of developing individual agency and an awareness of the importance of producing social goods and protecting the environment. It is an experiential approach that begins as early as primary school through what are called circles of interest programs, bringing children together with professionals from the field, often community members working in schools, community centres and other workplaces.

(c) **Democratic nature of Cuban education:** Family, community and society are seen as a whole in Cuba and encouraged to participate in all aspects of the educational process. This involvement manifests directly through parental involvement mechanisms at the school and political levels through the democratic processes built into Cuban socialism. Therefore, in these ways, people can be said to participate fully in the realization and control of education.

(d) **Diversity**: Access to educational and training centres is available to all equally. The concept of a school open to diversity cannot be understood merely as an educational space opening its doors to all regardless of race, sex, gender, economic situation, social group, religious beliefs, physical and mental capacity, or other characteristics. In Cuba, diversity is synonymous with inclusivity. It translates into a need for sufficient professional training and psycho-pedagogical and didactic resources to guarantee all students the maximum possible academic and social development. This is reflected in curricula devised and established by the Cuban Ministry of Education (Gayle Morejón et al., 2011).

(e) **Differentiated attention and school integration**: Specialized attention is provided to all school children according to their individual needs and potential. The aids and stimulations are appropriate and require students to foster maximum development and ensure they do not become or feel excluded or segregated within the educational sphere.

(f) **Free of charge** for all citizens at all levels, including postgraduate studies.

To guarantee the ongoing fulfillment of these principles, Martí's postulates on civic education as instrumental to strengthening the core, humanistic values of Cuban society are taken strictly into account. Values formation is given special attention at all levels, including at daycare centres. It begins with learning about José Martí and his work. Each daycare centre, primary school, secondary school, and university has a bust of José Martí, offering a place to pay homage to this apostle of Cuban independence, a great national hero of Cuba. One of the first poems Cuban children learn at home, in daycare, or in primary school is "Cultivo una rosa blanca" ("I cultivate a white rose") by Martí (1891). In this poem, Martí highlights the value of friendship and integrity and the importance of how our actions shape and define us. Martí tells us to cultivate a white rose even for those who would do us wrong.

Through civic education, primary and secondary students learn about and are encouraged to respect Cuban national heroes, which helps develop a sense of national belonging and pride. Schools organize guided educational visits to historical sites, such as local museums, mausoleums, cemeteries, and other sites of interest to access local and national history. These educational field trips help students understand that all the heroes and martyrs we read about in the history books are real flesh-and-blood people who risked their lives for independence. By way of example, visits to places related to Martí's life include the Santa Efigenia Cemetery in Santiago de Cuba, where a monument stands in his honour. Fidel Castro's monument is also here, and visitors can watch the changing of the guards.

Vocational training is another distinguishing feature of Cuban education. Different methods are used to boost student interest in knowledge acquisition. At school, outstanding students who show interest in a given subject become student monitors and assist teachers. This process is strengthened by our circles of interest programs, which introduce young students to research and career possibilities in their school's local territory. For example, they are attended by instructors from prioritized economic, technological, and social sectors, such as the agricultural, industrial, and mechanical sectors, and there are also pedagogical interest circles. From the earliest ages, children in primary and secondary schools are encouraged to identify and choose an area of interest and join a circle. There are also pedagogical classrooms, scientific societies, clubs at senior high schools, and "open door days" at universities. Such events familiarize students with various occupations including firefighting, butchering, carpentery, masonry, hairdressing, etc., to help them with career choices and personal development. This part of the educational process is to support children, adolescents, and young people establish life goals.

Circles of interest programs help students reflect on the present while projecting into their future, developing individual creativity and cooperation in a group setting. Circles of interest favour communication, mutual help, and collaboration to develop scientific curiosity and a desire and ability to learn and share knowledge about specific fields with others. These Circles of interest activities are managed by qualified personnel and organized by schools, pioneer palaces (i.e., community centres), military facilities, work centres, and research centres. Themes are organized and put in place by the school board, along with the other activities for the school year. Circles of interest are interactive endeavours that promote positive cognitive growth and contribute to developing positive personality traits in youth while keeping professionals in the various fields and related vocational training knowledgeable about social trends.

Currents and Tendencies in the Cuban Education System

The conceptualization of education in Cuba emanates from and builds upon the ideas of the Cuban pedagogues and thinkers mentioned previously in this chapter and upon those of notable pedagogues from other countries, including the famed Russian psychologist-educator Lev S. Vygotsky and the Brazilian critical pedagogue Paulo Freire, both of whose work has had a notable influence on modern Cuban pedagogy. Their educational approaches synchronize *avant garde* ideas of their day through a perspective of Latin American history into a rationale reaffirming the principles of national education as instruments of personal autonomy; of scientific and critical knowledge; of the relation between education and work; and of the principle of cognitive activity formation (self-conceptualization) so that learners can also use their own insights to guide their understanding.

The principle of cognitive activity implies that one's cognitive abilities are socially guided and created. It recognizes that social contexts and interactions have a relational influence on—to foster or impede—human cognitive growth; students learn from each other through interactions in their social environments, school, and their families and community.

Education is more than a right in Cuba; it is a responsibility. Thus, Cuban students must learn how to have agency, be aware of their behaviour towards others, and organize themselves within the given school structure to succeed in their learning and social development. They are afforded the direction, teaching, and support needed to decide what career might be the best fit for them. The importance of agency and support to help them develop cognitively cannot be overstated.

Through its application of these principles Cuba was the only country in Latin America and the Caribbean to meet all six of the Education for All Goals, according to the All-Monitoring Report on Education (UNESCO, 2015). This report put Cuba at the top of the Education for All Development Index for Latin America and the Caribbean, with a public education expenditure of 13 percent of its gross domestic product (GDP). Cuba has continued to fulfill these goals despite the economic difficulties faced by the country, and it has not renounced its commitment to obtain ever-higher results in terms of educational quality. The lowest expenditure on education was 5.62 percent of GDP in 1994, during the Special Period in Times of Peace, and the highest as of the writing of this chapter was 14.06 of GDP in 2008 (UNESCO Institute for Statistics (http://uis.unesco.org/).

International studies on primary education conducted by the Latin

American Laboratory for the Assessment of the Quality of Education, which is based in the Regional Office of Education for Latin America and the Caribbean and sponsored by UNESCO, have shown Cuba to achieve the best results for schoolchildren from third to sixth grade among the 13 countries in the given Latin American region.

The Third "Perfection Process" of the Cuban Education System Since the Revolution

The Cuban Ministry of Education works tirelessly to maintain and improve the national education system. The ICCP (Central Institute of Pedagogical Sciences) is the research centre responsible for conducting theoretical studies linked to the third "perfection process" of education in Cuba, which was first implemented in the 2012–13 school year. The changes implemented moved Cuban education in two fundamental directions: the transformation of the teaching methods and work culture/styles, and the elaboration of new curricula, workbooks, syllabi, and methodological guidelines. The aim was a more open and flexible course model to better meet the needs of new generations.

Teacher training in Cuba is carried out in pedagogical schools and polytechnic centres for professional technical education. Upon graduation from Grade 12, which means three years of pedagogical teaching following the three primary years, students begin working as teachers and can enroll in a higher education major as part-time students. This third perfection process also includes teacher training, and for this purpose, some 39 new pedagogical schools have opened across the country. These schools cover preschool, primary, special education, second-language teaching, and the gamut of secondary grades.

Current Challenges within the Cuban Education System

The participation and support of successive generations of Cuban citizens have been made possible through the extensive network of social, professional, and scientific organizations dedicated to learning since 1959. Cuba's government is well-positioned to continue improving the national education system's structure. It functions mainly through the Ministries of Education and Higher Education and territorial governments. Through this process, the word "schooling" takes on unique relational characteristics, whereby the human being is a resource (students, teachers, parents, community, among others) and a result or product (student learning, knowledge, norms, behaviour, values). This relation enables the fulfillment of the purpose and objectives of the Cuban education system.

Today, several factors beyond Cuban control threaten the nation's ability to maintain and augment these advancements in education while ensuring equal accessibility to all Cubans. One of the most pressing issues is the scarcity of financial resources, which impedes our country's ability to provide the necessary infrastructure to meet the needs of all students and teachers. The other problem is related to the lack of teachers the country has faced for many years. Due to low salaries in the education sector, some resigned from teaching and accepted employment in the tourism sector, which pays well and actively seeks qualified workers. This situation (i.e., low salaries for teachers) is also related to the country's financial crisis, which has intensified due to the COVID-19 pandemic but was already severe because of the longstanding U.S. embargo.

As the Cuban Minister of Education Ana Elsa Velazquez (August 2019) has explained, the teacher situation is changing gradually, thanks to salary increases for teachers and professors in July 2019. In response, more than 8,000 teachers decided to return to teaching in the 2019–20 school year. Of these, 2,200 had been applying for discharge from the education system, and 1,047 were planning to retire. The renewed viability of teaching has allowed the demand for teachers to be 95 percent met. The remaining 5 percent will be met through part-time teachers' alternatives, increased teaching hours, and allowing university students in Education and certain other majors to do pre-service practicums. The recent salary increases (January 1, 2021) and teacher motivation have made this possible.

Cuba has offered full scholarships to students from poor countries or minorities for whom higher education is not within reach in their countries of origin, including students (i.e., minority groups living under the poverty line) from the U.S. More than 56,000 students from 137 countries have completed a major in Cuba. In the 2019 school year, 9,580 international students studied in Cuban universities. More than 2,000 ministerial and inter-university agreements have been signed to date thanks to the participation of more than 3,000 academic and scientific networks (Cubadebate, 2019).

Since 1959, 37,333 students from 141 other countries have graduated in medicine and related health sciences in Cuba. Since its creation in 2005, Havana's Latin American School of Medicine (*Escuela Latinoamericana de Medicina*, or ELAM) has graduated more than 29,600 doctors from 103 countries in Africa, Asia, and the Americas. Almost 200 students from the U.S. have graduated from ELAM.

> Congratulations to the new #U.S. #ELAM graduates!!! More than 200 students from the USA, mainly from marginalized minorities and low-income families, have graduated from the Latin American

School of Medicine of Cuba (ELAM). They decided to work in their underserved communities. —Ana S. Rodriguez Abascal, @DPRCubaOnu, Cuban Twitter, Representative to the United Nations (2020)

According to a report by the Interreligious Foundation for Community Organization (IFCO) and its Pastors for Peace project, the first U.S. students came to ELAM in 2001; by 2010, 122 U.S. students from 29 states plus Puerto Rico were attending medical school in Cuba, and 33 had already completed their studies. To be accepted into the free program, graduates are asked to work several years in an underserved community in their own country. "Pastors for Peace is an interfaith organization created in 1988, pioneering humanitarian aid delivery to Latin America and the Caribbean … and initiating advocacy projects for a more just and moral U.S. foreign policy in our hemisphere. Reverend Lucius Walker led it till his death, and now [it is led] by its former Executive Director, Gail Walker. Pastors for Peace began to organize Cuba Caravans & Designations to fight the U.S. blockade against the island. 'Each Caravan is an endeavor of love rooted in social justice. It's a huge project linking people, vehicles and humanitarian aid'" (IFCO, 2021). In 2017, IFCO/Pastors for Peace showed solidarity with Cuba by posting a link to an article from the United Nations News Centre announcing the UN's resolution against the blockade (IFCO, 2017).

While the Cuban ideology spotlights education in general, and specifically higher education, as key to reaching development goals in the United Nation's 2030 Agenda for Sustainable Development (UN, 2015), the financial constraints imposed by the U.S. blockade remain a threat. Given the success to date of the Cuban education system, imagine what could be done if free of the neocolonial stranglehold imposed by this unilateral blockade.

Impact on Education of the U.S. Embargo Against Cuba
Cuban education is but one of the sectors highly impacted by the United States' longstanding blockade. For example, long-distance freight charges for items the Ministry of Education needs—such as paper, ink, didactic games, sports equipment, computers, books, etc.—cost a fortune. For the 2019–20 school year, the country had to import fabric to guarantee each primary and high school student a school uniform. Since goods cannot be imported from the U.S., which is 90 miles from Havana, or European countries that align to varying degrees with the U.S. blockade, although consistently voting against it, there is no choice but to pay the high shipping costs from faraway China. Although this made making the requisite

three million student uniforms much more expensive, they were made in record time. Every Cuban student also had notebooks, textbooks, pencils, and other necessary school materials.

The uniforms are sold at a low price, but the rest of the supplies and materials are distributed to students for free by the Cuban government (Resolution 11, 2012. Art. 8). Wearing a uniform to school has a unique social implication for Cuba. In the beginning, after the triumph of the Revolution, there was a time of scarcity. Among other shortages, not all students had adequate clothes for school. The uniform means that all students have clothes of equal style and quality, identifying them as students of a given level and school type. Upon arrival at university, the school uniform has served its purpose and is no longer needed.

Education as a Phenomenon of Social Justice

In Cuba, the complex socio-political and economic situation resulting from the U.S. blockade makes it more challenging to count on resources and specialized technologies needed to modernize educational centres' infrastructure. Despite these challenges, however, the state's prioritization of education has made it possible to keep every school in the country open and leave not one child without access.

The Achievement of Social Inclusion and Integration through Public Education

School inclusion and integration is a predominant objective of the Cuban education system. The idea of an inclusive or holistic school approach that does not segregate any child despite individual differences and integrates children having different types of disabilities has gained momentum in Cuba as elsewhere. As José Martí pointed out at the end of the 19th century, poetry is found in the universe's unity, which contains many different things yet is one (Martí, 1975 [1884], p. 218).

In Cuba, participation of all people in the search for solutions to social issues and in ensuring the right of citizens to access a full life, culture, education, health, sports, social security, and justice, without distinction based on social background, race, gender, cultural level, or psycho-physical characteristics, is vital. This implies commitment and cohesion around clearly enunciated shared values, family and community involvement, and a high-quality academic platform that successfully aims to help young students find their place in a society and country to build a socioeconomic model that leaves no one behind.

For this reason, priority care is afforded to schoolchildren who present any social disadvantage. Potential risk factors are identified from behaviour noticed at school, in the community, and within the family. In the case of misconduct, Decree Law No. 64 of 1982 regulates the treatment of minors who transgress any criminal norms and minors in conflict with the Cuban criminal justice system, such as those with severe disciplinary or behaviour disorders that impede learning and progress in the regular schools of the national education system.

Under this law, minors with disorders or problems that manifest as antisocial behaviours not considered significant signs of social deviance or threats to public safety but that throw off the minor's interpersonal relationships and their ability to succeed academically are enrolled in behavioural schools run by the Ministry of Education jointly with the Ministry of the Interior. There are also comprehensive training schools for teenagers who have committed felonies classified as crimes. Equipped with multidisciplinary teams, such educational centres can provide one-on-one attention and treatment and help these youth to reinsert themselves into the national education system.

Conclusions

The development of the Cuban educational system has advanced within the context of the nation's realities to promote the right to equal access to quality education. For the Cuban government, which is currently engaged in updating its model of socialist development, maintaining the standards in education achieved since 1959 represents a significant challenge given the socio-economic limitations situations the country faces. However, the Cuban education system remains genuinely universal. Cuba has taken concerted action in the development of education since 1959. The result is an efficient and effective education system with highly skilled teachers functioning within an infrastructure that, despite the fact it does not have all the "indispensable" material resources, makes education available to everyone and ensures quality and methodological innovation. This quality has been assessed many times by international organizations sponsored by UNESCO, continually with outstanding results. Cuba is also recognized as a country that devotes much of its national budget to education (UNESCO, 2019).

In Cuba, education is a process enabling the full development of society and each individual. The Cuban education experience consolidates the ideas of Jose Martí and Fidel Castro into the significant twin paradigms of Cuban educational and national development. Since the revolutionary triumph in 1959, education in Cuba has been imbued with a humanistic concept and developed as a key pillar of the Cuban state and society. The

Cuban educational system represents a central building block of the Cuban nation. Significantly, the success of Cuba's broad popular participation and democracy through the Assemblies of People's Power depends on an informed citizenry. The universal nature of education in Cuba is among the human rights protected by the Cuban state.

Educational praxis demonstrates the need for permanent improvements in education at different levels, always in correspondence with the immediate environment and the world's economic, political, and social conditions. The Cuban educational system has undergone three perfection processes since 1971, offering continuous transformations that are in line with Cuba's vision for social and economic development including the 2030 Agenda for Sustainable Development objectives. In this way, our education system has remained responsive to the needs of new generations of Cubans. Yet, this central tenet of Cuban sovereignty is threatened by the U.S. blockade.

In Cuba, a teacher is not conceived as a specialist using a manual but as a person capable of orienting independently, a consistent intellectual who can deeply fathom problems and propose solutions from a scientific viewpoint while considering the interests of individuals and society. Students are not knowledge repositories; they are living beings filled with potential but who need the ability to think for themselves and have the agency, skills, and knowledge to thrive in society. All this requires much study, a high cognitive level, professional skills development, learning self-awareness, and attaining a highly developed sense of social inclusion and commitment.

The preventive nature of Cuban education thus constitutes a system of actions aimed at guaranteeing and ensuring fulfillment of the educational and socio-environmental rights and needs of all children, adolescents, and young people. Several special education facilities exist for youth suffering from behavioural or physical disorders. The participation of parents is guaranteed at the legal level through the Cuban Family Code (1975; 2022).*

"To educate is to deposit in each man all the human work that has preceded him; it is to make each man a living summary of the world up until the day of his death; it is to raise him to the level of his times, so that he stays afloat and cannot be left behind; it is to prepare man for life" (Jose Martí, 1975 OC T.5 p 275). This quotation summarizes the ideal advocated by the Cuban educational system.

Despite challenges linked to the economic conditions caused by the U.S. blockade, Cuba has consistently invested in education. This is evidenced in everyday life by the levels of literacy among the masses (approximately 99.6

---

* Editors' note: The new Family Code (Law 156/2022) was voted on and approved in September 2022, after the writing of this chapter (see Chapter 8).

percent) and the high calibre of teaching and other professions, but also by the fact that Cuba, among the poorest countries in the world, was able to vaccinate her entire population in 2021 with COVID vaccines developed at biotechnology centres created by Fidel Castro in the 1960s along with the simultaneous creation of medical science programs in universities. As Martí believed, it is through education that we as a society will save our Cuba. While change is inevitable, the authors believe that Cuban education's fundamental principles remain ideologically sound and accessible to the masses.

References

Alonso, F. R. (2020). Universidades cubanas abrirán sus puertas el 1ro de septiembre. Havana, Cuba: Sitio Mesa Redonda. www.cubadebate.cu

¡ahora! [Elzy Fors Garzon, Prensa Latina]. (2023, July 21). Cuban Parliament approves policy aimed at children and youth. Holguín, Cuba: Casa Editora Periódico ¡ahora! https://www.ahora.cu/en/cuba-en/19302-cuban-parliament-approves-policy-aimed-at-children-and-youth.

Anuario Estadístico [Statistical Yearbook]. (2016–17) [1952]. [National statistics]. Chapter 18. Education. Havana, Cuba: Dirección General de Estadística.

ArrowMight. (n.d.). ArrowMight Canada Literacy/Numeracy Program Background. Ottawa: ArrowMight Canada. http://www.arrowmight.ca/docs/AM-FACT-History.pdf

ANPP. (2023, April 19). 10th legislature of the Asamblea Nacional del Poder Popular [Ordinary period of the X legislature of the Parliament—National Assembly of People's Power (ANPP)]. MINREX [Cuban Ministry of Foreign Affairs].

Batalla de Ideas (Battle of Ideas). (1999, December 5). ECURED. https://www.ecured.cu/Batalla_de_ideas

Boughton, B., and Durnan, D. (2014). Cuba's Yo, Si Puedo. A global literacy movement? *Postcolonial Directions in Education*, 3(2): 325–359. https://www.um.edu.mt/library/oar/handle/123456789/19932

Castro, R. F. [1953, October 16] (1968). *History Will Absolve Me: The Moncada Trial Defence Speech at Santiago de Cuba*. London: Cape.

-----. (1971, April 30). Fidel Castro's Closing Speech at the First Congress on Education and Culture, April 23–30, 1971. Havana, Cuba: Havana CTC Theatre and Domestic Radio Report. Published May 3, 1971. See Lanic Castro Speech Data Base: Speeches, Interviews, Articles 1959–1966. http:// lanic.utexas.edu/project/castro/db/1971/19710501.html

-----. (1975). Primer Congreso del Partido Comunista de Cuba. Havana, Cuba: Informe Central. Editorial Pueblo y Educación.

Cepal. (2019). Informe nacional sobre la implementación de la Agenda 2030 [implementation report]. Objetivos para el desarrollo sostenible. [Objectives of sustainable developement]. Informe Voluntario Nacional de Cuba, 2019. chrome-extension://efaidnbmnnnibpcajpcglclefindmkaj/https://cepei.org/wp-content/uploads/2020/01/informe_nacional_voluntario_de_cuba_sobre_implementacion_de_la_agenda_2030.pdf

Childhood and Youth Code. (1978). Law 16, art. 17. Havana, Cuba: Minister of Justice.

CIGB. (2021). [Cuban engineering and biotechnology centre (CIGB)]. Havana, Cuba: Centro de Ingeniería Genética y Biotecnología (CUGB). https://www.cigb.edu.cu/

Conversation, The. (2022, March 16). Big Pharma vs. Little Cuba: Why Cubans trust vaccines and how they're helping vaccinate the world. https://theconversation.com/big-pharma-vs-little-cuba-why-cubans-trust-vaccines-and-how-theyre-helping-vaccinate-the-world-178119

Cuba: Economic and Social Policy Guidelines of the Party and Revolution. (2011, April 18). Resolution on the Guidelines of the Economic and Social Policy of the Party and the Revolution. http://www.cuba.cu/gobierno/documentos/2011/ing/l160711i.html

Cuba: Economic and Social Policy Guidelines of the Party and Revolution. (2016). Communist Party of Cuba. Period 2016–2021. [Lineamientos de la Política Económica y Social del Partido y la Revolución para el período 2016–2021]. Havana, Cuba: www.gacetaoficial.gob.cu/es/lineamientos

Cubadebate. (2008). Aplican en Canadá método cubano de alfabetización [applying Cuban literacy program in Canada]. Cubadebate. www.cubadebate.cu>2009/05/08

-----.(October 26, 2015). Alfabetizadas alrededor de diez millones de personas con método ´Yo sí puedo´. [Cuba literacy program: Yes I can]. Cubadebate http://www.cubadebate.cu/etiquet/yo-si-puedo

-----. (June 24, 2019). El sueño de Fidel: reciben su título 500 médicos extranjeros. Havana, Cuba: Cubadebate. Cubadebate. El sueño de Fidel: reciben su título 500 médicos extranjeros. www.cubadebate.cu/noticias/2019/07/24

Cubadebate/[Ojito, Enrique]. (November 26, 2019). El dia que Fidel sono un polo científico en Sancti Spiritus [the day Fidel imagined a scientific hub in Cuba. Havana, Cuba: Cubadebate. http://www.cubadebate.cu/especiales/2019/11/26/el-dia-que-fidel-sono-un-polo-cientifico-en-sancti-spiritus/

Cubadebate. (August 8, 2016). Fidel Castro durante la fundación del Centro de Ingeniería y Biotecnología. YouTube video with Spanish captions. Havana, Cuba: Cubadebate.

Cuban Constitution [Constitución de la República]. (2019). Official Gazette of Cuba [Gaceta Oficial de la República de Cuba]. (2019). GOC-2019-406-EX5. Havana, Cuba: Minister of Justice. https://www.gacetaoficial.gob.cu/es/gaceta-oficial-no-5-extraordinaria-de-2019 [an unofficial English version of the Cuban constitutions is available at Constitute: The world's constitutions to read, search, and compare. https://www.constituteproject.org/]

Cuban Constitution [Constitución de la República]. (1992); (1976). Havana, Cuba: Editora Política. http://www.cubadebate.cu/noticias/2019/07/24/el-sueno-de-fidel-reciben-su-titulo-500-medicos-extranjeros/

Cuban Family Code [Código de Familia]. (1975). Law 1289. Havana, Cuba: Minister of Justice. www.parlamentocubano.gob.cu [the official Cuban translation into English of the Cuban Family Code originally appeared in Volume II, No. 4 of the CCS newsletter. New York: Centre for Cuban Studies. See UFDC: Digital Library of the Caribbean. 1976. https://original-ufdc.uflib.ufl.edu/AA00021904/00001/2j].

-----. (2022.) Law 156. Havana, Cuba: Minister of Justice. www.parlamentocubano.gob.cu.

Cuban Twitter of Representative to the United Nations [Ana S. Rodriguez Abascal @DPRCubaOnu]. (2020, July 29). 200 US Medical Students Graduate in Cuba. World Today News.

Cruz-Taura, G. (2008). Revolution and continuity in the history of education in Cuba. Association for the Study of the Cuban Economy. Annual Proceedings,Volume 18. https://ideas.repec.org/a/qba/annpro/v18y2008id741.html

Embassy of Canada to Cuba. (2020, February 25). Canada-Cuba relations. Havana, Cuba: Embassy of Canada. https://www.international.gc.ca/country-pays/cuba/havana-la_havane.aspx?lang=eng

Garcia Gallo, G.J. EcuRed. (1974). Bosquejo histórico de la educación en Cuba. (Dra. Aelia D,ou Riera. Havana, Cuba: Editorial Pueblo y Educación. https://www.ecured.cu/Bosquejo_hist%C3%B3rico_de_la_educaci%C3%B3n_en_Cuba#Fuente

Fariñas L. G. (2004). Maestro. Para una didáctica del aprender a aprender. Un punto de vista histórico culturalista. Havana, Cuba: Editorial Pueblo y Educación.

Fiske, J., and Wilson, J. G. (eds.) (1886–1900). *Appleton's Cyclopædia of American Biography*. New York: Appleton and Company.

Fole, A., and Canal C. (2020). Caribbean Channel. Cuban News Channel. Havana: Multimedia Creation Group. http://www.canalcaribe.icrt.cu/en/40-years-of-graduation-of-the-third-detachment-manuel-ascunce-domenech/

Gasperini, L. (2000). The Cuban Education System: Lessons and Dilemmas. *Country Studies: Education Reform and Management Publication Series* 1(5). Washington: The World Bank.

Gayle Morejón, A., et al. (2011). El currículo de la escuela cubana actual [current Cuban curriculum]. El tratamiento a la diversidad mediante estrategias educativas. [Treatment of diversity through education strategies for inclusivity]. Curso [Course] 54. ICCP. Rev. Cuban Education. Minister of Education. Havana, Cuba.

Granma correspondents. (2021, April 21). Havana clinics prepare for mass vaccination against covid-19. *Granma* newspaper. Havana, Cuba: Communist Party of Cuba.http://en.granma.cu/cuba/2021-04-21/havana-clinics-prepare-for-mass-vaccination-against-covid-19

Granma [Barbosa León, Nuria]. (2015, December 9). Fomenting Cuban scientific talent. [National Centre for Scientific Research (CNIC)]. *Granma* newspaper. Havana, Cuba: Communist Party of Cuba. http://en.granma.cu/cuba/2015-12-09/fomenting-cuban-scientific-talent

Granma. (2020, September 1/23). Un país como una escuela. *Granma* newspaper. Havana, Cuba. http://www.granma.cu/cuba/2020-09-01/un-pais-como-una-escuela-01-09-20 20-23-09-58

Granma. (2020, July 29). The Moncada illuminates Cuba's future. Havana, Cuba: Communist Party of Cuba (PCC). *Granma* Tabloid. Havana, Cuba. http://en.granma.cu/cuba/2020-07-29/the-moncada-illuminates-cubas-future

Granma [Silva Correa, Yenia]. Y. (2019, September 3). More than 1,400 new teachers for special education. *Granma* Tabloid. Havana, Cuba.. http://en.granma.cu/cuba/2019-09-03/more-than-1400-new-teachers-for-special-education

Harvard, T.H. Chan School of Public Health. (2022, November 3). Cuba's COVID-19 vaccine success could serve as global model. Report. Harvard T.H. Chan School of Public Health. https://www.hsph.harvard.edu/news/hsph-in-the-news/cubas-covid-19-vaccine-success-could-serve-as-global-model-report/

INDER. (February 23, 1961). Instituto Nacional de Deportes, Educación Física y Recreación de Cuba (INDER). Cuba. https://www.inder.gob.cu/Historia.

IFCO. (n.d.). Interreligious Foundation for Community Organization News. Pastors for Peace Story of the Latin American School of Medicine. https://ifconews.org/muedical-school

IFCO Pastors for Peace. (2017, November). UN once again denounces US blockade of Cuba. Interreligious Foundation for Community Organization (IFCO).

Kurt, Serhat. (2020, July 11). Lev Vygostky: Sociocultural theory of cognitive development. *Educational Technology*. https://educationaltechnology.net/lev-vygostky-sociocultural-theory-of-cognitive-development/

Ley [Law] 64. (1882) Decreto-Ley No. 64 del sistema de atención a menores con trastornos de conducta. Cuba Official Gazette No. 010/1982. Special edition. www.minint.gob.cu

López Mola, E.; Acevedo, B. E.; Silva R.; Torma, B.; Montero, R.; and L. Herrera. (2022, September 27). Development of Cuban biotechnology. *Journal of Commercial Biotechnology*. https://www.researchgate.net/publication/312518306_Development_of_Cuban_biotechnology.

Martí Pérez, José. [Cited in Who was José Martí? The International UNESCO/Jose Martí

Prize. (2020). UNESCO]. https://en.unesco.org/prizes/Jose-Marti#:~:text=People%20must%20live%20in%20the,York%20over%20a%20century%20ago.

———. (1975) [1884]. Cartas a María Mantilla. *Obras Completas*. [complete works]. 2nd Edición. Havana, Cuba: Ciencias Sociales. Tome 8, p. 218.

———. (1889). *Obras Completas*. [complete works]. 2nd Edición. Havana, Cuba: Ciencias Sociales. Tome 8, pp. 290–91.

———. (2020). [Cited in Who was Jose Martí? The International UNESCO/Jose Martí Prize. UNESCO]. https://www.unesco.org/en/prizes/jose-marti#:~:text=People%20must%20live%20in%20the,York%20over%20a%20century%20ago.

———. (1990). *Ideario Pedagógico*. Havana, Cuba: Editorial Pueblo y Educación.

———. (1965). *Obras Completas*. [complete works] Tome 11. Havana, Cuba: Editorial Nacional de Cuba.

Martínez, O'Farrill. (2018). La perspectiva filosófica sobre la Educación [in Enrique José Varona]. *Revista Atlante*. Havana, Cuba: Cuadernos de Educación y Desarrollo. https://www.eumed.net/rev/atlante/2017/05/enrique-jose-varona.html

MEDICC Report. (2022, October 31). Insights from Cuba's COVID-19 vaccine enterprise: Report from a high level fact-finding delegation to Cuba. Medical Education Cooperation with Cuba. *MEDICC Review July-October* (24):3ff. Executive Summary. Creative Commons. https://doi.org/10.37757/MR2022.V24.N3-4.13

MINED, Cuba. (2004). [The development of education in the Republic of Cuba]. El desarrollo de la Educación de la República de Cuba. [national report] Informe Nacional. Havana, Cuba: Ministerio de Educación [Minister of Education].

———. (2021, June). [Diagnostic and orientation Centre] Centro de diagnóstico y orientación (CDO) Servicios especiales. Havana, Cuba: Ministerio de Educación [Minister of Education]. www.mined.gob.cu/especial/servicios-especiales-legales-y-sociales/servicios-especiales/

———. (2017). Tarea Vida. Plan de Estado para el enfrentamiento al cambio climático [State plan on climate change]. Havana, Cuba: Ministerio de Educación [Minister of Education]. Council of Ministers. https://www.mined.gob.cu

———. (2012). Resolución [Resolution] 11. Art. 8. Gaceta Oficial No. 007 Extraordinaria de 16 de marzo de 2012 [Cuban Gazette, March 16, 2012]. Havana, Cuba: Ministerio de Educación [Minister of Education]. www.mined.gob.cu

———. (2019, August 26). Programa de alfabetización ´Yo sí puedo´: una idea de Fidel [Yes, I Can – Fidel's idea]. Havana, Cuba: Ministerio de Educación [Minister of Education]. Noticias. https://www.mined.gob.cu

———. (1999). Programa Director de Educación y Promoción para la Salud en el Sistema Nacional de Educación [program director of health promotion and education, national education system). Havana, Cuba: Ministerio de Educación [Minister of Education]. (1999). https://www.ecured.cu/educacion-para-la-salud-en-el-sistema-nacional-de-educacion

———. (1982). Decreto Ley [Decree-Law] 64, Atención a los escolares con alteraciones en el comportamiento [concerning schoolchildren with behavioural disorders]. Gaceta Oficial [Official Gazette] Havana, Cuba: Ministerio de Educación [Minister of Education]. https://www.mined.gob.cu/wp-content/uploads/2019/03/menores.pdf

———. (1985). Resolución Ministerial [ministerial resolution] no. 13. Atención de los maestros ambulantes en Cuba [itinerent schools in Cuba]. Havana, Cuba: Ministerio de Educación [Minister of Education]. http://www.mined.gob.cu

Navarro Quintero, S. M. (2009). El trabajo preventivo en el sistema educativo cubano. Edit. Ministerio de Educación [Cuban Minister of Education, Havana, Cuba].

Oppmann, Patrick. (2021, March 3). As the world vies for vaccines, Cuba's making its own. CNN. https://edition.cnn.com/2021/03/03/americas/cuba-covid-vaccine-soberana-intl-latam/index.html

Ortega Rodríguez, L. et al. (2011). Prevención educativa, un concepto a debate en el ámbito escolar, familiar y comunitario [Educational prevention, a concept under debate in the school, family and community sphere]. Curso 44 Pedagogía [Pedagogy, Course 44. Havana, Cuba: Educación cubana. www.cubaeduca.cu

Parra, Elena Diego. (2019, December 3). New contingent of the Manuel Ascunce Memenech Pedagogical Detachment. Las Tunas, Cuba: *26 Periodico* 26. http://periodico26.cu/index.php/en/education-2/1654-new-contingent-of-the-manuel-ascunce-domenech-pedagogical-detachment

Patterson Peña, M., et al. (2010). El método de alfabetización cubano "Yo sí puedo" en el contexto canadiense [Yes, I Can literacy method—in the Canadian context]. Memorias XIV Congreso Internacional de Informática en la Educación [XIV International Congres on computer technology and education]. Havana, Cuba: Editorial Universitaria [University of Havana Press,].

Relys Díaz, L. (2005) Yo, sí puedo [*Yes, I can.*]. Un Programa para poner fin al analfabetismo [a program to end illiteracy]. Havana, Cuba: Editorial Abril. http://www.ecured.cu/programa_cubano_de_alfabetizacion_yo_si_puedo /

Rivera Ferreiro, I., et al. (2012). Educa a Tu hijo. La experiencia cubana en la atención integral al desarrollo infantil en edades tempranas [Educate your child. The Cuban experience in comprehensive care for early childhood development]. Cuba: CEPAL. MINED-UNESCO. https://dds.cepal.org/proteccionsocial/pacto-social/2013-11-seminario-Costa-Rica/1_Rivera_Cuba.pdf

Rodriguez Abascal, A. S. (2020). La Escuela Latinoamericana de Medicina es una universidad internacional impulsada por Cuba. https://www.telesurtv.net/news/elam-200-medicos-estadounidenses--20200729-0033.html

Rojas, Laura Maria. (2023, June 6). Cuba's family code recognizes diversity in families expanding rights for children, women, and LGBTQI+ people. Inequality Solutions portal [Curated by the United Nations]. Inequality & Exclusion, curated by the Pathfinders for Peaceful, Just and Inclusive Societies; United Nations Economic and Social Commission for Western Asia (UNESCWA); London School of Economics' Atlantic Fellows for Social and Economic Equity (AFSEE), among others. https://www.sdg16.plus/policies/cubas-family-code-recognizes-diversity-in-families-expanding-rights-for-children-women-and-lgbtqi-people/#policy-reference-4

Statista. (2023, March 20). Rate of COVID-19 vaccine doses administered worldwide as of March 20, 2023, by select country, territory, or region. https://www.statista.com/statistics/1194939/rate-covid-vaccination-by-county-worldwide/

teleSUR.[HD] (2021, June 21). [Cuban President Miguel Diaz-Canal quoted in Latin American News (Cuba).] Cuban COVID-19 vaccine candidate Abdala is over 92% effective. Latin America: teleSUR[HD] English. https://www.telesurenglish.net/news/Cuban-COVID-19-Vaccine-Candidate-Abdala-Is-Over-92-Effective-20210621-0027.html

Torres Fernández, P., et al. (2009). *Evaluación de la calidad de la Educación en Cuba: Fundamentos, estructura y resultados* [Evaluation of the quality of education in Cuba, fundamentals, structure and results]. Havana, Cuba: Educación Cubana.

Turner Martí, L. et al. (1996). *Martí y la Educación*. Editorial Pueblo y Educación [Martí and education, people and education]. Havana, Cuba: Editorial Pueblo.

UNESCO. (1990). Education for All. Statistical Yearbook. http://unesdoc.UNESCO.org

-----. (1998). International Commission on Education for the Twenty-first Century. Informe a la UNESCO de la Comisión Internacional sobre la Educación para el siglo XXI (1998). UNESCO Digital Library. http://www.academia.edu

-----. (2006). Study on the effectiveness and feasibility of the [Yes, I Can] Literacy Training Method Yo Sí Puedo. Paris: UNESCO. http://unesdoc.UNESCO.org/images/0014/001468/146881e.pdf

-----. (2006). Premio Alfabetización 2006 Rey Sejong de la UNESCO [UNESCO King

Sejong Literacy Prize]. https://es.UNESCO.org/themes/literacy/prizes

—————. (2006). Segundo Estudio Regional Comparativo y Explicativo [second regional comparative and explanatory study]. https://es.unesco.org/fieldoffice/santiago/llece/SERCE2006

—————. (2013). Tercer Estudio Regional Comparativo y Explicativo [second regional comparative and explanatory study]. https://es.unesco.org/fieldoffice/santiago/llece/TERCE2013

—————. (2015). Informes sobre la calidad de la Educación [quality of education reports]. http://www.UNESCO.org/new/fileadmin/MULTIMEDIA/FIELD/Santiago/pdf/Informe-Regional-EFA2015.pdf

—————. (2015). La Educación para Todos 2000–2015. Logros y desafíos (Informe) [education for all 2000–2015 achievements and challenges (report)]. http://unesdoc.UNESCO.org

—————. (2019). Global education monitoring report. (2019). Migration, displacement and education: building bridges, not walls. UNESCO. https://en.unesco.org/gem-report/

United Nations. (1989). Convention on the Rights of the Child. Treaty Series, 1577, 3. Unicef. http://www.unicef.es

—————. (2015). 2030 Agenda for Sustainable Development. https://www.un.org/sustainabledevelopment/development-agenda

Yaffe, H. (2021, March 31). Cuba's five COVID-19 vaccines: The full story on Soberana 01/02/Plus, Abdala, and Mambisa. LSE Blogs. https://blogs.lse.ac.uk/latamcaribbean/2021/03/31/cubas-five-covid-19-vaccines-the-full-story-on-soberana-01-02-plus-abdala-and-mambisa/

Yo sí puedo. (2019, October 17). Program implemented in Saint Kitts and Nevis, Santa Lucia and Jamaica. Source: Cubadebate.cu, October 17, 2019.

CHAPTER ELEVEN

The Cultural Policy of the Cuban Revolution: Roots, Utopia, and Reality

Rolando Bellido Aguilera

Abstract

From a humanistic perspective and with faith in social and human improvement, this chapter will summarize the development periods of Cuban nationality (colony, neo-colony, and revolution) and assess their main characteristics, events, and works. The characteristics of cultural policy before and after 1959 in Cuba illustrate the importance of artistic and literary creation and the significance of the Battle of Symbols and Ideas in defending and consolidating identity and heritage. This process reflects active participation by intellectuals, artists, and institutions working within the principles of Cuban socialism against neoliberal, economic, and technocratic dogmas. The application of cultural policy during the so-called "five grey years" was fraught with challenges. In Cuba today, the fertility of cultural history flows into the need to develop critical discourse around consumerism, the pseudo-culture, and political, geographical, and economic determinism.

Keywords: art, culture, transculturation, third generation, neo-colony, five grey years.

Rolando Bellido Aguilera, PhD (Philosophical Sciences). MA (History and Culture). Professor and Researcher, Faculty of Social Sciences, University of Holguín. Member of the National Commission of Community Culture and co-founder/coordinator of the Cuban community cultural-work program "The Tree that Whistles and Sings."

Introduction

This chapter examines the Cuban socialist government's application of a humanist cultural policy within a development and implementation framework, achievements, obstacles, and errors from 1959 to the present day. The first section explains the late-18th-century roots of the theoretical-conceptual basis of national identity and culture that informs Cuba's cultural policy. The second section argues for the radical positioning against Spanish colonialism during the independence wars (the Republican Period) in the second half of the 19th century, when the early representatives of Cuban art and culture began to be recognized. Here the author spells out José Martí's contributions to the dignification of the political, ethical and cultural reality and argues for the continued relevance of his aesthetics (e.g., Martí's critical reflections on the interconnected nature of the relations of art and literature to culture).

The third section of this chapter will establish the historic continuity between Martí's humanism and the socialist humanism of the Cuban revolution, which triumphed in 1959. Finally, the chapter will explain the role of artistic and literary creation within conceptual frameworks of development and the need to preserve traditions. It analyzes the causes, key facts, and teachings of what has become known as the five grey years (1971–1976) as well as the importance of the Ministry of Culture (created in 1976) and how its network of institutions has been used to preserve the nation's historical-cultural identity, promote artistic-literary freedoms, and ensure the active participation of new generations. To this end, the author will define emancipatory concepts of creation, tradition, identity, nation, and national culture and explain the goals of the UNEAC (National Union of Writers and Artists of Cuba) and AHS (Hermanos Saíz Cultural Asociación) and the importance of such influential institutions as Casa de las Américas,* among others, within the broader framework of the cultural policy underlying Cuban socialism. The chapter concludes with a discussion of the significance of Fidel Castro's humanistic ideas for fostering the development of Cuban culture in radical opposition to economic and technocratic models.

Culture and Human Improvement: Nutrients of Cuban Cultural Thought

From the very first manifestations of nationalism, Cuban culture included teachers, essayists, artists, writers, and promoters so committed to Cubanness that their lives and works should be considered as roots or foundations of what has become the cultural policy of the Cuban Socialist Revolution.

The cultural revolution in Cuba was spearheaded by such notable indi-

---

* Casa de las Américas was founded in 1959, just months after the triumph of the Revolution, by the Cuban government as a publishing house and information centre to develop and foster socio-cultural relations with Latin American countries.

viduals as Felix Varela (1788-1853), José Antonio Saco (1797-1869), José de la Luz y Caballero (1800-1862), José María Heredia (1803-1839), Domingo del Monte (1804-1853), Gertrudis Gómez de Avellaneda (1814-1873), Adelaida del Mármol (1838-1857), Enrique José Varona (1849-1933), José Martí (1853-1895), and Julián del Casal (1863-1893). These intellectuals excelled in the fields of theological and philosophical reflection, poetry, knowledge promotion, journalism, literary criticism, scientific research, and pedagogy. Gómez de Avellaneda's writings stand out as early examples of Cuban poetry elucidating the emancipation of women, the abolition of slavery, secularization, and the role of religion in society.

In what can be described as second-generation Cuban cultural thought, the author Enrique José Varona (1849-1933) must be included, although he also belonged to the first generation along with Juan Gualberto Gómez (1854-1933), Fernando Ortiz (1881-1969), Medardo Vitier (1886-1960), Emilio Roig de Leuchsenring (1889-1964), Jorge Mañach (1898-1961), Rubén Martínez Villena (1899-1934), Lydia Cabrera Marcaida (1899-1991), and Julio Antonio Mella (1903-1929), to mention some of the most prominent cultural influencers.

Fernando Ortiz's work, for example, in the fields of cultural history, anthropology, and sociology is so substantial that some scholars have described him as the "third discoverer of Cuba." Ortiz' concept of "transculturation," with its metaphor of "*ajiaco*" (Cuban "vegetable and meat broth") expressing the critical role of fusion within Cuban culture, continues to inform identity studies. Lydia Cabrera Marcaida, an ethnologist who studied under Ortiz, infused Cuban literature and culture and enriched anthropological knowledge in Cuba with her knowledge of black folklore and language.

Where Nicolás Guillén (1902-1989) flooded the insular poetics with musicality and legitimate ethnic-African components, Jorge Mañach delved into some of the main materializations of superficiality present in Cuba without detracting from the substance of Cubanness. Samuel Feijóo (1914-1992) carried out the invaluable work of rescuing and conserving Cuban popular mythology, while Dulce María Loynaz (1902-27), Alejo Carpentier (1904-1980), Raúl Roa García (1907-1982), José Lezama Lima (1910-1976), Cintio Vitier (1921-2009), and others too numerous to mention carved out works of universal renown in novels, poetry, essays, and cultural criticism. Mirta Aguirre Carreras (1912-1980), a poet, novelist, journalist, professor, staunch supporter of the socio-cultural aims of the Cuban revolution—exiled in Mexico during Machido's reign—was an important political activist of the LGBT movement.

In terms of this third generation, it is practically impossible to observe a strict chronological order. The work of Guillén, Carpentier, Lezama Lima, Feijóo, Loynaz, and Vitier continued to enrich the cultural legacy of their predecessors, complemented by philosophical-reflective artistic creations in literary criticism and the cultural reflections of many others. Mirtha Aguirre became one of the top female academics in post-revolutionary Cuba. Dulce María Loynaz became the first Cuban woman ever to receive the Miguel de Cervantes Prize (1992), the highest literary recognition by the Royal Academy in Spain and other Spanish-speaking countries. The award had previously been won by Carpentier (1978).

Guillén was the first recipient of the Cuban National Prize for Literature (1983) while Lezame Lima won the UNEAC award (1968). Nancy Morejón (1944–) was winner of the Cuban National Literature Prize (2001) and President-Elect of the UNEAC for many years starting in 2008. Also, the first poet identifying as black to publish and be accepted widely as a writer, critic, and translator in Cuba, Morejón is the best-known and most widely translated female poet of post-revolutionary Cuba. This is to name only a few of the many awards within Cuba and internationally won by these and the other Cuban writers discussed in this chapter.

Cultural Policy in Cuba before 1959?

It would be an overstatement to speak of an official cultural policy in Cuba before 1959, if by this we mean a system of theoretical and operational principles that guide actions and processes in the sphere of culture based on an integral diagnosis of the internal reality and projections into the future. If, however, we believe that the official cultural model and policy (defined and driven by the state and its system of institutions) of a nation or country can co-exist with popular political dialogues and social movements, then we can acknowledge the existence of politics and cultural policies before the triumph of the Revolution in 1959.

Until 1898, the island of Cuba was a colony of Spain. Between 1898 and 1902, the country was subject to American military occupation. During this period of Yankee interventionism, the Cuban state was governed through U.S. "military orders" and plans and actions of a markedly pro-U.S. character. The period from May 20, 1902, to December 31, 1958, is considered by many historians of the revolutionary period as a neo-colonial or mediated republic. Other historians take a more socio-classist approach and call it either the republican period or the bourgeois or oligarchic-bourgeois republic.

In short, the official cultural policy before 1959 was elitist and strongly influenced by mercantilism with minimal state action in promoting culture or safeguarding artistic and literary traditions and values. Most authentic cultural actions and processes were "private" or consisted of local initiatives by associations, societies, or groups too numerous to mention. They included the famous Origins Group (*Grupo Orígenes*),* Studio Theatre, and José Martí Popular University (circa 1923–27), supported by Julio A. Mella† among others, and the *University of the Air*‡ (educational radio, 1932–1952), and the Alicia Alonso Ballet Company (1948), which later became the National Ballet of Cuba. There was also patronage or sponsorship by powerful companies and personalities. Life was generally precarious for artists and writers trying to survive on their art alone.

The Cultural Policy of the Revolution

With the revolutionary triumph of January 1, 1959, Cuban society began to be radically transformed through the implementation of popular anti-imperialist and socialist measures within the realms of politics, economy, and society. Special emphasis was put on the importance of education and culture in moving workers away from being objects of exploitation and into becoming the historical subjects of their own destinies.

The cultural policy of the Cuban Revolution was nourished by contributions from the colonial and neo-colonial periods. Making use of the fertile terrain prepared by José Martí, these contributions were enriched with the attempted and more-or-less happy synthesis between nation-world and the no less complex or exciting interrelation of tradition and modernity.

The political-cultural thought of Fidel Castro and Ernesto Che Guevara generated indispensable works for a profound understanding of local-universal relation and of the endless fruit of Martí's work in dialogue with the original Marxism of Karl Marx. This all was very different from the unfortunately widespread "dialectical materialism" of the Soviet manuals, as we will see later when analyzing the storm clouds and squalls of what we call the five-year grey period found in the work of certain orthophonic

---

* Origins Group. Group of intellectuals in Cuban culture that distinguished itself by the extraordinary richness of its contributions to culture and the diversity of styles. Founded in 1944 (Sainz, 2016).

† Julio Antonio Mella McPartland (1903–1929) was a Cuban political activist, writer, and founder of the Cuban Federation of University students and the Cuban youth magazine *Alma Mater* in 1922, the Jose Martí Popular University in 1923, and the original Communist Party of Cuba (1925).

‡ *La Universidad del Aire* (*University of the Air*) was a program for the dissemination of culture on the radio. It discussed historical, sociological, and literary topics, among others.

epigones (i.e., mediocre writers or artists enjoying the privilege of their academic credentials and positions).

Among the documents indispensable to understanding Cuba's revolutionary cultural policy are José Antonio Saco's writings against the U.S. annexation of Cuba; José Martí's essays, such as "Our America" (Martí, 1891) and "Wandering Teachers" (Martí, 1884) and most of his epistles, such as the letter to Federico Henríquez y Carvajal of March 25, 1895, and one to his friend Manuel Mercado dated May 18, 1895, just the day before Martí's death in combat; the aesthetic postulates of the Origins Group (Sainz, 2016), brought together particularly in Lezama's poetics and some of Cintio Vitier's essays, such as "Ese sol del mundo moral [Sun of the moral world]" (1975) and "Lo cubano en la poesía [The Cuban in poetry]" (1970, 1988). As well, all of Fidel's speeches on the role of art and literature, and culture in general, including his indispensable "Palabras a los intelectuales [Words to intellectuals]" (1961) and his speeches at UNEAC* congresses; Ernesto Che Guevara's articles, including the indispensable "Socialism and Man in Cuba" (1965); and essays and lectures by Carlos Rafael Rodríguez, such as his 1967 collection, "Problemas del arte en la Revolución [Art problems in the Revolution]"; the official documents from the First Congress of Education and Culture in 1971, and the "Theses and Resolutions on Cultural Policy" put forward at the Congresses of the Communist Party of Cuba, 1975.†

Regarding the importance of the cultural dimension and the artistic-literary and intellectual creators, as well as the specificities of art and literature, the following texts are cultural treasures: *La cigarra y la hormiga [The cicada/grasshopper and the ant]* (1996) and *Vanguardia y masividad [Vanguard and massivity‡]* (2010) by Abel Prieto; *Utilidad de la cultura* and *Al pueblo lo que es del pueblo [Utility of culture, To the people what belongs to the people]* (2011, 2012) by Miguel Barnet; *Política cultural [Cultural policy]*, *La difusión masiva de la cultura [Massive cultural diffusion]* and *Cultura, mecenazgo y subvención [Culture, patronage and subsidy]* (2016; 2012; 2006) by Graziella Pogolotti; *Espacios unitivos [Unitive spaces]* by Cintio Vitier (1988); *Vivir en Cuba, crear en Cuba: riesgo y desafío [Living in Cuba, creating in Cuba: risks and challenges]* by Leonardo Padura (2002); and "Palabras en la Feria" [*Words at the fair*] (2012) by Ambrosio Fornet; among others.

---

* UNEAC, acronym for the Union of Writers and Artists of Cuba, founded in 1961.

† PCC, acronym for the Communist Party of Cuba.

‡ "Massivity of sports and culture in Cuba" refers to a policy of the Revolution that guarantees access to and active participation in sports and culture as a right of all citizens.

Fidel Castro, Ernesto Che Guevara, Carlos Rafael Rodriguez, Nicolás Guillén, Alejo Carpentier, and José Lezama Lima, another significant group of political and intellectual leaders, were convinced of the importance of the participation of artists, writers, students, amateurs, researchers, and workers in general with the leaders of the Revolution. They believed not only in the practical application of cultural policy but also in its theoretical construction and continuous enrichment with the elements of cultural identity.

The aspiration was, from the very genesis of the Revolution, for the masses to cultivate themselves and rise together to create the most authentic cultural treasures of humanity, invaluable universal art and literature. Fidel's phrase, "We do not tell the people to believe, but to read" (1961), was as popular at the time as his "Homeland or Death!" slogan. It was not just a matter of forming a literal or literate culture but a deeply inspirational one, where theory and practice converge with knowledge and ethical and patriotic values. From the very beginning, the struggle was to develop fully educated human beings capable of being participatory and responsible subjects at the heart of a revolution, convinced that *the mother of decorum, the sap of freedom, the maintenance of the Republic and the remedy for vices, is, above all else, the propagation of culture* (José Martí, 1886).

Some hypercritics, today refugees in the bosom of the counter-revolution financed from the United States, exaggerate the errors and imperfections of the cultural policy of the Cuban Socialist Revolution. Responding to these distortions of fact meant not only having to demonstrate and promote the educational, social, and cultural work of Cuban socialism but honestly analyzing the mistakes made, aware that *"whoever brushes aside even a part of the truth, whether through intention or oversight, is doomed to fall. The truth he lacks thrives on negligence, and brings down whatever is built without it"* (José Martí, 1891a, Trans. 3 June, 2021).

On the basis of the social, educational, and cultural ideas of José Martí—who epitomizes the best and most advanced of Cuban thought and art during the 19th century and of the ideas of dignity and social justice, anti-imperialism, solidarity, and defence of Cuban identity and culture gathered in historical and political documents such as "History will absolve me" (Castro, 1953), "Words to the intellectuals" (Castro, 1961), the "First and Second Declaration of Havana" (Castro, 1960 and 1962) and in the essays or poetry of the most influential artists and writers of the 20th century in Cuba—the primary nuclei of the cultural policy of the Cuban Socialist Revolution were delimited.

As a system of ideas and principles, the cultural policy of the Revolution has been characterized by the definition and defence of culture as heritage and the right of every Cuban, promoting the most democratic access possible to the cultural goods. Culture was accorded the highest importance; this demanded a strong state presence, starting with the formulation of policy, managing it at the different levels of the nation and spurring sociocultural development for local people living in small towns or communities. Similarly, in the legitimate desire to avoid and overcome any potential or already known phenomena of bureaucracy and excessive state control over creation, it has been essential to foster the greatest possible respect for creators and to stimulate the need and benefits of maintaining a permanent dialogue with them in order to encourage the most active participation of intellectuals and artists, and of the people, at all levels; this ideal is easy to formulate at the political-theoretical level but extremely difficult and complex to bring into practice.

Other no less important features of the cultural policy of the Socialist Revolution are the free nature of artistic education and the maintenance of a climate of unity among all revolutionary forces as a historical learning process of more than one hundred years of struggle for national independence and sovereignty and, at the same time, freedom for writers, artists and intellectuals in general.

As referenced earlier, the most fertile nuclei of the cultural policy of the Cuban Socialist Revolution are in the ideas of José Martí and Fidel Castro. From Martí these apothegms have been taken as essential directions of our cultural policy: *culture is the only way to be free* (1891a); *teachers should educate children not only with science but with tenderness and love* (1891b); *Banana wine; even if it comes out sour, it's our wine!* (1891c); and *let the world be grafted into our republics; but the trunk must be our republics* (1891d).

The cultural policy of the socialist Revolution has been nourished by Fidel's enormous discursive work, furthering the awareness that the future lies in culture, and nothing spent on it is wasted; rather, everything invested in it comes back to society in the form of increased ethical and aesthetic values and a sense of meaning and happiness in life.

Fidel always defended the thesis of the decisive importance of culture. He had to repeatedly sustain that assertion against universal skepticisms and the glaring insular economists. He often entertained thoughts like, *Man must distance himself from rude and vulgar materialism. I do not say that we must forget about material needs; man has to eat, to have a roof, to dress, but we do not know where we are going to end up if we only seek happiness in material things* (Fidel Castro, 1999).

Fidel's ideas in "Words to the intellectuals" are admirable, for example: "We are going to wage a war against inculturation"; "The Revolution should reject only those incorrigible reactionaries who are incorrigible counter-revolutionaries"; "the development of art and culture is one of the goals and one of the basic objectives of the Revolution"; "we want to develop the conditions which will permit the satisfaction of all the cultural needs of the people" (Fidel, 1961; LANIC, n.d.); "The ... goods of the future are in culture; whoever does the math—and I like to do the math—knows that the future lies in culture" (Fidel Castro, 2001).

Hence, the bases of the cultural policy of the socialist revolution are expressed in a systematic and enlightening way, but this does not guarantee their successful practical application in all places and at all levels. A contextual clarification of its principles, understood as necessary and endless enrichments, must be an ongoing practice. Abel Prieto, for example, who served several years as president of UNEAC, and Minister of Culture for many more, has made important contributions that are briefly outlined below and help in the understanding of the enormous complexity of cultural life and creation. *While capitalism can function with pseudo culture, socialism by contrast can only be created and function with a culture of popular and human dignification* (Prieto, 2004).

The Grey Years in the Application of the Revolution's Cultural Policy

The most commonly used adjectives to refer to this stage of pettiness and dogmatism that materially and worst of all spiritually wounded Cuban culture include the "five grey years" (*The Five Grey Years: Revisiting the Term*, Ambrosio Fornet, 2007); "*Decenio negro*" [black decade] (César López, 2007); *Quinquenio gris* [bitter quinquennium] (Mario Coyula, 2007); and *Etapa de profunda dogmatización ideológica* [stage of deep ideological dogmatization] (Arturo Arango, 2007). Some qualify this as the *pavónato* ("paving") stage, explicitly referencing and condemning Luis Pavón Tamayo, who oversaw the National Council of Culture between 1971 and 1976.

Below is a succinct analysis of the causes that made possible this rarefied climate of dogmatism, intolerance, censorship, and prohibitions, not for the simple love of art, not gratuitously or capriciously, but rather believing it was the right thing to do, the most beneficial thing for the people, conceived by those who wrongly thought and acted as if the people were an unarmed, unthinking, uncultured mass that needed to be led along the best path.

Alfredo Guevara, in the "Declaration of Cuban Filmmakers," defines this grey five-year period as a time of *"entrenched dogmatists behind the bureaus [sic] of culture"* (Guevara, 2003). These dogmatists imposed a climate of intolerance and hardening against plurality and celebration of difference not only in an artistic-literary sense but also in philosophical, religious and moral terms. Meanwhile, Antón Arrufat, who suffered this obscuration for being a poet and homosexual has stated the following:

> In the seventies, the cultural bureaucracy of the time, fulfilling orders from the political leadership, had configured us in that "strange latitude" of being: death in life. It imposed on us to die as writers and to continue living as obedient citizens.... Our books stopped being published; those published were collected from bookstores and surreptitiously removed from the shelves of public libraries. The plays we had written disappeared from the stage. Our names stopped being pronounced in conferences and university classes, they were erased from the anthologies and from the histories of Cuban literature composed in that dismal decade.... We were removed from our jobs and sent to work where no one knew us, in libraries far from the city, at presses printing textbooks and foundries.... Where all cultural activity is an activity of the State, being marginalized by the State itself is destiny. (Arrufat, 1994)

Of course, none of this should have happened, but we must bear in mind that although Anton Arrufat (1994) was one of the most "repressed" during the grey years, he only spoke of imposed obedience, non-publication or circulation of his books, prohibition of theatrical premieres of his works, removal from his public jobs, and other forms of marginalization by the state. There is no evidence that any writer "branded" or "accused" of being a counterrevolutionary or "homosexual" has been subjected to torture or murder, or otherwise shunned in Cuban society.

Not everything can be reduced to a mediocrity of officials and much less to bureaucratic quarrels and dislikes; it is more a matter of ideological dogmas being turned into foundations to explain everything but ending up being as totalitarian and intolerant as religious fundamentalism.

Officially, officials did not accept the term "protest song,"* among oth-

---

* Protest song: music incorporating strong political and social themes. Examples of this movement are found in Chile and Cuba, where it began to be known as "new song" or *"nueva trova."* In 1967, from July 27 to August 8, the First International Meeting of the Protest Song was held at Casa de las Américas with the participation of 50 singers from 18

er reasons, because from their point of view, there was nothing to protest against in revolutionary Cuba; they were building a perfect society, and along that path of unstoppable progress, processes of "moral purification" also took place in the universities. The moral cleansing had to do, more than anything, with homosexuality, considered by some officials as a vice, disease, or scourge inherited from the past (Saruski and Mosquera, 1979), and those with religious beliefs.

In these years and those immediately following, the censorship was especially rigorous against anyone suspected of being homosexual or homoerotic. This is evidenced by Gerardo Fulleda's reference to the editorial policy of "El Caimán Barbudo":*

> ... the first generation of the first "El Caimán Barbudo" arose, [they] declared war, exterminating it not only from their pages, where it was not allowed to publish anyone suspected of homosexuality or of having a relationship with someone of the same gender, but where they did have the luxury of attacking everything that even came close to it, as well as launching insidious and low machinations that hurt more than one victim in the university purge. (Fulleda, 2007)

A few officials, out of conviction or opportunism, struggled to turn art into a weapon of the Revolution and to make monolithic unity a reality as quickly as possible. For this, artistic works had to shield against imperialist penetration and ideological diversionism and serve as effective didactic channels of collectivist formation and education. This implies denial of the critical role of the intellectual. The only criticism possible was to praise achievements and successes.

In 1975 the First Congress of the Communist Party of Cuba was held. The following year the Ministry of Culture was created and Armando Hart Dávalos (1930–2017) was placed at the helm. Hart was not only a decent person, but cultured and educated, of pure "Cubanness" and solid legal training, capable of believing more in the teachings of the history of the country than in the abstract regularities of the Marxist-Leninist theology found in the Soviet manuals. The year 1976 also saw the death of José Lezama Lima, who had seen most of his poetic work published by *Letras Cubanas* in 1970.

---

countries. Some of the well-known members of this movement are Silvio Rodríguez and Pablo Milanés (Cuba), Isabel Parra (Chile), Alfredo Zitarrosa (Uruguay), Barbara Dane (U.S.), among many others.

* *El Caimán Barbudo* [*The Bearded Caiman*]. Cultural magazine of Cuban youth committed to the most advanced and revolutionary elements of Cuban and international culture.

These dogmatic extremisms and unjustifiable and unacceptable errors brought about palpable consequences in some cases but for the most part intangible ones, which is to say impossible to fully gauge their extent and depth through traditional empirical proofs. Still today, some, from positions of extreme revolutionary intransigence, consider it above all else as a matter of whining, pettiness, and sensibilities more typical of bourgeois ladies than of militants, fighters, and the brave and selfless, stoical and anti-imperialist workers. In them, cultural prejudices and underestimations of the cultural field survived due either to their intellectual mediocrity or their practical betrayal of the ideals of socialist humanism.

The five grey years, or "paving" period, remains largely unknown and obscure even to the Cuban people. Across the many areas of artistic and literary culture, we find only shallow references or rather sentimental glimpses and no deep understandings about it. There was fear, and precaution, prejudice, and, still today, even apprehension. It's as though the fundamental archives for this period have not yet been opened, and the main participants have either decided not to speak or feel it is not to do so. It is like a pact of silence between gentlemen, or between bureaucrats, or between one and the other. The point to bear in mind is that no comprehensive research has been done on those years. This author thinks that study of the attitudes assumed by the Cuban intelligentsia and its institutions during those years of ideological repression has yet to be effected. As Arturo Arango (2007) pointed out, *years of ideological repression* can provoke not only scandal but upheaval if taken to open public discussion while we remain surrounded by the enemy; the analysis is being postponed in order to prevent greater ill.

Fidel Castro often verbalized his conviction that knowledge of divergences and errors in the application of the Revolution's cultural policy makes for a profitable learning experience, prevents them from recurring, and strengthens the same cultural policy. He also shared Martí's idea that hiding the truth is a crime; hiding only the part of it that impels and animates is a crime; hiding what is not convenient for the adversary and saying only what is convenient is a crime (Martí, 1892P);[*] and there is also an always urgent need to promote, through education and the implementation of correct cultural policies, a true ethical revolution in man (Castro, 1999).

The principles of socialist cultural policy support the need for sociocultural research within which the history of culture is a dimension of decisive

---

[*] Open letter to Enrique Collazo, published in *El Porvenir,* January 20, 1892. Of the many letters left to us by this national hero of Cuba, the author considers that this one constitutes one of the great political lessons of human sensitivity and culture.

importance. Socialist cultural policy also demands asking metaphysical questions, not in the non-pejorative sense of this philosophical occupation, but as essential human labour, which has to do with consciousness, with our capacity for glimpsing that our thoughts and works can only transcend themselves through culture. Must we human beings live to produce, alienating ourselves through complete submission to work like a punishment, or can we produce through free labour (emancipated, Marx would say), something that does not exclude the joy and exaltation of culture (and beauty, José Martí would add)?

The economy itself, in the sense of organizing production to fulfil social objectives and meanings, belongs to the cultural world as, from a material point of view, a means to make spiritual or symbolic life fuller. To deify the economy would be doing the same thing as the dogmatic capitalists, who deify "capital" to hide the exploitation of the living (wage-earning) labour that is the creator of "social wealth." We must ask ourselves both types of questions; in all reflections and practices, we must strive to maintain body-spirit/spirit-body unity and the economy-culture/culture-economy dialectic.

Paulo Freire (1970) said that *man is not given, but in the process of becoming*; while Martí says, "*the proud are pitiful, the world has never stopped.*" When human beings stop, when they stop searching and struggling, they become animalized; they return to the state of nature. We have art at our disposal—not to stop, not to conform, but to constantly imagine new horizons. A cultural history is not only possible, but also necessary to give an account of the intangible in the present and the future.

Neither the economy nor the means of production produce; human beings, society, and living labour are what produce. When the economy takes over, as happens under fundamentalist capitalism—commodities are fetishized and fundamental human needs go unaddressed in the frenzy to satisfy the appetites of the owners of capital—then the living labour, which is the worker, and in the long run, human society and the natural environment, end up badly damaged.

Consider the broad sense of culture as "poiesis" (that is, as creation/production for social and human improvement) (Bellido, 2003). José Martí used this concept in his essay on Walt Whitman in which he argues that poetry is the most distinctive and important expression of human life:

> Who is the ignorant person who maintains that poetry is not indispensable to people? There are people so short-sighted they believe that the peel is all there is to a fruit. Poetry is more important than industry because it gives people life-force desire and motivation,

which is more than mere survival. Poetry has the power to build up or cause anguish, support or throw down souls, give or take faith and consideration. (Martí, 1887c)

Within the Revolutionary context, art is the song celebrating life. We work because there is art. The economy is produced, organized, and developed only with culture in mind. There is an economic structure because there is an organized human society. The economy is manufactured. The real thing is the artist, the creator. This is the Martían and Lezamian myth of the poiesis and the praxis of Marxist emancipation. The opposite is sterile or unproductive manualism. The economy counts, art gives. The economy reaps, art shows. The economy lands, art soars. The economy bleeds, art heals. The economy subtracts, art adds; economy and money divide, art unites. We must pay attention to the economy, organize production, and save everything that can be saved, etc.—but we must never say, or accept, that culture is secondary to the economy.

One of the pillars of Cuban cultural policy is the assertion that culture can be led but not administered. In the cultural field, fortunately, the war has been far more complex and in the battle between symbolic value (given by a work of art) and price (decided by the market) the victory has not totally been with chrematistics or administration. This has to do with what Leslie White (1965: 17–18) once observed: culture is not determined in an absolute way, which means it is relatively autonomous.

To continue on the path of emancipation requires a reflection and practices that integrate politics, ethics, and culture without disregarding or submitting to the imperatives of economic determinism. To give another potential meaning to life, different from the globalization of the free market—waste and banality—with a comprehensive and enriching dialogue between cultures, in communion with the environment and inviting the broadest popular (mass) participation. Therefore, culture demands a belief in ethical and patriotic values and human solidarity, and an optimistic struggle for its theoretical and practical propagation.

The Cuban national hero penned that, *I don't know if I'm crazy, because I am a complete idealist.* Martí's "idealism" is not a negation of objective reality; it emphasizes that although the human being is body and spirit, and both are important, what is essential, makes him a "subject" (a term that Martí does not use), is his subjectivity.

Where specialized science errs by excess analysis; where neo-liberalism errs by excess immediacy; where economics errs by excess appetite; emancipatory politics, ethics and culture intuit and reorient with the correct words. The centre of the emancipating cultural policy is the social human being. Within the context of the Cuban revolutionary principle, this makes sense because the policy is created by and for everyone in Cuban socialism, where people are not seen as commodities.

Can anyone appraise the value of national identity and the significance of internationalism practiced for the benefit of so many peoples of the world? Can the embrace of a mother be bought or sold, or the kiss on the forehead of a child, or the emotion of a patriot while listening to the Bayamo Anthem (Cuba's national anthem), *The Beautiful Cuban,* or the opening of the novel *Cecilia Valdés*?

Conclusion

The cultural policy of the Cuban Revolution, like the famous "Scream" by the Norwegian painter Edvard Munch (1863–1944), launches a colossal but hopeful *scream* over the bridge, proclaiming that under both capitalism and bureaucratism, the most valuable thing is creation. This means that the poiesis which criticizes, proposes, and seeks the new system of values (i.e., post–Cuban Revolution cultural policy) is one more step along the path of social and human improvement.

References

Arango, A. (2007). Pasar por joven. [Posing as a youth]. Havana, Cuba: *Criterios*. http://www.archivocubano.org/pasar_por_joven.pdf

Arrufat, A. (2002) [1994]. Virgilio Piñera, entre él y yo. [Between Piñera and me], p. 56. Havana, Cuba: Editorial Letras Cubanas [Havana, Cuba: Ediciones UNIÓN, 1994].

Barnet, M. (1999, September). Utilidad de la cultura. In *En la cultura está el porvenir*. Encuentro Nacional de Directores Municipales de Cultura. Havana, Cuba: Ministry of Culture.

Barnet, M. (2019). Al pueblo lo que es del pueblo. In *Nuevos autógrafos cubanos*, pp. 39–44. Havana, Cuba: Editorial Letras Cubanas.

Bellido, R. (2003). El mito de la poiesis. [The myth of poiesis]. Holguín, Cuba: Editions Holguín. https://isbn.cloud/9789592211421/el-mito-de-la-poiesis/

Castro, F. (1960). *The Havana declaration* (translation). LANIC Castro Speech Database. http://lanic.utexas.edu/project/castro/db/1960/19600902-2.html

Castro, F. (2001) [1961]. *Palabras a los intelectuales* [*Words to intellectuals*], pp. 9–30. 40th anniversary tribute edition. Havana, Cuba: Letras Cubanas.

Castro, F. (1962). *The second declaration of Havana*. [Editorial note from *Fidel Castro Speaks*, James Petras and Martin Kenner (Eds.). New York: Grove Press/Evergreen Black Cat Books, 1969). Scanned by Jon Flanders, January 2007. Edited by Walter Lippmann based on the Cuban English language edition of 1962.] PDF of this speech: http://www.walterlippmann.com/fc-02-04-1962.pdf

Castro, F. (1999, September 14, 15, and 16). "Palabras en el Encuentro Nacional de Directores Municipales de Cultura" [Speech at the national meeting of municipal culture directors]. Havana, Cuba: Published as *En la cultura está el porvenir* [The future lies in culture], p. 8. Havana, Cuba: Cuban Ministry of Culture.

Castro, F. (1999, June 11). Discurso en la Clausura del Primer Congreso Internacional de Cultura y Desarrollo. [Speech at the Closing Ceremony of the First International

Congress on Culture and Development]. Havana, Cuba. http://www.cuba.cu/gobierno/discursos/1999/esp/f110699e.html

Coyula, Mario. (2007, March 19). [English paraphrase of the Bitter trinquennium and the dystopian city: autopsy of a utopia. Read by the author at the Higher Institute of Art (Havana) as part of "The cultural policy of the Revolution: memory and reflection" cycle. Havana, Cuba: organized by the Criterios Theoretical-Cultural Center]. El Trinquenio Amargo y la ciudad distópica: autopsia de una utopía. Conferencia leída por su autor el 19 de marzo del 2007 en el Instituto Superior de Arte (La Habana) como parte del ciclo *La política cultural de la Revolución: memoria y reflexión*. La Habana: organizado por el Centro Teórico-Cultural Criterios. Retrieved from: http://www.debatecultural.net.ve/Observatorio/CoyulaElTrinquenioAmargo.pdf

Fornet, A. (2007, January 30). The five gray years: revisiting the term. Revista *Casa de las Américas*, 246 (Jan.–Feb.): 3–16. Havana, Cuba. http://www.casadelasamericas.org/publicaciones/revistacasa/246/flechas.pdf

Fornet, A. (2012, February). Palabras de Ambrosio Fornet en su homenaje en la Feria del Libro de Havana, Cuba. https://www.youtube.com/watch?v=8N2BHc-zmEQ

Freire, P. (1970). *Pedagogy of the oppressed*. Myra Bergman Ramos et al. (Trans.). 30th anniversary ed. Continuum International Publishing Group. Originally published (in Spanish) in Portugal in 1968. https://envs.ucsc.edu/internships/internship-readings/freire-pedagogy-of-the-oppressed.pdf

Fulleda, G. (2007). In *Los juegos de la Escritura o la (re)escritura de la Historia, Alberto Abreu Arcia* [The writing game or rewriting history by Alberto Aubreu Arcia]. Havana, Cuba: Casa de las Américas [English paraphrase of Spanish text quoted on pp. 81–82].

Guevara, A. (2003). *Tiempo de fundación* [Time of foundation], p. 174. Seville, Spain: Iberoautor Promociones Culturales S. L.

LANIC. (n.d.). Castro, Fidel. (June 30, 1961). "Words to Intellectuals." Castro Speech Data Base. Speeches, interviews, articles: 1959–1966. Latin American Network Information Center. English.

LANIC. (n.d.b). Castro, Fidel. (September 2, 1960). "The Havana Declaration." Castro Speech Data Base. Speeches, interviews, articles: 1959–1966. Latin American Network Information Center. English.

Martí, J. (1975). *Obras completas* [*Complete works*], vol. 19, p. 429. Havana, Cuba: Ciencias Sociales.

Martí, J. (1884a and 1884b). Maestros ambulantes [Mobile/itinerant teachers]. *La América*. New York. In Martí, J. *Complete works*, vol. 8. Havana, Cuba: Editorial de Ciencias Sociales, 1975.

Martí, J. (1887). "El poeta Walt Whitman" [The poetry of Walt Whitman]. Mexico: El Partido Liberal. In *Obras completas*, vol. 13, p. 135.

Martí, J. (1892, January 12). Letter to Enrique Collazo, New York (in fact this is an open letter to Collazo, published in *El Porvenir*, January 20, 1892). Published in its entirety on page 291 of Martí's *Obras completas* [*Complete works*], vol. 1, pp. 288–293. http://www.damisela.com/literatura/pais/cuba/autores/marti/epistolario/collazo/1892_01_12.htm

Martí, J. (1891a and 1891b). Nuestra América [Our America]. In *La Revista Ilustrada*. New York. http://bibliotecavirtual.clacso.org.ar/ar/libros/osal/osal27/14Marti.pdf

Martí, J. (1891c and 1891d). Nuestra América [Our America]. In *Obras completas* (1975), vol. 6, p. 18. El Partido Liberal, Mexico, January 30, 1891. Havana, Cuba: Ciencias Sociales. Quotation in English retrieved from: https://quotepark.com/quotes/1907551-jose-marti-newspapers-universities-and-schools-should-encour/

Martí, J. (1886). "Tilden." In *Diario la República*, *Honduras*. In *Obras completas*, vol. 13, p. 301. Havana, Cuba: Editorial Nacional de Cuba (1963–1975).

Padura, L. (2002). Vivir en Cuba, crear en Cuba: riesgo y desafío. In *La cultura y la Revolución cubana. Conversaciones en La Habana*. John M. Kirk and Leonardo Padura Fuentes

(Eds.). San Juan: Editorial Plaza Mayor, 2002.
Pogolotti, G. (2012). La difusión masiva de la cultura [Massive cultural diffusion]. In *Espacios unitivos*, pp. 10–16. Báguanos, Cuba: Casa del Joven Creador, Hermanos Saiz Association (AHS).
Pogolotti, G. (2006). Cultura, mecenazgo y subvención. In *Los polémicos sesenta* [Culture, patronage and subsidies]. Havana, Cuba: Editorial Letras Cubana.
Prieto, A. (1997). La cigarra y la hormiga: Un remake al final del milenio [The cicada and the ant: A retake at the end of the millennium]. In *La Gaceta de Cuba*, 1 [Cuba official Gazette, No. 1]. Havana, Cuba: Edited by the UNEAC.
Prieto, A. (2009). *Vanguardia y masividad* [Avant-garde and massive]. In *La cultura es lo primero que hay que salvar* [Culture is the first thing to save]. Closing speech of the VII Congress of UNEAC. June, 2008. Havana, Cuba: MINCULT.
Prieto, A. (2004). Interview with Abel Prieto, Cuban Culture Minister, by Alejandro Massia and Julio Otero. *Tiempo de Cuba* [Time in Cuba]. Trans. Ana Portela (for CubaNews). Edited by Walter Lippmann. http://www.walterlippmann.com/abelprieto-11-7-2004.html
Sainz, E. (2016). El Grupo Orígenes en la cultura cubana. *Espacio laical*. http://espaciolaical.net/wp-content/uploads/2016/11/101107.pdf
Vitier, C. (1958). *Lo cubano en la poesía*. Havana, Cuba: Editorial Letras Cubanas. La Habana.
White, L. (1965). *La ciencia de la cultura* [Science and culture], pp. 17–18. Buenos Aries: Ediciones Paidós.
Saruski, J. and G. Mosquera. (1979). The Cultural policy of Cuba. *Studies and documents on Cultural policies*. Paris: UNESCO.

EPILOGUE

An "Outsiders'" Perspective

Nancy Wright* and John Winterdyk[†]

Despite media coverage and various journal articles and books by Western academics about Cuba in recent decades, the Cuban system remains somewhat of a mystery to the world. To address this problem, we sought to bring together a written collection from Cuba about its legal, political, and economic systems and associated cultural and social structures from the end of the 19th century. When we started this project, we were uncertain how things would unfold across the two languages and cultures, let alone the physical distance between us in Canada, and our co-editor Vilma Páez Pérez and all the authors in Cuba.

Drawing on the experiences of the lead editor, it was clear the timing of such a reader might represent a valued contribution on several fronts. First, the history of Cuba in English has historically been told by people outside the nation. Second, the history of Cuba is not readily referenced without an understanding of Fernando Ortiz's cultural model of transculturation. Third, the impact of colonialism on the development of the modern world and the construction of a Third World to serve it have become increasingly essential foci of research across settler-colonial nations in many fields, including literary criticism and criminological inquiry, not to mention history. Fourth, the current impetus for research across the West seeks insight into perceived neo-colonial tendencies or colonial legacies, such as sys-

---

* Nancy Wright, MA, is an independent professional editor, writer, and researcher located in Quebec's Eastern Townships, and also brings extensive experience as a translator. She has presented regularly at the WEFLA-SECAN conference in Holguín, Cuba, since 2016, independently undertook a special doctoral-level course in transculturation at the University of Holguín in 2017, and in 2018–19 made several one-month trips to Cuba to consult with the authors. Since 2012, she has held the position of editor-in-chief of *Actualités JUSTICE Report*, the national publication of the Canadian Criminal Justice Association.

† John Winterdyk, PhD, is an internationally recognized Canadian criminologist based in Calgary, Alberta, where he taught at Mount Royal University for 37 years before retiring in 2023. Winterdyk has attended several conferences in Cuba, including WEFLA-SECAN, as well as conducting several sessions with the authors, and is the author of over 38 published books and a wide array of scholarly articles.

temic racism in post-colonial/post-settler nations. Finally, the highly contested U.S. embargo and the U.S.-controlled naval station at Guantanamo Bay, Cuba, offer a modern-day look at how "old world" international politics of the colonial period may still be in play. Contextual editing ensured sufficient background details where a frame of reference was needed to make some of the complex concepts more accessible to foreign audiences (i.e., outside of Cuba). The authors, with our co-editor Vilma Páez-Perez in Cuba, always returned perfectly appropriate texts.

Nancy Wright is a professional editor with an advanced understanding of the colonial system and pitfalls of revolution derived from the theory of researchers such as Jacques Roumain (Haiti, 1944), Alejo Carpentier (Cuba, 1949), Aimé Césaire and Édouard Glissant (Martinique, 1950/1957), Albert Memmi (Tunisia, 1957) and Orlando Patterson (Jamaica, 1957). Their early explorations of post-colonialism and neo-colonial legacies were foundational to our current understandings. John Winterdyk brings insights as a Canadian criminologist and author, along with his understanding of justice systems internationally and links to academia in Canada and internationally. Vilma Páez Pérez brings in-depth knowledge of Cuba today, its history and that of the Cuban education system, expertise in Cuban-Canadian studies, and links to academia in Cuba and internationally.

This collection represents the most comprehensive and the only contextualized overview of Cuban history written in Cuba, and we trust it will stimulate further inquiry. While there may be certain omissions in the coverage, the authors of this reader offer an integral, critical understanding of Cuban history and the Cuban system and its underlying ideologies within a framework of colonial, post-colonial, and neo-colonial influences by Spain and the United States. This anthology will also afford the reader a basic understanding of the complex concept of transculturation, which is relevant to every aspect of development in Cuba, including the pre-independence formation of the "Cuban nation." Appreciating the challenges faced by the Cuban contributors, all of whom were born, reside, and work in Cuba, we are profoundly grateful to everyone who agreed to participate.

In addition to Cuba's being the largest Caribbean island, its capital, Havana, lies just over 90 miles (approximately 150 km) south of Key West, Florida. As the Cuban anthropology professor José Vega Suñol points out in Chapter 9, Cuba became part of the historical perspective of European expansionism the moment Admiral Christopher Columbus set foot on its coast. Technically speaking, Cuba is part of North America, located on the North American continental shelf and not on the Caribbean tectonic plate. More importantly to many, Cuba's deep port at Guantanamo Bay represents the gateway to Latin America. Cuba has always been of heightened regional and global geopolitical interest.

As is well documented throughout this book, Cuba has long experienced a complex and problematic relationship with the United States. Cuba was once a well-known playground where U.S. citizens, including members of the mafia, could get around U.S. laws, such as drinking—before and after amendments to the U.S. Constitution created Prohibition (1920–33)—and prostitution, among other activities considered illegal or immoral in the United States at that time. Through ingenuity and resilience, Cuba remains comparatively homogeneous and free of the many problems afflicting some countries in the Caribbean, such as Jamaica.

By all accounts, Cuba's biggest export is professional labour and expertise; it is said that doctors working in other countries benefit the Cuban economy more than tourism (GIS, 2019). Cuba has the best education system in Latin America and the Caribbean and, since the early 1960s, has one of the highest literacy rates in the world. However, many people worldwide would arguably agree that "dictatorship," "communism," and "oppression" are the three most prevalent words in the Western social imagination and media when it comes to Cuba.

Overall, Cuba is a country of contrast characterized partly by its history of fusion, explained by Ortiz's transculturation. As described in various contexts throughout this collection, Cuba has developed a unique social and political justice model, making this small country harder for most Westerners to understand but especially worthy of closer inquiry. The emphasis on contextualization in this book is also warranted by the amount of propaganda prevalent in the West about Cuba and alleged human rights violations from time immemorial. Semantics also plays a role because the mere mention of communism evokes negative connotations seemingly inerasable from Western memory.

Although Cuba gained independence in 1902, true sovereignty was inhibited by U.S. interference, and this has been perpetuated not just through the U.S. embargo against Cuba (1958; 1962 to present) but also the U.S. "toehold" at Guantanamo Bay, Cuba. As Vilma Páez Pérez and Salvador Escalante Batista point out in Chapter 5, U.S. control over the 45 square miles (116.5 square km) territory at Guantanamo has been a "thorn in Cuba's side" throughout its evolution as a country and highly contested, especially since 1959.

U.S. Propaganda in 2021 Recalls 19th-Century News Coverage of Cuba

Escalante Batista and Sarmiento Blanco point out in Chapter 4 that "yellow journalism" (i.e., news based on little or no research and intended to be sensational) was born in 1898 with coverage of the USS *Maine*'s explosion off Cuba's shores. The U.S. claimed it had positioned the battleship to protect Cuban shipping interests. According to U.S. State Department archives, coverage by Hearst newspapers denounced Spain and blamed it for the explosion. In reality, however, this was no more than an unsubstantiated rumour spread by the media.

During the summer of 2020, amid the COVID-19 pandemic, the world again observed yellow journalism in the U.S. targeting Cuba. On July 16 and the following day, rare protests had sprung up in cities across the island. Disturbances saw protestors attacking police with sticks, stones, broken bottles, etc. There were several lootings at shopping malls. Keep in mind the period since the pandemic's onset had been extremely rough for Cuba amid COVID-19 spikes and increasingly severe shortages of the most necessities. As noted in this book, in 2020—at the height of the pandemic—then President Donald Trump imposed 243 measures strengthening the U.S. embargo against Cuba, which some had already termed genocidal given its long duration and devastating economic effects.

The Cuban government met some protesters' demands, such as temporarily removing particular medicine and food import duties. Any calls for an end to the dictatorship were wildly over-reported by the media yet voiced by an infinitesimally small percentage of Cubans; they would bear little discussion in any democracy. "Fake" news appeared on social media and was sensationalized through repetition by certain broadcast networks worldwide (e.g., in the U.S., Spain, and Canada). Miami Mayor Francis Suarez suggested that an airstrike by the U.S. against Cuba might be an option worth exploring in response to the protests. Is the world expected to just ignore this, not to mention President Joe Biden's announcement of new sanctions on Cuba because lawbreakers were arrested during the protests?

Decolonizing Political States

"The greatest crimes are caused by excess and not by necessity."
—Aristotle, *Politics* (cited in Braithwaite, 2022).

Reverence for Cuban heroes is omnipresent in Cuba. Every town is marked with signs, paintings, murals, and other honorary acknowledgements of local and national heroes who served in the Cuban War of Independence and, later, the Cuban Revolution. If fortunate enough to visit Santiago de

Cuba, the original capital city, and visit the resting place of Fidel Castro, you will be struck by the sense of reverence and love also given to fallen heroes such as Jose Martí.

Reflections on the impact of U.S. interference in Cuba—especially the state of severe economic crisis unavoidable under the U.S. embargo following the fall of European communism in the early 1990s—appear in almost every chapter of this book. Equally clear, however, is an awareness that even the relative poverty wrought by this extra-territorial policy of the United States has not destroyed the Cuban nation's resilience. Instead, Cuban resilience has been bolstered by the return on human potential from the government's ceaseless investment in human development through popular policy and an informed citizenry that is almost entirely literate.

Anyone who ventures off the resort in Cuba can readily see how the effects of the economic, political, and social "quarantine" or embargo have limited Cuba's advancement at a material level. However, Cuba is far from being "frozen in time." As Yohannia Ochoa Ardite and Vilma Páez Pérez point out in Chapter 10, Cuba's investment in education roars with the revolutionary Cuban sentiment of leaving no one behind. The country has even created its COVID-19 vaccines—something most Western countries are not equipped to do. Most of Cuba's population was fully vaccinated by the end of 2021 with its Abdala or Soberana 02 vaccines. Both were exported to developing countries, creating revenue streams and aligning with Cuba's tradition of medical solidarity.

As the chapters in this book illustrate, Cuba's early post-colonial national development, from 1902 to 1959, was characterized by military interventions and other authoritarian influences by the U.S. aimed at destabilization and domination. In chapter 8, Manuel Alberto Leyva Estupiñán, Larisbel Lugo Arteaga, and Luis Manuel Probance Labrada explain that one of the impacts of the U.S. policies, which also caused widespread poverty and economic uncertainty, was increased crime and highly overcrowded prisons rife with black-market cannabis and alcohol sales, and practically being "run" by the prisoners before 1959. Disturbingly, this recalls most of the Western world's prison systems today.

It is equally important to note that the social equality produced through this collective struggle has become a mantle of national pride, perseverance, and resolve. For example, gender equality has succeeded "[i]n Cuba, [where] women held 49 percent of seats in the national legislature during the past decade—a higher proportion than for all Western capitalist societies, according to the World Bank (2016)" (Braithwaite, 2022: 46). Therefore, within a North American context, Cuba's social, economic, and political climate is not marked by the effects of colonialism in the same way as are most former colonies of France, Spain, or Britain. It is, however, indelibly marked by the U.S. embargo against Cuba and much of the world's compliance with it.

As they say, "No man is an island." In Chapter 3, Miguel Torrez Pérez points out that the current critical lack of foreign exchange—brought about by the fall of Cuba's key trade partner (the Soviet Union) in 1991, subsequent intensifications of the long-standing U.S. embargo, and the more recent supply effects wrought by the pandemic—have stifled Cuba's ability to take advantage of regular international trade opportunities. These events, among other punitive geopolitical actions against Cuba, robbed the national currency (CUP) of the buying power needed to ensure adequate supply for the island. This, and the associated inflation, erodes infrastructures and profoundly impacts the government's ability to deliver, let alone further develop, the totality of services, supports, and nutrition guaranteed under Cuban socialism. In Chapter 2, the Cuban sociologist Luis Orlando Aguilera García explains the economy's relational impact on social values.

The "proximity hypotheses" of the lifestyle model developed by Hindelang, Gottfredson, and Garafalo (1978) can be helpful at the macro-international level to show how small, vulnerable nations have been positioned and conditioned over time by powerful nations to be dominated through unfair trade practices or invasion. According to such a theoretical perspective concerning Cuba, this form of victimization can be seen in the way the United States (the offender/dominator) appropriated the Cuban War of Independence against Spain by intervening militarily in Cuba (the victim/survivor) through the Spanish-American War to emerge three months later, against the provisions of its own War Measures Act, holding a protectorate over Cuba. Using this foothold, the United States managed to keep the contested naval base at Guantanamo, support more than one dictator in Cuba, and generally establish neo-colonial relations with Cuba through economic domination. This book, however, also shows how the virtue of Cuban resilience is inspired by Jose Martí's white rose ideology and commitment to individual human development (i.e., full potential).

The Cuban people have also remained resilient in the face of internal difficulties, and the government has openly apologized for and corrected mistakes, such as the initial move toward communism. Another example lies in how Castro long ago apologized and took the blame for gay persecutions in Cuba during the 1960s. The 2019 constitutional debates in Cuba suggested that gay marriage would soon be on the table, and same-sex marriage has since been legalized along with other changes to the Cuban Family Code via a secret ballot public referendum. It is perhaps noteworthy that several U.S. states today practice various forms of persecution and criminalization based on "ethnicity" through anti-LGBTQ2+ or erasure legislation. Fidel Castro realized long ago that such views are prejudicial and inconsistent with the inherent equality of human beings. In other words, as with Western courts, to be balanced, we need to be able to see legislation's effects in both increasing and suppressing freedom (Braithwaite, 2022).

Braithwaite's "proposed freedom theory of crime argues that a normative order that is legitimate because it guarantees freedom and minimizes domination lays a pathway to low-crime societies" and the opposite is also true (2022: 23–24). Braithwaite's 2022 *Macrocriminology and Freedom* explores the criminological concept of *anomie* (née strain theory) and an ensuing "'relentless promotion of self-interest' at the expense of citizenship values" (Braithwaite, 2022: 85; internal quotation from Farrall and Karstedt, 2019) as a risk for countries, such as Jamaica, that fail to meaningfully distribute among their citizenry the wealth created by capitalistic market structures (Braithwaite, 2022: 84–85). Arguably, although articulated by the father of modern economics, Adam Smith, as a necessary adjustment of the free market system, such failure besieges many Western nations. For Braithwaite, "Commodification, a marketized mentality, drives capitalism forward at the same time as it risks its destabilization" (85).

In "the Caribbean, the level of inequality is the only variable showing a robust causal effect across national and subnational levels to predict which are the hot spots of crime within the region as measured by victimization surveys as well as homicide rates" (Braithwaite, 2022: 141). Hence, "These supranational dynamics of the contestation of feudal power are also a key to understanding why feudalism continued to dominate so many Eastern European societies until Napoleon's armies and France's legal code abolished feudalism" (Braithwaite, 2022: 7). *Our Cuba: Contextualizing a Vibrant History* will offer readers a clearer picture of how extreme capitalist dogma is working to keep the dominating forces of colonialism alive in the present day.

Cuba is the least commercialized island and the most drug-free nation in the Americas. Consider, for example, Barbados, Trinidad and Tobago, the Dominican Republic, Jamaica, the Yucatan Peninsula, and Belize, where the drug trade (e.g., for international smuggling and domestic sales to tourists) and the associated demand for drugs or money characterizes much of the crime problems plaguing the United States, Canada, and most Western countries. Related to such organized crime, "the former British colony of Jamaica has [for decades] ranked in the top few countries for homicide rates for the South American and the Caribbean regions (Harriott, 2011)," and "the offshore wings of Jamaican drug traffickers murder more people overseas than in Jamacia, particularly in the United States, but also in Canada and the United Kingdom." Another result of "the regional problem" in the Caribbean and South America is the fact that Jamaica has "among the highest rates of killings by police in the world." Cuba and Chile are the only Caribbean and Latin American societies "that have avoided the very highest homicide rates in recent decades" (Braithwaite, 2022: 142).

Cuba's success in the protection and development of children and adolescents stands in stark contrast to Jamaica's persistent failures to fulfill even the most basic needs and safety of children, let alone the tenets of the Jamaican-ratified UN Convention on the Rights of the Child (CPRI—Caribbean Policy Research Institute, 2018). In 2019, Cuba's population was over 11 million, and tourism accounted for around 10 percent of the country's GDP. The same year, Jamaica's population was just under 3 million, and tourism accounted for over 35 percent of its GDP. The Cuban landmass is about 90 percent larger than Jamaica's.

The U.S. Embargo Against Cuba: After the Fall of the East European Bloc

When the rationale for the embargo fell away with the demise of the entire East European bloc in the early 1990s, one would think the time had come to dissolve the embargo and possibly initiate friendly relations with Cuba. The United States instead adopted a new rationale based on an assault on Cuban socialism, in 1992 expanding the embargo through the Cuban Democracy Act (Chapter 4). This period of history, remembered in Cuba as the "Special Period in Times of Peace," was characterized by extreme poverty and undernutrition for Cubans but also continued investment in education. Ultimately, the Cuban government adjusted the Cuban economic system to include some foreign investment, skirting the embargo restrictions, and the Cuban people rallied successfully.

As also discussed in this book, for more than 30 years, Cuba has repeatedly called for a vote in the UN General Assembly urging an end to the U.S. embargo against Cuba. This has been the Cuban response since the U.S. intensified the embargo in 1992 and again in 1995 with the Helms-Burton Act, both moves ironically prompted by the fall of the Eastern bloc. In 1997, Canada reinforced its opposition to the now 62-year-old embargo by amending our Foreign Extraterritorial Measures Act (FEMA) to make the Helms-Burton Act unenforceable for Canadians. However, many corporations face challenges in fully utilizing this mitigating mechanism due to the complexities of extraterritorial enforcement and legal exposure, as evidenced by FEMA's 2019 update aiming to "prevent or offset the legal exposure of Canadians to the Title III regime."

In an era when globalization seems to be the term used to describe the evolving nature of what is happening around the world, Cuba has not only remained comparatively isolated from what has been happening elsewhere, but it has done so despite being such close neighbours to the United States and many other vibrant countries in the region. One sees the phases of Cuban history rolling by every day on the city streets: a procession of horse-drawn buggies, bicycle taxis, bicycles, motorcycles, American cars and heavy vehicles from the 1950s, lots of Ladas (a former iconic Soviet car), and a wide range of modern vehicles including the yellow taxi. In short, while there is noticeable austerity everywhere, happiness, pride, intelligence, and a palatable passion for life starkly contrast with the simplicity that is also evident everywhere you go.

Although John Winterdyk attempted to visit the various elements of the criminal justice system (i.e., police, courts, and corrections), the opportunities never materialized over the past few years while co-working on this project. We know this was not through any lack of good will or intention and had heard of such visits being carried out in Havana, a possibility we unfortunately did not pursue. As our Cuban co-editor Vilma Páez Pérez has commented, this book may help people understand why Cuba holds its cards very close—to avoid exposing its internal affairs and plans to the global community.

Looking Ahead

As Vladimir Pita illustrates in Chapter 6, the once-stated goal of attaining communism in Cuba was long ago discarded in favour of the proprietary political system known as "Cuban socialism." There is nothing to suggest that Cubans want a market economy or a democracy that holds public elections at the presidential level. In Cuba, the people elect by free election/secret ballot, and through their mass organizations, the National Assembly of People's Power deputies entrusted to elect the president. During the almost complete support of the Cuban people throughout Fidel Castro's reign, there was no need for more than one presidential candidate. As the legal-political transculturation process embraced in Cuba continues, any changes will likely be innovative and in line with the democratic mechanisms of Cuban socialism. Since we started this book, Cuba has significantly changed its economic policy. In chapters finalized before the constitutional changes were consolidated in 2019, the authors made all efforts—such as José Augusto de Rio Ochoa in Chapter 7—to provide at least the most essential updates.

Cuba is a comparatively small country, and in a global context, its social, economic, and geopolitical transitions might be viewed as an odd anomaly ("off the beaten path"). However, as reflected throughout this book, Cuba represents a unique opportunity to study how soft resistance—and a decolonization of colonial structures as evidenced by the redistribution of wealth through Cuba's proprietary brand of socialism—has, since 1959, infused Cuba and the Cuban people with a resilience to the anomie brought about elsewhere in the Caribbean/Latin America through the colonial structures and systems of the world's capitalist markets. Indeed, there is a dire need for macro explanations in criminology, criminal justice, and other fields about how the impact of these types of "authoritarian" foreign policies of certain nations might still be infringing on the rights of those in poorer nations and contributing to the unfair status quo, a paradigm that Braithwaite (2022) says is helping feed crime around the globe.

While this anthology offers a unique opportunity to understand how Cuba has weathered the geopolitical storm for almost two centuries and can serve as an example for studying various elements of socio-economic justice, how Cuba will withstand potential social upset created by individual wealth accumulation remains critical. As visiting Harvard law professor Rafael Cox Alomar recently opined, "Cuba stands today at the verge of a complex and uncertain crossroads. Cuba's challenges are both exogenous and endogenous" (Neal, 2021). Many of the points Cox raises in his article are discussed throughout this book, *Our Cuba: Contextualizing a Vibrant History*, but the myriad of social and political changes both internally and internationally, along with the socio-economic pressures currently facing all countries, suggests that Cuba will most likely remain a fertile environment for describing, understanding, examining, and foreshadowing not only the topics covered in this book but those themes and issues that are certain to arise.

It is difficult to imagine that the impact of political domination related to and ensuing from colonial times can be properly fathomed without similar engagement by professionals in other fields, such as sociology, economics, education, literature, criminology, and political science. The relational social angst brought about by the pockets of wealth amassed by some Cubans in tourist gratuities (since the end of the 1970s) has been a subject of debate and concern in Cuba. It will undoubtedly be interesting to see how Cuban policy might offset any further relational social angst that may arise from individual wealth accumulation ensuing from Cuba's recent legalization of independent ("contract") workers and small businesses or from the "greed" that Braithwaite (2022: 74, 85, 98) says is motivating white-collar crime in nations around the globe. In effect, the world may learn a lesson from how Cuba makes its mixed system function within the revolutionary framework of leaving no one behind.

Cuba's respect for the arts is evident (Chapter 11). It clearly uses its relatively small tourist sector to provide venues for rising actors, musicians, and artists. In the cities, you might hear an outdoor opera at night, see a play performed on a park square, or be surprised when a statue in the park reveals itself as an actor! Thus, what most "Third Worlders," such as people in Jamaica, experience as poor educational outcomes, extreme poverty, and associated high crime rates is overridden in Cuba by solidarity and a sense of inclusion that most world citizens would envy. This solidarity is both the saving grace and the result of guaranteed free education, healthcare, housing, and a portion of every month's food, and is a testament to the elasticity of Cuban political and legal structures. In Chapter 1, the Cuban historian and author José Novoa Betancourt contextualizes the complex process that led to the construction of Cuba's national model as unprecedented in the western hemisphere. There has been nothing in Cuba's history since 1959 to suggest anything but a commitment to furthering the Cuban dream of human development and equity. This book illustrates how, despite persistent anti-Cuba rhetoric and extreme financial constrictions imposed on the Cuban economy by the U.S., Cuba has emerged as a leader (see also Braithwaite, 2022).

As detailed in this book, the U.S. embargo persists even though the vast majority of countries with the UN have consistently voted against it annually since the early 1990s. Given the perceived limitations of the International Court of Justice (located in The Hague), many feel that only pressure from the international community can help break the age-old U.S. chains on Cuban sovereignty. When European communism took its final breath in 1991, the United States "simply" adjusted its rationale for the embargo from a communist threat to a lack of democracy in Cuba. At the same time, the U.S. and its allies embrace trade with countries such as China, a decidedly communist country, and the Kingdom of Saudi Arabia, which has no democratic mechanisms at all and is rife with human rights restrictions, especially for women. As *Our Cuba: Contextualizing a Vibrant History* clearly illustrates, the U.S. trade embargo and lease/treaty governing the highly contested naval base at Guantanamo Bay, Cuba, today have no objective validity, legal or otherwise, and contravene Cuba's sovereign right as a nation to be its own supreme authority.

References

Braithwaite, John. (2022). *Macrocriminology and freedom*. Australian National University Press. Open access available via OAPEN at chrome-extension://efaidnbmnnnibpcajpcglclefindmkaj/https://library.oapen.org/bitstream/handle/20.500.12657/53117/1/book.pdf

Carpentier, A. (1949). [1957]. *El reino de este mundo*. Edición y Havana, Cuba: Distribución Iberoamericana de Publicaciones. [Trans. Harriet de Onis. *The Kingdom of this World*. New York: Alfred A. Knopf].

Césaire, Aimé. (1950). [1972]. *Discours sur le colonialisme*. Paris: Éditions Présence Africaine. [Trans. Joan Pinkham. *Discourse on colonialism*. New York: Monthly Review Press.].

Glissant, É. (1958) [1959]. *La lézarde*. Paris : Éditions de Seuil. [Trans. Francis Frenaye. *The ripening*. New York: G. Brazilier.].

-----. (1981). [1989]. *Le discours antillais*. [Trans. Michael Dash. *Caribbean discourse: Selected essays*. Charlottesville: University Press of Virginia.].

Memmi, A. (1957). [1965]. *Portrait du colonisé précédé de portrait de colonisateur*. Paris: Éditions Corrêa. Introduction by Jean-Paul Sartre. [Trans. Howard Greenfeld. (Portraits of) *The colonizer and the colonized*. Boston: Beacon Press.]

Roumain, J. (1944) [1977]. *Gouverneurs de la rosée*. Port au Prince, Haiti: Imprimerie de l'état. (1946). Paris: La bibliothèque des Éditeurs Français Réunis. [Trans. Langston Hughes and Mercer Cook. *Masters of the dew*. New York: Collier Books, 1971]

Cox Alomar, R. Cuba's "'uncertain future.'" *Harvard Law Today*. https://hls.harvard.edu/today/cubas-uncertain-future/

GIS. (2019, October 11). Is Cuba entering another "Special Period"? GIS. https://www.gis-reportsonline.com/who-we-are/

Neal, J., and HLS News Staff. (2021, July 19). Cuba's "uncertain future." *Harvard Law Today (HLS)*. Faculty Scholarship. Harvard Law School. https://today.law.harvard.edu/cubas-uncertain-future/

Patterson, Orlando. (1964). *The children of Sisyphus*. London: New Authors Limited.

ABOUT THE COVER

Marina con galeón prestado de Cosme
("Marina with Galleon," inspired by Cosme)

This painting by **Victor Manuel Velázquez Mirabal** of Holguín, Cuba, is part of a private collection in Havana and appears on the cover of this book by permission of the artist. In it, the artist pays homage to his teacher and close friend, Cosme Proenza Almaguer (Holguín, Cuba, 1948–2022), recipient of the National Prize for Fine Arts and one of the most renowned Cuban artists—the "pride of Holguín," from which city he created a universal body of work exhibited worldwide, including at the Vatican. The painting serves as a metaphor: the galleon represents Cuba, an island navigating the Caribbean, just as each of us is an island, carrying our own memories and dreams. It also evokes the theme of migration—people coming, people going, carrying their hopes and dreams. What do visitors seek? What do those who leave take away from us?
(2007, oil on canvas, 40 cm x 70 cm)

THE TEAM

Above (photograph 1, April 2017, Universidad de Holguín). I (Nancy Wright) pursued a multi-pronged doctoral course on transculturation in Cuba during the winter trimester, facilitated by Vilma I. Páez Pérez, then Head of Canadian Studies at UHo and organizer of the annual springtime WEFLA-SECAN conference at Guardalavaca. The photo above shows my professors, some of whom (their names in **bold**)—as well as Vilma—became founding/contributing authors of *Our Cuba*. From the left: **Manuel L. Estupiñán** (Criminal Justice), Alejandro Torres Gómez de Cádiz Hernández (Religion), **Vladimir Pita Simón** (Cuban Socialist Democracy), **José A. Ochoa** (Legal System and Constitution), Vilma I. Páez Pérez, Nancy Wright, **José Vega Suñol** (Anthropology), Yusimi Borjas Algeciras (Spanish-SFL), and Anabel González González, an interpreter for some of my classes who later refined the early translations of certain chapters. Not pictured is **José Novoa Betancourt** (History). They showed me that understanding Cuban history in all its facets is integral to grasping transculturation—this realization inspired the idea for *Our Cuba*, and led to an enriching intercultural journey (2017–2025) with the authors and others not pictured above, including John Winterdyk (Canadian co-editor, Mount Royal University).

Above left (photograph 2, taken in December 2017). Seated, left to right: José A. Ochoa, Manuel Leyva Estupiñán, Carlos Córdova Martínez, Nancy Wright. Standing, left to right: John Winterdyk, José Novoa Betancourt, Vilma I. Páez Pérez, Vladmir Pita Simón. This photograph was taken at the Union of Writers and Artists of Cuba (UNEAC) in Holguín, Cuba.

Above right (photograph 3, taken in April 2022). Seated, left to right: Vilma Páez Pérez, Paul Sarmiento, Salvador Escalante Batista, Luis O. Aguilera García, John Winterdyk, Yohannia Ochoa Ardite, Violeta Rosa Mejías Rojas, Vladmir Pita Simón; standing, left to right: Manuel Leyva Estupiñán, José A. Ochoa del Rio.

Right: Rolando Bellido Aguilera.
Far right: Miguel Ramón Torres Pérez.

www.ingramcontent.com/pod-product-compliance
Lightning Source LLC
Chambersburg PA
CBHW071953070526
44583CB00015B/1173